David V. Herlihy

Bicycle THE HISTORY

Yale University Press   New Haven and London

Frontispiece: Waverley Belle, circa 1896, a lady's model by the Indiana Bicycle Company, with a steel frame and wooden handlebars, fender, and chain guard. (Pryor Dodge Collection)

Designed by Sonia Shannon
Set in Bulmer type by BW&A Books, Inc.
Printed in China through World Print Ltd.

The Library of Congress has cataloged the hardcover edition as follows:
Herlihy, David V.
    Bicycle : the history / David V. Herlihy.
        p.   cm.
Includes bibliographical references and index.
ISBN 978-0-300-10418-9 (alk. paper)
1. Bicycles—History. I. Title.
TL410.H43 2004
629.227'2'09—dc22   2004012992
ISBN 978-0-300-12047-9 (pbk. alk. paper)

A catalog record for this book is available from the British Library.

This paper meets the requirements of ANSI/NISO Z39.48-1992 (Permanence of Paper).

10 9 8 7 6 5 4 3 2

In memory of my father, David Herlihy

Contents

Introduction

Think back to your first cycling experience, the moment you wobbled beyond the clutches of an anxious parent, without recourse to training wheels. Chances are, it rates as a highlight of childhood—your first real taste of freedom and even pride in ownership. It was your bike—and you were free to go wherever your spinning feet could take you, or so it seemed. And it was indeed a true love affair, likely to lure you back time and time again, even when you thought you had moved on. My own reawakening began as a teenager in the early 1970s, in the midst of a budding American craze for European-style ten-speeds. Like the main character in *Breaking Away*, a college-bound cyclist obsessed with his racing aspirations, I cherished my Italian racer and its exhilarating ride.

Much has changed in the cycling world since then. Many of the familiar American and European brands have disappeared in a market dominated by Asian manufacturers. What were then frills, such as alloy rims, are now standard equipment. Lightweight, affordable frames come in a variety of high-tech materials, including titanium and aluminum alloys. Tubular tires have given way to high-performance clinchers. You no longer have to reach down to change finicky gears by deftly adjusting the shifting lever; now you simply twist a handlebar grip or nudge a brake lever, and the chain dutifully snaps into place. A new concept designed for off-road use, the mountain bike, dominates the recreational market. Jerseys are made of Lycra, not wool. Helmets are light and airy. You can even take a cell phone along for the ride.

Albert Einstein taking a spin at a friend's house in Santa Barbara, California, in 1933, a time when recreational cycling was enjoying a revival

Yet so much remains the same. Millions of people around the world still rely on their trusty clunkers for cheap and efficient transportation. In fact, the global fleet approaches a billion, with the vast majority circulating in developing countries like Cuba and China where automobiles remain a luxury. Recreational riders continue to take to their wheels for exercise, adventure, and companionship, often participating in mass rallies like the MS Bike Tours and the AIDS ride. Every July, the Tour de France still draws millions of spectators to the roadside, eager to catch a glimpse of their heroes. Evidently, the bicycle retains the same inherent appeal that drove the great boom of the 1890s. Little wonder, then, why our ancestors counted the modern bicycle among their greatest achievements, along with the steamship, the railroad, the telegraph, and the telephone.

But the simple mechanical marvel we know today as the bicycle was actually the culmination of a long and elusive quest for a human-powered vehicle, a remarkable story that has yet to be told in full detail. The first clumsy attempts to tap human power went nowhere. "The proudest triumph of mechanics," declared one British journalist in 1819, "will be the completion of a machine or carriage for travelling, without horses or other animals to drag it." Not until the 1860s, in fact, did the basic bicycle emerge in Paris—under mysterious circumstances. Featuring pedals attached directly to the front hub, it demonstrated the surprising principle that a slender vehicle with but two wheels could be indefinitely balanced and propelled by means of a mechanical drive. Although it was soon saddled with the unflattering appellation "boneshaker" once better-built bicycles came along, the primitive bicycle unleashed a frenzy of experimentation and quickly captured the world's imagination. "Never before in the history of manufactures in this country," marveled the *New York Times* in early 1869, "has there arisen such a demand for an article."

For the first time, people could truly imagine a world in which the horse—a beloved but demanding creature—no longer bore the brunt of personal transportation. An exciting new era of road travel loomed ahead, one that would enable even a poor man or woman to travel afar and at will. Still, the euphoria proved premature, and yet another generation passed before the two-wheeler assumed a truly practical and inviting form. To be sure, the majestic high wheeler of the 1870s and 1880s was already a road-worthy vehicle of remarkable construction, one that gave great joy to legions of privileged young men the world over. But its intimidating form and prohibitive cost betrayed the original objective of a "people's nag." Nevertheless, high-wheel production established the technical and social foundation for the practical "safety" bicycle complete with a chain drive and pneumatic tires.

The introduction of the modern-style two-wheeler triggered revolutions both social and technological. One contemporary in the midst of the 1890s boom wrote, "It is well nigh impossible to calculate the far-reaching effects of [the bicycle's] influence." For one thing, the seductive low-mount bicycle encouraged an increasingly sedentary population, including housebound women, to exercise outdoors. Although some social guardians and medical authorities fretted about the consequences, most observers agreed that moderate cycling was a universal blessing. "As she [the New Woman] is becoming a co-worker with man," affirmed one feminist in 1896, "she needs a man's opportunities for physical development." And women did take to the wheel in vast numbers, forcing reforms in the rigid Victorian dress code as had no other pastime. "Since women have taken up the bicycle," another feminist of the period remarked, "it has become more and more apparent that its use demands a radical change in costume."

The technological consequences of the boom were also profound. During the peak

A German caricature from *Simplicissimus* in 1897, suggesting how much the bicycle helped loosen Victorian standards of dress and gave female cyclists greater independence. The caption read:

HE: But Miss Elsa, are you so carried away with your women's liberation work that you would never consider an engagement?

SHE: An engagement? Why, heavens no—that's far too conventional for me!

An automotive plant in the United States from about 1910, already showing a large, systematic operation. The American bicycle industry of the 1890s developed methods of mass production that led to factories like this and helped usher in the automotive age.

year of 1896, some three hundred firms in the United States alone produced more than a million bicycles, making it one of the country's largest industries. The cycling trade not only launched the Good Roads Movement, culminating years later in a great national network of highways, it also provided the foundation for the automotive industry. In particular, the advanced techniques used to assemble millions of bicycles were readily adapted to automobile production. Even the vast nationwide network of bicycle repair shops evolved into the first gasoline stations. Literally and figuratively, the bicycle paved the way for the automobile.

The bicycle trade also produced the first motorized two-wheelers at the turn of the century, and for some time the two industries remained closely aligned. Many bicycles of the 1910s, in fact, sported head badges with motorcycle brands like Harley-Davidson and Indian. Bicycle mechanics likewise played an important role in early aviation. Wilbur and Orville Wright themselves operated a small bike repair shop in Dayton, Ohio. They used bicycles to conduct their first wind tunnel experiments, and they built the 1903 Wright Flyer in their workshop using familiar tools and materials. Glenn Cur-

The Wright brothers' bicycle shop in Dayton in 1897, with Orville, right, and his assistant Edwin H. Sines. The brothers built the Wright Flyer in this workshop in 1903.

tiss was another former bicycle mechanic who developed some of the first successful airplanes.

The bicycle as we know it was largely a product of the Victorian imagination and the tremendous ingenuity that characterized that age. By the end of the nineteenth century, in fact, nearly all the main features of the contemporary machine were already in place: the familiar low-mount profile, wheels of equal size, rear-wheel drive powered by a chain, and inflatable rubber tires. Consequently, the greater part of this book is devoted to tracing the events that ultimately led to the breakthrough bicycle in the mid-1860s and its sustained development throughout the balance of the nineteenth century. This material is divided into four sections, covering the pre-history and the three devel-

A mail-order catalog from Sears, Roebuck, in 1914. By this time department stores were selling reliable bicycles at a fraction of the boom-era price, making them at last affordable to the masses.

opmental phases of the pedal-powered two-wheeler: the boneshaker, the high wheeler, and the safety bicycle. The fifth and final section reviews how the bicycle successfully adapted itself to the needs of the motorized age—a remarkable story in its own right and one that has been largely neglected, even in the most recent cycling histories.

The bicycle, in fact, did not truly complete its transition from a rich man's toy to a poor man's carriage until the early part of the twentieth century. Before the boom, the first safety models had cost about $150—well beyond the means of the average worker who made only about $12 a week. But shortly afterward, reliable vehicles were selling for around $25 through discount department stores and mail-order houses. Bicycles became more practical, too, with the addition of freewheels, brakes, hub gears, and electric lights. And though recreational interest in cycling had waned in the United States as automobiles began to take over the roads, Europeans continued to look with favor upon the bicycle as a means to good exercise as well as cheap transportation.

In the 1920s and 1930s, the touring bicycle developed in Europe, acquiring a light-

Messenger boys like this one in Danville, Virginia, in 1911, circulated on bicycles in many cities throughout the first half of the twentieth century

weight frame, aluminum alloy parts, and derailleur gears. Cycle camping became a popular weekend activity, while a growing network of youth hostels, born in Germany, offered cyclists cheap overnight accommodations. In the United States, the bicycle became primarily a child's vehicle, laden with automotive-style gadgets. Yet the country experienced a brisk bicycle revival in the 1930s when the Great Depression curbed automobile sales and Hollywood actors took up the sport. Meanwhile, in the developing world, demand for utilitarian cycles rose rapidly, keeping Raleigh's huge plant in Nottingham humming year-round.

During World War II, the bicycle played an even larger role in everyday life in Europe. Even gasoline-pinched Americans turned to the lowly two-wheeler for basic transportation, and following the conflict they rediscovered the joys of cycling. Many of the five million soldiers returning from Britain had used English lightweights during the war, and had acquired a newfound appreciation for the bicycle. At the same time, the domestic trade vigorously promoted adult pleasure cycling. By the late 1960s, following a fad for Sting-Rays among youngsters, Americans began to covet the even lighter and more versatile ten-speed, sparking the second boom. Suppliers worldwide worked frantically to meet the surprising and overwhelming demand, producing some forty million bicycles between 1972 and 1974. Although sales eventually tapered off, cycling reestablished itself as a popular adult pastime on both sides of the Atlantic.

Since then, the versatile new mountain bike, conceived in California, has injected fresh life into cycling by cleverly packaging lightness and multiple gears in the form of a

A painting by Norman Rockwell in the *Saturday Evening Post,* 1 April 1921, captures the sheer joy of cycling from a juvenile perspective

Lance Armstrong of the United States Postal Service team making his way through France's Basque country in 2003, the centennial edition of the Tour de France. A year later, the reigning American champion claimed a record sixth title.

rugged yet comfortable machine that can go just about anywhere. Meanwhile, cycling advocates have spearheaded construction of hundreds of miles of bike paths and trails for commuting and recreation. Increasingly, congested cities are promoting the bicycle as a green machine, even mounting their officers on police bikes. And the bicycle is still widely used throughout the developing world. Countries like China, India, and Brazil that once relied heavily on bicycle imports now boast massive cycle industries of their own, and have themselves become leading exporters.

Today, cycling is riding a new crest of popularity. Bicycle touring, in small or large groups, for day trips or extended rides, has become a popular activity worldwide. Numerous firms now offer guided bicycle tours in scenic locations and scores of nonprofit organizations host cycling events to raise money for their causes. Many localities stage annual community rides, such as the thirty-year-old RAGBRAI, a popular jaunt across Iowa sponsored by the *Des Moines Register*. Every August, some fifteen thousand French cyclists converge in a designated region for a week of fun and riding known as *la semaine féderale*. They tour at their own pace, sleeping en masse on institutional floors. One of the largest cycling events in the world is the annual sixty-mile Argus Cycle Tour around the spectacular coast near Cape Town, South Africa. The thirty thousand or so entrants are officially engaged in a race, but the vast majority are out for pure enjoyment.

The competitive sport also continues to captivate the public, pushing the upper limits of cycle technology and the capabilities of the human body itself. Track racing, including the notorious six-day marathon, remained a popular sport in America well into the twentieth century and is still practiced today, especially in Europe and Japan. More recently, mountain bike and BMX racing have created exciting new spectator sports. And despite persistent drug scandals, road racing retains its immense popularity, enjoying even greater exposure with the rise of triathlons. The legendary Tour de France has gained even more international luster in recent years with the superhuman exploits of the Spaniard Miguel Indurain and the Americans Greg LeMond and Lance Armstrong.

But the story of the bicycle is an ongoing adventure, and the book's conclusion explores a few intriguing possibilities for future development. Some believe the two-wheeler is due for a major overhaul, given the superior speed of low-slung aerodynamic models known as recumbents. One sleek variation with a fiberglass shell recently surpassed 80 miles an hour—still a far cry from John Howard's mark of 152 miles per hour, achieved on a specially designed bicycle trailing a rocket car on a salt flat in Utah. Other observers predict that the bicycle of the future will be a power-assisted vehicle, offering the traditional pleasures of cycling as well as the capacity to engage an auxiliary electric motor whenever the will to pedal wanes. Regardless of what lies ahead of us, the bicycle's rich and colorful history projects a future as bright as its past.

Part One The Pre-History

ONE *The Elusive Mechanical Horse*

More than three centuries ago, the distinguished French mathematician Jacques Ozanam spelled out the theoretical advantages of a human-powered carriage "in which one can drive oneself wherever one pleases, without horses." Its owner could freely roam along the roads without having to care for an animal and might even enjoy a healthy exercise in the process. Moreover, this particular type of "self-moving" vehicle, in contrast to those that called for wind or steam for propulsion, would run on that most abundant and accessible of all resources: willpower. But how to construct such a valuable vehicle? That was the twenty-third of some fifty "useful and entertaining" problems Ozanam identified and addressed in his famous *Récréations Mathématiques et Physiques*, published in 1696.

Ozanam not only issued an important challenge to the inventive community, one that would ultimately yield the modern bicycle, he also proudly revealed his own "solution" in the book's frontispiece: a massive four-wheeled carriage designed by Dr. Elie Richard, a physician from La Rochelle. According to Richard's plan, a gentleman seated comfortably in front has only to steer the front axle using a pair of reins. Meanwhile, his servant standing at the rear drives the vehicle forward by stepping up and down on two reciprocating planks tangential to the rear axle. The planks were spring-loaded and suspended by a rope-and-pulley system so that when one sank under pressure from the driver the other rose until reaching its apogee, whereupon the planks reversed direction. Each plank, in turn, activated a gear affixed to the rear axle, causing the axle to turn, thereby rotating the wheels. The entire driving apparatus was neatly

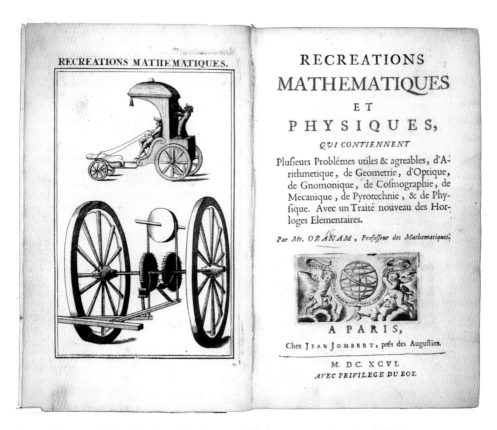

Jacques Ozanam articulated the theoretical advantages of the human-powered carriage in his famous compendium of scientific riddles, published in Paris in 1696, with its frontispiece showing an example built by Dr. Elie Richard of La Rochelle

hidden within the body of the carriage. Never mind that the pair would be better off walking, especially the poor lackey!

Richard's carriage, despite its dubious potential, served for more than a century as the working model of the human-powered vehicle. Several variations were built in Europe over the years, presumably with technical improvements, but to little avail. Finally, in 1774, a London journal pronounced a local entry "the best that has hitherto been invented." The handiwork of a Mr. Ovenden, it reportedly cruised at six miles an hour, or faster if the footman expended a "particular exertion." It could even surmount "considerable hills," provided they had a "sound bottom." Yet even this worthy initiative appears to have gone nowhere.

A few years later, in 1779, a prolific French inventor, Jean-Pierre Blanchard, created a similar carriage with the help of a M. Masurier. Blanchard and his servant rode it around Louis XV Square in Paris, exciting a curious crowd. The pair even coaxed the

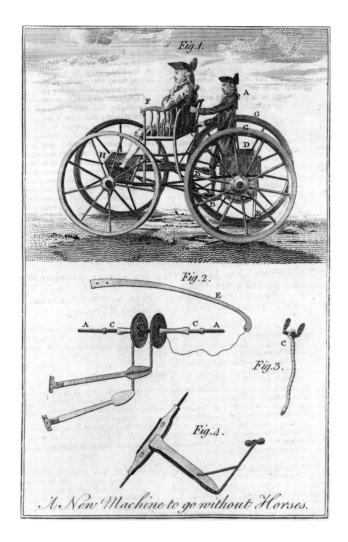

In Ovenden's carriage, depicted in the *Universal Magazine* of December 1774, a gentleman seated in the front steers while his lackey in back does all the legwork. For more than a century, inventors tried in vain to develop a practical mechanical vehicle along these lines.

vehicle a dozen miles to Versailles—the first recorded long-distance journey on a human-powered vehicle. The *Journal de Paris,* noting that the carriage drew praise wherever it appeared, urged Blanchard to give his invention greater exposure. He obliged by holding regular exhibitions in a courtyard by the Champs-Elysées. Alas, he too failed to generate a demand. Blanchard went on to more profitable pursuits, becoming a famed balloonist.

Even the New World recognized the need for a practical human-powered vehicle. In 1804, an obscure American mechanic named J. Bolton patented a four-wheeled carriage designed to carry up to six idle passengers who sat comfortably on three upholstered benches. In addition, two men operated the vehicle. One sat in front and steered the smaller front wheels, each about two feet in diameter. The other stood in the middle

"The First Balloon Crossing of the English Channel" (1785), an artist's rendering of Jean-Pierre Blanchard sailing over the Norman countryside. A few years earlier, this inventive Frenchman displayed his own variation of a mechanical four-wheeler in Paris.

of the platform facing the rear and two of the benches. With both hands, he rotated a lever bar that activated a series of four progressively larger interlocking cogwheels on either side of the vehicle. The last ones were affixed directly to the rear wheels, which measured about four feet in diameter, and turned them forward. The system was designed to augment the driver's natural arm strength by improving leverage, the last cogwheels being almost as large as the rear wheels themselves. In contrast to his European counterparts, Bolton flaunted his driving gear. Nevertheless, for obvious reasons, his idea likewise failed to catch on.

By this time, however, the Industrial Revolution was picking up steam in Great Britain and elsewhere, energizing inventors and prompting fresh initiatives on all fronts. Indeed, thanks to a variety of useful new products and more efficient production techniques, many citizens were beginning to enjoy better living conditions, more leisure time, and greater life expectancies. Humanity was gradually freeing itself from the oppressive need to eke out a hard living off the land. Even the landscape itself was rapidly changing, as bustling factories of all sorts sprouted up within cities.

But where in all this exciting technological tumult was Ozanam's elusive horseless

J. Bolton, an American mechanic, filed this drawing for a patent issued in 1804. Nearly a century later, during the great bicycle boom, a British writer ridiculed this clumsy attempt to tap human power, suggesting that the lax helmsman in the drawing "has pulled his hat over his eyes as though rather ashamed of himself for so using a fellow-creature. As well he may be."

carriage? Alas, for all the marvelous advances of the age, the seductive concept of the human-powered vehicle had barely budged. Nor were many people optimistic about its prospects. "A machine of this kind will afford a salutary recreation in a garden, or park, or on any plain ground," opined one skeptic, "but in a rough or deep road must be attended with more pain than pleasure."

One determined individual nonetheless set out to end this saga of failure and frustration. He was Karl von Drais, an eccentric German baron from a distinguished family in Karlsruhe. A forest master employed by the Grand Duchy of Baden, he perhaps coveted a practical human-powered vehicle as a means to facilitate his own regular inspection tours of the land he oversaw. In any event, he clearly appreciated the need to improve existing means of personal transportation. In 1813, he built a mechanical four-wheeled vehicle that would carry two to four passengers. One or more riders supplied the motive power by working a cranked axle with their legs and feet, while another handled the steering by means of a tiller.

Convinced that he had finally met the challenge of the horseless carriage, Drais sought public approval. Several journals dutifully published accounts of his invention, and some luminaries offered accolades, notably the Russian tsar, Alexander I. But despite Drais's modicum of success, the patent offices of both Baden and Austria swiftly rejected his pleas for patent protection. The examiner from his native Baden, Johann Tulla, issued a particularly harsh evaluation of the carriage and even denied that Drais had gained any ground whatsoever. Man, insisted Tulla, was ill equipped to apply his motive powers in any context other than the God-given means of walking.

Unrepentant, Drais made one last spirited push to establish his invention. In the fall of 1814, to the embarrassment of some of his colleagues at the forest ministry, Drais paraded his carriage before delegates attending the Congress of Vienna, convened to partition Europe following the downfall of Napoleon, emperor of France. Drais failed,

Muscular effort was not the only way to power a horseless carriage. But unlike this "Sailing Chariot" depicted in *Curiosities of the Ingenious* (London, 1822), the human-powered vehicle requires no special weather conditions, nor does it consume external resources, such as water or coal. Moreover, a vehicle propelled by the rider could conceivably provide healthy exercise as well as cheap transportation.

however, to win their approval. He returned to Baden disheartened, whereupon he shifted his creative energies to other worthy scientific endeavors, notably the development of a periscope and a device for speed-writing.

Yet within a few years, the stubborn Drais would revisit the vexing problem of the horseless carriage. But this time he proposed a radically different solution: the "laufmaschine" (running machine), soon to be known as a "draisine" or "velocipede" (from the Latin words meaning fast foot). This curious concept, unveiled in the summer of 1817, would become the first human-powered land vehicle to mount a serious bid for public acceptance. Moreover, the draisine marks the first significant step toward the basic bicycle, the compact, pedal-powered vehicle that ultimately solved Ozanam's riddle.

The slender vehicle Drais commissioned reflected the carriage technology of the time. Save for its iron tires, the machine was made almost entirely of wood and had but two miniature carriage wheels in a line, connected by a perch that supported a single cushioned seat. The rider sat nearly erect and propelled the machine by pushing off the ground with one foot, then the other, as if walking or running. A long pivoting pole at

The mechanical horse offered personal mobility, but to gain popular acceptance it would have to prove distinct advantages over the animate variety. In an English print from 1819 the hobbyhorse is shown edging out its rival.

the foremost end of the frame allowed the rider to turn the front wheel in the desired direction of travel. A small padded board was affixed in front of the seat, at waist height, for the rider to rest the elbows or forearms on, shifting pressure as needed to keep the vehicle from tipping to one side or the other. The entire affair weighed about fifty pounds and cost the princely sum of four Carolins.

According to Drais, his new machine facilitated and accelerated the natural acts of walking and running. Compared to a runner or a pedestrian, the rider purportedly covered a given distance with less labor. For in the act of striding along, the rider not only advanced in the conventional manner but also imparted a velocity to the machine. It thus carried both forward on its own accord, even when the rider was between steps and not normally progressing. As one source explained, the rider "pushes the wheels along when they won't go alone—and rides them when they will." Those who took advantage of this machine thus covered extra ground with every "step," routinely advancing four or five yards with each impulsion, about twice the distance of a normal stride.

Moreover, according to Drais, a stride atop a velocipede was actually less taxing on the feet, since the machine supported the bulk of the rider's weight. He compared the velocipede rider to a horse that pulls an attached cart, pointing out that the horse carries a given load much more easily in the cart than it does directly on its back. In the same way, he argued, the velocipede rider's own weight is effectively rolled along with the support of the machine, relieving the rider from having to carry the full load on the feet. Drais insisted further that the velocipede was not merely a pedestrian "facilitator," but also an "accelerator." On a good road with minimal effort, Drais found that he could bowl along at five or six miles an hour, about twice a normal walking gait. If he ran with his machine instead, he could reach a speed up to twelve miles an hour, comparable to a galloping horse—the fastest thing on the road at that time.

Actual performance, Drais conceded, depended on a variety of factors, including the condition and the incline of the road, and the force with which the rider pushed off. In principle, the velocipede was most effective when used on good roads as a running machine. As one enthusiast explained, in the normal act of running, in contrast to walking, the entire upper body is brought into play. The runner often falters not because the legs give out, but because a cramp, or some other problem, develops elsewhere in the body. But when running atop a velocipede, the rider who reposes the chest on the padded board works only the legs, "whilst the other parts are in a state of rest"— presumably protecting them from a breakdown. In effect, riders were free to run as fast as their legs could carry them.

An expert could further economize time and effort, and maximize speed, by coasting during reasonably steep descents. For, as Drais discovered, once the machine reached a certain velocity on account of gravity, the rider could safely lift the feet up off

Why Not a "Bicycle"?

Although some historians call the draisine the first bicycle, to emphasize what they see as a direct evolutionary link between the original aid-to-walking and the pedal-powered two-wheeler, the two vehicles are actually quite distinct—both historically and conceptually. The term "bicycle" was not introduced until the 1860s, when it was coined in France to describe a new kind of two-wheeler with a mechanical drive. Ever since then, "bicycle" has been used in French and English to designate a two-wheeler with pedals.

Admittedly, "bicycle" was perhaps an ambiguous choice of terms to distinguish the new-style two-wheeler from the original variety, given that a literal interpretation of "two wheels" would evidently apply to the draisine as well. But since the aid-to-walking was already obsolete by the 1860s, there was little doubt about what one meant by the term. Moreover, explained the lawyer Charles Pratt in 1884, "words made for French and English use do not always have the meaning exactly of the combined words from which they are derived." Rather, he noted in defense of Lallement's original bicycle patent of 1866, a new term like bicycle "has more usually a special meaning which a word was needed to express."

A more general term was "velocipede," introduced by Drais (or perhaps his French agent, Louis Dineur) in 1818 to designate his kick-propelled two-wheeler. The term quickly became the generic word for a human-powered vehicle with two or more wheels, and it remained in use until about the early 1870s, when it yielded to the more succinct and precise expressions "bicycle," "tricycle," and even "quadricycle." Initially, however, bicycles were commonly referred to as velocipedes, despite some objections. "*Velocipede* (velox pedis, swift of foot) is very inappropriate," protested one Scottish newspaper in 1869, "seeing that the traveller does not go on foot at all, and that the motion of his feet cannot fairly be said to be swift." Nevertheless, the fact that "velocipede" became the general term for a human-powered vehicle and remained in use for over half a century affirms Drais's catalytic role in energizing the elusive search for a practical mechanical horse.

the ground and let the machine roll along on its own. When it finally slowed down beyond the base of the hill and began to falter, the rider's feet reestablished contact with the ground and pushed off once again. In the meantime, however, the rider had accomplished what amounted to a giant step with minimal exertion. Drais also insisted that riders incurred no harsh penalty driving the velocipede to the top of the hill in the first place. Even if they had to dismount on account of a severe incline and proceed by foot, they could easily push their vehicles along at a normal walking pace, and might even lean on them for support, as one might a cane.

Exactly how Drais came upon this simple and novel scheme is unclear. Some have suggested that he drew his inspiration from the art of skating, since he likened the two movements in his brochure. Drais, however, never actually revealed the circumstances of his epiphany. But he did explain why he found the new design so compelling. As he wrote to one royal patron, compared with his original carriage, his running machine was simpler, more functional, and "better supported by nature herself." He was particularly keen on its motive system. Like his first vehicle, the draisine engaged the legs, which he recognized as the stronger set of limbs. But this time they performed natural work, not awkward motions to activate cumbersome machinery. He no doubt hoped that this new approach would appease those who objected to the mechanical carriage on philosophical grounds.

Drais apparently arrived at the compact configuration following his rejection of the mechanical drive. For if he no longer needed any sort of lever system to convey human power to the wheels—a process he had come to distrust—then he had no need for a platform on three or four wheels to support such a mechanism. He could thus reduce the profile of the machine to a minimal form consisting of only two wheels in a line, to act as an adjunct to the human body itself. This new approach transformed the very nature of the human-powered vehicle. It was no longer a mechanical "chariot" carrying multiple passengers, but rather a single "horse" that obeyed only one master. The personal nature of the draisine introduced an unprecedented degree of practicality and appeal.

To critics, however, the velocipede was a "strange invention" that "turned a man into a horse and carriage" and thus compelled the rider to do work formerly performed by animals. John Keats, the famed English Romantic poet, was among those who dismissed the novelty as the "Nothing of the Day." One American pundit summarily dismissed the velocipede, scoffing that "every species of transatlantic nonsense, it would seem, is capable of exciting curiosity, no matter how ridiculous." Some derided its mechanical assumptions, likening velocipede riding to "working a passage up a canal by towing the boat." Others took aim at the riders themselves, lampooning them as idle and vain "dandies."

Indeed, one skeptic in Philadelphia deemed the machine "a mere apology for a de-

Velocipede riders were commonly portrayed in the European satirical press as vain attention-seekers, as in this print published in London in 1819

cent man to take a race by himself." As he saw it, no respectable gentleman would ever "run a mile for diversion . . . as nature made him," since the spectacle would inevitably "astonish the natives" and "bring the heads of the good people at their windows," perhaps even generating a trail of boys yelling "Stop Thief!" Yet, he concluded, "if a man only has a wheel at his back, or appears to have some machinery on foot, he may run till dooms-day, and no body will molest him."

Others, however, welcomed the velocipede as a serious scientific proposal, in perfect step with the fast times. "Velocity is the fashionable mania of the present day," read one London advertisement for lottery tickets. "We walk with a Velocipede, are whirled along in a light Post Coach, or run into Fortune in five minutes by a successful speculation." A writer in Maryland insisted that the velocipede meshed well with the pervasive spirit of innovation. "We teach the dumb to speak, and can make one sheet of paper as long as from here to Boston. Our Grist Mills take in the grain themselves, carry it up half a dozen stories, grind it, deposit it, and almost make the barrels and pack it away without the visible agency of man. Next comes the Velocipede, a substitute for a horse. By the slightest pressure of his foot upon the ground, the machine is propelled and bears the rider, in good, smooth, level roads, at the rate of seven or eight miles an hour. This travelling poney costs about eight dollars, and as he requires no food, Curry Comb or Bridle, may be considered the cheapest conveyance ever known."

Still others greeted the velocipede with cautious optimism. While few anticipated that the new vehicle would ever deliver true utilitarian service, many held out hope that it would at least furnish harmless amusement, if not healthy exercise. An editor in Cincinnati professed not to know "whether these machines can be applied to useful purposes as the admirers of them say they can," but added, "this is certain, they are calculated for much amusement and the promotion of health by the peculiar exercise they afford." Another writer in that western city, after viewing some velocipede lessons, agreed. He found that the exercise "brings into full action every muscle of the body, and opens the chest." He foresaw a bright future for the velocipede as an athletic instrument. "There are multitudes who go to the grave simply from want of exercise," he observed. "They acquire sedentary habits which give no alarm, but silently weaken the system. It is highly important in large cities that some innocent, simple, and not overexpensive mode of exercise should be afforded to the public."

Even those who questioned the practicality of the velocipede as a road vehicle refused to rule out the possibility of significant improvement. One editor in Westchester, Pennsylvania, expressed his own doubts about the pretentious little machine called a velocipede, accelerator, hobbyhorse, and "seven other names." Yet he urged that it be given a fair trial, "for there is no knowing what the ingenuity of this wonderful age may bring forth." Moreover, he added, "there is no reasoning against facts. So we will wait awhile with patience—assured if there is any use in the machines our enterprising Coach maker, Mr. Work, will soon introduce them."

Clearly, the fate of the draisine would hinge on its actual performance on the road. And thanks to the spirited efforts made by Drais himself, the machine got off to a fast start. At his first demonstration in Mannheim in the summer of 1817, Drais covered nine miles on a road in one hour, less than half the normal walking time. A month later, he performed a similar feat with an improved machine, ascending a steep hill between Gernsbach and Baden. The German press took due note of Drais's prowess as a runner atop his invention, and generated a wave of favorable publicity. Before long, mechanics in Dresden, Leipzig, and Frankfurt were pushing draisine knockoffs.

Meanwhile, to encourage development, Drais issued a promotional pamphlet with a price list and ordering instructions. It described several models, notably a tandem and a three-wheeler with a second seat in front to accommodate a lady passenger. Optional accessories included an umbrella and a sail for windy days. Drais also specified his royalty terms. Upon payment of one Carolin from a maker, he would supply a badge with his family coat of arms, to be affixed to every authorized machine. Drais explained that he was setting liberal terms to be collected on a voluntary basis in advance of any patent, so as not to delay exploitation of this truly important discovery.

Indeed, the velocipede had vast and undeniable possibilities, should it prove practical. As a "facilitator," it could enable the less agile, including women and the elderly, to make their rounds with less effort or to go farther under their own speed than they had ever imagined possible. As an "accelerator," it could attract scores of young sportsmen eager for exercise and amusement. Its superior speed could even serve useful functions, such as the delivery of time-sensitive messages. In his brochure, Drais pointedly pictured a military courier astride the machine.

The draisine continued to pick up momentum in early 1818. In January, the state of Baden granted Drais his first patent, despite new objections from Tulla. A month later Drais secured a French patent as well, in the name of his agent, Louis Dineur. The draisine, or draisienne as it was called in France, quickly became a cause célèbre among the European elite, appearing in parks and on stages. As Drais's prestige grew, he was admitted to several learned societies, and he even lectured one on the merits of his latest invention. Still, it remained to be seen whether the velocipede would truly deliver compelling practical or recreational benefits.

Drais stressed the practical benefits of his "running machine" in his pamphlet from 1817, showing a military courier atop a velocipede as he delivers a time-sensitive message

The velocipede demonstration held in the Luxembourg Gardens of Paris in April 1818, as seen by a French artist. Many who observed the curious performance doubted that the invention would prove of any practical value.

Many Europeans who saw the machine in action came away disappointed. The *Journal de Paris* derided the sorry performance by Drais's servant in the Luxembourg Gardens that April. It noted that a band of children on foot had no trouble keeping up with his machine. When a brave spectator tried to run atop it, he fell with such force that he broke a bolt, disabling the vehicle. For the newspaper, this curious invention was just as futile as Blanchard's short-lived four-wheeler some forty years earlier. Cracked a contemporary, "Mr. Drais deserves the gratitude of cobblers, for he has found an optimal way to wear out shoes."

Another demonstration, in Burgundy that summer, drew only mixed reviews. François Lagrange, a turner from Beaune, reportedly rode a velocipede of his own construction thirty miles to Dijon in only two and half hours. The next day, he and a partner rode "every which way" around the main square, exciting a crowd. A Dijon paper pronounced the affair a success, but a contemporary in Beaune concluded that the velocipede was no more practical than the mechanical wings another German had exhibited the year before. It charged that Drais had "tortured his mind" in a vain effort to replace the coach. In its view, his machine required a custom-made "hard and dry" road. On any other surface, travelers were apt to find themselves in the unhappy situation of proceeding on foot with the added weight of the machine on their shoulders.

Drais, meanwhile, did his best to silence his critics and establish a velocipede trade. In April 1818, he rode his invention more than fifty miles from Mannheim to Frankfurt, returning two weeks later. But the press, having lost interest in the novelty, paid scant notice. In October, he traveled to France to revive flagging interest, stopping first at Nancy. A local paper praised his skillful handling of the velocipede, and the "grace and speed" with which he descended a hill. But it also noted that the baron's legs had "plenty to do" when he tried to mount the machine on the muddy grounds. Drais fared little better in Paris, where his demonstration in the Tivoli Gardens drew only a small crowd. The *Journal de Paris*, while acknowledging Drais's superior skill, reiterated its position that the draisine was of no practical value. Elsewhere in Europe, mechanics gradually and reluctantly reached the same conclusion.

Yet the running machine was not necessarily doomed. Conceivably, it could still create a permanent, if modest, demand as a recreational tool. After all, even those who had questioned or denied its utilitarian value were inclined to believe it might serve as a pleasant and healthful diversion. "In the final analysis," conceded the critical *Journal de Paris*, "we believe velocipedes are capable of providing healthy exercise in a park or

Hills were a chief concern to prospective velocipede riders, as this English print from 1819 suggests. One risked having to haul the machine on the way up or losing control of it on the way down.

on solid ground." Indeed, during the summer of 1818, velocipede races were among the chief attractions at festivals in and around the French capital. At Monceaux Park, Drais's agent Dineur rented out the machines by the half hour, and similar services were offered in Germany and elsewhere in Europe. In Vienna, Anton Burg, a maker of agricultural tools, equipped and operated a popular outdoor rink for riding draisines.

In spite of these initiatives, the sport failed to establish itself on the European continent, where the velocipede all but vanished by the end of 1818. One might suppose that the failure of the velocipede to prove itself on the road created a stigma that overshadowed its genuine recreational possibilities. Yet had these vehicles truly afforded compelling exercise and amusement, some fun-lovers would no doubt have continued to ride them from time to time. Evidently, the draisine commanded little lasting appeal in its primary role as a rink vehicle or "path putter." It was no doubt more amusing when used outdoors as a downhill coaster, a sort of summertime sled. But such a fleeting pleasure entailed a significant initial investment, a fair amount of work trudging up the hill, and a high risk of injury or damage to the machine.

In the end, as a mere toy, the draisine lost much of its theoretical appeal. In its original utilitarian context, as a substitute for a horse, the vehicle's cost seemed moderate and its size admirably compact. But as an article of amusement, compared with kites, sleds, and skates, the velocipede was both costly and cumbersome. Clearly, the draisine would require substantial improvements before it could provide any compelling service, whether utilitarian or recreational.

T W O *The Draisine Abroad*

Development of the draisine might have all but ended in 1818 had it not been for an ambitious Londoner named Denis Johnson. Why this long-established coachmaker, nearing sixty years of age, decided to start his own velocipede production is uncertain. He may have been aiming to cash in on the latest continental novelty; or perhaps he genuinely believed in the vehicle's long-term prospects. Whatever his motivation, he announced in late 1818 that he would soon market an improved model. Some months later, he unveiled his "hobby-horse," as it came to be known. It did indeed set new standards of elegance and performance, and sparked an unprecedented flurry of experimentation with human-powered vehicles.

Like the draisine, Johnson's hobbyhorse featured two wheels in a line connected by a wooden perch. The body, however, was dipped in the center below the seat to accommodate larger wheels, meant to enable faster speeds. To support the frame on the hubs, Johnson used an iron fork in front and two iron stays in the rear, doing away with Drais's bulky wooden braces. He simplified the steering mechanism by providing a steering bar perpendicular to the frame with wooden handgrips at each end. Originally the bar was connected to a long semicircular piece of iron that projected from the frame

A.D.1818. Dec. 22. N.º 4321.
JOHNSON'S Specification

(1 SHEET)

FIG. 1

FIG. 2

Examined
Victor Indore Henry
Robert Lucas

The enrolled drawing is colored.

Drawn on Stone by Malby & Sons.

and forked at the base to make room for the front wheel, with each prong pivoted to one side of the hub. Johnson eventually affixed a much shorter rod directly to the steering column. Some models featured footrests at the lower ends of the fork blades where riders could rest their feet during descents. Compared with a draisine, Johnson's hobby-horse had a much more elegant appearance and, at forty to fifty pounds, it was also somewhat lighter.

In February or March of 1819, Johnson opened a riding school near his workshop on Long Acre, charging a shilling for admission. The curious came in droves to observe the latest sensation, while others earnestly prepared for springtime excursions on the open road, taking lessons from the instructors on hand. Johnson happily took orders for velocipedes, charging the goodly sum of eight pounds. He also solicited the rider's

facing page: Denis Johnson of London submitted this drawing to complement his patent specification, originally filed in December 1818. He improved the draisine and sparked an unprecedented interest in human-powered vehicles.

below: An elegant hobbyhorse made by Johnson for George Spencer, fifth duke of Marlborough (1766–1840), preserved at the London Science Museum. It features a breastplate, iron braces suspending the wheels from the frame, and an ornate dome above the front fork reminiscent of Saint Paul's Cathedral near Johnson's workshop on Long Acre.

weight, so that he could custom build each machine to be as light as possible without compromising its structure. The seat, which rested on two iron supports, could also be raised or lowered according to the rider's inseam.

When spring finally arrived, however, many neophytes hesitated to venture out in public atop their strange mounts. One newspaper attributed their timidity to the "fear of ill success and the quiz of novelty," and suggested that they would defer their debuts "until they have become so well drilled as not to fear the exhibition of a *somersot*." The bold few who did set forth for the great outdoors promptly ran into trouble. In London, one unfortunate "velocipeder" found himself surrounded by a hostile mob. He frantically hailed a stagecoach, flung his machine on its rooftop, jumped in, and sped off to safety. Three men who intended to exhibit their riding skills in Hyde Park found themselves surrounded by several dozen agitated boys.

Evidently, as long as the velocipede commanded such intense public scrutiny, outdoor jaunts would be no walk in the park. Still, if growing numbers adopted the vehicle over time, the public would presumably grow accustomed to its sight and even encourage its use and development. The first opportunity to win a strong measure of popular sympathy came on the first of April, when numerous exhibitions were announced across

Pedestrians travelling on the New Invented Hobby horse!

An English print from 1819 projected a positive image of the velocipede as a traveling machine, yet all three vehicles sport an extra rear wheel, suggesting that the artist distrusted a vehicle having only two wheels

England. Many citizens eagerly expected to catch their first glimpse of the celebrated pedestrian accelerator on that particular day.

In Canterbury, "crowds of the lower and middling classes" lined the main road to witness the anticipated five-mile run. "There being only one of those machines in the place, and that not having been much seen," recounted a local paper, "the curiosity of the inhabitants was excited to a great degree." When the machine failed to appear at the appointed hour, however, "spectators began to betray considerable symptoms of impatience." They were soon reassured that the velocipede "was broken and gone to be repaired, but would be there in the course of half an hour." More time elapsed, however, and still no sign of a velocipede. Finally, the gullible public learned that "the proprietor of the machine had no intention of exhibiting it publicly" and "the whole transaction was intended to make them remember the first of April."

Before long, however, velocipedes did materialize on roads throughout the kingdom. But problems persisted. For one thing, the riders—generally young men of leisure—were not always well received. A "charger" in Liverpool, for one, had to endure "the censures and remarks of the illiberal and the illiterate." Many also encountered difficulty trying to advance over rough roads. Some took to the smooth sidewalks, prompting a slew of arrests at the behest of indignant pedestrians. One luckless Londoner, apprehended on Leather Lane, begged the magistrate to waive the two-pound fine since he had "laid out all his money in the purchase of his charger." But the merciless judge impounded the vehicle and ordered the defendant to pay in full.

Clearly, the hobbyhorse was off to a difficult start in its bold bid to win a measure of public acceptance, let alone broad approval. But not all early reports were discouraging. In Yarmouth that spring, two locally made machines were exhibited every evening, becoming "the general topic of conversation." A Winchester newspaper reported that velocipedes were becoming "very general," frequently arriving from towns "forty and fifty miles distant." Several makers and enterprising individuals staged crowd-pleasing exhibitions in large cities, including Liverpool, Manchester, and Sheffield. For one shilling, the public could inspect the machine close up, and even learn to ride one. A Leeds paper noted that "the working of those [velocipedes] now exhibiting in the Cloth-Hall are much better understood than during the first week. A gentleman has gone 120 yards at one spring, and has run a quarter of a mile in two minutes."

That April, Denis Johnson himself appeared at the Stork Hotel in Birmingham to demonstrate his "truly unique vehicle." A month later, he took his act to Music Hall in Liverpool. "Before we saw the performance," confessed one journalist, "we had no conception of the graceful movements of which [the velocipede] is capable in skilful hands." Johnson's production soon reached approximately twenty machines a week. Meanwhile, other makers began to enjoy a brisk business as well, although they did not always meet with Johnson's approval. The Londoner vigorously denounced the "spurious imitations" and the "imperfectly skilled" exhibitions that had preceded his own appearance in Liverpool.

In June came the encouraging news that four gentlemen on velocipedes had easily covered the sixty miles between Brighton and London in only twelve hours. By summer, the ever-present vehicle had even won over a few pundits. A sympathetic writer in York chastised those who refrained from velocipede riding strictly for fear of public ridicule. He praised those "sensible and modest enough to make no fuss about the matter, who mount and set off at once, with a sense, not of themselves, and what others shall think of them, but of the utility and pleasure of so desirable an invention." Indeed, "if numbers of persons were to adopt this new invention," he insisted, "it would make considerable change in the health of the community. . . . We hope in the course of the summer to see [velocipedes] scuddling about in all directions, to the great discomfiture of indigestion, bad spirits, paleness, leanness and corpulency."

But critics charged that the pesky velocipede was more likely to attack unsuspecting pedestrians than any human ailment. Groused one newspaper in Hull, "We have again to remark on the growing nuisance of running Velocipedes upon the foot pavements in almost every part of this town." A week later, the newspaper gleefully reported the arrest of one such offender, John Gould. "Upon any further complaints," warned the paper, "the Magistrates are determined to levy the full penalty of five pounds."

Meanwhile, a few spontaneous velocipede contests on the open road drew large crowds, but did little to dispel the public's growing misgivings. One ten-mile contest in York pitted a dandy charger against an opponent mounted on a jackass. "At starting," reported the local newspaper, "bets were in favour of the ass." But the velocipede soon made a surprising "speed a-head." Its lead proved short-lived, however, once its rider became footsore. "The race was now expected to be keen and well contested," the newspaper recounted. "But, to the great mortification of the dandy horse and his rider, [the velocipede] came down while at full speed, breaking its own fore-leg, and cutting the rider on the forehead. Needless to say, the prize went to the 'long-eared competitor.' "

Velocipede advocates soon recognized that if races were to advance their cause, they would have to be well planned and promoted, like the many crowd-pleasing contests featuring horses and pedestrians. Only by attracting the ablest riders with the best vehicles could these events rescue the velocipede "from the disgrace and odium of Dandyism" while establishing its merits as a legitimate source of exercise and amusement. Moreover, the public's faith in the practical potential of the machine might grow as competition gradually improved its construction.

Starting in May 1819, several organizers announced velocipede races to feature competitors in colorful jockey attire. Alas, the contests either fizzled or failed to come off. A

Organized races, such as the one depicted in this English print from 1819, could conceivably demonstrate the practicality of the invention and encourage its development. Yet they failed to hold a lasting appeal.

race held in Ipswich that July, coinciding with the annual horse derby, drew but three contestants. "So great was the eagerness of the multitude to be near them," reported the local paper, "the riders, for want of scope, had no opportunity for showing their skill either in speed or jockeyism." Another event, set to take place in York that summer, was to have united an unprecedented two hundred riders. But it apparently fell through, judging from the conspicuous absence of any follow-up report.

Undaunted by these failures, one visionary outlined an elaborate program for a velocipede race slated to take place in Lincoln that September. To win over the public, he urged organizers to scrap the proposed monetary awards in favor of "more ennobling" prizes that would be "better worthy a dandy striving for." He prescribed practical items such as looking-glasses, scissors, and smelling-bottles. For the grand prize, he suggested a corset "richly embroidered with gold and silver" to be "suspended from the Grand Stand during the whole of the races" for the public's admiration. At the closing ceremony, the "glorious victor" would receive the precious prize from "the fair hands of approving beauty." Alas, the race never came off.

As the summer wore on, rather than gaining in popularity as the York writer had hoped, the velocipede faced mounting opposition. A struggling Denis Johnson began to push a special model for ladies, no doubt hoping to revive public sympathy and demand. "The principal difference," explained the *Liverpool Mercury*, "consists in the

The author of this 1819 English print ridiculed the idea that proper ladies would ever ride a two-wheeler in public. Denis Johnson nonetheless proposed a special model for women.

horizontal bar which unites the two wheels [being] below instead of above, [so that] the drapery flows loosely and elegantly to the ground." This bold initiative failed, however, and the public continued to spurn the mechanical horse.

The final straw for the beleaguered velocipede movement in England was the announcement in August that the London College of Surgeons had condemned the machine. According to this prestigious body, riding on the two-wheeler was dangerous to the rider and liable to cause "ruptures," meaning hernias or severe cramps. Only a fool would persist. By fall, Johnson's advertisements had ceased, and he resumed production of conventional carriages. His former rivals were likewise in retreat. The once promising two-wheeler had evidently run its course throughout Europe.

While the velocipede was being put to the test in Britain, Americans gave it a go as well. To be sure, their experiment unfolded on a much smaller scale, with probably no more than a hundred machines, less than a third of the estimated number produced by Johnson alone. Yet the young nation prided itself on its technological prowess and was not about to ignore an invention that had captivated the Old World. Indeed, with the vast and ever-expanding distances they inhabited, Americans were particularly keen on any proposal that promised to improve transportation. Robert Fulton's celebrated steamboats were already chugging along the nation's major waterways, and the very spring that the velocipede arrived, in 1819, the *Savannah* left New York for Liverpool on what became the first steam-assisted transatlantic crossing.

Over land, too, America was increasingly well connected. Mail coaches—light-weight horse-drawn carriages holding up to six passengers—made regular excursions from one city to another. One editor in New York marveled how he could leave town at dawn, travel one hundred miles to Philadelphia in eight hours, transact business there for an hour or two, and still return home by midnight. Benjamin Dearborn of Boston even envisioned a means to apply steam power to land vehicles, proposing a self-moving carriage to travel on a "level rail-road." In his estimation, such a vehicle could carry up to thirty passengers in complete comfort, at the extraordinary speed of twenty miles an hour.

The first American to test the velocipede was J. Stewart of Baltimore, a musical instrument maker. In late 1818, he built a specimen based on a European technical drawing and called it a Tracena, a corruption of the term draisine. The following February, he displayed his device at Concert Hall, inviting "ladies and families." One reviewer granted that Stewart's machine might rival the newly introduced kaleidoscope for curiosity value, but questioned its practical possibilities. "The constructor feels very confident that [the velocipede] may answer all the purposes of a land carriage," he reported, "but in this we fear he is too sanguine. It appears to be suited only for good level roads; and cannot, therefore, be introduced in that character here, at least for some time." The writer nonetheless concluded that the machine deserved consideration "as an instrument of graceful and manly exercise," noting that "Mr. Stewart has already had orders for a number of young gentlemen." Local interest apparently dissipated, however, as the press made no further mention of Stewart's machine.

Several months passed before another American velocipede maker emerged. He was Ambrose Salisbury of Boston, a wheelwright and chaise maker. In late April, he demonstrated his vehicle on the city's mall and main streets, where it attracted packs of boys and "the gaze of the crowd" on account of "the rapidity of its motion" and "the singularity of its shape." Within a month, Salisbury invited the public to inspect his first two specimens at his workshop. One wag conceded that the machine might temporarily displace that "old fashioned animal called a horse," given that "Boston folks are always fond of novelty." But he predicted that the humble creature would ultimately prevail since it was "more serviceable in climbing a hill, or passing a snowdrift." Indeed, Salisbury's enterprise likewise faded.

The velocipede at last found a receptive market in Philadelphia, thanks in large part to a leading senior citizen, the famed portrait artist Charles Willson Peale. After inspecting Stewart's velocipede in Baltimore, Peale decided to have one made for himself, despite being nearly eighty years of age. He engaged an "indifferent blacksmith" in Germantown, providing him with a drawing from a London journal and scrap iron from an old threshing machine. When it was completed in early May, his velocipede topped fifty-five pounds, five more than the average weight quoted in the article.

Peale was immensely proud of his acquisition, but increasingly troubled by its apparent overload. At first, as if to reassure himself, he declared to his son Rembrandt, "a few pounds additional is of little consequence as being borne on the wheels." He soon concluded, however, that his machine was "heavier than it might have been" and "cannot go without labour uphill." Several times he had his velocipede modified to shed the offending pounds, until there was "very little of the original machine left." As his repair bills mounted, he groused that what was supposed to be a modest investment was rapidly turning into a major expenditure.

Peale's financial frustrations were mercifully alleviated once he cashed in on the novelty value of his new device. Shortly after its completion, he put the oddity on display in his "museum," a well-known repository in Philadelphia where he exhibited his artwork along with his vast collection of natural curiosities gathered from his many explorations around the world. To Peale's great satisfaction, the mechanical marvel quickly produced "a very considerable profit, as a great deal of Company has visited the museum on purpose to see it, being the first made in Pennsylvania."

Almost immediately, more specimens materialized in Philadelphia. One journalist counted two others "which are exhibited everyday for the amusements of the spectators at the public squares and gardens—any person rides them that pleases." One belonged to a Mr. Chambers, who hired out velocipedes in Vauxhall Gardens. Another was the handiwork of J. Stewart, who was now plying his trade in Philadelphia and exhibiting at Federal Hall. Peale's youngest son, twenty-three-year old Franklin, soon added yet another to the local fleet. Patterned after Stewart's original model, Franklin's machine was made of wood and weighed barely half as much as his father's iron monster.

One Saturday night in May, a journalist had occasion to witness both Peale machines in action. He happened to be in the vicinity of Washington Square when he heard rumors that one of those strange new vehicles was heading his way. Anxiously he awaited its arrival until at last, at about half past ten, the "curious machine made its appearance." The rider was Rubens Peale, another of the painter's sons. He was mounted on his father's clunker, which he had retrieved from the museum. The journalist promptly gave it chase, but was soon distracted. "My ears were assailed with the cry of 'Here comes another!'" he recounted, "and before I had time to look round it passed like lightning."

Indeed, as the senior Peale would proudly record, Franklin descended on the scene that evening atop his superior wooden mount and tore around the square in only two

The Artist in His Museum, a self-portrait painted by Charles Willson Peale in 1822. In the background is his personal museum stocked with exotic artifacts. A few years earlier, Peale displayed his own velocipede to the delight of curious crowds.

and half minutes. Moreover, to the journalist's astonishment, "the rider seemed to sit with as much ease as if in an elbow chair." The journalist finally managed to catch up with the fleeter velocipede, but only after Franklin came to a complete halt. Peering through the dense crowd that had encircled the novelty, the journalist studied its form. "It seems to differ entirely from . . . those constructed here," he reported—"it appears to be more manageable, and can turn in a smaller space."

While the Peales evidently valued the velocipede primarily as a recreational tool, they also gave some thought to its practical possibilities. That summer, the elder Peale noted that Franklin had used his new mount to visit a friend some distance away, taking three-quarters of an hour. He held out hope that, with further refinements, the machine might be able to reach "six or seven miles an hour without incurring much fatigue." He conceded, however, that this projection would have to be borne out by practice, adding that "we will be able to make a correct and exact estimation shortly."

Local officials, however, took a dim view of the velocipede. In June, one rider who dared to stray onto the smooth sidewalks was fined three dollars, a harsh retribution that stifled local use of the velocipede on public streets. Even the Peales began to confine their rides to the friendly confines of the family farm in Belfield, on the outskirts of town. For despite the public's general disapproval, the patriarch continued to use his machine as a welcome diversion from his arduous painting projects. Whenever his back began to ache, he would take a few spins atop his velocipede in the "salubrious air" of his garden, and return to his easel thoroughly invigorated.

The elder Peale also encouraged his family, including his daughters Sybil and Elizabeth, to indulge in the exercise. He particularly admired the reckless abandon of his sons and their friends when they flung their feet over the armrests and charged downhill "at the speed of a running horse"—with a "swiftness that dazzles the sight." Although Peale's son Charles found his father's machine "too heavy" for serious road use, he noted with some satisfaction that it went "down hill like the very devil." By mid-1820, however, Peale ceased to mention the velocipede in his correspondence. Apparently even the old master and his family tired of the activity. Philadelphia's brief experiment with the velocipede came to an unceremonious end.

By mid-May 1819, three of the country's largest cities—Baltimore, Boston, and Philadelphia—had all tried the two-wheeler, with little lasting enthusiasm. Yet the American experiment would hardly have been complete without the participation of the largest metropolis, New York. Surprisingly, it had yet to encounter the novelty firsthand. Finally, a local newspaper reported that the velocipede "was exhibited yesterday, for the first time in this city, by an unidentified English gentleman who brought it out on the *Criterion* from London."

Although most attendants "came away satisfied," one reporter insisted that New

Yorkers were being taken for a ride. He pronounced the Englishman's half-dollar admission "outrageous" given that many had already seen the novelty a full three weeks earlier in Boston. Moreover, he revealed, an ingenious local mechanic was about to unveil an improved model made entirely of tin "without charging the moderate price which the self-styled proprietor thought proper to ask." Even more infuriating, the English visitor reportedly had the gall to demand an exclusive American patent.

Undaunted by such criticism, the English entrepreneur continued his personal campaign to promote the velocipede on the other side of the Atlantic. He promptly made two or three public appearances on his mount, and "immediately collected a crowd which [he] easily outran." Gushed one local paper, "This whimsical new hobby has furnished much conversation in every circle." Further stoking the public's curiosity, a Mr. Parker from the Liverpool Theater rode a velocipede on stage "and kept the house in continual roar."

That June, the entrepreneur opened a velocipede rink near Bowling Green in lower Manhattan "fitted up at considerable expense." The rink operated every day but Sunday from six in the morning to noon and from six in the evening to ten at night, when the room was gas lit. Admission was a quarter, with monthly subscriptions costing five dollars. The facility offered an entire fleet of machines. Whether the proprietor had brought them all from England, or had some made locally, is not known. In any event, his advertisements boasted that patrons could travel "between six and twelve miles an hour, free of any molestation or danger, on a circumference of nearly 200 feet." They also stressed health benefits, claiming the exercise could "promote digestion, invigorate the corporate system, and ensure health to those that are indisposed."

If the ample advertisements in the local newspapers are any indication, the rink enjoyed a healthy patronage during the summer of 1819. It also appears to have graduated a fair number of riders who migrated to city streets to exhibit their newfound dexterity. That fall, the city declared the contingent of velocipede riders a public nuisance and banned the vehicle from public ways. As was the case in Philadelphia, this restrictive measure appears to have brought about an abrupt end to public exhibitions. The rink never reopened, and the velocipede vanished.

In spite of the public's failure to adopt the two-wheeler in the largest cities, Americans were not quite through with their experiment. Across the country, a smattering of artisans made velocipedes for their own use or for retail. In Troy, New York, the mechanics Davis and Rogers reportedly built as many as three specimens. In the western outpost of Cincinnati, the coachmaker Westervelt fitted up several "animal machines." The honor of demonstrating the first one fell to a clown, who entertained a charitable gathering. Similar devices were also exhibited in a few locales that charged admission, such as a pub in Georgetown and a hotel in Norwalk, Connecticut. Some lucky citizens in Hudson, New York, saw one on the open road, free of charge. But the rider "met with so little encouragement, he took [his velocipede] on his shoulders and bent his course northwardly, hoping to find the people there more public spirited."

The following report from Savannah, Georgia, suggests that a local demonstration fell flat. "A Velocipede made an appearance in Broad-street on Friday last. We understand it was not finished, but it attracted a reasonable portion of public attention—workmen left their employment to behold it, and merchants, deserted their counters and desks to witness its movement. It progressed with considerable speed when the propelling power was properly applied. The art of balancing was not in all cases understood by the riders, [however,] and the Velocipede was occasionally overturned—and now and then the rider, from an erect position, was found in a horizontal situation. We understand it is to receive some additional touches, when it will again, we presume, move through our streets with a gravity and speed proportioned to its utility."

The increasingly maligned velocipede nonetheless received one last spirited trial, in New Haven, Connecticut. Although the Elm City was only the tenth largest in the nation, with a population of ten thousand, it afforded an ideal opportunity to validate the new invention. Local mechanics were well schooled in the art of carriage making, and a large body of Yale students provided a natural clientele. Most important, an energetic promoter, John Mix, took up the cause. Like Peale, he ran a museum "stocked with curiosities." He commissioned several specimens from local carriage makers, and starting in June he rented them out "from

John Mix of New Haven placed this advertisement in the *Connecticut Herald* of 15 June 1819 and for a brief spell ran a successful business renting velocipedes to Yale students. Note the addendum soliciting a versatile young man who could not only manage a velocipede but also fix a drink.

sunrise to sunset" in the adjacent Columbian Gardens, a bucolic refuge where weary citizens indulged in summertime treats.

Before long, New Haven became the only American city where velocipedes combed the streets "in great numbers." The local reaction, however, was less than encouraging. One paper allowed that velocipedes "possess some advantages for exercise, and may answer a useful purpose," but it decried the "sundry and wild riders" who routinely dashed along the sidewalks after dark. So great was their "heedlessness and impetuosity," they annoyed all those who had not, like themselves, "the good fortune to be mounted on wooden horses." The newspaper noted that accidents had already occurred owing either to the faulty construction of the vehicles or the ineptitude of their riders; it knew not which. The paper implored the young riders to "keep in the middle of the streets, and leave the pavements to those who are willing to walk without wheels."

Another newspaper was even less forgiving. It vigorously denied that "these machines, with certain animals attached to them, should be allowed to run on the sidewalks of our cities, to the great annoyance of infirm persons, women, children, &tc." Pending the formal imposition of restrictions, the paper affirmed the right of citizens "to put common law into practice." It urged the populace to "seize, break, destroy, or convert to their own use as good prize, all such machines found running on the sidewalks—taking care not to beat or in any wise injure the poor innocent *jack-asses*." By fall, Mix's advertisements had ceased, and the streets of New Haven were clear of the dreaded nuisance. The New World, too, had at last given up on the two-wheeler that had once held so much promise. Alas, the velocipede had nowhere else to go but into oblivion.

For the next fifty years, before the introduction of the bicycle proper, a small number of mechanics, mostly in Britain, continued to pursue the elusive mechanical horse now known by the generic term "velocipede." Few, however, saw any need to resurrect the discredited two-wheeler, or to apply its awkward kick-propulsion scheme to other configurations. Mechanics focused instead on developing three- and four-wheelers powered by some combination of limbs and levers. By all accounts, the draisine itself sank into nearly complete obsolescence, whereupon it "lingered in and out of occasional use," in the words of one American historian. In Britain, a few bold draisine riders appeared from time to time. In France, carpenter apprentices purportedly used draisines for some years to travel from one town to another. Yet no specialized trade ever emerged, nor did the two-wheeler establish a lasting recreational market.

Still, over the years, some sympathizers pushed for a revival of the original velocipede. In 1829, *The Kaleidoscope* of Liverpool, a popular newspaper with a scientific bent, pronounced the neglected two-wheeler "greatly underrated." The same year, a contributor to *Mechanics' Magazine* lamented that "one of the most promising inventions" had been so quickly written off as an "obsolete triffle." Some years later, the distinguished mathematician Thomas Davies implored inventors to give the draisine a second chance.

Indeed, a few did suggest improvements to revive its use. Perhaps the most ingenious proposal came from Lewis Gompertz of London, a noted scientist and animal-rights activist who later founded the Society for the Prevention of Cruelty to Animals. In 1821, he modified the steering bar of a hobbyhorse so that it not only turned the front fork but also rocked back and forth in such a way that the arms supplied a motive force supplementing the rider's regular walking motion. By pulling the steering handle toward the body, the rider engaged a gear that powered the front wheel. Pushing out, however, disengaged the gear so that the front wheel would not spin backward. This clever arrangement effectively prolonged the distance one could travel with each stride, and allowed for faster speeds. And although the rider now worked the upper body rather than resting it, Gompertz insisted that the additional chore did not overtax the body nor did it detract from riding pleasure. Several technical journals discussed the plan, but little came of it.

Drais himself appears to have rejected Gompertz's solution, perhaps because it introduced a movement of the arms foreign to the natural act of walking. In Drais's view, his machine had failed in Britain simply because it had not been correctly constructed. He insisted that the two-wheeler, as he originally conceived it, needed nothing more than better materials. In 1832, to prove his point, he brought a velocipede with an improved seat spring to London. The editor of *Mechanics' Magazine* dutifully related Drais's new proposal, but he vehemently denied that his countrymen—or anyone else—

A few years after the draisine fell from favor, Lewis Gompertz tried to revive its use by adding an auxiliary hand crank. This image of his improved velocipede appeared in the *Polytechnisches Journal* of June 1821. A scientist and animal lover, Gompertz maintained a lifelong interest in human-powered vehicles, though he abandoned the two-wheeler in subsequent proposals.

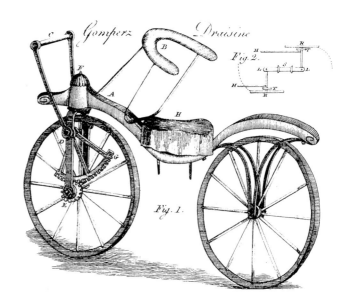

had prematurely rejected the original machine. "The velocipedes," insisted the editor, "had as fair a trial as invention ever had; and [yet] they were universally abandoned, simply because it was found there was nothing to be gained by them."

The two-wheeler thus languished, until at last it suddenly reappeared in the 1860s in the form of the original French bicycle. Although the new vehicle promptly caused a sensation, it struck many observers as little more than a draisine with pedals attached to its front axle. A stunned editor at the *New York Clipper,* writing in the fall of 1868, described the new pedals as a "mechanism so simple that everybody wonders [why] he had not thought of it before." Historians, too, have long struggled to explain an obvious enigma. Why, for nearly half a century, did inventors apparently overlook a seemingly straightforward modification to the original two-wheeler, one that presumably would have sustained and greatly accelerated its development?

Historians are apt to attribute the long lag in two-wheel advancement to the public's hostile disposition to the vehicle. They point out that Drais had all but established the bicycle proper, with its mechanical drive, by showing that a rider could coast downhill on a two-wheeler with the feet off the ground. The inescapable conclusion, as they see it, is that the promising draisine would almost certainly have acquired pedals much sooner than the 1860s if only the public had been more receptive to it. After all, the velocipede of 1819 was ridiculed in the press, harassed on the road, and legislated off the smooth sidewalks.

At face value, it seems reasonable to conclude that public hostility toward the draisine did, in fact, retard its natural pace of progression. From a contemporary perspective, we are apt to view the pedal-less two-wheeler as simply a "bicycle-in-waiting." Hence the lining up of two wheels in 1817 strikes us as the logical starting point to a predictable, if slow, process destined to yield the modern bicycle, constantly driven forward by incremental improvements. Accordingly, after 1817, the addition of a mechanical drive should have loomed to any sensible mechanic as the next logical step in the development of the two-wheeler—a virtual no-brainer. If that step took an inordinate amount of time, the reasoning goes, then the unenlightened public must surely shoulder the blame.

In truth, however, public intolerance was not necessarily the primary obstacle impeding development of the two-wheeler. The transition from the draisine to the bicycle proper was not an evident direction, let alone a simple task. For Drais in particular, his primitive propulsion scheme was not a makeshift measure to kick-start the two-wheeler pending the application of a suitable mechanical drive. Rather, kick-propulsion, not the optional two-wheel arrangement, was the very heart of his system. He genuinely believed that the natural motions of walking or running were the best, if not the only, ways to propel a practical human-powered vehicle. In 1820 he denounced ongoing

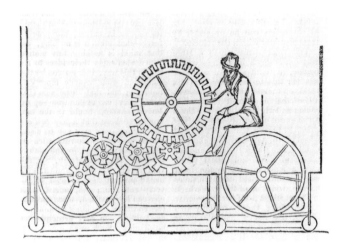

"Idea of a Manu-motive Carriage." The inventor of this curious vehicle, depicted in *Mechanics' Magazine* of 3 December 1825, adopted Drais's plan for two wheels in a line but favored a mechanical drive over kick propulsion. He added four small balancing wheels on each side to keep the contraption upright.

efforts to develop treadle-driven three-wheelers, insisting on the futility of the mechanical drive. Clearly, he would not have considered the addition of pedals to his running machine a natural extension of his thinking. Indeed, historians have largely overlooked a fundamental irony. Drais proposed the two-wheeler to do away with mechanical drives; yet his design would ultimately inspire the very machine that actually proved their merit.

Nor is it likely that Drais and his contemporaries would have instinctively thought to mechanize the two-wheelers upon which they gleefully coasted downhill. In that limited context, their draisines were in fact emulating bicycles as we know them. And, like contemporary cyclists, the coasters had learned, intuitively, to shift their weight and make subtle steering adjustments to keep their vehicles upright. But they evidently did not recognize that this coasting capability was a powerful principle to build on, one that called for the addition of some sort of mechanical drive to sustain the balancing act when gravity was no longer at play. Drais, after all, did not cite the ability to coast downhill as one of the machine's chief merits. On the contrary, he stressed in his brochure that only experts should attempt the risky act of suspending their feet while in descent. Others could take full advantage of the machine simply by using it in the conventional manner, with the feet striking the ground.

It is clear why Drais would have downplayed his machine's coasting capability. However surprised he may have been to discover that his two-wheeler could in fact coast downhill, this property alone did not give his invention any natural advantage over other configurations that could likewise coast downhill—with considerably less effort and greater stability. For Drais, the happy fact that his slender machine could roll along without falling over was simply a bonus that allowed the experienced rider an occasional reprieve from kicking chores. But it was by no means a basis to rethink the very nature of his running machine.

To be sure, the original two-wheeler did face significant social obstacles that may well have discouraged its development. As many historians have pointed out, caricaturists mocked the velocipede, especially in England, where they produced some eighty prints depicting the novelty in an unflattering light. Conceivably, these negative images may have deterred some would-be riders by linking velocipedes with vain, self-absorbed dandies. And the medium was indeed powerful. "The works of the caricaturists," noted one contemporary, "meet the broad gaze of the world from the windows of print stores and barber shops."

Yet it seems unlikely that ridicule alone thwarted the draisine's development. Even Gompertz refused to blame satirists for the machine's speedy demise. He reasoned that their scorn must inevitably "yield to the advantages which [velocipedes] will bestow on the world." On balance, satirical prints may have actually promoted velocipede development by giving the novelty greater exposure. Even its notoriety as an elitist toy may have attracted a few would-be dandies. A newspaper in Albany, New York, recalled such a case in 1869 when the bicycle proper arrived. An English stranger, it seems, had vis-

Collegians at their Exercise! _ or Brazen Nose Hobbies! _

This 1819 satirical print by I. R. Cruikshank gave a fine view of the Oxford skyline, but a rather unfavorable image of velocipede riders. What effect such ridicule had on velocipede development is unclear.

ited the town a half-century before, calling himself Lord Mortimer. He immediately ordered the then celebrated velocipede, as if to underscore his royal lineage. After being feted by the local elite for some weeks, he suddenly skipped town, leaving behind his dandy prop and unpaid hotel bills.

A more ominous obstacle to draisine development was no doubt the open hostility riders sometimes faced on the road. Even verbal abuse alone might have been sufficient to discourage the more sensitive from appearing in public on their mounts. Still, some riders were no doubt true believers who would not have been swayed by a few negative remarks. Presumably, what mattered most to these pioneers of privilege was not the reaction of the rabble, but rather the estimation of their peers, as well as their own self-image. As long as they believed in the destiny of the velocipede, they could hold their heads high and flaunt their progressive colors. That even the most devoted riders gave up the practice suggests that they themselves had lost faith in the vehicle.

The banning of sidewalk riding may also have deterred velocipede development. As Gompertz noted, such restrictions forced the machines off smooth lanes and onto rough roads where they had to compete with wide carriages and excitable horses. No doubt, as Gompertz suggested, the creation of special velocipede lanes on the roads themselves would have compensated for this setback and might even have prolonged the career of the draisine. Still, even the banishment from sidewalks would not by itself have precluded further experimentation. After all, velocipede inventors had known from the start that any successful design would ultimately have to cope with inferior roads, while also sharing them with other vehicles.

Constructing a roadworthy velocipede was, of course, an enormous technical challenge given the poor state of the roads, a problem that persisted throughout the nineteenth century. Yet, as Drais himself pointed out, the two-wheeler enjoys a natural advantage over other designs in that the rider can more easily direct its single track to the better parts of the road. Moreover, even in Drais's time, such promising technologies as macadamized surfaces were already emerging, offering hope for gradual road improvement. Surely inventors would not have given up so easily on the two-wheeler had they continued to believe in its basic merits.

In sum, a lack of public support did not necessarily doom the draisine. After all, in the fall of 1868, the original French bicycle, composed of similar materials and ridden on roads that had scarcely improved at all in fifty years, provoked the very same negative reactions. Yet it continued to develop, sparking an extraordinary outpouring of worldwide interest. And even more important, once that initial craze subsided, a small community of devotees continued to improve the bicycle, quickly establishing its practicality. The draisine evidently failed to sustain a similar development not because the public blindly rejected it but because its technical shortcomings were seemingly insurmountable.

EVERY ONE HIS HOBBY plate 1.

An English print from 1819 that humorously suggested different ways to customize velocipedes to suit various gentlemen, careerists, and tradesmen

Inventors, to be sure, might well have prolonged the draisine's run in 1819 had they applied some obvious improvements. Brakes, for example, might have better enabled riders to control their machines during descents, when they were most vulnerable to serious injury. Yet no minor adjustment could possibly have overcome the public's deep dissatisfaction with the "running machine." After all, riders would still have to strike the ground continually with the soles of their shoes, an awkward process that reportedly wore out boots, led to crashes, and provoked "ruptures," while failing to deliver compelling efficiency or amusement.

So what, then, did Drais actually achieve in the development of the bicycle? Although he failed to establish the pedal-powered two-wheeler, he nevertheless made three distinct and valuable contributions to its eventual emergence. First, he injected life into what had been till then a lethargic search for a human-powered vehicle. Second, he gave that search a distinct new direction, the pursuit of the personal mechanical horse. Third, he proposed a plan that would eventually provide the chief inspiration for the breakthrough bicycle.

But to get from the draisine to the basic bicycle, the prospective inventor would have to be willing to contemplate the two-wheeler in a context quite distinct from the running machine Drais originally proposed. Moreover, to prove the validity of the new concept, this inquisitive individual would have to develop and apply a functional drive to the two-wheeler, by no means a trivial task. Finally, the ingenious mechanic would have to gain confidence, through extensive experiments, that the system was indeed practical, while convincing others to adopt the plan as a basis for development. All told, these steps constituted a significant technological hurdle, one that would take many years to overcome.

Of course, once mechanics had generally dismissed the draisine as a dead end, few were likely to revisit and rethink the obsolete two-wheeler. After all, to do so would be to defy conventional wisdom. Yet, as the years elapsed and no compelling alternative design emerged, many sensed that the velocipede, in all its various forms, was missing something quite basic, even if they could not pinpoint the problem. "You have given sketches and descriptions of various forms and contrivances for manumotive or pedomotive machines," wrote one frustrated correspondent to *Mechanics' Magazine* in 1843; "still it is very rare to see such a machine in use." He drew two inferences from these observations: first, "there is a continued desire in the public mind to have such machines," and, second, "there is still something wanting to render them useful."

THREE *Wheels and Woes*

In the wake of the lamented draisine, many observers, inside and outside the inventive community, reluctantly concluded that humanity had drawn no closer to the elusive mechanical horse. Even those who were sympathetic to the objective began to wonder openly if the highly prized creature was not in fact a wild goose, the object of a vexing and fruitless chase. Still, while mechanics had largely written off the draisine, a few, primarily in Britain, continued to pursue alternative velocipede designs. After all, if nothing else, Drais had established the vast potential market for a practical human-powered vehicle, even if its basic form was yet to be determined. But where to go from here?

The draisine had barely been introduced when scores of dissatisfied mechanics began to propose a wealth of alternative plans involving three or more wheels and a mechanical drive. In Canterbury, England, the locals admired a French-built tricycle that advanced by means of a pre-wound spring. A young man reportedly tore around New York's Battery Park at the astonishing clip of fifteen miles per hour, riding a self-made tricycle "propelled by the feet working two paddles, which are connected with the after

The Velocimano tricycle, proposed by Gaetano Brianza of Milan in 1819, featuring wings that were designed to flap as the operator worked the drive, apparently to help the vehicle progress

wheels." In Dumfries, Scotland, a mechanic devised a treadle-driven four-wheeler steered by means of a pole in the center. But perhaps the first alternative design to gain international publicity was the Velocimano tricycle, introduced in early 1819 by Gaetano Brianza of Milan. By pushing and pulling a pair of lateral levers by hand, the operator worked the drive connected to the rear axle and also flapped a pair of wings, presumably to assist the forward motion.

Initially, while the draisine still captivated the public's imagination, the press paid little attention to these more elaborate schemes. *The Kaleidoscope* even dismissed them outright. "Wheel carriages, to be impelled by the passengers themselves, acting by means of cranks, levers, etc [have been] repeatedly attempted with very little success ... we have no hesitation in saying that all such attempts will be abortive." Once the draisine began to falter, however, the press began to take a closer look at other proposals.

In the fall of 1819, the *Monthly Magazine,* an early proponent of the draisine, reviewed three novel tricycles by J. Birch of London. One, called the Trivector, carried three passengers, each of whom participated in the propulsion by working a hand crank. The foremost had the additional chore of steering with the feet, using the footrests protruding at the base of the front fork. The magazine reported that three men had recently left London one morning in the carriage and successfully drove it fifty-four miles to Brighton in only seven hours. After dining, they went another thirteen miles that same day. The magazine calculated that it would be possible to ride the tricycle up to one hundred and twenty miles in a single day "without distressing the men." It concluded that Birch's tricycles "cannot fail, from their elegance, safety, and power to command extensive patronage."

The Trivector, illustrated in the *Monthly Magazine* of 1 November 1819, was one of several tricycles produced by the coachmaker J. Birch of London shortly after the demise of the draisine. Despite a favorable review, it failed to catch on.

Alas, Birch's carriages, and other similar vehicles, soon fell by the wayside. Such substantial structures evidently lacked the simplicity, compactness, and convenience of a personal vehicle on the order of the draisine. The public soon realized that the void left by the original velocipede would not be easily or quickly filled. As the ongoing saga of the human-powered vehicle faded into the background, the community of amateur mechanics, based primarily in Britain, quietly took over the unmet challenge. In specialized journals such as *Mechanics' Magazine,* founded in 1822, contributors submitted velocipede designs from time to time, while hashing out such basic issues as which limbs are most powerful and how best to use them. Presumably, if ever they found a compelling design, they could revive the public's interest and reenlist its support.

But skepticism abounded, even among inventors. Since many shared Drais's aversion to mechanical drives, yet had also written off kick propulsion, they saw nowhere else to turn. The sporadic velocipede proposals, of all shapes and sizes, most with wild and unworkable propulsion schemes, offered little encouragement. Nor did the occasional sightings of actual velocipedes as they inched their way along country roads. By 1832, even the editor of *Mechanics' Magazine* had sided with those who had long ago dismissed the theoretical possibility of a practical mechanical horse. He affirmed that it is "impossible for an individual to travel faster in the long run, in a machine propelled by his own personal strength," relative to the pace he would achieve by using his limbs in the "usual and natural way." Echoing Tulla, he insisted, "Man is a locomotive machine of Nature's own making, not to be improved by the addition of any cranks or wheels of mortal invention."

An Italian counterpart, writing for the scientific journal *Antologia* in 1826, took an equally dim view of the velocipede. He reported that a certain Mr. Barret of Lyon, France, had recently invented a mechanical carriage that had gained some renown. "Not only is it not new," opined the editor, "it is evidently incapable of delivering any useful service, except perhaps to a man with vigorous arms and stout legs." He scoffed at the inventor's rosy long-distance projections based on performances over "a short tract on an extremely level road." Who is to say," asked the editor, "if an extraordinary fatigue that one can endure for a few minutes can be equally sustained over many hours?" His conclusion: "To see men occupy themselves with researches of this type makes one think that they are possessed by the strange persuasion that they can create force by means of purely mechanical combinations."

Some nevertheless continued to hold out hope that a practical human-powered vehicle would eventually emerge. Still, they longed for some empirical encouragement. One perplexed contributor to *Mechanics' Magazine* asked the brotherhood whether some sort of "mechanical intervention" could truly make better use of human muscular power, "or has nature placed a limit that no ingenuity can pass?" Even the velocipede designers themselves, it seems, were uncertain. Noted one contributor in 1839, "We occasionally meet with some one of these numerous contrivances for aiding and extending the locomotive powers of man, wending their solitary way through unfrequented roads . . . as if the owners were more than half ashamed of their production or of its performance." The writer, William Baddeley, expressed what was perhaps the prevailing view. "As an amusement and agreeable gymnastic exercise these machines have a limited range of usefulness." But, he cautioned, "to imagine they can ever be made extensively or usefully . . . is a chimera unworthy of this mechanical age."

Yet to many, even a satisfying recreational vehicle seemed hopelessly out of reach. In the 1830s, more than a decade after the demise of the draisine, velocipede designers were still at an apparent standstill. One would-be velocipede rider expressed his utter frustration to *Mechanics' Magazine* in 1841. He had seen "sundry schemes for accelerating pedestrian paces" over the years in the pages of that esteemed journal, "but like steam on the common roads, all appear to be 'no go.'" He pleaded, "Can any of your correspondents inform me of any really useful and economical velocipede which has borne the test of practice?"

During the 1840s and 1850s, a modest velocipede trade finally emerged in the United States and Europe as a branch of the carriage industry. But its main products were not designed for able-bodied adults, nor did they envision practical road use. Rather, they were wheelchairs for the disabled and lever-driven tricycles for children. These specialty products, in fact, did little to dispel the prevailing notion that velocipedes were mere toys or adjutants ill suited for practical purposes. Nonetheless, the

William Baddeley's proposed "Exercising Carriage," in *Mechanics' Magazine* of 13 April 1839. The drawing omitted the second rear wheel, mirroring the other, to provide a better view of the vehicle's construction. The rider used the arms to propel the machine much like the modern cyclist uses the legs, for inventors had yet to discover that the lower limbs could generate much greater power with a similar rotary motion.

emergence of a steady demand for small carriages encouraged a few enterprising makers to experiment with mechanized three- and four-wheelers intended for general adult use.

The American velocipede trade in this period was centered in Philadelphia. E. W. Bushnell of that city introduced "small coaches for children's gratification" as early as 1835. Thirty years later, during the Civil War era, the new owner of the firm, Jacob Yost, employed some forty workmen and supplied children's velocipedes to the entire country. William Quinn, meanwhile, began producing "invalid carriages" in 1856. American firms, however, do not appear to have actively pursued the development of adult human-powered vehicles until the bicycle was introduced in 1868.

In England, however, at least one maker of small carriages dedicated himself to that task. Indeed, before the introduction of the bicycle, Willard Sawyer of Dover was perhaps the only specialized maker of adult human-powered vehicles. Originally a carpenter, he began to produce four-wheel carriages in the early 1840s. In his first models, the

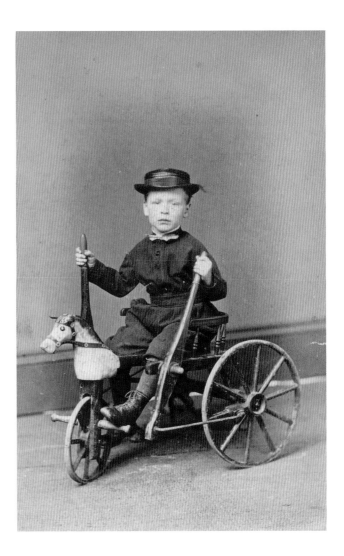

A toddler sitting on a velocipede, in a photograph from
about 1850. This style of toy
was popular among American
children of privilege in the mid-
nineteenth century but was not
conceived for serious road
travel.

rider powered the rear wheels by shifting foot treadles back and forth while steering the
smaller front wheels by means of a tiller. The design recalled the invention of the late
Edmund Cartwright, a former area resident famed for his power looms. Cartwright had
presented his carriage during the time of the draisine. When he died a few years later, in
1823, *Mechanics' Weekly Journal* recalled how he had "astonished the natives of London
by working and steering his carriage through the streets. He expressed himself with
great confidence, that this child of his old age would come into general use, and that carriages of every kind would in a few years travel the road without the aid of horses."

Whether Sawyer consciously adopted the earlier design, taking it upon himself to
fulfill Cartwright's mission, is unknown. In any case, Sawyer no doubt achieved a supe-

rior product by applying more advanced carriage-making technology. His frames were made from lightweight steel bars and his parts were manufactured to great precision. Typically, his carriages weighed less than seventy pounds. Moreover, Sawyer soon improved Cartwright's original design. He found that if the rider made a sharp turn, one of the front wheels could brush against a leg, possibly ripping the rider's pants or, worse, causing a spill. Sawyer thus reversed the wheel configuration, placing the larger driving wheels in front, and the smaller steering wheels in the rear, activated by means of a rope and pulley system. The new arrangement eliminated any possible contact between the rider's legs and the wheels.

In 1851, Sawyer rode one of his improved carriages to London's Great Exhibition, the inaugural World's Fair. Along with two other velocipede makers, including an American firm that produced children's models, Sawyer exhibited his handiwork. "A more beautiful piece of workmanship . . . I never saw," wrote one admirer. "The wheels were about 3 feet 6 inches high, and made of rosewood, the spokes not much thicker than lead pencils. . . . The regular easy speed seemed about eight miles an hour, and the

Willard Sawyer of Dover introduced his four-wheel velocipede in the early 1840s and continued production for about forty years. On later models like this one, the rider propelled the front wheels and steered the rear ones, so that the legs did not interfere with the wheels during turns. The wooden seat opens up to provide a handy storage compartment. Thomas Kelsey of Margate, Sawyer's brother-in-law, assembled this specimen, now at the Canada Science and Technology Museum in Ottawa.

The Draisine's Lingering Influence

After the demise of the draisine, most velocipede designers abandoned its kick-propulsion scheme and explored alternative designs employing various combinations of limbs and levers. One exception was G. R. Gooch of Lakenham, England. In 1842, he presented a new-style "walking machine" with the lofty-sounding name Aeripedis. Twenty years later, one writer recalled it as "a cross between the old dandy horse and the modern [read Sawyer-type] velocipede." Though it had already disappeared from circulation, the writer duly noted that "considerable voyages were performed by its means."

Ironically, Gooch himself had initially rejected the draisine in 1819 to pursue various multiwheeled vehicles with mechanical drives. Indulging in "pleasing dreams of rail-road speed," he tried "again and again . . . the treadle, the winch, the crank, and the hand lever"—all to no avail. He described the frustration of those who, like himself, spent a great deal of time developing a mechanical velocipede only to find "to his great mortification" something still wanting. "What is amiss? Some crank, some lever, some unfortunate wheel is not rightly applied; it must be altered, it must be modified. And so it is, till at last it is laid aside, perhaps hurled headlong into a garret or lumber-room, as waste material, the result of the inventor's folly."

Finally, after twenty years of futility, Gooch concluded that the combined weight of the rider and machine, totaling as much as 250 pounds, was simply too much for a person to propel efficiently by mechanical means. He thus came around, full circle, to Drais's original concept of the running machine. Although he used four wheels rather than two, for greater stability, Gooch reluctantly agreed

cranks were constructed to work with a very ingenious forward and downward movement combined."

This valuable international exposure no doubt enabled Sawyer to develop a wide reputation and a far-flung clientele. Three years later, he sent a model to an exhibition in New York. By then, his machines were also rented out at London's Crystal Palace

with Drais that kick propulsion was the most efficient way to tap human power. "Man . . . is certainly a progressive animal, but at the same time is but a walking animal; and I fear he can never become anything else by his own exertion. I do, therefore, consider, that the nearer we can come to the natural movement of man, to aid his progress, the nearer we shall come to the proper method."

Gooch's Aeripedis, depicted in the *Magazine of Science* of 16 July 1842, was one of the few velocipedes of that period to retain Drais's kick-propulsion scheme. Like Drais, Gooch reluctantly concluded that mechanical drives were inherently inefficient.

and to local beachgoers during the summertime. Yet despite Sawyer's growing prominence, he still struggled to turn a profit. In 1856, he complained to the Dover town council that its anti-velocipede ordinance had made him "unable to obtain a livelihood." Pointing out that he relied exclusively on the "hire and sale of velocipedes," he threatened to leave town.

Sawyer got a huge break the following summer, however, when the prince of Wales stopped by to place an order. Sawyer's first known catalog, published about 1858, cites a rapid succession of royal clients, including the emperor of Russia, the prince imperial of France, and the crown prince of Hanover. To what extent these notables actually used their novel vehicles is uncertain. Some may have patronized Sawyer simply to encourage velocipede development. Others may have done little more than showcase their elegant acquisitions, which cost up to forty pounds. Still others may have actually used their vehicles to patrol their estates. After all, like the draisine, Sawyer's velocipedes were well suited for travel on hard, level surfaces. But unlike the fickle two-wheeler, the steady four-wheeler allowed one to cruise or stop without risking indignity.

Sawyer's clientele was not, however, limited to royalty. He sold cheaper models coated in glossy black paint (the "Japan finish") for between fifteen and twenty-five pounds, and secondhand machines for as little as five pounds. Nor did all his clients confine their journeys to short jaunts through private gardens. A certain J. C. Skeffington claimed to have toured southern England during twenty consecutive days, covering 526 miles, including hills. According to Sawyer's brochures, a rider could easily travel up to 60 miles a day on common roads. Some suburbanites even used their vehicles to commute into the city. *The Builder* of London observed in 1858 that human-powered "miniature carriages" were starting to enable "workmen living some distance from their employment . . . to live in healthful localities." It expressed hope that the trend would continue, noting that a postman in Wales had just received a velocipede by subscription, "which greatly facilitates his labours along the country roads."

"The Tourist" and (at right) "The Racer," from Sawyer's catalog of 1863. The Tourist offered "great strength and durability" and could be built for one or two drivers; Sawyer claimed one could travel up to sixty miles in a day "with as little fatigue as if a dozen miles had been journeyed on foot."

THE TOURIST.

In effect, Sawyer appears to have cornered the promising but tenuous market for adult velocipedes. His domination of that field enabled him to develop a diverse product line. His 1863 catalog illustrates a wide assortment of machines for men, women, and children, including both racing and touring models. Most were geared for individual use, but some could be modified to accommodate a second passenger or even a co-driver. One model carried as many as six individuals, with two to four furnishing the motive power. Only one Sawyer contemporary, a certain H. Cadot, of Lyon, France, appears to have offered anything like Sawyer's rich array of velocipedes. And only one serious rival design, the Rantoone, had appeared in England by the mid-1860s. This miniature carriage, which employed all four limbs, created a mild stir but managed only mixed reviews. One Brooklyn newspaper groused: "It would seem it required an engineer to run it."

Yet for all his apparent success, Sawyer largely failed to convince the public that his velocipedes were truly practical. In 1863, one writer lamented the fact that Sawyer's machines had not achieved "general adoption." Noting that the vehicles were rented out at London's Crystal Palace, he charged that they "merely attained to the rank of a machine by affording an hour's amusement to the holiday elevated Londoner." He suggested that the pleasant diversion they provided under those circumstances was "almost enough to deter us from going into the question of their real practical utility."

Indeed, many complained that the Sawyer machine took considerable practice to master, that it was impossible to work against a strong wind or after a heavy rain, and that it had to be dragged up a steep hill. Moreover, it was dangerously unstable during

THE RACER.

The Racer was calculated to provide "the highest point of speed consistent with safety" to gentlemen "inclined for sportive recreation"

Mechanical Minds

During the brief run of the draisine, the stubborn problem of the human-powered vehicle engaged some of the most distinguished technical and scientific minds of the period, notably Nicéphore Nièpce, the French pioneer photographer, and the Reverend Edmund Cartwright, the celebrated English inventor of the power loom. Following the disappointing failure of the draisine, however, the velocipede receded from the forefront of scientific inquiry. Still, a few leading scientific figures occasionally revisited the challenge, perhaps simply to amuse themselves, without entertaining great expectations.

Two of the leading proponents of the draisine, Lewis Gompertz and Drais himself, continued to explore new forms of vehicles, although neither returned to the two-wheeler after 1832. Gompertz presented two more velocipedes, in 1847 and 1861, both with four wheels and hand cranks. In 1837, Drais appeared in the streets of Mannheim driving a curious carriage, described by one reporter as "the proverb realized—the cart before the horse." The passengers sat in front facing forward, while the coachman sat on the roof looking backward at the four attached horses, steering with the help of a mirror. As with his earlier vehicle, Drais enumerated its advantages: The horses cannot run away or kick dust into the passengers' faces, and the travelers enjoy an unobstructed view of what's ahead. Moreover, the driver cannot overhear their conversations or subject them to tobacco descents. Even satisfied customers readily acknowledged its severe limitations. "Even on the best of our high roads," noted one rider, "the rattling and shaking of such slight machines is dreadful at the speed of anything over seven or eight miles an hour and if driven constantly at this rate they cannot last long."

In spite of Sawyer's best efforts to develop a practical velocipede, the public's sense of frustration lingered. Complained one writer to *Mechanics' Magazine* in 1860, "In these days of invention, improvement, and locomotion, why cannot we poor pedestrians be helped forward by some new kind of velocipede or accelerator?" The writer acknowledged the existence of Sawyer-type velocipedes, but noted that these were "few and far between" and that none came "up to the mark." He proposed that the magazine offer a monetary reward to stimulate the search for a breakthrough design. Shortly

fumes. In 1843, Drais also returned to the human-powered vehicle, proposing a four-wheel velocipede with a mechanical drive to ride on railroads.

In Britain, meanwhile, scores of inventors turned their attention to the railroad, helping build an extensive network interconnecting the entire kingdom by the 1850s. This remarkable development, however, offered little consolation to those still struggling with the velocipede. "Perhaps the general speed of the railways," noted one sympathizer in 1863, "has thrown discouragement on the more humble modes of progression." Moreover, as time went on and no convincing human-powered vehicle emerged, even the most technical minds were inclined to suspect that a truly practical mechanical horse was simply beyond the reach of ingenuity.

Some, however, continued to dabble in velocipede experimentation. In the 1830s, the chemist Michael Faraday, acclaimed for his pioneering work in electricity and magnetism, reportedly operated a four-wheeled kick-propelled velocipede of his own design. At about the same time, the prominent British railroad pioneer Isambard Kingdom Brunel designed and built a velocipede that ran on train tracks. On one occasion, he and a friend rode it twenty miles from Paddington to Slough. "We can only hope," quipped the *Great Western Magazine,* "that they had well-timed themselves with regard to the trains."

thereafter, just before the introduction of the bicycle, a contributor to the *English Mechanic* called for the formation of a velocipede club to encourage development of more practical models.

In sum, the fifty-year period separating the draisine from the basic bicycle was interspersed with largely futile attempts to develop a compelling new velocipede with three or four wheels. Yet during the great bicycle boom of the 1890s, some would claim knowledge of pedal-powered two-wheelers pre-dating the original French bicycle of the 1860s. Several murky "priority claims" asserted, in effect, that certain individuals in the interim period had indeed built mechanized two-wheelers for their own personal use, only to be ignored by the general public.

To be sure, these purported machines amount to historical footnotes at best, since they evidently exerted no influence on development. Moreover, they must have been exceedingly rare, given the conspicuous lack of any recorded commentary. In particular, the technical literature of the interim period contains no discussion of mechanized two-wheelers—not even reports of failed experiments. Nevertheless, the possible existence of a few isolated bicycle prototypes before the 1860s is an intriguing proposition.

One obvious impediment to the development of a bicycle after 1817 was the need to devise a simple yet efficient drive system. Of course, a practical propulsion scheme was desirable for any velocipede, but it was imperative on a bicycle. Without one, the rider simply could not generate sufficient speed to get started and establish equilibrium. Yet many of the first drives proposed for three- and four-wheelers were preposterously unworkable. Rotary cranks, a simple and powerful solution, were not introduced until the 1860s. Clearly, even if a few clever inventors had previously thought to mechanize the kick-propelled two-wheeler, they would have been hard pressed to find a practical drive.

By the 1840s, some mechanics had developed reasonably efficient treadles for tricycles that were capable of driving two-wheelers. But the question remains, did anyone at that time think to apply these drives to the obsolete draisine? Conventional accounts since the boom respond affirmatively, crediting at least three Scottish tradesmen with rear-drive bicycles. Collectively, they appear to reveal a surprisingly active "Scottish bicycle school" that predates the French machine by some three decades. Still, these belated claims warrant scrutiny.

The first Scotsman to gain posthumous recognition as the original bicycle inventor was the cooper Gavin Dalzell, who reportedly built a rear-drive machine as early as 1845. His son eventually donated what was purported to be the original bicycle to the Transport Museum in Glasgow, where it remains today. An even earlier claim soon emerged, crediting the blacksmith Kirkpatrick MacMillan with a similar machine. Although none of his supposed bicycles survive, the wheelwright Thomas McCall was said to have replicated MacMillan's design in the 1850s. Indeed, McCall was known to have produced and marketed a rear-drive bicycle in 1869 as an alternative to the then popular French direct-pedal velocipede.

In 1888, when Dalzell's son presented the bicycle he claimed his father had made forty years before, he also submitted documentation to prove its age. Two repair bills from 1847 did indeed show that a local blacksmith had tinkered with his father's "horse," while two letters from the same period refer to his father's "riding machine." Yet none of the documents actually specified that the machine had only two wheels, and the omission of any such reference in the letters is particularly troubling. In one, a certain Francis Forrest asked Dalzell at what rate his machine could travel a mile uphill, as well as "the lengths of the different parts." But he did not pose the obvious questions a novice would ask of the intimidating mechanical two-wheeler, namely: how long will it take to learn the knack of balancing, and is there any danger of falling? These were, after all, typical queries put to Michaux of Paris, the pioneer bicycle company, in early 1868.

We are thus left with the distinct possibility that Dalzell's son may have converted his father's original tricycle into a two-wheeler sometime after 1868 when the French bicycle was well known. Or perhaps the younger Dalzell built the entire bicycle himself in that later period, adopting a treadle drive his father had once used on a tricycle. Either way, the locals may have genuinely confused two distinct machines, sparking false rumors that the elder Dalzell had built the world's first bicycle in the 1840s. When the press first approached the son in the late 1870s for confirmation, he may have succumbed to temptation by presenting what was essentially an 1860s machine as that coveted "first bicycle."

The claim that MacMillan built a similar bicycle in 1840 surfaced a full fifty years after the supposed fact. A cycling enthusiast named James Johnston set out to undercut the newly accepted Dalzell claim, asserting that the latter had merely copied MacMillan. Yet despite his lengthy investigation, all that Johnston could muster in the way of direct evidence was a brief report of a velocipede accident in 1842 from a Glasgow paper. He claimed it referenced MacMillan and his bicycle, but the article neither named the rider nor described the machine as a two-wheeler; in fact, it referred to hand cranks rather than foot treadles, suggesting a tricycle. Johnston excused his glaring lack of documentary support, pleading "newspapers and letters in those days were not so common." Yet ample sources from that period do exist, and it is hardly unreasonable to expect at least one clear-cut account of MacMillan's alleged bicycle. After all, before 1869, bicycles of any construction were both bizarre and noteworthy.

Despite his paucity of supporting evidence, Johnston prevailed in the Scottish press. His "star witness" was none other than Thomas McCall of Kilmarnock, the mechanic who made rear-drive bicycles during the velocipede craze of 1869. McCall in fact stated that, as a child around 1845, he had seen MacMillan atop a velocipede of an unspecified construction. He further acknowledged that, years later, before he built his bicycles in 1869, he had made copies of MacMillan's machine. But he pointedly did not state that his first velocipedes had only two wheels. On the contrary, he described his bicycle of 1869 as an entirely new pattern of his own design. In effect, McCall does not appear to have truly endorsed the MacMillan claim to bicycle priority.

Curiously, in the spring of 1869, when McCall advertised his new bicycle in the *Kilmarnock Standard*, he appears to have alluded to his earlier MacMillan-inspired machines. "Having made velocipedes thirteen years ago," he noted, "[I am] prepared to make them to order upon the very best principle." But again he did not specify that those earlier machines were bicycles. Rather, he appears only to have implied that he had general experience building velocipedes. Presumably, the machines in question were tricycles, similar to others of that period. Indeed, another velocipede advertisement in the same issue refers to the bicycle as a "novel mode of locomotion." McCall's own recent demonstration is described in terms that underscore the novelty of the mechanized two-wheeler. "On Saturday afternoon last, Mr. McCall . . . drove his specimen velocipede . . . for more than an hour in the presence of a large number of spectators . . . at a considerable rate of speed with apparently but moderate exertion. . . . The experiment as a whole appeared to be highly satisfactory."

Two articles in the *English Mechanic* from the spring of 1869 provide further evidence that McCall's bicycle was not a sudden reprise of a decades-old design but rather a new construction inspired by the recently introduced French bicycle. The articles presented the rear-drive pattern as the latest bicycle innovation, one that offers certain advantages over the original French design. A number of contributors also discussed

Thomas McCall built this rear-drive bicycle, now at the London Science Museum, in the late 1860s. Some later claimed that various Scotsmen, including McCall, had made similar machines as early as the 1840s—well before the first French bicycles.

McCall's invention, but none alluded to any prior rear-drive bicycle designs, Scottish or otherwise.

If the rear-drive bicycle of 1869 had in fact already enjoyed a thirty-year track record in Scotland, it is surprising that neither McCall nor anyone else at the time appears to have alluded to it. After all, the memory of a Scottish bicycle school from the 1840s and 1850s should still have been palpable a generation later when the French bicycle arrived. Yet the ample Scottish reaction to the French novelty recalled only three- and four-wheelers similar to English patterns known to have existed at that time. A newspaper in Hamilton, outside Glasgow, for example, noted that "the colporteur that travels in the Moffat district has, we are told, for many years used a tricycle, which, in addition to himself, carries a great quantity of books."

In the summer of 1869, the same paper even appears to have alluded to the velocipede built by the elder Dalzell. "A merchant in this town [Hawksland], sometime deceased," it reported, "constructed [a velocipede] so far back as 1845, and used it for many years. It is still occasionally to be seen on the road." Dalzell senior had in fact expired in 1863, and the sketchy details in the article appear to agree with those put forth by his son some years later—save for the fact that the writer makes no mention of the machine having only two wheels. Had he known that to be the case, he had no apparent reason not to mention the point since it would have underscored his basic argument that velocipedes, French or otherwise, were nothing new to the district. In all probability, the velocipede in question was therefore a tricycle similar to the Moffat machine.

By all contemporary accounts, Scotsmen of the late 1860s were just as mesmerized as any other people by the novel sight of riders balancing and propelling themselves on French-style two-wheelers. In 1869, a newspaper in Dumfries, near MacMillan's hometown, reported that a crowd assembled every evening to admire the bicycles in motion. "No little amusement is occasionally furnished by the riders being dismounted," it observed, "but on the whole they manage to keep [on] their little saddle astonishingly well." No one seems to have recalled MacMillan's supposed performances on a similar machine some twenty years before, although he was still alive at the time. Nor did the local press make any mention of his purported interest in bicycles when he died in 1877, despite the fact that bicycling had by then developed into a major sport.

The early Michaux company correspondence from 1868 provides further evidence that the bicycle was still a complete novelty to Scotsmen at that time. A velocipedist from the northern city of Inverness wrote to assert the superiority of his own self-made tricycle, offering to race it against the new Michaux bicycle. Presumably, if he had any knowledge of prior Scottish experiments with mechanized two-wheelers he might have added that similar vehicles had already been tried and discounted in his homeland. Another

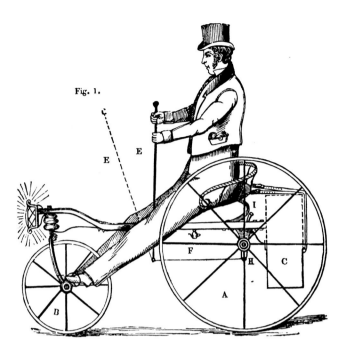

Fig. 1.

A hand-driven tricycle, illustrated in *Mechanics' Magazine* of 13 November 1841, that was among the many velocipede proposals pre-dating the French bicycle. The mechanical literature of the period, however, makes no mention of mechanized two-wheelers.

Scotsman wrote from Leith, just outside Edinburgh, to order a bicycle. He mentioned that he belonged to a local velocipede club that rode two or three times a week, and he was eager to introduce his companions to the two-wheeled novelty. "Your system is unknown here," he noted, adding, "[our velocipedes] are almost all four-wheelers."

Of course, given the sporadic ongoing velocipede experimentation in Scotland and elsewhere between 1820 and 1869, a mechanic here or there might well have experimented with mechanized two-wheelers before the introduction of the French bicycle. In 1871, well before the Dalzell or MacMillan claims surfaced, a contributor to the *English Mechanic* insisted that he had seen a rear-drive bicycle built by a millwright in Strathaven "twenty or thirty year ago." In response, another correspondent conceded "a solitary [rear-drive bicycle] may have existed." But he also insisted that "the principle was never really known." As he saw it, the mechanics like McCall who were then developing rear-drive bicycles were not reviving an older bicycle plan, but simply applying the "superior action" of Sawyer-type four-wheelers to the new French velocipede.

Historians may yet substantiate a bicycle claim that pre-dates the French machine. But it is safe to conclude that any such vehicles must have been isolated experiments rather than part of a wider, collective effort to develop a mechanized two-wheeler. After all, a single French-style bicycle in the United States in 1866 led to both a clear-cut description of the article in a local newspaper and a patent application. It seems highly improbable that an arbitrary number of equally eye-catching machines could have operated in and around Scotland's largest cities—or anywhere else for that matter—for nearly thirty years without leaving the slightest paper trail. And even if a few isolated bicycles were built before the 1860s, they evidently failed to establish a sufficient degree of functionality to warrant development. Clearly, the true breakthrough in the quest for a mechanical horse awaited the original Parisian bicycle.

Part Two The "Boneshaker" Era

FOUR *The Bicycle Breakthrough*

Decades after the demise of the draisine, mechanics were still struggling to fill its void. Finally, in 1867, the original bicycle burst on the Parisian scene and broke the impasse. Although velocipede designers had long dismissed the compact two-wheeler as a dead end, the revelation that it could be steadily and continuously driven by means of a simple mechanical crank opened a new and exciting path for development. Even in its most primitive form, the pedal-powered two-wheeler could sustain speeds of up to eight miles an hour, and it did away with that awkward and cumbersome need to strike the ground, the bane of the original two-wheeler. The addition of pedals, *Scientific American* noted, "completely changes the character of the vehicle . . . it glides along as though it were alive, and with a smooth grace alike exhilarating and beautiful to behold." Moreover, riders discovered that the knack of balancing could be learned in a few lessons, after which they could travel four or five miles with as much exertion as if walking only one. Bicycle development was under way.

Surprisingly, the key pedal breakthrough occurred not in Britain, which had long led the elusive quest for a practical mechanical horse, but in France, where the problem of human locomotion had received comparatively little attention. As late as April 1867, *Le Moniteur Universel du Soir,* the official evening newspaper of the Empire of France, lamented the country's lack of enthusiasm for velocipedes. While such machines were common in England, it noted, only an occasional amateur dared to promenade in the French capital. Yet only a month later, the same paper carried a brief advertisement for "pedal velocipedes" by Pierre Michaux of Paris, an obscure blacksmith who made iron parts for the carriage trade clustered around his small workshop by the Champs-Elysées. Few readers could have imagined then that this cryptic item would soon provoke an extraordinary worldwide reaction.

Michaux's velocipede, as it turned out, was a novel two-wheeler propelled by pedals and cranks attached directly to the front hub, which transformed it from a draisine-style aid-to-walking into a veritable vehicle. The construction was surprisingly reminiscent of Johnson's obsolete hobbyhorse from nearly half a century before. It was bolted together in like fashion and made of similar materials, except that its serpentine perch was solid iron, not wood. Its wheels were also placed much more closely together, almost abutting each other, and were slightly larger, the rear one measuring about thirty-four inches, the front one a few inches more for improved gearing. To mount, the velocipedist generally stood beside the machine, grasped both handlebar ends, and began to run ahead before vaulting onto the saddle. The rider then sat erect, the arms stretched out to the handbars, seeking out the flat sides of the spinning pedals with the feet. Once in control, the rider flailed the legs forward to keep the machine in motion. The entire contraption weighed about seventy pounds and cost the princely sum of 250 francs.

This curiosity, soon to be known as a bicycle, included such thoughtful refinements as an elongated spring stretching across the serpentine frame and serving as suspension for the leather seat, to absorb road shock. The frame itself featured an extension over the front wheel to receive the rider's calves during descents, so that the feet would not have to follow the rapidly spinning pedals, for the hub had no freewheel mechanism. Some cranks were slotted, so that the pedals could be slid up or down and affixed at the optimal distance from the seat to fit the rider's inseam. The seat itself could be slid backward or forward along the spring, enabling a given velocipede to accommodate a wide range of statures. The rider could always stop by pedaling backward. Fancier models, however, included a brake, which was activated by twisting a handlebar end, thereby pulling on a cord that applied a metal spoon to the iron tire of the rear wheel. The rear end of the spring sported the Michaux nameplate with the company's address.

The Michaux machine caught on fast, despite its high cost and the public's initial skepticism. When the first solitary riders appeared on the Parisian boulevards in the course of 1867, recalled one journalist a few years later, the public scoffed. "Bah," said the passersby, "It's just Paris at play again. First balloons, now velocipedes—one more

LE VÉLOCIPÈDE

A PÉDALES ET A FREIN

DE M. MICHAUX

PAR UN AMATEUR

The cover of the first Michaux promotional pamphlet, printed in the spring of 1868, suggested both practical and recreational uses by showing a hunter, a soldier, and a gentleman, all mounted on Michaux bicycles. The title refers to the new velocipede "with pedals and brake" to distinguish it from the original draisine.

capricious fantasy!" But within days, entire groups of velocipedists sprouted up in every quarter, "cutting across the capital's great arteries, passing like whirlwinds, leaving behind pedestrians, carriages and horsemen." Amusement gave way to awe, as the public discovered the surprising "prowess of an iron cavalcade."

Among Michaux's first customers were the leaders of the bicycle movement, about twenty in all, most with noble titles. "Struck with the importance of the idea," explained one journalist, these "young men of leisure" aimed to establish the velocipede as a "common mode of locomotion." Every evening they gathered to practice their strange art by the cascades in the Bois de Boulogne, the expansive park on the west side of Paris not far from the Michaux shop. From there, they invaded the fairgrounds of the ongoing Universal Exhibition, determined to show the world that a practical mechanical horse was at last at hand. *Le Sport* described their evangelical spirit: "On your velocipede! That is the rallying cry loudly repeated of late by a few intrepid Parisians, fanatics of this new means of locomotion.... [It will reach] every exhibitor booth and [from there] all corners of the earth."

Indeed, the world quickly took note of the bizarre novelty. Under the heading "A Revolution in Locomotion," the Paris correspondent of the *New York Times* marveled how the "scarcely visible" velocipede could eclipse twelve miles an hour, giving the rider "the comical appearance of flying through the air." Among its many advantages were "great economy of time as well as money," "immense development of muscle and lung," and the fostering of "independence of character." For women, it would "force adoption of the bloomer or some other more convenient costume." For urbanites, it would provide much-needed mobility. "Is it not absurd, is it not a disgrace to the inventive age we live in," concluded the writer, "to see a man obliged to employ, in order to get through the street, a great vehicle, as large almost as a house? So let us have the velocipedes."

The bicycle movement quickly gained momentum as the year 1867 progressed. Although Michaux bicycles had not been formally admitted to the Universal Exhibition, under way since April, they were already in evidence at the fairgrounds that summer. Several foreign visitors purchased specimens and shipped them back to their homelands. By fall, a firm in Lyon and another near Grenoble had initiated production of the new-style two-wheeler. In September, *La Vie Parisienne* observed that "everyone is talking velocipedes." In December, some one hundred riders, including several prominent citizens, departed Paris en masse on their way to Versailles as part of a novel "tourist excursion."

Still, as the inaugural year came to a close, it was unclear just how much farther the newfangled vehicle would go. To be sure, the Michaux company had already largely assuaged any misgivings about the respectability of the sport, at least for the time being. After all, one could hardly fear ridicule or condemnation traveling in such distinguished

A Letter to Michaux

Neuvy, near Esternay, Marne, France

22 February 1868

Sir,

Last year, at the time of the universal exhibition, in the midst of all its amazing wonders, I was surprised to see pass and disappear before my eyes two young men mounted on contraptions I could not fathom. A few weeks later, I saw arrive at the train station of Bezancours a man, mounted on the same object. This time, I could make out two wheels, a small one placed before a large one, a small seat, two hand grips, and two stirrups. The man descended, but the whistle of the locomotive prevented me from obtaining the name of this strange, I would almost say fantastic, machine. Recently, a sporting magazine fell into my hands. It spoke with much praise about a certain velocipede that I immediately recognized as my strange horse-vehicle. I shared the issue with my colleagues, and our small committee has authorized me to ask you, sir, the following:

1. The price of a velocipede without frills but solid and able to go a long time without repairs.
2. If one can learn to ride the velocipede alone, and if the training is long, and if at the beginning one does not risk more or less dangerous falls.
3. Can the velocipede climb steep hills, and is there any danger in descending mountains? Can one easily make sharp turns?
4. Can one travel on unpaved roads, in mud, on sand, etc.? How much time do you allow for the payment?

These questions resolved, sir, you may expect another letter with an order.

Your devoted Servant,

A. Picart, Primary school teacher at Neuvy (Marne)

"La Revanche des Vélocipèdes," satirical image from *Le Charivari*, 10 July 1867, and the first known depiction of a pedal-powered two-wheeler in the popular press. The velocipedists are shown encircling a horse-drawn carriage, blocking its passage. During the ongoing Universal Exhibition, many citizens complained of rude and obnoxious cab drivers, hence the title "The Revenge of the Velocipedists." Curiously, the gentleman in the middle is riding a rear-drive machine resembling an American Star, which was not introduced until fifteen years later. Perhaps the artist exercised his own technical imagination.

company. Yet if the machine was to gain broad circulation and acceptance, the company still had to dispel two more common misgivings: first, the novice's natural fear of being injured or embarrassed while learning the art, and second, the purchaser's concern that such a substantial investment might prove an unmitigated waste.

A number of Michaux correspondents in early 1868 expressed reservations about the safety of the machine. "Many persons around here are captivated by this new means of locomotion," wrote one man near Grenoble. "They know perfectly well, as I do, that the two-wheel velocipede is more advantageous in many respects. But, being of a certain age, they are afraid of the learning difficulties, and they believe that for traveling on good road a velocipede with three wheels would do just fine." A more daring client in London sprang for a bicycle, but pleaded to Michaux: "Make it low, so that we can learn to ride it without accident." Nevertheless, he complained after receiving his order: "I tried the machine with two of my friends, they took turns on it as well, but we made no progress at all." A customer in Bilbao, Spain, tried to teach himself in secluded spots but likewise met with "very little success."

The cost of a Michaux machine was another sore point with numerous correspondents who prodded the blacksmith for more favorable terms. "I find your price a bit steep," protested one bargainer. "I was sure that I could get one for about 180 or 200 francs, especially when I am coming to you, that is, to the factory, and I might be sending a few friends your way." "Would you agree to sell me one for twenty francs a month?" propositioned a young Parisian clerk. "There are about eighty-five colleagues at the office where I work, mostly young men, the majority of whom would certainly become purchasers under such conditions." Another asked if he and two friends could rent a velocipede for a month, hinting that they would buy it once they learned to ride it "perfectly and without danger." And while some grudgingly agreed to pay the asking price, others held out hope for future relief. "Can you tell me if at some point down the road," asked one gingerly, "you will make velocipedes more accessible?"

By offering free lessons to purchasers, the Michaux company helped allay their fears about balancing. Moreover, it declared, one needed only "five or six lessons" to make good use of the vehicle. Even upscale women, dressed in stylish gymnastic outfits, were turning up at the Michaux shop ready and willing to pedal. And, naturally, the more the number of velocipedists grew, the more prospective purchasers gained confidence in their own ability to control the machine. As one American observer concluded, contrary to first impressions, the art was evidently well within the reach of "ordinary" people and not a special gift "vouchsafed only to the few, like painting, or music, or sculpture."

The high price of a Michaux velocipede, however, remained a formidable obstacle to ownership. Nevertheless, hundreds succumbed to the irresistible urge to buy a

A French doll on a tricycle, from about 1869, reflecting the pervasive popular interest in the new-style velocipede with rotary pedals. Although this prudent young lady has opted for the more stable three-wheel variation,
she sports earrings shaped as bicycles.

bicycle personalized to their specifications. One buyer, obsessed by technical details, stipulated that his front wheel was to be exactly 0.95 meters in diameter, only to lambaste Michaux when he received one that measured a full meter. But many were more concerned about aesthetics. "As to the colors I discussed in my last letter," wrote one finicky customer, "instead of the two thin stripes you usually do please make only one a centimeter wide. And don't paint the handle ends." Another, slightly more flexible in his demands, let it be known that he preferred a black velocipede with blue stripes. He would nonetheless accept any ninety-centimeter machine in stock so as to expedite his order. "I don't care about the color," he assured Michaux, "as long as it's not yellow."

By the spring of 1868, the Michaux bicycle had become, in the words of *La Vie Parisienne,* "the amusement of golden youth and the dream of employees." The Michaux workforce had swelled to about sixty, all with their hands full trying to keep up with orders from across France and beyond. Meanwhile, other Parisian firms rushed into the new trade to meet the surging demand. More and more bicycles rumbled along the boulevards, causing much commotion and more than a few accidents. Both friends

A caricature from *Le Journal Amusant* of 1 August 1868 showing the return home of a wealthy velocipedist who gets a stern scolding from his wife for his overexertion, while the butler wheels away the offensive vehicle with a look of detached amusement. The first velocipedists were in fact generally young men of privilege.

and foes of the movement soon sensed that it was in fact no passing fancy but rather the beginnings of a bold experiment, far exceeding the scale of the original velocipede craze.

This new breed of horsemen even managed to infiltrate a cherished annual ritual, the Easter parade on Longchamps. There, in the center of the Bois de Boulogne, their curious vehicles vied for public approval, alongside fine carriages and elegant society women. One spectator, writing for the satirical review *Le Charivari*, described how, then and there, he joined the growing ranks of the velocipedists. "My attention was drawn to a man who failed to knock me over. He was mounted on a velocipede and went like the wind. He stopped about fifty feet in front of me, to return his beast to Michaux . . . making me curious to examine more closely these charming vehicles that are cheaper to maintain than a horse or carriage. . . . Believe it or not, as a result of my visit, I, too, bought a velocipede. Starting tomorrow, in my capacity as a purchaser, I will return to take my free riding lessons. Ah, a little bit of exercise is such a good thing!"

The Parisian press gave frequent updates on the rapid rise of the velocipede. One paper reported the case of two velocipedists who were exercising along the Champs-Elysées when suddenly they spotted a thief outrunning his pursuers. The gallant pair caught up with the culprit and detained him until the police arrived. "In 1868," declared *Paris-Caprice* that spring, "man, woman and child can play with this instrument, without shocking anyone. The velocipede is no longer a fashion, it's a rage. In six months' time, it will be an epidemic. One sees them by the hundreds on the public promenades, hurtling down the streets, and sailing through the parks."

But the bicycle invasion was by no means confined to cities. On the contrary, many believed the vehicle would render the greatest service on smooth and deserted country roads, enabling fortunate owners to travel afar and at will. In May, the public learned of an extraordinary ride across southern France. In two weeks' time, two gymnastic teachers covered five hundred miles from Nice to Clermont-Ferrand, the future home of Michelin bicycle tires. Along the way, they demonstrated their new vehicles in city centers before stunned onlookers. "Velocipede mania" was indeed in full swing.

Obviously, the pioneer firm Michaux had started something big by the spring of 1868. But how did it get its own start in the bicycle business? Michaux's first advertisements from the previous year alluded to a patent on the pedal velocipede but offered no background information. The early articles in the press were equally vague, suggesting only that the clever blacksmith had conceived and patented the basic bicycle some years before. One, published in *Le Sport* of July 1867, nevertheless implied that the year of discovery was 1864, asserting that Michaux's four sons were the world's first velocipedists, having had about three years of experience. Indeed, one would expect that Michaux had required a certain amount of time to produce such a polished article, with fine touches like weighted bobs on the pedals to keep their flat sides facing the soles of the rider's feet.

Left unexplained, however, were the circumstances that led to the surprising invention, what Michaux had done with the idea in the interim, and why it was only then coming to light. One sketchy report that reached the United States from Paris in April 1869 maintained that "for years [Michaux] starved while trying to introduce the vehicle. The money he gained at his anvil was absorbed by the new invention, and it was only after sending his sons and workmen for a year driving through the streets, that the public eye became familiar enough with [the velocipede] to venture to buy it. It is only eighteen months since M. Michaux commenced to sell seriously to the public."

That broad public awareness of the bicycle dated from the fall of 1867 is supported by the evidence—but what does not mesh is the image of Michaux as a heroic inventor who had struggled for years to draw attention to the bicycle, with no luck at all. After all, if his sons were already accomplished velocipede riders in 1864, he hardly had to wait two years before setting them loose on the streets of Paris where they were certain to generate free publicity. Before 1867, in fact, Michaux appears to have made no attempt whatsoever to announce or promote the novelty. Nor is there any record of commercial bicycle production taking place during that span. According to city records, it was not until 1867 that Michaux liberated the two floors above his shop for velocipede production. And even then he continued his regular line of business in the carriage trade on the ground floor, suggesting that, despite appearances, he was less than devoted to the bicycle.

Deepening the mystery behind the invention, Michaux's initial claims to a bicycle patent turned out to be false. In 1867, when he announced his product, he had only one unrelated patent to his name. Filed in 1855, it described a mundane set of shears, which he exhibited at the Universal Exhibition that year. And however cash poor the Michaux family might have been a decade later, Pierre's eldest son and co-worker Ernest managed to secure a series of patents between 1864 and 1865 in France and abroad relating to a miniature steam engine for amusement parks. Although some would later suggest that Ernest had a hand in the bicycle invention at about the same time, his early mechanical interests appear to have been confined to steam power.

Even more perplexing, the middle-aged blacksmith with an established business and a large family to support hardly seemed a likely source for such a curious and demanding invention. "The individual who first rode one of these crank bicycles," surmised one American journalist in 1869, "must have had much leisure time on his hands and considerable confidence in his ability to maintain his equilibrium under difficult circumstances." A far more likely candidate would be a young mechanic, not easily deterred by falls, who was directly involved in the construction of small carriages.

Aimé, left, and René Olivier at a costume ball in the early 1870s, after the demise of their velocipede enterprise. As sons of a wealthy industrialist, they enjoyed an active social life. Aimé described his younger brother René as the "heart and soul" of the original Michaux company. René died in a carriage accident shortly after this photograph was taken; Aimé went on to become an African explorer.

A further piece of evidence undermining Michaux's supposed leadership role in the launching of the pioneer company is the charter filed in May of 1868, which reveals that Michaux merely supervised bicycle production in his spare time. The other three signatories to the contract, the brothers Marius, Aimé, and René Olivier, were the ones who discreetly controlled commercial and technical development. These sons of a prominent industrialist from Lyon, who had amassed a fortune from a network of chemical plants, had in fact supplied the entire capital of fifty thousand francs. The brothers also controlled 70 percent of company profits.

As it turned out, the sole patent covering the basic bicycle was filed in the United States in April 1866, about a year before the launching of the Michaux bicycle operation. The patentee, Pierre Lallement, later testified that he had conceived the bicycle in 1862, as a nineteen-year-old living in Nancy, in the eastern part of France. At the time, he was employed in the construction of perambulators and children's tricycles. One day, he saw a man go by on a draisine, a bizarre sight that riveted his attention. After considerable experimentation, he hit on the idea of a mechanized two-wheeler with rotary cranks attached to the front hub.

Lallement soon moved to Paris where he landed a job with Strohmeyer, a maker of children's vehicles. He went about building a bicycle prototype in his spare time, enlisting the help of his shop mates. Finally, in the summer of 1863, he completed his vehicle. He learned to ride it in his shop's long corridor, before he took to the boulevards "and all the people saw it." In July of 1865, he left for America, toting the makings of an improved bicycle. Curiously, the machine depicted in his patent was nearly identical to the one Michaux marketed a year later, minus a few improvements such as a brake.

Evidently, the primitive bicycle was initially developed behind the scenes at two distinct locations in Paris before it even reached the Michaux shop: Lallement's work-

An engraving published in the *Wheelman Illustrated* of October 1883, showing Pierre Lallement on a bicycle in Paris making his first rounds along the Boulevard Saint-Martin twenty years earlier. Lallement built his original machine in a nearby shop where he assembled children's carriages.

Tapping Human Power

In the summer of 1863, when Pierre Lallement built his first bicycle in Paris, the United States was deeply immersed in its great Civil War. A band of Confederate engineers was busy developing a very different type of human-powered vehicle: a state-of-the-art submarine to be named the *H. L. Hunley*. This forty-foot long cast-iron vessel, with a circular cross-section only about four feet high, carried a commander who sat alone in front facing the helm, and seven crewmen seated on a long bench with their backs against the wall. Directly in front of the crew, through the center of the craft, passed a heavy iron shaft. As each man cranked a pair of hand levers, the shaft slowly spun around and turned the outer propeller at the stern, nudging the craft forward.

In early 1864, during the Union's debilitating blockade of the Southern coast, the *Hunley* and its crew crept silently beneath Charleston harbor toward an unsuspecting steam sloop, the USS *Housatonic,* stationed about four miles offshore. The captain navigated with the help of a periscope, and once the *Hunley* came within striking distance of the enemy ship he fired the vessel's single torpedo. It struck its target, scoring the first recorded sinking by a submarine.

For its day, the *Hunley* was a true marvel of engineering. Yet despite its successful strike, it failed to prove an effective weapon. The submersion system repeatedly malfunctioned, causing numerous fatalities. Even before the attack on the *Housatonic,* two crews totaling thirteen men had already perished, trapped within the submerged vessel. Shortly after its one triumph, at about the same location, the *Hunley* mysteriously sank for a third and final time, sending another

shop in the Faubourg Saint-Martin, and the nearby Ecole Centrale (now the Picasso Museum), where Aimé and René Olivier were enrolled. (Marius, the eldest brother, had already graduated and was not involved in the early development.) Although neither Lallement nor the Oliviers expressly acknowledged a joint collaboration, it seems likely that the two parties developed some sort of relationship in late 1863 or early 1864, following Lallement's public exhibitions. A few years later, after the Oliviers fell out with

eight men to their deaths. Salvagers in the year 2000 finally retrieved their remains, along with the historic vessel itself.

In spite of its evident flaws, the human-powered submarine might well have played a far greater role in the Civil War had its engineers employed more efficient propulsion. By using hand cranks, the crew had to labor for hours just to move the vessel a few miles underwater, seriously limiting its range. Had the bicycle already been established, the designers might have realized that rotary pedals powered by the legs offered a much more powerful means to spin a crank. Conceivably, a revamped, pedal-powered submarine could have covered greater distances at faster speeds with less manpower—a superior arrangement that no doubt would have furnished a much more lethal weapon.

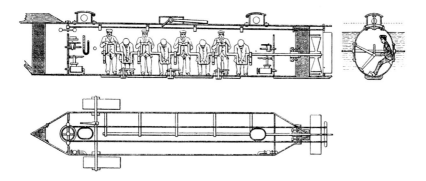

A sketch of the interior of the Confederate submarine *Hunley*, retrieved from Charleston harbor in 2000, along with the remains of the commander, Lieutenant George Dixon, and his crew. In 2004, using DNA evidence, researchers identified all seven of the men who powered the submarine, although the exact cause of its sinking is still unknown.

Michaux in the spring of 1869 and initiated a lawsuit against the blacksmith, René allowed in court that the original inventor was not his former partner after all, but rather an unidentified workman. For his part, Lallement confirmed that, despite his failure to attract an investor in Paris, "there were a few who took note" of his invention.

However René encountered the bicycle, he and a classmate, Georges de la Bouglise, quickly formulated their own plans to commercialize the invention. In René's words, they were "fanatics" of the velocipede, determined to win over the public. They were so keen on its possibilities, in fact, that they hatched an ambitious plan to produce the novelty on a large scale using malleable cast iron. This advanced process required special ore, expensive equipment, and highly specialized skills. But because parts could be made in series from molds, rather than individually as with traditional hand-wrought iron, this approach offered significant labor and cost savings on large-volume production.

To be sure, technologists were then debating to what extent malleable cast iron could adequately replace wrought iron. In particular, some warned that large pieces made of malleable cast iron, as opposed to the more pliable wrought iron, were subject to snapping under stress. René and Georges nonetheless concluded that the largest piece of the bicycle, its serpentine frame, could be composed of two curved parts of malleable cast iron securely bolted together at the base.

In all probability, it was René who then enlisted Michaux to set up production and build the materials, since the blacksmith offered the essential technical expertise as well as production facilities conveniently located in the heart of the Parisian carriage trade. René would later testify that he met Michaux in 1864, when the blacksmith had only a few employees and was deep in debt. By that summer, Michaux had produced an initial experimental batch of bicycles. That fall, René sent a specimen to his brother Aimé, in Lyon, who had recently moved back to the family homestead following his graduation from the Ecole Centrale.

Aimé, in turn, showed the curious machine to a certain Gabert, a trusted mechanic who worked for the family's chemical concern. Together, they developed useful accessories such as brakes, as well as a lighter and more rigid frame featuring a main bar sloping from the handlebars to the rear hub. This so-called diagonal pattern did not call for malleable cast iron, however, since it would have to be built as one long piece—one

A picador on a velocipede featuring the original serpentine frame design, in Bilbao, Spain, a French drawing that was reprinted in *Frank Leslie's Illustrated Newspaper* of 8 August 1868. The Michaux bicycle was already in demand abroad at the time of this performance in the spring of 1868.

that might snap under pressure with disastrous results. René evidently faced a difficult decision, whether to pursue production of the serpentine frame of malleable cast iron, with its perceived advantages of economy, or switch to the more rigid—but also more costly and labor-intensive—diagonal frame of wrought iron.

René, Aimé, and Georges put both models to the test in August 1865, when they made an unpublicized trial run on bicycles. The three set off from Paris on Michaux-built machines of malleable cast iron, bound for Avignon, some five hundred miles to the south. As they passed through small towns along the way, the astonished citizenry gave them chase. Although Georges dropped out after a few days for unknown reasons, the brothers carried on. By the time they reached Lyon, however, about halfway through their journey, their serpentine bicycles had shaken themselves apart. The brothers then switched to wooden prototypes of Gabert's diagonal model. A few days later, they reached the home of their uncle, Michel Perret, in Tullins, near Grenoble. After a brief rest, on the eighth day of their sojourn, René purportedly covered the remaining 120 miles to his father's house in Avignon in a grueling but triumphant twenty-three-hour marathon.

The Oliviers' trip may not have resolved their frame dilemma, but it did clarify at least two essential points that made their prospective bicycle venture look promising. First, a rider could traverse great distances at a good clip, and, second, one could indefinitely withstand, and even enjoy, the rotary pedal action. In the spring of 1866, his last year at school, an enthused René planted himself at the Michaux shop to plan the launching of a new industry. But he faced major obstacles at the onset of his bold bid. In particular, Aimé eventually revealed, their own family did not approve of the venture, and indeed treated them for years "as fools for having been involved in such a thing."

Without the family's backing, the brothers were hard pressed to raise the necessary capital for such an ambitious undertaking. At least one bank turned down their initial request for a loan, citing the novelty of their proposition. Further complicating matters, René himself would soon be moving back to the homestead in Lyon after his own graduation that summer, no doubt to take a position with the family enterprise. He knew it would be some time before he could settle back in Paris and personally preside over the bicycle operation. Aimé was likewise preoccupied by family affairs outside Paris. Nor did the Oliviers, or their partner Michaux, possess a controlling patent that might have enabled them to defer commercial exploitation of the bicycle without risking premature competition. Indeed, even before they initiated their production, they may have learned of Lallement's patent, a potential embarrassment if not a legal liability.

In spite of these various impediments, René followed through with his original plan to produce bicycles of malleable cast iron. He perhaps calculated that this material offered the fastest and cheapest way to build up a large stock, and that the serpentine

A wooden prototype of a diagonal-frame bicycle, apparently one of the vehicles the Olivier brothers used in their inaugural ride from Paris to Avignon in the summer of 1865, built by the mechanic Gabert of Lyon. Aimé Olivier's son Georges donated this bicycle to the Touring Club of France in 1926; it was later transferred to the Musée Nationale de la Voiture et du Tourisme in Compiègne, where it remains today.

frame was sufficiently functional to establish the product and his company's pioneer status. But he faced a difficult struggle ahead. As a journal recounted a few years later, when the velocipede was in vogue, René and his brother, "desiring to launch this industry in a grandiose manner . . . made great personal sacrifices to overcome all obstacles in their way."

To get things started, René put Georges in charge of designing and building the production machinery. He also arranged to have his friend supervise the operation in his absence. In the meantime, to assist Michaux with his preparations, René lent the blacksmith ten thousand francs, payable in installments. René would collect 6 percent interest, as well as five francs for every velocipede sold, payable every six months. Michaux, for his part, agreed to put aside a third of his profits to extinguish his prior debt so that he could achieve financial stability.

In setting up his bicycle operation under the Michaux banner, René was evidently hedging his bets. If the venture failed, he risked neither his family's good name nor his own capital. He had safely concealed his own unauthorized leadership of the project, and he also stood to recoup his initial loan with interest. If bicycle sales took off, René would not only collect a healthy commission, he could also easily displace the vulnerable Michaux and assume control of the budding operation once his circumstances permitted. At a time of his choosing, René would emerge as the prestigious "founding father" and leader of a vibrant new trade. Indeed, as Aimé later explained, René was the true "heart and soul" of the Michaux operation, whereas Michaux was merely a "pseudonym" covering René's accomplishments.

After its strong start in the second half of 1867 and the spring of 1868, the upstart Michaux company appeared to be on a successful course. A robust demand for bicycles had quickly materialized, just as René and Georges had anticipated. The press showed growing interest in the novelty, and more and more inquiries arrived each day from all over Europe. Moreover, sufficient capital was finally materializing. Both Olivier brothers had recently married into the same wealthy family from Marseille, and a strong backer finally emerged in the person of their common father-in-law, the shipping magnate Jean-Baptiste Pastré.

But despite appearances, the company was already suffering from internal friction and technical glitches. Not only were the absentee Oliviers increasingly at odds with their supervisor Michaux, they also discovered that their malleable cast-iron frames were prone to catastrophic failures after all. Moreover, the owners of the broken machines were highly displeased to learn that their vital hardware was made of cast, rather than forged, iron. "Please tell me if you can make [the bicycle] with wrought iron," pleaded one customer in the spring of 1868, "because cast iron cannot be repaired." Another correspondent noted with thinly veiled contempt that his offer of 160 francs should be sufficient payment for a machine "made entirely of cast iron."

To make matters worse, the serpentine frame was not delivering the anticipated economy of scale. A ledger from early 1868 suggests that Michaux, despite a heavy reliance on outside vendors, struggled to produce a few machines a day, hardly sufficient to meet surging demand. Meanwhile, numerous customers groused about their unfulfilled orders. In April, a member of the newly formed velocipede club in Valence advised Michaux that his tardy delivery had cost him dearly: "I finally received your velocipede this morning, after a two month delay. Let me say first of all that this is not the way you should be acting. You kept postponing my order, week after week. These delays and lack of rectitude will not encourage my peers to buy from you. Many of my friends were waiting to see your improved velocipede before buying one of their own. But since they became impatient, and mine never came, they went elsewhere, where they were satisfied in little time. In the past month, eight velocipedes were purchased in Valence, five at least would have been bought from you if you hadn't made me wait as long as you did."

While the Michaux company struggled to meet a rising demand, rivals were fast emerging to take up the slack. One of the most prominent was A. Favre of Voiron, near Grenoble, the supplier of the Valence club and a major vendor throughout the south of France. Favre first encountered the novelty in early 1867, when he spotted a bicycle trundling along a country lane near his home. The rider turned out to be none other than the noted scientist Michel Perret, the Oliviers' uncle, who had been privy to the boys' early experiments in Paris. Quickly persuaded of its practical benefits, an enthusiastic Favre initiated his own bicycle production later in the year. In February 1868, Favre published *Le Vélocipède: Sa Structure, ses Accessoires Indispensables* (The Velocipede: Its Structure, Its Indispensable Accessories), the first primer on how to select and ride a bicycle.

But rather than imitate the sensational Michaux serpentine frame, Favre adopted the diagonal model René had initially rejected. Other early makers did so as well, notably H. Cadot of Lyon. Perhaps aware of Gabert's early experiments in the same city, Cadot introduced a wooden diagonal frame in the spring of 1867. Though bulkier in appearance, it was somewhat cheaper and no heavier than the Michaux model. Several local newspapers gave it favorable reviews. A number of Parisian firms likewise adopted diagonal models, notably Claude Jacquier, one of Lallement's former employers. In the spring of 1868, Jacquier presented his novelties at the international maritime exhibition in Le Havre.

René, recognizing his mistake, scrambled to shift production to the increasingly popular diagonal frame of wrought iron. But Michaux resisted, according to René. Worse, the blacksmith allegedly took advantage of René's chronic absence by exploiting company resources behind his back. In May 1868, René finally consolidated his control over the troubled affair through a company charter that brought in his brothers as investors. His friend Georges, meanwhile, who had apparently favored the serpentine frame, quietly left the company. The charter, signed by the three Olivier brothers and Pierre Michaux, ensured that the brothers would have exclusive control over commercial and technical development. Indeed, Michaux was expressly forbidden from interfering in these matters.

Curiously, despite their flawed initial product and their struggles to rein in the rogue blacksmith, the Oliviers opted to retain the original brand name, formally pro-

The Velocipede in the Service of Love

From *Le Gaulois,* Paris, 21 October 1868

All lovers will be thrilled to learn what services the velocipede can render, and I am certain that they will soon take advantage of this precious instrument. In a small country village a young man fell in love with a young girl whose hair was as blonde as wheat. Up to there, nothing unusual. But the beauty lived ten miles from his town and that distance made encounters very difficult. To walk the road was very long indeed; to take a carriage meant drawing attention in a small town where the slightest curiosity gives rise to rumors. Our lover heard talk of velocipedes and it occurred to him to use one to travel faster and easier to the one he loved. He thus procured one, and after some training, he became the master of this difficult art. Almost every evening at dusk, he quietly left on his engine, as if he were making a small tour. Then, once out of the village, he devoured space, bolting to the agreed upon place where his love anxiously awaited him. When this new Leander arrived, she wiped his sweaty brow with her caressing hand.

But after a few days a jealous rival discovered the lovers' rendezvous. Not daring to take revenge himself, he scurried, with rage in his heart, to her parents. No need to describe their anger when they learned of their daughter's escapades. They quickly agreed on a plan. The next day, as soon as our Leander set foot to the ground, he saw black shadows arise from all directions, quickly advancing upon him while making threatening gestures. Without a moment's hesitation, he remounted his saddle and took off. The others gave chase and threw rocks at him. But they had barely taken a few steps when the lover disappeared into the darkness of the night, fleeing with dizzying speed while blessing his velocipede, which had snatched him from the claws of his persecutors.

Cupid on a velocipede, from *Paris-Caprice* of 25 April 1868

nouncing the pioneer company Michaux et Compagnie. René would later insist that they did so out of sympathy for the blacksmith and his large clan, but it seems more likely that the brothers valued the Michaux name for its unique cachet as the first in the field. Indeed, the charter preserved for posterity their own distinct connection with the pioneer firm. Whatever motivated the brothers to keep the Michaux name, they were evidently confident that the blacksmith would cause them no further trouble. As velocipede mania took hold, René was poised to preside over a far more cohesive and profitable affair.

At last, the Oliviers implemented the long overdue transition to the superior wrought-iron frame. By the fall of 1868, amid growing competition from dozens of firms across the country, the new diagonal Michaux frame was widely recognized as the industry standard. Most, if not all, were built in Marseille, at a large shipbuilding foundry belonging to Pastré, the Oliviers' father-in-law. They were shipped in bulk to the ever more expansive Michaux factory, where they were painted and converted into complete machines. The new production process slashed turnaround time and enabled far greater volume, up to twenty units a day.

In the meantime, the newly reorganized company developed racing as a means to promote the trade. On the last day of May in 1868, Michaux et Compagnie sponsored the first official races, held in the Parisian suburb of Saint-Cloud. In what would become a familiar format, the program featured a series of contests engaging between three and seven racers. The first event admitted velocipedes with front wheels measuring less than a meter (about thirty-six inches) in diameter, while the second, won by a young Englishman named James Moore, showcased those with larger wheels. The third and most important race of the day was open to all comers. The winning times over the half-kilometer course hovered around two minutes and thirty-five seconds, an impressive speed of about fourteen miles an hour. In addition, a "slow" race provided comic relief, as contestants struggled to creep forward as slowly as possible without tumbling. The winner was the last still standing to cross the finish line. The imperial prince reportedly observed the entire affair from his nearby carriage, and the results were widely reported in France and even abroad.

The success of the races at Saint-Cloud inspired other contests that summer in and around the French capital. In July, Toulouse hosted the first major races outside the Paris area. A month later, the Michaux company spearheaded two series of races in Le Havre, drawing large crowds from the ongoing international maritime exhibition. In the first, Pierre Michaux's son Edmond won a medal for fancy riding. A local journalist who interviewed him related that the Michaux workforce had already grown to two hundred employees, "only a year after the invention." In the second series, James Moore collected another first-place medal from a host city. This time, he edged out two Pari-

This French print from about 1869 confirms that even children participated in the velocipede craze. The aspiring young velocipedists depicted here have rented bicycles in a Parisian park, under the watchful supervision of their guardians.

sians, including an adept twelve-year-old who later won the slow race. In a rematch for the official exhibition medal, however, Moore was disqualified after falling to the ground and taking down a competitor. Such mishaps were common in early competitions, as racers struggled to master their unwieldy machines.

Although the Michaux name enjoyed the greatest acclaim, other makers did their part to promote the new sport. In July, a Favre-built bicycle figured in the most highly publicized velocipede event since the races at Saint-Cloud. A velocipedist from the town of Castres named A. Carconade raced against a horse and buggy forty-five miles to Toulouse over rough roads. His opponent beat him by twenty-five minutes, arriving in

An engraving from *La Vie Parisienne* of 10 October 1868 announcing the "inauguration of the Michaux rink," where the fashionable gathered to learn the new art of bicycle riding, and also showing a bustling Michaux factory and showroom stocked with examples of both the original serpentine model and the newly introduced diagonal variety

The idea that a person should perform work previously relegated to animals struck some as comical, if not regressive. This caricature from *Le Journal Amusant* of 29 October 1868 lampooned the curious role reversal.

six hours flat. Nevertheless, Carconade's gutsy performance was widely heralded as a stirring moral victory for the mechanical horse, one that signaled its imminent triumph. At a banquet honoring the contestants, the host rose amid thunderous applause to toast not only Carconade but also the invention of the hour: "To the velocipede, gentlemen, that ingenious and charming machine, by now a faithful friend and inseparable companion to the solitary and weary traveler. To that useful invention, bequeathed by science to a stunned and grateful world. Yes, gentlemen, let us drink to this carriage of the future. To its perfection, to its success, and to its long and useful existence."

That fall, the velocipede craze reached new heights throughout France. A British correspondent in Paris noted: "It is extraordinary what strides the mania for these machines is making here. Not only does one meet them flying down the Champs Elysées and along the Rue de Rivoli, but many miles from Notre Dame one sees them scudding along interminable white country roads." In the second edition of his primer, Favre revealed that he had already sold some two thousand machines, mostly in southern France. The post office, meanwhile, contemplated furnishing tricycles to rural carriers. Journals depicted distinguished citizens on velocipedes, including the imperial prince. Artists, musicians, and playwrights celebrated the novelty. The Hippodrome of Paris, famous for its novel and entertaining acts, staged regular bicycle performances.

A French engraving of a women's velocipede race reprinted in *Harper's Weekly* of 19 December 1868. Held in Bordeaux a month earlier, the affair drew some three thousand spectators. Women's races soon became regular attractions.

But perhaps the most extraordinary event of all took place that November in Bordeaux, where the novel prospect of a women's race brought thousands of curious citizens to a local park. Four fashionable contestants took their positions on the field wearing unusually short skirts. The excited mob burst through the barriers to get a closer look, enveloping the course. Undaunted, these "heroines of the bicycle" dutifully took off at the sound of the gun. Miss Louise surged to the front, but Miss Julie made a "superhuman effort" and overtook her down the stretch, winning by a nose. An etching of this epic battle soon circulated around the world, giving many foreigners their first glimpse of the novel French bicycle.

Unfortunately, as had happened in so many other places, some civic leaders began to complain that velocipedes were running amok, prompting communities to impose restrictive ordinances. Nevertheless, the French public was clearly enraptured by the ambitious little mechanical horse. That year, 1868, would go down in French annals as the "year of the velocipede." Indeed, by the year's conclusion, the diagonal machine was a familiar sight throughout the country. In his popular annual summary of scientific achievements that year, Louis Figurier praised the "democratic" new vehicle and welcomed its promise to provide "cheap, personal transportation."

Figurier cautioned, nonetheless, that the young colt was not quite ready for general use, given its tender state of development. He urged patience, noting that overexposure and inflated expectations could stunt its growth. But proponents of the French movement vowed to see the challenge through, until at last the bicycle was established as a common means of locomotion. Nor would they have to act alone. The primitive machine was already making its way across Europe and the United States, and, indeed, around the world.

F I V E *The American Adventure*

Well before a bicycle craze erupted in Paris, the novelty reached American shores. In July of 1865, one month before the Oliviers made their trial run to Avignon, the mechanic Pierre Lallement brought the makings of a wrought-iron bicycle from Paris to Brooklyn aboard the steamship *City of London*. Although he was to secure a patent—the world's first published specification of a bicycle—a little over a year later, his bold bid to launch a new industry was unsuccessful in the end. Nevertheless, once the velocipede mania swept France shortly thereafter, it would indeed strike the United States as well—sparking an extraordinary adventure.

Lallement found a manufacturing job in the prosperous town of Ansonia, Connecticut. That fall, he assembled his machine and made a five-mile ride to Birmingham (now a section of Derby) and back. Years later, a co-worker recalled the Frenchman as a pleasant young fellow whose contortions on his strange vehicle after working hours provoked laughter. Undaunted, Lallement rode his creation some twelve miles to New Haven in the spring of 1866, prompting an observant journalist to record the first known report of a bicycle in action. "An enterprising individual propelled himself about the Green last evening on a curious frame sustained by two wheels, one before the other, and driven by foot cranks." The odd display induced a certain James Carroll to fund a patent application together with Lallement, and the patent was granted that November. But the hapless pair failed to enlist a manufacturer.

Lallement, apparently conceding defeat, retreated to France in early 1868. Ironically, shortly afterward, Americans began to receive regular reports on the quickly developing Parisian craze. Thousands soon saw the novelty for themselves. Starting in the summer of 1868, three of the Hanlon Brothers, part of a famous acrobatic troupe, raced bicycles down an incline on stages across North America. The trio also regularly rode outdoors before large crowds, starting with a romp through the Boston Common. In Savannah, where a demonstration of the draisine a half century earlier had failed to elicit confidence, the Hanlons "were followed everywhere by great crowds anxious to observe the proper method of managing the 'critters.'" Anticipating a demand for the novelty, the Hanlons secured the second American bicycle patent, claiming such improvements as an adjustable crank and seat. Meanwhile, they engaged Calvin Witty, a carriage maker in Brooklyn, to produce their model.

Before long, several New York firms joined the nascent trade. One, G. H. Mercer and Monad, offered a French-style diagonal bicycle, while a rival maker, Pickering and Davis, presented the "American velocipede." Especially designed by Thomas R. Pickering to cope with the country's notoriously bad roads, it featured smaller wheels, sprung handlebars, and a lower frame. Riders activated the novel brake by pushing down on their seats with their derrieres, using the handlebars for leverage. For greater strength and lightness, Pickering introduced an iron tube for the frame's main horizontal component (called a backbone) to take the place of a solid iron bar. The tube's round ends were brazed into cast bronze fittings. The weight savings were modest on account of the heavy materials, but the tubing idea eventually proved fundamental to bicycle design. Pickering also made the parts interchangeable to facilitate repairs.

Several large carriage makers along the Eastern seaboard also began to produce bicycles as a sideline, notably J. M. Quimbly of Newark, New Jersey; the Wood Brothers of Bridgeport, Connecticut; and George L. Brownell of New Bedford, Massachusetts. Most models resembled the French style and came in a variety of colors with contrasting stripes. Others in the trade, however, took a more cautious approach, waiting to see if the novelty was more than just a passing phenomenon. A few firms imported French bicycles for study, but many held off on making costly production preparations, fearing "the excitement may die out before they can get profitably at it."

Such concerns were justified, for the labor-intensive bicycle was costly to produce. A newspaper in Newport, Rhode Island, explained, "every part has to be made by hand," given that "experiments substituting cast iron for wrought iron, or steel, have uniformly proved disastrous to the rider and also to the manufacturer." And with the price of a new bicycle ranging from $75 to $150, there was no guarantee that the Ameri-

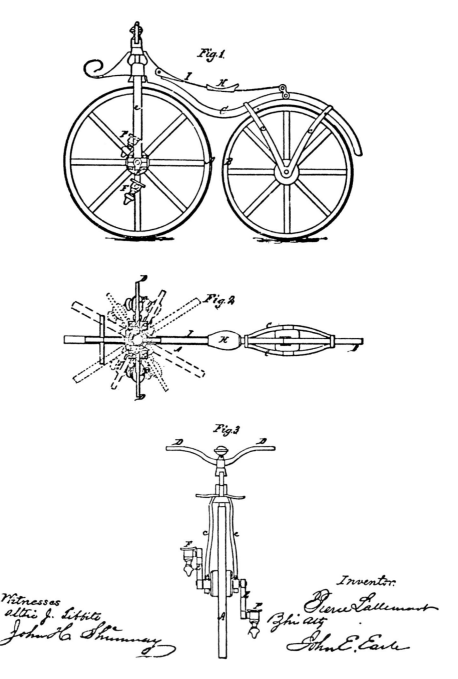

The serpentine machine delineated in Lallement's original bicycle patent (no. 59915, granted 20 November 1866) was strikingly similar to the first ones marketed by Michaux of Paris some six months later. As was then required, Lallement submitted a wooden model, on which this drawing was based. "After a little practice," Lallement asserted in the accompanying text, "the rider is enabled to drive the same at an incredible velocity with the greatest ease."

SINGULAR APPEARANCE IN THE CENTRAL PARK.
N.B. It is only a Gentleman on a Velocipede coming over the Brow of a Hill.

Harper's Bazaar of 20 March 1869 featured this silhouette of a solitary velocipedist making his way through Central Park, where the first American-made bicycles had appeared six months earlier

can public would bite. At a time when $10 a week was considered a good working wage, the cost of a bicycle was a considerable investment for an article that had yet to prove itself. One paper exhorted the public to resist the temptation to buy a velocipede until the inevitable improvements, along with increased competition, drove down its "exorbitant price."

But New Yorkers, at least, were unwilling to wait for more favorable terms. In the fall of 1868, a furor erupted in Manhattan. A local athletic club hosted an inaugural bicycle contest in November, and specimens began to appear in Central Park, to the astonishment of strollers. In December, the Pearsall brothers opened a riding school on Broadway that immediately attracted several hundred prominent citizens, including doctors, lawyers, merchants, and ladies. Meanwhile, the carriage makers that had initially hesitated to join the trade rushed into bicycle production to satisfy the surging demand. A young Winslow Homer aptly depicted the New Year arriving on a bicycle.

Barely a month later, the craze had spread across the land. In Portland, Maine, hundreds admired the first specimens produced by a local sleigh maker. Pickering's machine was the star of the Mechanics' Fair in Hartford. In Cincinnati, Chicago, and New Bedford, hundreds watched indoor velocipede races. More schools opened in and around New York and Boston, as well as in Syracuse, Detroit, and San Francisco. A few machines even appeared outdoors. In Fall River, Massachusetts, two young men raced down Main Street, captivating a crowd of onlookers. In Indianapolis, a young attorney

A young Winslow Homer aptly depicted the New Year arriving on a velocipede in this sketch from *Harper's Weekly* of 9 January 1869. The craze was soon to engulf the entire country.

reportedly "ate, drank, and slept velocipedes" for three months before he finally got hold of a machine. He spent another ten days "practicing by moonlight and lantern" before making his street debut.

Among the early champions of the bicycle who helped fan the flames of passion were the minister Henry Ward Beecher and the journalist Charles A. Dana. The famous clergyman from Brooklyn revealed to his congregation that he had given each of his two sons a bicycle, and had even learned to ride one himself. He pronounced the sport a "rational recreation" and predicted that his flock would soon pedal its way to his services. Dana praised the bicycle's "brilliant prospects," asserting it would soon be "naturalized in every part of the world." To promote local use, he proposed an elevated bicycle path to run the length of Manhattan.

By February 1869, the leading makers were producing as many as fifteen bicycles a day. Even village blacksmiths began to make small batches to satisfy the demand. "The velocipede mania is becoming serious," marveled one journalist, "and is a joke no longer." But the thriving manufacturers "were doomed to sudden disappointment." Calvin Witty, the Hanlons' former partner, announced that he owned a controlling patent on bicycle manufacturing and would assess a fee of at least ten dollars for every machine sold, effective retroactively. The producers were stunned. "It being under-

"Bicycles on the Rampage"

As the velocipede craze raged across the United States in early 1869, curious citizens eagerly awaited the arrival of the celebrated machine that seemed to defy nature itself. As *Scientific American* pointed out, "That a velocipede should maintain an upright position is one of the most surprising feats of practical mechanics." Viewing the machine for the first time, an editor in Oswego, New York, was duly amazed. "The first impression is that it won't go. But there was never a greater mistake. It will go, and that, too, at a speed reaching anywhere between six and fifteen or twenty miles an hour." An editor in Cincinnati pronounced the novelty "one of the funniest, queerest and most interesting machines that has ever been invented."

Under the heading "Bicycles on the Rampage," a paper in Cincinnati described the velocipede's stunning debut in Pike's Hall.

> Notwithstanding the sloppiness of the streets and the inclemency of the weather, the Hall was well filled with a crowd of spectators, all agog to fathom the mysteries of the wondrous bicycle. All ears were deaf and all eyes were strained toward the door through which the great unknown was expected to appear. Presently, the door opened and in sailed Mr. Gosling upon the great mysterious, circling around the hall, now creeping slowly along, and now darting forward with a recklessness which seemed to endanger his neck. He made the occupants of chairs skirting the course draw up their feet and hold their breath as he sped swiftly by them; yet [he was] perfectly self-possessed and secure. He fully demonstrated to the audience that the marvelous stories they heard of the mystic machine were not myths but verities.

> Moreover, the writer was confident that the bicycle would outlive its novelty and develop into a truly useful and enjoyable article. "It will always have a fascination for those who enjoy athletic sports," he predicted; "there is an oddity, a mirth-provoking quaintness and audacity about the machine that will commend it to that large, and, we trust, growing class who love fun."

stood that it was a French invention," explained one journalist, "no one supposed there was or would be any patent on it in this country."

Yet the crafty Witty had discovered otherwise. In the fall of 1868, after he had made about seventy-five bicycles for the Hanlons, a New Haven firm connected with the carriage trade approached him to broker a settlement. The company had learned from one of its employees, James Carroll, that he was the part owner, with Lallement, of a controlling patent. A mystified Witty promptly hired investigators to conduct a thorough review at home and abroad to confirm the validity of the Lallement patent. A few months later, satisfied that the Frenchman was indeed the original inventor, Witty purchased Carroll's share. He then wired instructions to an agent in Paris to track down the absentee inventor and buy his remaining half interest. Lallement readily complied, and Witty emerged as the sole owner of the bicycle patent.

In the wake of Witty's "ominous circular," some manufacturers hastily settled with him, while others suspended operations and sought legal counsel. The leading makers met in New York City to review Witty's demands, reluctantly concluding that his patent was valid. A French newspaper in New York, claiming familiarity with the case, concurred with their judgment. "The monopoly Witty purchased belongs to him . . . there is nothing more to say." It predicted two inevitable consequences. First, Witty would grow richer, and, second, the public would continue to pay a premium for bicycles. Indeed, Witty collected about forty thousand dollars in back royalties over the next few weeks. Bicycle makers, meanwhile, promptly raised their prices to cover the outlay, despite widespread complaints that American bicycles were now twice the price of comparable machines in France.

Yet still the American trade appeared poised to prosper from the seemingly insatiable demand. The carriage maker George C. Eliot of Providence, shortly after taking out a license with Witty, doubled his weekly production capacity to 250 units. Clubs formed in several cities, while scores of rinks sprouted up across the country to prepare the eager public for road riding come spring. Newspapers and magazines were filled with articles about the two-wheel wonder, and the young trade even acquired its own monthly, *The Velocipedist,* funded by Pickering. So pervasive was the craze, noted a paper in Evansville, Indiana, "that everything new is called 'velocipede.' In walking about town, we notice in a shoe store the 'velocipede' boots for young ladies; at a music store, 'Velocipede' Gallop, and we suppose we shall soon have the 'velocipede' hat, the 'velocipede' necktie, &c., &c."

facing page: Velocipede mania generated a profusion of popular songbooks and sheet music celebrating the novel two-wheeler

AS SUNG BY
BILLY SHEPPERD
OF
HOOLEY'S MINSTRELS.

THE GAY
VELOCIPEDE

WORDS BY
GEO. COOPER

Music arranged by
HARRY MILLER.

NEW YORK.   ST. LOUIS.
J. L. PETERS.   J. L. PETERS & CO.

Cincinnati.   Chicago.   Galveston.   Boston.
M. A. DOBMEYER & CO.   DE MOTTE BROS.   T. GOGGAN.   WHITE SMITH & PERRY.

Entered according to Act of Congress A.D. 1869 by J.L. Peters in the Clerk's Office of the Dist. Ct. of N. J.

Why such extraordinary enthusiasm? The bicycle promised two basic but highly prized functions: first, cheap and efficient personal transportation, and, second, a healthy recreational outlet. To be sure, critics charged that the new vehicle was nothing more than a thinly veiled draisine destined to fail on both counts. "When we reflect that the whole effort of this utilitarian age is to get away from labor, and not into it," declared one skeptic, "we can guess what the fate of the velocipede will ultimately be." Others derided its recreational value, dismissing the primitive bicycle as an infernal machine calculated to break necks. Even those who conceded a certain conceptual appeal denied its prospects. "They may be very pleasant things to sport with on Boulevards and Central Parks," chortled one, "but how about the sandy roads and steep hills of the country?"

But others held that the bicycle, over time, would indeed prove an indispensable "poor man's carriage" and not an ephemeral "rich man's toy." They insisted that it represented nothing less than the dawn of a new "era of road travel." Businessmen would soon discard their carriages, or forgo the train, and commute on bicycles between their suburban homes and downtown offices, saving money if not time. Clergymen, doctors, and lawyers would likewise make their rounds more efficiently, as would missionaries, postmen, and telegram boys. One visionary declared, "The velocipede is the forerunner of a new conveyance—namely, the little passenger locomotive—for common roads [to be] propelled without the aid of muscle, animal or human."

Others defended the recreational possibilities of the bicycle, asserting that it would give sedentary urbanites much needed exercise and a "glow of health." A Boston writer praised the vehicle for breaking "the fearful habit of joining drinking with every amusement," while another affirmed that the slender machine "would hardly be safe to use when returning from a convivial party." An enthusiast in Lynn, Massachusetts, predicted that the bicycle "will take men away from the gambling rooms and rum shops, out into God's light and sunshine." He even suggested that bicycle riding could provide the same thrill as alcohol, but without its "sting." Susan B. Anthony, a pupil at the Hanlons' rink, envisioned a "graceful, healthy and useful exercise for all women." But even proponents conceded that the bicycle was unlikely to endure if it failed to deliver any real service. "As a toy it cannot be long lived," warned one realist; "it must be put to practical account or it will not remain long in use."

Yet many were confident that the famed "Yankee ingenuity" would do just that, resulting in "the real working, every day velocipede." Enthusiasts were already prescribing what had to be done. "We want something that can cross the tracks of our city street railroads as well as wade through the sloughs of mud provided by city fathers," explained the *Detroit Free Press*. "Future generations, when they have vastly improved upon our velocipedes," asserted one optimist, "will refer to those of the present day as rude contrivances." Still another boldly predicted: "The practicality of velocipedes is merely a

"A Hint to Fat and Consumptive Policemen," ridiculing the notion that policemen would trade in their horses for velocipedes, from the *Illustrated Sporting and Theatrical News* of 27 March 1869. In spite of caricatures like this, proponents fully expected the bicycle to develop into a useful machine.

matter of time. Twenty years from now, as a means of transportation, the bicycle will be in general use." One writer expressed supreme confidence that Americans would soon transform the bicycle "beyond the Frenchman's wildest dreams," adding smugly, "We can whip [the French] out of their boots in mechanical contrivances."

The prognoses varied, but most observers agreed that the experiment was worthwhile. Even if the sport failed to displace baseball as the national pastime, as some were already predicting, it might at least furnish harmless amusement in rinks or parks. And why not give American inventors a chance to render the thing of some use? After all, a practical velocipede may not have been within easy reach, but at least it no longer seemed an utter impossibility. "What will be the final result of the new method of locomotion we cannot pretend to foretell," mused one journalist in Providence, "but as matters are tending now the 'feedless horse' . . . promises to become an important element in modern civilization." Another reporter wrote, "The question is getting to be an interesting one, as to how extensively the social system is to be revolutionized."

At least one thing was certain: American mechanics would not shy from the challenge of perfecting the crude velocipede. During January and February 1869, the patent office received about one hundred velocipede-related applications. It granted about half—more than the sum total it had previously issued for human-powered vehicles in its eighty-year history. Moreover, by early March over one hundred more applications had been either filed or announced. Not all of these velocipede proposals concerned

"The Velocipede Mania—What It May Come To," a caricature by Thomas Worth mocking the idea that the bicycle was destined to become a popular means of conveyance, from *Harper's Weekly* of 1 May 1869

two-wheelers, but the bicycle was the dominant design and the one that had sparked such an extraordinary interest in human-powered vehicles. One contemporary marveled that, apart from the wave of proposals for new weapons at the outbreak of the Civil War, "nothing was ever known like this velocipede rush."

Meanwhile, as inventors pondered how to improve the machine, the craze continued unabated. More rinks sprang up in cities large and small to accommodate demand. Many were hastily contrived in abandoned churches, empty offices, or wherever adequate space could be found. One resourceful promoter in Lynn, Massachusetts, established the "Pierre Lallement Rink" under a giant canvas tent. The best facilities, however, were converted ice-skating or roller-skating rinks with smooth wooden floors —sometimes sprinkled with sawdust for an outdoorsy effect. If the riding space contained pillars, they were usually padded to soften the inevitable collisions.

The novice who tries to "kick his way through the world," observed one wit, inevitably ends up "sprawling on the floor, trying to extricate himself from the wheels of his vehicle, with bruised shins and elbows." To shield these "Timid Toddlers" from the jeers of onlookers, managers of velocipede rinks often trained them in isolation. This prudent policy also protected the more experienced riders, classed progressively as "Wary Wobblers," "Go-it-Gracefuls," and the "Fancy Few," from the like of Chad Chalk of Brooklyn. An urban legend, this would-be velocipedist reportedly "runs into every-thing that can't get out of his way." At last, the exasperated manager offered Chad a ve-locipede and a cash payment to "stay away from the Academy and do his practicing elsewhere."

Enterprising young men not only founded rinks in their own towns, they fanned out from velocipede hotbeds in search of localities where the novelty was as yet under-represented. Once they found a promising location, they had three or four velocipedes sent from home via train. Parties from southeastern Massachusetts were especially ac-tive in spreading the craze, establishing schools throughout New England, upstate New York, eastern Canada, and the South. The *New Bedford Mercury* likened the exodus to the Gold Rush, noting that "if a man or boy is missed from the community, it is quite safe to conclude that he has embarked in velocipeding."

While some rink entrepreneurs received a warm welcome, others faced hostility. A newspaper in Montpelier, Vermont, charged that these young men were "too shiftless to get a living by honest labor" and aimed instead to "wheedle money out of the people." The editor of a newspaper in Gardiner, Maine, complained bitterly when a rink sud-denly appeared on the floor above his office. "Greenhorns come fumbling at our doors, inquiring 'is this the Veelosh-eye-peedee School?'" Worse, he asserted: "The building trembles to the foundation. The gas fixtures rattle. The window sashes dance. The plas-tering is bulged down. Our hair is full of sand and lime." Determined to stick it out, he implored his readers, "if the building comes down, and our cold remains are found among the ruins, let our friends remember that we died at the post of duty."

In spite of such heated objections, rinks continued to sprout up across the land. By spring 1869, the largest cities hosted a dozen or more of these "academies." Most mid-sized cities had at least two. Even small towns were rarely deprived of a facility. Eau Claire, Wisconsin, had but one rink with two bicycles, yet it still managed to stage an ex-citing race. Some of the larger rinks had as many as fifty machines, including the top New York models. But a typical fleet comprised about a dozen machines.

The potential revenue from a rink was indeed enticing. Managers generally charged fifteen cents for admission, plus a penny for every minute spent on a saddle. A proprietor in Petersburg, Virginia, reportedly made a tidy thirty to forty dollars a day with only five machines. Some patrons, however, pronounced the going rates exorbitant and de-manded reductions. "One dollar per hour makes the exercise both aristocratic and ex-clusive," warned one writer from Newark. He urged that the rate be halved to democra-tize the sport, arguing that "many deserving and respectable young men, who earn but a little more than a dollar a day, are now debarred from patronizing the institution."

Managers also collected windfalls from special events like grand openings and races, usually featuring a live band and refreshments. At the inauguration of the "Ve-

You Are a Velocipedist

Learning to ride a velocipede was no easy task, even at a rink, as one journalist from Malden, Massachusetts, discovered. (From the the Malden Messenger, *13 February 1869)*

Velocipedes are pretty things to look upon as they whirl along so swiftly and gracefully, operated by some practiced hand. But did you ever try to ride one? If not, you have an experience before you. It seems an easy thing to sit on the little carpeted seat, put your feet upon the treadles, and astonish everybody by your speed; but just try it! And don't invite your lady friends to witness that first performance either. You mount the machine with a great deal of dignity and confidence, you see that all is clear, you undertake to place your feet in the proper position, and—the trouble begins. Your first half hour is spent in [determining] which shall be uppermost, yourself or the machine, and the machine exhibits an amount of skill and perseverance that astonishes you. Surely, you think, no one was ever so clumsy, and the tittering of the lookers on does not help the matter any. You bump your head, jam your feet, and cover yourself with dust and perspiration. You would be discouraged, but here all your native grit comes to the rescue. Give it up? No! You will break your neck first! You balance as well as possible, summon your remaining strength, and give a desperate kick at the treadle! You give a succession of kicks, you have actually ridden a short distance. The vic-

locipedrome" in Jersey City, for example, some two thousand spectators heard the showman P. T. Barnum, ever on the alert for novelties, expound on the virtues of the velocipede. Championship races at large rinks in New York, Boston, Philadelphia, and San Francisco drew as many as five thousand spectators, and even local contests were often spirited affairs that attracted hundreds of curious citizens.

Typically, four or five contestants raced multiple times around the rink, covering anywhere from an eighth of a mile to a full mile. In the event of a crowded field, or a narrow circuit, the contests were sometimes staggered in heats. Winners usually rode about twelve miles an hour, and netted a silver cup for their efforts. One lively contest in Lew-

tory is yours. You have the knack now. Your courage is up. You are a velocipedist. Soon we will see you looking with contempt upon amateurs, wondering how they can be so awkward.

The Wood Brothers made velocipedes in Bridgeport, Connecticut, and operated a riding rink in Manhattan, shown here in *Harper's Weekly* of 13 February 1869. Evidently, chaos was the order of the day.

iston, Maine, drew thirteen competitors who had to complete seven circuits measuring two hundred feet each, a distance of just over a quarter mile. Four racers strayed into the inner rope and were disqualified. Jackson Lewis, a young black man, prevailed by the length of a velocipede, finishing in one minute thirteen and a half seconds. "Amid great applause," the local newspaper reported, "he took off his hat, made a low bow and walked off triumphant with the [silver] pitcher under his arm."

Some events featured fancy riders who dazzled the crowd with their skill. A performer in Wilmington, Delaware, "unscrewed the handle of his velocipede while in rapid motion" and "threw it on the floor" while his partner, billed as Master Willie, sat

THE FIRST
GYMNACYCLIDIUM
FOR LADIES AND GENTLEMEN.

COPYRIGHT SECURED BY PEARSALL BROS.

CLARRY & REILLY

OPENING EXHIBITION AND HOP AT THE
GRAND VELOCIPEDE ACADEMY

Or Gymnacyclidium, containing over 8,000 square feet for Riding, with Gallery and Se
for about 1,500 people, by the

PEARSALL BROTHERS
Originators of Velocipede Schools in this Country, at the
APOLLO BUILDING
CORNER BROADWAY & 28th STREET,
Main entrance on 28th Street,

On MONDAY EVENING, APRIL 5th, 186
Commencing at 8 o'clock.
MUSIC BY DODWORTH'S BAND.

The Pearsall brothers of New York opened a popular rink equipped with the latest models, including some specially designed to accommodate women

on his shoulders. In Albany, "five riders mounted a single velocipede, two perched on the shoulders of their companions, made a successful trip across the hall amid the applause of the three thousand spectators." One popular performer was Carrie Moore, a skating champion, whose repertoire included standing on the machine with one foot. She wore a feathered cap over her flowing blonde hair, a blue velvet blouse embroidered in gold with matching trousers to her knees, white tights, and tall bronze boots.

While rinks prospered, however, bicycle makers faced an increasingly chaotic and oppressive patent situation. By April, Witty had issued more than thirty licenses in ten states, collecting another forty thousand dollars in royalties as domestic production climbed to an estimated sixteen thousand units, about a quarter of them in New York City alone. But Witty had barely issued his chilling decree when the Hanlon brothers demanded an additional five dollars per machine for their own patented improvements. The Hanlons' lawyer purchased his clients' patent himself, then turned the tables on Witty, charging him with patent infringements. The *New York Sun* warned that any more royalty demands on the nascent trade "would destroy the business pretty effectively. Indeed, $10 [per machine] is quite as much as it can stand."

Further muddling matters, a certain Stephen W. Smith announced that he, not Witty, held the true controlling patent. In fact this patent, awarded some years earlier to Phillip W. MacKenzie, covered a child's rocking horse. The *New York Sun* chortled, "it has about as much applicability to velocipedes as it has to railroad locomotives." Yet by baiting the beleaguered manufacturers with the promise of a single, reduced royalty fee, Smith managed to create even more havoc. The consortium of makers who had initially settled with Witty announced that they would henceforth pay only the Hanlons while Witty and Smith sorted things out. Not to be thwarted, the opportunistic pair hastily joined forces.

By late spring 1869, rinks were in sharp decline. Some cited the arrival of good weather, although at least one owner blamed the demise of his rink on his "woodenheaded" manager. But in truth rinks had simply lost their allure. The public had no more appetite for lessons, nor did it develop a taste for crash-plagued races. The press increasingly decried the dangers of the rink. One wit claimed he could recognize patrons walking down the street "with their legs spread apart . . . ready for a fall in a soft place." Desperate rink owners slashed their rates. Some offered increasingly outlandish fare, including female riders in risqué attire, "introduced merely to gratify prurient tastes." Irate citizens clamored for closures. But most managers shut their rinks voluntarily on account of dwindling attendance, selling off their stock at a fraction of its original cost.

Riders recognized that if the vehicle was to survive for a second season, it would have to prove itself on the road—and quickly. But neither they nor their machines were up to the task. A velocipedist in Portland, Maine, after drawing a curious crowd,

"Velocipede Belle," a smartly dressed and up-to-date young lady who leaves her suitors in the dust, featured in the *Illuminated Western World* of 13 March 1869. Her short skirt and visible leggings were avant-garde for the period.

promptly slid into a pile of snow, scaring a horse. In Frankfort, Kentucky, "clerks struggled with might and main to harness the captious steed," but it proved "a difficult animal to master." In Indianapolis, a rider suddenly "struck a snag," sending his spokes flying in all directions "as if they had been stuck in the hubs with Spalding's glue." In San Jose, a fallen velocipedist made "half a dozen fruitless efforts" to remount his machine. In Saint Paul, a disgusted individual who "couldn't make his wooden horse go," hired a boy to wheel the thing home, "loudly mentioning a place not believed in by Universalists."

Even those who got to their destination often failed to prove the merit of the bicycle as a road vehicle. After two weary souls rode ten miles from Albany to Troy, a local paper scoffed, "Judging from their jaded appearance, an invitation to ride back in a carriage would have been thankfully accepted." In April, the well-known racers Frank Swift and James Boyle left Syracuse on state-of-the-art bicycles, bound for a rink in Rochester, eighty-five miles away, where a crowd anxiously awaited their arrival. To keep the welcoming committee apprised of their progress, the proud pair sent periodic telegrams. Two days later, after fifteen hours in the saddle, they finally arrived. Swift,

"Beauty on a Bicycle," from the *Illustrated Sporting and Theatrical News* of 20 February 1869. Apparently the sight of an actress roaming a public street on a velocipede—sitting sidesaddle no less—was startling even to a horse. The artist, however, seems to have forgotten to include the pedals on the front wheel.

A Victim of the Velocipede

One victim of the velocipede craze was Louis Rinaldo Ehrich, a twenty-year-old student at Yale College. In the spring of 1869, he set out to learn the art at a local rink. "I am just beginning to get the idea," he noted in his diary, adding "I caught my foot in the wheel and sprained it somewhat." A few days later, he practiced for a full forty-five minutes, proudly recording, "I can ride about 18 feet." Throughout April, he took regular breaks from his intensive studies to enjoy up to an hour of "splendid fun" at the velocipede rink. He even attended an exhibition in which the performers "seem to do almost everything on the bicycle."

But Ehrich's true passion was to pedal along in the great outdoors. In early May, he took a long ride with his friend Sam. "How I love to dash along drinking in the beauty of Spring," he mused, although the next day he took a long bath, admitting to himself, "I feel sore from my ride." Two weeks later, still faithful to his iron steed, he rode about New Haven with another companion. "Call it foolish, childish, what you will," he wrote defensively, "I believe velocipede riding is a pleasant, invigorating exercise."

however, was too exhausted to present himself. One writer sneered that they would have done better had they walked.

Increasingly, road-wary velocipede riders gravitated toward smooth sidewalks, prompting a slew of protests and restrictive ordinances. One irate pedestrian in Indianapolis made a personal stand against velocipedes. His brush with a bicycle landed the rider a $12.75 fine, even though, the court found, the target "could have avoided the vehicle, but made no attempt to do so." In Lawrence, Massachusetts, five young cyclists were apprehended and charged with sidewalk riding. Their lawyer argued that they had caused no obstruction since there were no pedestrians on the walkway at the time of the alleged offense. The court, however, ruled that the presence of the machines had deterred would-be occupants and fined each defendant $5.55. One outraged journalist denounced the harsh decision, pointing out that "persons convicted of actual crimes are daily let off free in the same court."

One heroic velocipedist in Hartford, Austin T. Ashmead, fought back. Mounted on his bicycle, he deliberately sailed past the police commissioner himself. Ashmead's sympathizers packed the courtroom, but the judge levied a whopping fifteen-dollar fine. Other cities applied similar crackdowns. In Utica, five boys were arrested after they terrorized pedestrians for an hour with a rented velocipede, driving it into fences, gutters, front stoops, lampposts, and even trees. A few days later, the police nabbed the son of a wealthy citizen as he rode by on his velocipede. The indignant lad argued that they were "exceeding their duty in attempting to interfere with him." When the officers refused to let him proceed on his steed, the boy "vented some wrath in a manner not particularly acceptable to the policemen," leading to his arrest and a stiff fine.

Such a clampdown may have seemed heavy-handed, but velocipede accidents were alarmingly common. In Indianapolis, a "young colored man" knocked over a colonel. In Saint Louis a "gay and indefatigable" amateur decked a burly Irishman, and would have incurred bodily injury himself had he not issued a "prompt apology." A newspaper in Dayton, Ohio, reported that a velocipedist had scared two hitched horses, prompting them to take off down the street "at a fearful rate" as they strewed the wreckage of a wagon. The horses "had very much the appearance of trying a race against time." When last seen, they "were heading for Greene county, without any apparent signs of fatigue." Their owner, who was inside a pharmacy at the time making a delivery, was described as a "poor man [who] can ill afford the loss of his wagon and the probable ruin of his horses."

But velocipedists were perhaps first and foremost a threat to themselves. A Pittsburgh man who had "the misfortune to run into a fireplug" broke not only his machine but also both his legs. Doctors who had once extolled bicycle riding as a healthy activity increasingly decried its evident dangers. Some medical authorities even asserted that the activity curved spines, stooped shoulders, and collapsed lungs. Dr. Van Wyck, a noted surgeon, warned that the "severe jar of the small hard seat" upon "the most tender parts of the anatomy" threatened "the powers of manhood." Constant practice, echoed another, would "prevent [the rider] from holding a paternal relation to the bicyclist of the future."

Colorful French-style races might well have eased mounting public objections, and would no doubt have encouraged much-needed technical development. Unfortunately, however, most outdoor contests only exacerbated the sense of imminent doom. Of the twelve racers who competed in a one-mile competition at the Union Course on Long Island in April 1869, only one barely beat six minutes, prompting the once sympathetic Charles A. Dana to brand the bicycle a failure. A race in Morristown, New Jersey, a few weeks later did little to redeem the machine. One contestant was thrown "up and over his velocipede," landing on his head and hands, with heels in the air, in the middle of the track." That acrobatic feat earned him "a round of applause for his agility," but led one observer to judge the sport "more laughable than exciting."

Still, despite the rising tide of bad press, some Americans actually achieved encouraging results on indoor tracks using the better class of machines. On several occasions, George Thudium of Indianapolis completed a mile in just over three minutes, setting national records. James Boyle of Syracuse made two miles in less than eight minutes. At the Empire Rink in New York, the oarsman Walter Brown covered fifty miles in just over four and a half hours, shaving nearly an hour off his time from only a week before. A contestant in Pittsburgh accomplished one hundred miles in a little more than ten hours. Most astonishingly, in July, A. P. Messinger of New York reportedly rode five hundred miles on an indoor track within fifty hours, resting for about seven of those hours and losing seven pounds in the process.

Some racers even achieved impressive results outdoors. Before a large crowd at the Open Air Velocipede Park in Albany that May, the winner completed a mile in just 4:37. A month later, at the Capitoline grounds in Brooklyn, James Boyle and Frank Swift registered mile times ranging from 4:15 to 4:25 using lightweight Rochester-made machines with wire-spoked wheels. A full year later, the best racers in England would fare no better. Some Americans even kept up a comparable pace on the road. In California, about a dozen velocipedists raced four miles from San Jose to Santa Clara, with the winner arriving in about seventeen minutes. Two thousand spectators in Newburyport, Massachusetts, cheered on fifteen-year-old Henry T. Moody, Jr., as he devoured three miles in less than thirteen minutes.

Even tourists routinely covered between five and eight miles an hour, easily double a normal walking clip. Perhaps the longest day trip was a ninety-mile run in Ohio from Akron to Toledo, accomplished in fifteen hours. One man rode from Wheeling, West Virginia, to Washington, Pennsylvania, and back, covering sixty miles in about twelve hours. He reported that he was slowed not by fatigue but by excited townsfolk who impeded his way. Indeed, upon his arrival in Washington, according to a local journalist, "the rush of men, women, children and dogs could not have been greater had half the town been on fire." Another velocipede rider easily pedaled from Northampton, Massachusetts, to Boston, covering one hundred miles in two days. In Indianapolis, four "neatly dressed" velocipedists set off for Richmond, Indiana, "in the highest spirits," toting "all needful articles." In three days, they covered 150 miles and were reportedly "so well satisfied with the journey that they want to do it some more."

Yet negative press largely overshadowed these encouraging developments. One paper went so far as to pronounce the craze "the most senseless and ridiculous mania that ever took hold of the public." As summer wore on, the bicycle movement quickly lost steam. The few rinks left were increasingly dependent on stunts, such as velocipede

TO
ED. R. LORING ESQ.
(of the N.O. School of the Velocipede.)

THE UNLUCKY

Velocipedist.

Song ☆   Galop ☆

BY

S. LOW COACH.

Quick Step ☆   NEW ORLEANS,   March ☆
Published by BLACKMAR & Co. 201 Canal St.

The title of this ditty would seem a fitting epitaph for the short-lived American bicycle trade. The machine shown is a Demarest bicycle that put the rider in a more reclined position. Manufacturers sometimes published sheet music themselves as a form of advertisement.

riding on tightropes, and other "superlatively foolish antics." To be sure, velocipedists still roamed a few cities. The *Indianapolis Sentinel* detected "a great many persons living some distance from their places of business who ride to and fro half a dozen times a day." In several southern cities youths met in the evenings for bicycle jaunts by moonlight. But with public disapproval mounting, even these limited activities soon ceased.

Defenders of the bicycle movement nonetheless held out hope. "Bicycle exercise is too fascinating a sport, and too good an exercise not to become popular," insisted New York's *Sunday Mercury* in August 1869. *Scientific American* reaffirmed its faith in the future of the bicycle and, noting the continued interest in the British Empire, gamely predicted the return of the American bicycle come "cool and delightful autumn weather." Alas, the anticipated revival never materialized. A velocipede festival in Brooklyn that October drew a respectable crowd but only one exhibitor, Calvin Witty. Conceded one sympathizer, "Velocipeding is acknowledged to be dead."

The year 1869 has been remembered ever since as a milestone in the history of American transportation—thanks not to the abandoned velocipede but to the golden spike that completed the transcontinental railroad. Why did Americans give up so quickly on the primitive bicycle after such a fast and furious start? Historians have often cited a technical impasse. Yet the American bicycle actually made impressive progress in a short time. Right away, Thomas R. Pickering introduced the stronger and lighter tubular frame—one satisfied owner claimed to have ridden it regularly outdoors over a six-month period with no trouble. George L. Brownell of New Bedford applied solid rubber tires to cushion the ride. Virgil Price of New York introduced what was perhaps the most important improvement of all, the lightweight and elastic wire wheel.

Similar innovations in Britain were soon to yield the extremely successful high-wheel bicycle. Even in America, some inventors had already anticipated its profile, building front wheels exceeding fifty inches in diameter. Other promising designs included the American Improved Velocipede by Tomlinson, Demarest, and Company of New York. The Demarest, as it was commonly known, featured a front fork and steering column tilted toward the rider at about a forty-five-degree angle, allowing for a nearly fifty-inch driving wheel while still keeping the rider's feet within striking distance of the ground. The more reclined position was also said to provide a more even distribution of weight, greater comfort, and better leverage on the cranks for uphill climbing or fast pedaling. The Dexter bicycle, patented by William Van Anden of Poughkeepsie, New York, included a freewheel mechanism in the front hub to enable riders to rest their feet on the pedals even as the front wheel rotated. Calvin Witty of Brooklyn experimented with lever-activated rear-wheel drives and built a bicycle with a geared hub that turned the front wheel three times for every revolution of the cranks.

Clearly, other factors besides technical discouragement contributed to the prema-

"Price's Improved Bicycle," featuring wire wheels patented by Virgil Price mounted on a Pickering frame, itself an advanced design, with finely engraved lugs. Wire wheels, a key improvement, were just beginning to appear in the United States when the velocipede craze fizzled. The inset in this sketch, which appeared in the *Scientific American* of 12 June 1869, shows how the iron rim is grooved to admit a rubber tire.

ture cessation of velocipede development in the United States, including poor roads, safety concerns, and inflated popular expectations. In the end, however, the patent mess was probably the greatest deterrent to sustained advancement. The hefty fees imposed by patent holders demoralized both riders and makers, stalling the development and application of key improvements. Moreover, the trade suffered from a glaring lack of leadership. Its captain, widely reviled as "Royalty" Witty, assisted by a dozen legal clerks, was too busy enforcing his inflated demands for fees to tend to the long-term interests of the trade.

Before long, a get-rich-quick mentality sank in, as unlicensed makers flooded the market with inferior machines and opportunistic rink managers charged outlandish fees. The public, in turn, came to resent the exorbitant prices they had paid to purchase or rent the velocipede, only to discover that it was of little or no practical value—a "great humbug," as one commentator put it. Even those who felt a lingering attachment to the primitive bicycle bowed to public pressure and dismounted. The beleaguered trade was powerless to defend itself against the backlash, and the bold Yankee experiment ended in an abrupt and decisive failure.

SIX *European Development*

During the brief American craze, the bicycle continued to thrive in France. By the spring of 1869, the country hosted thirty clubs, frequent races, and as many as fifty thousand machines. In April, just as Americans were losing interest in the novelty, the weekly *Le Vélocipède Illustré* appeared to spearhead the growing velocipede movement. "The velocipede is not a fad born yesterday, in vogue today, to be forgotten tomorrow," insisted the editor. "Along with its seductive qualities, it has an undeniably practical character. It supplants the raw and unintelligent speed of the masses with the speed of the individual. This horse of wood and iron fills a void in modern life; it responds not only to our needs but also to our aspirations." Its masthead, featuring Lady Progress on a velocipede, symbolized a widespread determination to transform the bicycle into something truly useful.

The booming French bicycle trade, meanwhile, was gearing up for a banner year in 1869. By summer, it counted more than one hundred makers. Paris alone had at least nine specialists, most with ties to the carriage or toy trades. One was Pierre Lallement,

1re ANNÉE — N° 1. LE NUMÉRO : **DIX** CENTIMES 1er AVRIL 1869

ABONNEMENTS
POUR
PARIS
ET LES
DÉPARTEMENTS
—
Un an 5 fr.
Six mois. 3 fr.

BUREAUX
19, rue des Martyrs
A PARIS
On ne reçoit que
les lettres affranchies

DÉPOTS
DANS LES
DÉPARTEMENTS
CHEZ LES
Principaux Libraires
ET LES
Correspondants
DU
Petit Journal

RÉDACTION
ET
ADMINISTRATION
—
L. G. JACQUES
19, rue des Martyrs
A PARIS

DÉPÔT GÉNÉRAL
à Paris
CHEZ
M. MADRE
r. du Croissant, 16

LE
VÉLOCIPÈDE
ILLUSTRÉ
Paraît
tous les Jeudis.

LE VÉLOCIPÈDE ILLUSTRÉ

The first issue of the weekly French trade journal *Le Vélocipède Illustré,* launched in the spring of 1869, with Lady Progress on its masthead. The four-page journal reported race results and featured many velocipede-related articles and advertisements. Starting in July 1869, it was issued twice a week until its suspension in September 1870 on account of the Franco-Prussian War.

who opened a store near the Champs-Elysées using the proceeds from the sale of his American patent. The industry leader, however, remained the original Michaux company, now renamed the Compagnie Parisienne. The blacksmith himself, however, was no longer involved in its operations. René Olivier later explained that his relationship with Michaux had only gotten worse after the two parties chartered the pioneer company in May of 1868. Far from falling in line, René asserted, the blacksmith continued to exploit the company name on his own and thwart the long-overdue transition to the diagonal frame. Worse, he purportedly embezzled funds and incited the workmen against the Oliviers. In the spring of 1869, the brothers finally engineered his departure, underwriting a lucrative severance package.

René, now overtly in charge, hired a new manager named Jean-Baptiste Gobert, expanded the factory, opened a massive new rink, and adopted the English slogan "Time is Money." His workforce soon swelled to some five hundred employees, and production reached hundreds of machines a week, which were exported around the world.

Pierre Lallement posing on a diagonal-frame velocipede in Paris, probably in the second half of 1869. He had opened a velocipede shop near the Champs-Elysées that spring.

The press cited the operation as a shining example of industrial progress. "Its fabrication is formidable," gushed one visitor, adding that it would be perfect "were it not for the daily improvements implemented by the inventive genius of its leaders." He found the massive stock simply overwhelming. "Imagine a field of velocipedes, a horizon full of pedals and wheels, a profusion of colors. Every thing is green, red, gray, yellow or blue; with shiny wheels and glistening steel. There they are, all neatly lined up, destined for the most distant and disparate lands."

At last, René had emerged from the shadows of Michaux to bask in the limelight as the founder and leader of this dynamic new industry. In numerous interviews he gave to the press that spring, René claimed full responsibility for the inception and direction of the original bicycle company. In June, *Le Vélocipède Illustré,* closely aligned with René's new company, sketched the Oliviers' pivotal role. "For many years, the founders of the Compagnie Parisienne, anticipating the present bicycle craze, dedicated themselves to studying the possible [business] organization and [technical] improvements. Finally, two years ago, confident that they had attained a perfection sufficient to render this in-

A poster for the Compagnie Parisienne showing its operation in 1869, with its new and expansive rink, and featuring the motto "Time is Money" in the center along with references to branch houses in England, Ireland, and Scotland

strument practical, they hired the most skilled workers, adopted all the best innovations, and placed themselves at the head of this industry founding the firm Michaux et Cie."

But even though the bicycle appeared on the road to technical improvement, the trade still faced significant obstacles. For one thing, the cost of a bicycle remained discouragingly high. "Show me the employee, the worker, the rural postman who can put aside 200 or 250 francs for a velocipede," huffed one indignant journalist. "Why, you can almost buy a carriage for that sum! We will therefore patiently await for a factory to appear that can deliver velocipedes for only 100 francs." How long that might take he could not say, but he had no doubt where the bicycle was headed in the long run. "The velocipede will amuse the idle rich for a while, but they will abandon it one day, for the simple reason that they all own horses and carriages. The velocipede will thus become the carriage of the poor. That is its true destiny."

One group dedicated to reducing the cost of a velocipede while improving its usefulness was the Practical Society for the Velocipede. It was founded in December 1868 by some twenty Parisians who aimed to "render the bicycle practical and to win public

Patent Problems

René Olivier observed, around the time of his trial against Michaux in late 1869, that others had "hesitated at first" to enter the velocipede trade, "believing in the existence of a patent." But he neglected to add that his own company had created that false impression by presenting Michaux as the patentee in its early advertisements. No doubt that ploy was intended to discourage potential rivals for a spell, while the Oliviers established the Michaux name as the pioneer brand. In March of 1868, a suspicious lawyer in Bordeaux wrote to Michaux for clarification. "I would be greatly obliged, sir, if you would let me know the dates, numbers, and classifications of the various patents you are exploiting." The ledger fails to note if he received a reply.

The Oliviers, however, had a real patent problem of their own. Although Lallement's American patent, the only one claiming the basic bicycle, did not bear directly on the French trade, it effectively sealed off what was to the Oliviers a potentially lucrative market. Calvin Witty's advertisements in the spring of 1869, in fact, expressly forbade importation of bicycles from Paris. Moreover, should the public come to learn of the Lallement patent, the Michaux company stood to suffer considerable embarrassment. A Parisian journalist, Lèo Lespés, using the pen name Timothée Trimm, did allude to Lallement, but to deny rather than confirm the existence of a foreign patent. After touring the Compagnie Parisienne with its director, M. Gobert, in May 1869, Lespés related: "We are told that in North America a foreigner presented himself as the inventor of the velocipede. His trickery was short-lived . . . and he fled without obtaining a patent."

Naturally, Gobert and the Oliviers would have known full well that Lallement had in fact received a patent. In fact, when René applied for his own American patent a few months later, covering a fork suspension system, he engaged John E. Earle of New Haven—Lallement's patent attorney. That curious choice suggests that René was perhaps simultaneously maneuvering to buy the vexing Lallement patent himself. Witty had reportedly already turned down at least one offer for $75,000 from an unidentified source. René, as head of the world's largest bicycle concern, might well have been among those interested in acquiring the patent. That might explain why, during the Michaux trial, he was so coy about the origins of the bicycle, alluding to the inventor only as a "workman" distinct from Michaux. By neither confirming nor denying the validity of the Lallement patent, he was perhaps keeping open the option to acquire it himself.

acceptance of it as a means of transportation." Its president noted in the spring of 1869, with evident satisfaction, that velocipedes had proliferated over the past year. Yet the vehicle was still "widely regarded as an instrument of pleasure," not utility. Moreover, its construction, so meticulous from an aesthetic point of view, "leaves everything to be desired in terms of solidity and affordability." To steer the trade in the right direction, the society's technical committee issued medals to those who had found ways to either improve the quality of the velocipede or reduce its cost. The first winners were A. Berruyer, a maker of kickstands, and the newly independent Pierre Michaux, who was marketing a four-wheeled velocipede his son Ernest had patented in November 1868.

But while the trade struggled to improve the construction of the velocipede and reduce its prohibitive cost, the movement faced a growing public backlash. Many citizens resented the prosperous young men who rode velocipedes, while others disparaged the machine itself as a pricey gymnastic toy, if not a harmful instrument. Indeed, riders often suffered serious injuries when their machines slammed to the ground, or when they collided with each other. Some accidents were even fatal. One fifteen-year-old in central France, for example, lost control of his machine as he sped downhill. He plunged into the Rhone River, and though he repeatedly resurfaced he was unable to reach the shore and no one could save him from drowning.

Some people argued that velocipedists had the right to imperil their own necks if they so chose. But others charged that their reckless driving also threatened the well-being of those who chose to travel by other means. Bicycle riders often collided with pedestrians, especially in dense urban areas. Velocipedists were also said to frighten horses, and were blamed for a number of serious carriage accidents. Further tarnishing the riders' reputation were widespread reports of hit-and-run accidents. Many citizens implored local authorities to curb velocipede riding in the name of public safety.

By the summer of 1869, numerous cities had responded with restrictive measures. A typical ordinance was the one issued by the mayor of Dôle, in central France. "Considering that the use of velocipedes is becoming more general," he declared, "access to public promenades and to sidewalks is hereby prohibited." Elsewhere in the city, velocipedists were not to exceed a "very moderate pace," nor were they to make any maneuvers that might obstruct carriages, horses, or pedestrians. At night, they were required to use a lantern, just like carriage drivers.

By forming clubs, velocipedists defended their interests collectively, while drawing companionship and support from their peers. A typical organization was that of Marseille. It had thirty male members between the ages of twenty and forty-four, and they included landlords, merchants, an architect, a pharmacist, and a bicycle maker. Clubs organized regular rides and publicized the results so that the public would better appreciate the value of the bicycle. In February 1869, for example, the press dutifully reported

The Compagnie Parisienne, formerly Michaux, offered a variety of bicycle styles by 1869. This one was designed with the tourist in mind; the strap shown on the ground could be secured to the front of the bicycle and wrapped around the back, allowing the rider to lean backward for better leverage on the pedals while ascending hills.

that a large group from Auch had ridden forty-four miles to Agen in just six hours. Traveling in numbers also enabled riders to cope with the frequent mechanical breakdowns and accidents that plagued their machines. Moreover, hostile locals, prone to pelting lone velocipedists with stones or planting obstacles in their way, were less likely to harass an entire group.

To curry public favor and encourage technical development, clubs organized outdoor races in conjunction with city festivals, with the proceeds earmarked for charities. The clubs booked bands, raised prize monies, and publicized their programs. At times, they even secured discounts on train travel for out-of-town visitors and arranged their accommodations. Typically, the course was a half-mile loop over a dirt track or smooth road wide enough to allow competitors to pass one another. Racers generally made several circuits for a total of one or two miles. Local dignitaries and their lady guests watched the proceedings from a grandstand at the starting line. As many as a thousand spectators paid to enter the field. Many more—up to ten thousand—crowded the periphery. The programs featured live music and often concluded with fireworks and lavish banquets.

In March 1869, a club from Carpentras, outside Avignon, resumed the budding tradition of city-sponsored races. Its well-publicized program drew fifty of the best racers from across France. The proud velocipedists, wearing colorful jockey attire, paraded along the main street toward the battlefield amid a profusion of flags and flowers. Hundreds lined the streets, filled windows, and flooded balconies to witness the procession.

French velocipede races, such as this one that took place in the summer of 1869 near the palace of Fontainebleau, were colorful affairs organized by clubs with the patronage of the host city. This French engraving was reprinted in London's *Illustrated Times* of 7 August 1869.

Once the competition commenced, the crowd invaded the field itself, forcing organizers to postpone the championship race. The competitors reconvened at seven o'clock the next morning, in a vain effort to evade further congestion. The local press pronounced the entire affair a stunning success.

Soon, similar spectacles took place all over France, stirring widespread sympathy for the velocipede. A journalist in Laval, in central France, pronounced the local contests "graceful and charming," adding that races were "one of the most pleasant distractions that a city's idle youth can give to their people." A race in eastern France that June created a palpable sense of excitement. "Never before was the theater of a struggle more beautifully situated," declared a local journalist. "Surrounded by pretty houses, beside the cathedral of Thann, hemmed in at the four corners by superb mountains, Napoleon Square was chock full of spectators. All around, on rooftops, in trees, on neighboring hills, hundreds of curious citizens took their positions to observe the gyrations of the velocipedists." On one day alone—the centennial of Napoleon's birth on the fifteenth of August—more than twenty French cities held velocipede races.

By fall, nearly every corner of France had hosted at least one series of these novel contests. The results were often impressive. One journalist in Lyon marveled at how a racer had covered a mile at the speed of a local train. But above all the races were exciting and entertaining. In Dunkirk, for example, Jacques Pedro, a black man of Brazilian descent, closed with a furious burst to nip his rival at the finish line, whereupon he was carried off on the shoulders of enthusiastic fans. "Slow" races and juvenile contests provided added diversion, along with open races where the winner collected all the entry fees. Another popular format was the obstacle race, which required riders to make sharp turns, ascend steps, and leap over water-filled troughs.

But the chief draw, at times even overshadowing the main contest of the day, were women's races. Introduced in late 1868 at Bordeaux, these novel spectacles became increasingly popular in 1869 and virtually obligatory by 1870. At first, organizers struggled, however, to repeat the Bordeaux success. Several of them announced women's races that failed to draw any contestants. The competitors who did appear at one race in Lyon in the spring of 1869, according to a local paper, had no clue how to manage their machines. But soon a small contingent of highly adept female riders enlivened the French racing circuit and endeared themselves to an adoring public.

The sizable cash prizes, up to five hundred francs, encouraged the best riders of both sexes to earn at least a partial living from the sport. The public came to recognize, and seek out, an elite tier of professionals that included James Moore, Edmond Moret, Louis Tribout, and André Castera. Some were admired as much for their style as for their speed. One writer marveled how Moret could sit "comfortably and gracefully" on his instrument, almost immobile, without betraying any effort while he "sliced through space like an arrow." Mused the writer, "One wonders if it is really he who pushes his machine, or if it is rather the machine who pushes him, blown along by some mischievous spirit."

Several women racers also became popular celebrities. In August 1869, two veterans of the Bordeaux match, Amélie and Julie, raced again in nearby La Réole. They amazed the overflowing crowd with their dexterity. But the true star of the circuit was "Miss America." Originally from Lyon, possibly of English descent, she was married to Rowley B. Turner, himself a noted velocipedist who hailed from England. Despite her petite stature, she earned a reputation as a fierce competitor. In November 1869, she was the only woman to complete the entire course in the first long-distance road race from Paris to Rouen. In June 1870, she won a first-place prize in Rouen, then took an overnight train to Blois where, the next day, she dispensed with the local competition with embarrassing ease.

In spite of the popularity of city-sponsored races, not all observers lent their approval. Some citizens decried the road closures that were enforced on race days. One grouch in Fontainebleau chastised the city for spending its scarce resources on race decorations. Some officials even refused to sanction the events. When a bicycle maker in Clermont-Ferrand proposed races in conjunction with a musical festival planned for the spring of 1869, the mayor withheld his support. He insisted that the program schedule was already full, nor would the budget allow for any prizes.

Races were also plagued by frequent logistical and technical mishaps. On several occasions, unruly crowds invaded the field, causing delays, accidents, and cancellations. And even when unmolested, the riders often faltered on their own, by misplacing their feet on the pedals or failing to make a turn. With alarming regularity they fell, usually taking down others in the process. Longer races over regular roads were particularly problematic. The winner of one eight-mile run in Le Neubourg, Normandy, arrived in less than an hour, but four of the twelve entrants failed to finish.

Still, these contests gave mechanics a valuable opportunity to test new products and gradually improve the machine. Many programs also included exhibitions where bicycle makers could display and sell their products, while providing a lively forum for the exchange of technical ideas. To further encourage development, sometimes a jury would award prizes to the best machines and accessories. To be sure, the racers themselves were not always receptive to promising propositions. They spurned, for example, a nifty freewheel mechanism by A. Boeuf of Tarare, no doubt out of fear that the device would add needless complexity. Like the Dexter hub previously introduced in the United States, this mechanism would have enabled them to adjust their pedaling cadence at will, while the front wheel spun on its own accord.

Nevertheless, racers widely adopted at least one critical improvement in the course

The Hippodrome in the Bois de Boulogne of Paris, a wooden stadium holding up to fifteen thousand spectators, was well known for its novel and entertaining acts. Starting in the fall of 1868, this popular venue regularly presented women velocipedists, as seen in a print from about 1869.

of 1869: the inch-thick solid rubber tire designed to give a more comfortable ride than the standard iron variety. Initially proposed by Clément Ader, a future aviation pioneer, the idea was slow to catch on. Even *Le Vélocipède Illustré* at first dismissed rubber tires as an impractical luxury, likely to wear out quickly or even fall off the rims to which they were crudely attached with wire strands or rivets. But bicycle makers soon introduced metal rims with U- and V-shaped cross-sections that allowed tires to be securely cemented or wedged into place. Racers quickly proved that these tires not only were durable and comfortable, they also increased speed. Soon tourists adopted them as well, and they became standard accessories on all varieties of cycles.

Racers also began to adopt larger front wheels so that the bicycle would go farther with every revolution of the cranks. The large driving wheel, however, created a flap on

Women and the Velocipede

In the 1860s, Western women were still largely second-class citizens confined to the home or the factory. Conventional garb—tight corsets, long dresses, hats and gloves—restricted their bodies and discouraged recreational exercise. Yet reform was already in the air. Suffragettes clamored for the right to vote, while dress reformers such as Amelia Bloomer proposed simpler, lighter, and more comfortable clothing. Even the medical community was starting to encourage women to exercise and spend more time outdoors. Little wonder, then, why so many women took a keen interest in the velocipede.

In Paris, the Michaux bicycle had barely debuted when *La Vie Parisienne* wondered how society women would take to the novelty. It predicted, correctly, that they would sooner shorten their skirts than pass on the bicycle. American women likewise relished the new sport. Some makers experimented with ladies' tricycles, but one source warned, "The fair sex will not wait until a velocipede is invented especially for their use." Indeed, scores of women showed their interest in the bicycle, prompting Pickering to propose a woman's model with a "drop

An American label for Velocipede Tobacco from about 1874. Although attractive female velocipedists were often depicted purely for product promotion, many women showed a genuine interest in the first bicycles. Conventional dress and attitudes, however, along with mechanical flaws, often discouraged them from riding.

frame" and a "basket saddle." Women also patronized rinks, enlisting in ladies-only classes. Calvin Witty hired Carrie Moore, the "Velocipede Queen" herself, to serve as chief instructor, and his advertisements declared, "Garments of the Bloomer pattern will be kept on hand for those who wish to ride." Nor would any gentlemen be admitted to the room, to protect "sensitive and bashful ladies."

For a woman to ride a bicycle in public was nonetheless a bold gesture. "The very appearance of a lady on such a machine would be obviously incongruous and out of place," huffed one matron, "excepting as a joke or mere piece of bravado." Nevertheless, some women did venture forth on their velocipedes. In April 1869, some three years after Pierre Lallement rode his bicycle around the green in New Haven, that same venue hosted another "novel spectacle." A local newspaper reported: "A young woman in fancy attire amused the crowd on the velocipede. The only difficulty she experienced was in getting a good start and making a graceful halt." The curious display was nonetheless "too questionable to meet the approbation of the ladies who happened to be crossing the green at the time." Even the paper concluded, "The performance would have looked better if it had come off in a circus ring."

In Great Britain, women appear to have been more reluctant than their French and American counterparts to mount the intimidating bicycle. The *Englishwoman's Domestic Magazine* concluded that bicycles "are not for us" and favored a tandem that would let a woman sit sidesaddle. It nonetheless conceded, "The evolutions of actresses mounted on bicycles on the Parisian boards are described as simply marvelous." It also refused to rule out favorable development. "A thousand questions rise up in connection with the velocipede. Will they really become the rage? If so, are we to go shopping as well as promenading on them? At all events, they would allow us to see more of the 'wide, wide world' and afford plenty of exercise to lungs and muscles, for it be known that ladies are not altogether such ethereal creatures as certain poets have divined."

the racing circuit. Some organizers banned bicycles with wheels exceeding thirty-eight inches to ensure that the contests hinged on superior skill rather than equipment. Proponents of the bigger wheel, however, claimed that such restrictions impeded technical progress. The issue boiled over at a race in Marennes. A competitor from nearby Rochefort showed up with an objectionably large front wheel, prompting the local competitors to storm off the field in protest. Eventually, organizers resolved the matter by restricting the wheel size in some events while leaving others open-ended. This policy effectively forced the dominant Parisian professionals to compete among themselves, mercifully saving the local competitors from certain embarrassment.

By the fall of 1869, the bicycle's novelty value was starting to wear thin. Many wealthy individuals who had once indulged in the fashion were no longer active riders, and many specialized firms had already folded. Still, there were some encouraging signs. Races, though fewer, still drew large crowds, and affirmed that the velocipede was making steady technical progress. There were even indications that the elevated price of a good machine would soon descend to a more affordable level. One maker in Clermont-Ferrand, who advertised his velocipedes at 225 francs in May, listed them at 150 francs by September, proudly announcing that he had "finally resolved the problem of how to bring the velocipede within the public's means."

The Compagnie Parisienne, meanwhile, valiantly carried on as the industry leader. Yet even in his moment of glory, René was still haunted by his former associate. The terms of Michaux's departure that spring required the Oliviers to pay the blacksmith a whopping 150,000 francs. For his part, Michaux agreed to desist from using his family name in connection with velocipedes. Nevertheless, shortly after his exit, the blacksmith launched a new bicycle company under the Michaux banner. He even billed himself, once again, as the original inventor and developer, while asserting that he alone provided genuine Michaux bicycles. Compounding the problem for the Oliviers, Michaux's machines were virtually identical to their own. The exasperated Oliviers sued Michaux for breach of contract, waging a court battle over the summer of 1869.

In October, the Oliviers finally won their case, driving the Michaux family out of the trade and into bankruptcy. Yet, even with Michaux out of the picture, the company suffered from chronic mismanagement. Aimé, who presided over the family's chemical concerns in western France, occasionally dropped by the Parisian factory to check up on things and lend his brother a hand. On one such occasion, he sent his other brother and fellow investor Marius a blistering report. "Our enthusiasm," he bemoaned, "is matched only by our ignorance." In his estimation, René was merely "amusing himself" rather than buckling down to business. Aimé recounted how large stockpiles of useless materials flowed into the factory on a daily basis. Yet the day before, after making six bicycle sales in short order, Aimé found himself scrounging around for pedals to complete the machines. Desperate, he finally lifted them off the rink vehicles. "This business could be quite profitable," he lamented, "if only we imposed a measure of order."

Yet however lax René may have been as a plant manager, he was by all accounts an effective champion of the bicycle. His crowning achievement was no doubt the eighty-mile Paris-to-Rouen road race, a precursor to the Tour de France, over which he presided. Held for the first time on November 7, 1869, it was the most ambitious large-scale test of the bicycle ever undertaken. Thousands gathered at the Arc de Triomphe early in the morning, as more than a hundred velocipedists assembled for the historic journey, including many amateurs who intended to go only partway. The lineup included virtually all the top male racers, Miss America, and at least one tricyclist. Even a retrograde pedestrian, later disqualified, took his position, insisting that he could outrun the machines.

The winner, James Moore, arrived in Rouen after ten and a half hours in the saddle, coping with rather hilly terrain and roads muddied by recent rain. The Vélo-Club of Rouen was on hand to greet the champion, as were cheering spectators. His advanced machine featured solid rubber tires and an oversized front wheel with ball bearings in the hub for smooth rolling. A dozen more racers drifted in before midnight, and another eighteen trickled in by dawn. In all, some thirty contestants successfully finished the course in under twenty-four hours. Eugène Chapus, editor of *Le Sport*, pronounced the affair "a remarkable and brilliant performance." He foresaw a rosy future for this "rapid means of locomotion" to be built upon "progressive improvements."

In fact, velocipede construction continued to improve in the 1870 season. The general adoption of rubber tires spawned another vital improvement: the all-metal wheel with tensioned spokes built on the suspension principle. Although the carriage trade had repeatedly experimented with metal wheels as a possible alternative to conventional wooden wheels, with little success, bicycle constructors were eager to revisit this idea. They recognized that the metal wheel was ideally suited for the bicycle because it was considerably lighter than the wooden variety and also more elastic, both crucial properties that could further accelerate the bicycle and soften its bone-jarring ride. Wire wheels were also less likely to get out of true, and easier to adjust when they did.

Among the first to devise and market a practical all-metal bicycle wheel was a master craftsman, Eugène Meyer of Paris. In August 1869, he patented a system featuring individually adjustable spokes. Meyer's own wire-wheeled bicycles weighed just forty-four pounds, easily twenty-five pounds lighter than a standard velocipede with wooden wheels. Meanwhile, other Parisian makers such as Jules Camus and William Jackson exploited wire wheels to build tricycles that weighed no more than conventional bicycles while offering greater stability. The highly advantageous wire construction was soon widely adopted in Great Britain as well, where it became known as the "spider" wheel.

James Moore, right, winner of the first road race from Paris to Rouen, with the runner-up, André Castera. It is not known if the photograph was taken before or after the race but these suits are presumably what they wore that day. Castera's machine displays the typical profile of 1869, but Moore's rear wheel is only half the size of his front one. By the spring of 1870 wire wheels had largely replaced the wooden variety shown here, and Moore's profile became the standard.

As was the case with rubber tires, some velocipede riders initially greeted the wire wheel with skepticism. But once again, impressive race results helped prove its practical advantages. At the start of the 1870 season, the Compagnie Parisienne, which had initially promoted fork springs as the best way to cushion road shock, abruptly changed course and introduced a wire wheel of its own. The top French racers promptly switched to bicycles with wire wheels and rubber tires. Mechanics connected with the racing circuit thus continued to make the bicycle an ever fleeter and smoother vehicle, redefining standard equipment.

Spider wheels, in turn, accelerated the trend toward larger driving wheels. Riders were increasingly dissatisfied with the conventional thirty-six-inch front wheel, because it forced them to pedal furiously to gain any speed. Although makers had understood all along that larger wheels would improve gearing and enhance speed, they found that wooden wheels simply could not be safely constructed beyond about forty inches in diameter. Some French makers, notably Emile Roux of Paris, initially attacked the problem as Witty had, by devising a front hub with an internal gear mechanism that rotated the wheel two or three times with every revolution of the crank. Such mechanisms, however, added weight, cost, and complexity without providing a compelling competitive advantage.

Meyer and other makers of wire wheels happily discovered that the new construction imposed no such upper limit. Indeed, the diameter of the wire wheel could be arbitrarily extended without compromising its structural integrity or adding significant weight. They affirmed that the simplest and most economical way to solve the gearing problem was to enlarge the direct-drive front wheel built with tensioned metal spokes. Naturally, the gearing possibilities were limited by the need to keep the front wheel to a reasonable size. Nevertheless, a larger yet still manageable front wheel increased the distance the vehicle traveled with every revolution of the pedals, and thus allowed for faster speeds.

Between the fall of 1869 and the spring of 1870, most French racers adopted front wheels exceeding forty inches in diameter. At the same time, bicycle makers discovered that they could safely reduce the rear wheel to about half the size of the front, thereby saving weight and keeping the length of the vehicle in check. They thus tilted the backbone and slid the seat forward to keep the rider's legs within reach of the pedals. This new configuration—which some would later call transitional in that it served as a stepping-stone to the full-blown "high wheeler"—quickly asserted itself on the racing scene. In the summer of 1870, in the Norman town of Le Neubourg, André Castera used such a machine to cover five miles in less than twenty minutes, averaging more than fifteen miles an hour. He took about 20 percent less time than James Moore had needed to cover the same course the year before using an old-style bicycle.

Races in 1870 were neither as frequent nor as popular as they had been the year before. Yet the movement still boasted its own journal, numerous clubs, and a large and enthusiastic following. Moreover, the success of the Paris-to-Rouen event encouraged road racing. In January 1870, thirty contestants raced twenty miles around the periphery of Paris in about two and half hours. A month later, the gymnast Jules Léotard, famed for his acrobatic feats and the tight slacks that would one day bear his name, rode forty miles in under four hours. A journalist in Dijon admired the tenacity of the bicycle boosters who gathered for a race that May. "With the velocipede craze behind us," he asserted, "it's high time for another machine to take its place. Yet the [recent] races drew seventeen amateurs who remain faithful to their instrument. They know its feel, its whims and its speed. Mention horses, and they all shrug their shoulders and vigorously deny that the bicycle is a proven failure."

In spite of the inevitable decline of the furor, the French movement had largely succeeded in establishing the bicycle as a useful and enjoyable vehicle. Moreover, its immediate survival was assured, and its prospects for improvement were encouraging. The outbreak of war with Prussia that July, however, knocked France out of the leadership position it had enjoyed since the inception of the bicycle industry three years earlier. French velocipedists would eventually regroup, but not the Compagnie Parisienne. In 1874, having exhausted their family's tolerance, the Oliviers formally dissolved the money-bleeding operation and sold its remaining stock. Others would have to carry on the unfinished work of perfecting the still rudimentary machine.

At least the bicycle was not short on exposure. Between 1869 and 1870, the primitive bicycle had appeared the world over: in Asia, the Pacific, northern and southern Africa, and even Central and South America. In the same period, many European countries hosted crowd-pleasing outdoor races, including Austria, Belgium, the Netherlands, Switzerland, and Spain. German makers had supplied not only the lively home market but also neighbors such as Russia. Italians were also active developers, having figured among Michaux's first customers. As early as the fall of 1868, Florentines watched with amazement as A. Favre, the French maker, rode his machine through their streets. By 1870, Florence had a club of its own. In February of that year, a sixteen-year-old American named Rynner Van Hest won an inaugural road race between Florence and Pistoia. He covered the twenty-one miles on a Compagnie Parisienne velocipede in an impressive time of two hours and twelve minutes.

But Great Britain, with its strong metalworking tradition and network of fine roads, furnished the most fertile ground for development. There, mechanics gradually transformed the still-crude bicycle into a truly roadworthy vehicle. As early as mid-1867, the French bicycle was already stirring interest in the inventive community across the channel. The *English Mechanic* published a sketch of the curious little Parisian vehicle. In November, a writer from *The Field*, a widely read sporting paper, visited the Michaux factory for a firsthand tour. His glowing report prompted a number of curious Englishmen to contact the pioneer firm and import the first bicycles to England and its colonies.

One early Michaux customer who had learned of the novelty from *The Field* was Charles Bowen, a royal engineer stationed in Madras, India. He promptly dashed off a letter requesting "at an early date, round the Cape, a good two wheeled velocipede." Other early correspondents with ties to England had come across the bicycle during their travels abroad. "Having seen a velocipede bought from your house of business at Paris when I last visited Gibralter," wrote thirty-two-year-old ship captain William W. Vine from Portsmouth, "I took such a fancy to it, that I should like to purchase one."

By the spring of 1868, a few Englishmen had already received their orders. E. W. Martin of Devonshire, for one, was entirely satisfied with his acquisition and sent his compliments to Michaux. "The whole machine, I must say, is an exquisite piece of work-

A balloon-assisted "mountain velocipede" drawn by a German artist for *Illustrirte Zeitung* of 3 July 1869, demonstrating how widely the primitive bicycle captured the world's imagination

manship and does great credit to you and the workmen." James Collinge of Chester, having "completely mastered" his bicycle, was so pleased with it that he promptly ordered a second one. He confessed to Michaux, however, that he sometimes struggled with his machine given that "this part of the country is very hilly." The day before he had ridden about twenty-two miles in four straight hours, but "fully seven miles of it I had to walk." He therefore implored Michaux to make sure that his next bicycle came equipped with all the latest improvements.

Yet despite this initial wave of interest, England experienced no immediate outbreak of "velocipede fever." To be sure, the technical press increasingly discussed the French novelty, but many remained skeptical of its merits. After all, the two-wheeler had been tried and dismissed nearly a half century before. Not until the fall of 1868, with

Though billed as American, the bicycle in this poster was actually made in England by the Coventry Sewing Machine Company. Rowley B. Turner, the Paris agent for the firm, took an early interest in bicycles and persuaded his home office to begin producing them. The initial shipment went to Turner's partner in Paris, Louis Pascaud, owner of the Pascaud gymnasium and the father of bicycle racer and performer Henri Pascaud.

France already deeply immersed in the craze and Americans about to follow suit, did various English concerns develop firm plans to exploit the bicycle. A. Davis of London was one of the first to import the machine from France, while the Coventry Sewing Machine Company prepared for its own large-scale production. Its agent in Paris, Rowley B. Turner, persuaded the company directors, which included his uncle Josiah Turner, to start a bicycle line. Rowley Turner himself placed the first order for some three hundred machines on behalf of his partners, the Pascaud gymnasium of Paris.

In contrast to the United States, however, rinks did not proliferate in Britain that winter. Nevertheless, starting in early 1869, various reports signaled that the velocipede would indeed progress rapidly in England. In January, four velocipedists raced two miles down London's Dulwich road, the winner arriving in under ten minutes. A month later, Rowley Turner and two friends, Charles Spencer and John Mayall, rode their bicycles fifty-three miles from London to Brighton, the same route Birch's Trivector had covered a half century before. Mayall, who went as fast as eight miles an hour, arrived in about twelve hours. Moreover, he felt in such "good condition" upon his arrival that he dined out and caught the second half of a musical performance.

In March, an agency in Liverpool began to import Pickering and Davis bicycles from New York, and a local velocipede club sprang into existence. Two members promptly strapped "carpetbags" to their machines, and rode over two hundred miles to London in just four days, astonishing townsmen along the way and underscoring the bicycle's practical possibilities. In April, the fever hit in earnest. An inaugural road race between Chester and Rock Ferry, over a macadamized road, drew "thousands of people, rich and poor," eager to see the novelty. They mobbed the exhausted winner, a member of the Liverpool club named Henry Eaton, who had to be carried into a nearby garden and resuscitated with the help of "a little brandy."

This colorful contest was indeed a promising start to the velocipede movement in Great Britain. Not only did the public show great enthusiasm, Eaton's performance was quite remarkable. Despite "a strong headwind and a crowded road," he managed to cover thirteen miles in one hour and twenty-seven minutes. That pace, approaching nine miles an hour, far surpassed any comparable American result and was impressive even by French standards. Meanwhile, London, too, began to show symptoms of a growing mania. Hundreds flocked to the Crystal Palace to watch velocipede races, while riding schools sprouted up across the capital.

At first, English riders looked to French experts for guidance. The veterans Edmond Moret and Henry Michaux, Pierre's sixteen-year-old son, dominated the early competitions in London. Another French teenager, Henri Pascaud, dazzled spectators at Spencer's gymnasium with his extraordinary riding skills. According to one report, he rode around "whilst his arms were folded, his hands unemployed, and his face and

eyes apparently turned in every direction but that in which ordinary riders would find themselves compelled to look."

But Pascaud's skill was never more evident than when he played a game of tag with John Mayall. The Englishman, likewise mounted on a velocipede, was to chase after the young Frenchman and tap his shoulder. "It is not a question of mere racing," explained a reporter. "The Frenchman's tactics are much more wily." Indeed, Pascaud repeatedly led the ill-fated Mayall into a corner within inches of the wall, only to make "a dexterous twist in direction only he could execute." Whenever the beleaguered Mayall seemed at last poised to tap his adversary, Pascaud "eluded his grasp in a way which seemed little short of miraculous." Finally, the Englishman made a "bold push," and "succeeded in giving the necessary pat, amid loud cheers."

Before long, thanks to a growing number of schools and makers, England raised its own army of expert velocipedists. They eagerly took to the road, routinely venturing out on day trips to towns where the bicycle was as yet unknown. Two riders from Manchester, for example, rode thirty-six miles to Bakewell, where they spent the night. Their unexpected arrival caused the locals "considerable excitement," and the following morning, after word had spread that the riders were headed to Derby, "vast numbers came to inspect the velocipedes, and the start." Another group rode twenty miles from Wolverhampton to Stafford, "without violent exertion in a very reasonable time." They concluded that anyone, with a little bit of practice, could make an enjoyable "fifteen or twenty mile trip into the country."

The Lancet, a prestigious medical journal, was inclined to agree that the new bicycle could provide healthy exercise. It found that the position of the rider and the motion of the legs "do not seem likely to produce that violent action of the abdominal muscles which was necessitated by the old velocipede." Although the journal cautioned that bicycling was not suited to anyone over forty with "diminished elasticity," it predicted that younger riders would find the sport "a very agreeable method of taking useful and healthful exercise." Others were intrigued by a possible practical payoff. A correspondent with the *Church Review* suggested that the bicycle might spare the "country and mission clergy the cost of a horse." Perhaps anticipating a controversy on that point, he reminded his readers, "What now seems a folly for the vain and frivolous may become a useful means of rapid communication."

As spring advanced, however, many began to have second thoughts about the wisdom of bicycle riding, whether for recreation or utility. The press reported numerous ac-

facing page: The Compagnie Parisienne enjoyed a brisk business in Britain starting in the spring of 1869. Its most expensive models, like this one, featured frames with elaborate etchings.

cidents on the road, often involving broken bones. Many citizens complained that velocipedes were nuisances, especially on sidewalks. But whereas those very objections
had already hastened the demise of the American trade, in England the fervor merely intensified. Merchants continued to import bicycles in great numbers, mainly from France,
while numerous artisans took up the trade. By June, at least a dozen manufacturers in
London alone, including another sewing-machine maker, Newton and Wilson, produced four hundred machines a week, and still they could not keep pace with orders.

Most British bicycle makers imitated the standard French-style diagonal pattern.
But several novel propositions addressed a dangerous drawback to the front-drive design that often led to injuries and spills—namely, the difficulty of turning the front wheel
while keeping the legs and feet free and clear. The sharper the angle, the more one leg
had to bend while the other extended, and the more likely it was that the tire would
brush against a thigh. Moreover, the fact that one also had to pedal during turns meant
that a foot could easily slip into the spokes. In an attempt to solve the problem, a London firm introduced the Phantom, a curious frame with a central hinge. To make a turn,
the rider angled the front wheel only half the usual distance, and the frame pivoted to
follow it. The less severe angle, and the additional bars between the rider and the wheel,
reduced the risk of an accident. The Improved Bicycle by Peyton and Peyton of Birmingham did away with the front drive altogether, placing up-and-down foot levers between the wheels. The maker claimed that this arrangement made for a safer and more
efficient bicycle.

The velocipede fever persisted in Britain throughout the summer, as the press continued to report encouraging feats. In July, R. J. Klamroth, of Newton and Wilson, rode
nearly five hundred miles from London to Edinburgh in just six days. In all, he spent
sixty-five hours in the saddle, averaging seven and half miles an hour. For breakfast, he
consumed "half a dozen eggs beat up together, and a pound of steak," capped by "a pint
of sherry." He stopped for lunch about noon, then napped for two hours. He continued
on for another four or five hours, before enjoying an evening meal and a good night's
sleep. For refreshment along the way, he continued to sip sherry, which he carried along
in a small flask.

Klamroth's extraordinary performance largely confirmed the value of the bicycle as
a touring machine. To be sure, he had suffered some discomfort along the way. After the
first day, three of his fingers felt cramped. The pain eventually disappeared, and he sailed
along in fine form through the third and fourth days, despite heavy rain and slick roads.
But suddenly he developed severe pain in his knees, which intensified through the re-
mainder of his journey. He nonetheless arrived at his destination in satisfactory condition and in high spirits. Clearly, mechanics had something substantial to build on.

PEYTON & PEYTON,

BORDESLEY WORKS, BIRMINGHAM,

MANUFACTURERS OF THE

IMPROVED BICYCLE.

BOURNE'S

PATENT.

Advantages as compared with the ordinary Bicycle—

1. Increased power. The rider can mount hills, and go along rough roads.
2. On account of the hind wheel being the driving wheel, there is no strain on the arms and shoulders.
3. There is an easy seat instead of a saddle, by means of which a serious objection, raised by the medical profession, is removed.
4. The action of the legs is easier and much more natural, resembling walking, and the legs are not dirtied, nor are they liable to be injured by the action of the guide wheel.
5. It is easier to mount *at any time*. It can be started *up-hill*, *even* without assistance. It has not to be started before mounting, but in the act of mounting, as the rider takes his seat.
6. It is easier to learn, because it is easier to mount, to start, and to work.

Most early English bicycles imitated the French diagonal design. Peyton and Peyton of Birmingham, however, marketed a distinct configuration targeted at women, advertised in *The Ironmonger* of 30 October 1869. The rear-wheel treadle drive supposedly made it easier to mount, steer, and propel the bicycle.

The public, meanwhile, continued to lend its support to the velocipede movement, renting out machines at such venues as the Crystal Palace and regularly attending performances. More than three thousand spectators watched a "cirque" at Agricultural Hall in Islington featuring women cyclists and trick riders in June 1869. One skeptic who observed the proceedings reluctantly granted of the bicycle, "There must be something in it." Large and enthusiastic crowds also attended exhibitions held in conjunction with popular events, such as flower shows and cricket matches. In September, the Crystal Palace hosted the International Velocipede and Loco-machine Exhibition,

The Bicycle in Scotland

For more than a century, Scotland has been closely identified with the invention of the bicycle. Nevertheless, the Scottish introduction to the pedal-powered two-wheeler appears to have paralleled the English experience. In the early part of 1868, a few Scotsmen obtained the novel Michaux bicycle from Paris. That fall, a Mr. Alsing of Glasgow, a dealer in foreign novelties, imported a few specimens for resale. In February 1869, according to a local newspaper, he began to exhibit them at a hall "in the presence of a wondering company." He soon opened a riding rink, attracting scores of patrons. By April, several more schools were flourishing in Glasgow, including one catering to ladies. Four local carriage makers scurried to make French-style bicycles, and the Glasgow Velocipede Club came into being. In Edinburgh, a velocipede school opened as well, although elsewhere in Scotland the bicycle was as yet "almost unknown."

Before long, however, velocipedists took to the road in great numbers. There were the usual arrests for sidewalk riding, and of course accidents. But some performances were impressive—even heroic. One rider left Bonhill at six in the morning, and arrived in Oban by ten that evening—a distance of eighty-three miles. He pedaled for fully twelve hours, averaging seven miles an hour, and rested for four. A bold young man from Largs raced a steamer for eight miles. As soon as the hands threw off the lines, he took off up the coast road, while the passengers gathered on deck to cheer him on. Remarkably, he was the first to arrive at Wemyas Bay. "This was excellent work," admitted the local newspaper, "considering that the Lancelot is one of the fastest steamers on the Clyde, and had only one stoppage on the way."

And of course Scotland had races too. Some were in small towns like Jedburgh, where hundreds of people assembled to watch a two-mile race with four bicycles and were "astonished at the ready way in which the different competitors mounted and set off." In August, some ten thousand spectators jammed the grounds of Edinburgh's Royal Patent Gymnasium, to watch the local champion A. Bathgate take on R. J. Klamroth, who had just ridden four hundred miles from London. Klamroth had an "elegant style," conceded one observer, but not "stamina enough to compete with a first-class performer." Bathgate prevailed, covering five miles in just over thirty minutes. At the championship of Scotland a month later in Dundee, however, it was Bathgate who faltered as Mr. Stiles, a local, beat another opponent by six inches. Still, for all the excitement, the velocipede craze soon fizzled in Scotland, as the deficiencies of the machine became discouragingly clear.

Fancy riding was a staple of velocipede entertainment, as shown in a scene from the Bicycle Circus at Agricultural Hall, Islington, published in the *Penny Illustrated Paper* of 18 September 1869. Many of the most dexterous performers were teenagers.

featuring more than two hundred machines from Britain, France, Belgium, Germany, and the United States.

Most important for the future of the machine, sporting grounds across the country hosted velocipede races. These popular outdoor establishments offered a variety of entertainment ranging from marathon pedestrian contests to rabbit racing. Patrons, generally considered a respectable cross-section of society, paid an admission and often wagered on the outcomes. Velocipede racing was thus a natural fit, at least while the craze raged. Some enthusiastic promoters even anticipated that the popular sport would outlive the mania.

Indeed, the prospect of regular professional contests offering attractive cash prizes boded well for the long-term development of the machine. Although many French clubs and host cities also offered significant financial rewards, these events were largely tied to infrequent and inflexible popular festivals. Clubs generally had to plan the program well in advance, at considerable trouble and expense. The proprietors of sporting grounds, in contrast, could readily organize and host races while adjusting their formats to suit popular tastes. They could also offer competitors attractive prizes based on the expected gate. Racers could even issue their own challenges to their rivals through the sporting reviews, setting terms involving distance, handicaps, and technical restrictions. This open-ended system encouraged talented riders to become professionals, since they could expect to earn a good and steady income, as well as a certain celebrity cachet.

At the same time, of course, racers acquired a greater incentive to improve their machines so they could gain a competitive edge. Working closely with the makers of their machines, the racers explored a wide range of technical innovations to reduce the weight of the bicycle and make it run smoother. Many of the early champions, notably John Henry Palmer and Alfred Forder, were themselves directly connected to carriage firms that made bicycles as a sideline. Moreover, regular track racing gave makers an opportunity not only to test new products but also to promote their wares. Some proprietors encouraged product exhibitions and even awarded prizes for the most innovative articles.

By the fall of 1869, even as the popular craze began to fade, velocipede races had become regular events at numerous sporting grounds, especially in the London area and in the Midland counties, where many of the provincial makers were based. After some experimentation, proprietors settled on the mile as the ideal distance, which usually required five or six laps around the track. The races were typically run in heats matching two riders, and the contests often extended to several days. Wheels were generally restricted to thirty-six inches in diameter; riders of larger machines, if admitted, usually had to cover an extra twenty or thirty yards. At first, organizers also required racers with machines under fifty pounds to carry extra weight to make up the difference. At the Championship of the Midland Counties in Wolverhampton that October, the winner of one heat was disqualified when rivals discovered that his bicycle weighed only forty-nine pounds.

The contests were often exciting seesaw affairs, reflecting the capriciousness of the machines as much as the skill of the riders. At times, the leader suddenly "came to grief" as a result of missing the pedals or failing to turn properly, only to regain the advantage when a rival made a similar miscue. At one race in Birmingham that August, the champion John Henry Palmer of Birmingham was heading into the stretch with a six-yard lead when he suddenly came to a standstill and nearly capsized, "his trousers coming in contact with the spindle." Alfred Forder, the Wolverhampton star, surged ahead "and got just a shade in front." Palmer, however, recovered his form and made a "fine spurt" to nip his rival at the finish line.

In spite of England's enduring interest in the velocipede, the fever was evidently on the wane as 1869 drew to a close. For all its improvements, the bicycle still fell far short of initial expectations, and it didn't appear destined to come into general use in the near future. Still, few could deny its progress. The Oxford correspondent of the sporting review *Land and Water* noted that the bicycle had gained much popularity in the six months since a local entrepreneur began to rent out a few machines. And now, in contrast to the early days of the craze, riders could promptly obtain a bicycle of their own. Moreover, a local club was in formation, velocipede races had become "a new feature in most of the late athletic meetings," and the sport would probably be "adopted in the programme of the University."

Yet the key question of practicality remained unresolved. Pondered the Oxford writer, "Are these bicycles likely to last long as a really useful means of conveyance?" Indeed, the signs were conflicting. "On one side we hear of [bicycles] being adopted into systematic use, and of manufacturers still favored by orders for thousands," he noted. "And on the other, that owners are soon weary of them, and that the pawnbrokers' shops are full of them." Yet while some skeptics fully expected the British public to sour on the bicycle, as the Americans had, the journalist predicted otherwise. "We shall by no means, as some people think, soon see the last of them." On the contrary, he asserted, the bicycle still offered great practical possibilities. "Judging from our own experience, and from accounts that we have seen, and also from the skill which is still being expended on improvements, the modern velocipede is deservedly, for many reasons, taking its place as a very serviceable vehicle."

But just how far and how fast—and in what direction—would the improved bicycle go in Britain? These remained open questions, ones that would be largely resolved on the sporting grounds of the Midland counties during the course of the second season. But at least one point was already clear by the spring of 1870. The pioneer period of highly touted but clumsy solid-iron affairs teetering on wooden wheels was over. A new era, one that featured precision-built all-metal machines, had already begun. To what extent these would ever serve the general population was as yet unclear. But, for the time being at least, they satisfied the recreational interests of an exclusive clientele—namely, young athletic males of certain means.

Part Three The "High Wheel" Era

SEVEN

The High Mount Prevails

The velocipede craze had largely subsided in Great Britain by the end of 1869, as it had in France and elsewhere. Nevertheless, a small but energetic community of makers, racers, and riders remained intact and resolved to keep improving the vehicle, now generally called a bicycle as opposed to the more pretentious term "velocipede." The number of makers had dwindled to a handful by this time, but they were highly skilled specialists who applied the latest technology, notably wire wheels and rubber tires. And they still catered to a palpable demand. Racers, who retained public interest, were as eager as ever to ride the fastest machines. Meanwhile, a growing number of "gentlemen riders" continued to practice and promote the recreational sport. For its part, the public, though no longer enraptured by the two-wheeler, was largely tolerant of the community's ongoing efforts to improve the bicycle as an instrument of pleasure, if not utility. By the mid-1870s, the majestic high-wheeler emerged as the standard bicycle, attracting a devoted following in Britain among athletic young men of means.

The 1870 racing season promised to be an interesting experiment, as the best racers gradually upgraded to new-style bicycles using spider wheels with rubber tires. The early results that spring were encouraging, as mile times quickly fell from around five minutes to four and half. Meanwhile, the public continued to favor the competitions with their presence, proving that the sport had in fact outlasted the mania. That April, an unprecedented four thousand spectators invaded Birmingham's Aston Cross grounds to watch seven of the "best performers of the Kingdom." The highlight was a mile heat between John Henry Palmer, the dominant force of 1869, and John Prince of Derby, a rising star. *The Sportsman* gave this rousing account of the duel:

After a very indifferent start, in which Palmer got best away, he showed half a dozen yards in front on first passing the referee. Prince, however, [got] on even terms down the straight, and they paddled away in close company for a lap. On entering the second, the Derbyite put on such a brilliant spurt as was never yet witnessed in the inclosure, and shot right away, quickly making a gap of twenty yards. In the succeeding lap he still further increased it to thirty, retaining his position to the end of the fourth lap. Here, Palmer, whose friends were looking anything but comfortable at the turn things had taken, began to decrease the gap, and by almost superhuman exertions, aided by the most determined pluck, succeeded in coming up with his opponent. On turning into the straight run home, [they put on] the most brilliant finish ever witnessed at the grounds, resulting in favour of the Derbyite by half a yard. Time: 4:25.5.

Several more gifted athletes soon joined the professional circuit, elevating the competition and stimulating technical development. One was John Keen of Surbiton, near London, who proved a graceful and powerful performer, as well as a brilliant mechanic. Another was J. T. Johnson, an Englishman who had spent the previous year racing in continental Europe, where he earned the lofty title Champion of Belgium. But the one who would exert the most immediate and profound impact was the veteran James Moore. Following the outbreak of war in France, he returned to his native land where he pursued a veterinary degree while competing as a bicycle racer.

In August 1870, Moore turned up at the Midland Counties Championship in Wolverhampton with a sensational oversized racing bicycle he had been using in Paris for the previous three months, with notable success. Made by the master craftsman Eugène Meyer, it featured all the latest continental improvements, including a hollow backbone and lightweight rubber pedals replacing the iron or wooden variety. As Moore soon demonstrated, these pedals received the balls of the rider's feet rather than the insoles, improving leverage and bringing the ankles into play. But the most striking feature of Moore's mount was its enormous front wheel. With a diameter of forty-three inches, it was easily four or five inches higher than those of his peers, who were generally taller than he. Equally novel was the forward position of Moore's seat, which was placed almost directly over the front wheel.

Moore easily won his first two heats, exerting powerful downward thrusts on his pedals. He appeared set to win the match in record time, when he fell while trying to turn his oversized wheel. Moore nonetheless demonstrated the compelling advantages of the new configuration and prompted others to follow suit. "What a revolution and transformation after my visit!" he recalled years later, adding that his peers "weren't satisfied" with wheels measuring forty-three inches but soon migrated to even larger sizes.

James Moore standing beside a transitional machine, at left, with a front wheel measuring around forty-eight inches in diameter, about twice the size of the rear, the profile he introduced to the English racing circuit in the summer of 1870. The photograph at right, taken around 1874, shows a high wheeler with a front wheel about fifty-four inches in diameter and a trailing wheel of only eighteen inches.

Indeed, E. Shelton, a teenager from Wolverhampton, who had been riding a standard thirty-six-inch machine, suddenly appeared on what one journalist labeled a "gigantic" wheel measuring almost fifty inches in diameter. Shelton promptly eclipsed the four-minute mile, and others who switched to high mounts registered equally impressive gains. Promoters quickly recognized the superior speed and appeal of the new configuration, and they dropped diameter and weight restrictions.

The surprising success of the high mount at the close of 1870 energized the modest English bicycle trade. Two men connected with the pioneer Coventry Machinists, James Starley and William Hillman, started their own bicycle firm, Starley and Company. In 1871, they introduced the all-metal Ariel with an improved steering column, a hollow steel backbone, and a new wire-wheel system with a tangential "lever bar" designed to tighten all the spokes at once. The profile was unmistakably that of an early high-wheeler, with the driving wheel about forty-eight inches high. Priced as low as eight pounds, it soon became one of the most popular new-style bicycles. Other notable

The Ariel of the early 1870s adopted a profile similar to Moore's 1870 bicycle. Produced in Coventry by James Starley and William Hillman, it featured a tubular steel backbone and a solid fork, a shorter and stiffer seat spring, slotted cranks, a rear brake operated by turning the handlebar grips, wire wheels, and solid rubber tires. Tightening the lever bar on each wheel adjusted all the spokes at once to keep the wheel in true. This design, priced competitively, helped establish the high wheeler as the preferred bicycle profile, even among recreational riders. This early advertisement was published in *Mechanics' Magazine* of 5 October 1872.

provincial makers were Thomas Humber of Nottingham and Daniel Rudge of Wolver-hampton. The best-known makers in and around London were the racer John Keen, F. Noble and Company, makers of the Tension model, and the Phantom Wheel Company, a holdover from 1869. Only the Phantom, with its distinctive pivoting frame, still offered front wheels under forty inches.

The bigger bicycle also enlivened the recreational market. In spite of the high mount's sensitivity to crosswinds, and its alarming tendency to tip over in reaction to a bump on the riding surface, it proved fairly roadworthy. Its large front wheel, padded with a rubber tire, effectively absorbed shocks while suspending the rider above the dust of the unpaved roads. In the spring of 1870, Palmer rode his racing mount from Newcastle-on-Tyne to his home in Birmingham, covering 220 miles in just three days. That summer, another tourist easily pedaled over one hundred miles between London and Bath in two days, at a clip approaching seven miles an hour. Another pair rode from Aberdeen, Scotland, to London averaging seventy miles a day over ten days.

Over the next few years, the English racing bicycle continued to evolve into an ever lighter, smoother, taller, and swifter vehicle—indeed, the fastest thing on the road. As heavy iron tubes gave way to thinner and lighter steel tubes, bicycles shed nearly half their original bulk, and weighed as little as forty pounds by 1873. Meanwhile, snugger bearings in the steering column and wheel axles gave the machines a more solid feel, and reduced the need for constant oiling. The preferred profile inched toward the full-blown high wheeler, featuring a front wheel up to sixty inches, maximized for speed, and a trailing wheel no greater than sixteen inches (a configuration later dubbed the "Penny Farthing" for the disparity in diameters). Mile times fell to just over three minutes, and racers kept up a fast pace over ever longer distances. "The riders of today may be justly proud of their instruments," declared *The Field,* noting that they provide "a wonderful combination of speed and silence."

One obvious problem with the towering profile, however, was the growing challenge riders faced when mounting and dismounting. Bicycle makers responded by affixing a small step to the left side of the frame, just over the rear wheel. The bicyclist could thus run alongside the vehicle, place the left foot on the step, and then pull the rest of the body up for the final leap onto the saddle. After landing, the rider had to catch the spinning pedals with the feet and quickly gain control of the moving machine. Alternatively, the bicyclist could stand behind the machine grasping the handlebars, raise the left foot up to the step, and kick the ground with the right foot to start the machine in motion before vaulting onto the saddle. The step also facilitated dismounts.

The fleet and flashy high mount proved an instant hit among both varieties of racers—professionals, who typically worked in the bicycle trade, and amateurs, who were of higher social standing and often independently wealthy. Atop such machines,

A scene from a 105-mile contest between Charles Spencer, left, and T. S. Carlyon of London, from the *Penny Illustrated Paper* of 6 January 1872, underscoring how road racing was becoming more popular in the early 1870s as bicycles improved. As Carlyon stumbled over a wayward pig in this race, Spencer surged ahead.

racers registered ever more impressive results. At the close of 1872, Keen rode ten miles in less than thirty-six minutes, averaging just three and a half minutes a mile. Three weeks later, James Moore rode fifty miles in under four hours. For its part, the English public welcomed the high mount as a racing machine. Hundreds of men and women, sometimes thousands, regularly assembled to watch bicycle races in London and the Midland counties. The programs often included curious contests that pitted crack racers against trotting horses and ponies, with the bicyclists generally prevailing over longer distances.

Given such success, racers were naturally ambivalent toward low-mount alternatives, which were more complicated, heavier, and costlier. During a one-mile race in Birmingham in 1872, J. T. Johnson rode a novel "speed-geared" Ariel. It had a front wheel measuring only thirty-four inches in diameter, but because the internal gears in the front

Champion bicyclists raced not only human challengers but also horses. A large crowd watched this ten-mile race at London's Alexandria Palace, shown in the *Pictorial World* of 24 July 1875, in which David Stanton briefly overtook a Mr. MacDonald and his mare, Lady Flora, after the sixth mile, but eventually lost the match by about forty seconds.

hub made the wheel spin faster than the pedals, it performed like a much larger machine. Johnson edged out James Moore by a foot in a respectable time of 3:39 1/2. But Moore's backers cried foul and denounced Johnson's machine as a "velocipede" as opposed to a proper bicycle. As construction of the high mount improved, geared machines quickly disappeared from competitions, ensuring the domination of the high wheeler. By mid-1873, Moore, for one, rode a fifty-two-inch machine, about ten inches higher than the oversized Parisian bicycle he had brought to Wolverhampton just three years earlier. Taller competitors such as Keen rode even bigger wheels. Indeed, most racers adopted the largest wheel their legs could manage and during sprints were reaching speeds approaching twenty miles an hour.

Meanwhile, the recreational market continued to grow. In 1870, London cyclists formed both the Pickwick Bicycle Club and the Amateur Bicycle Club. Within three years, over a dozen more sprang up across the kingdom. For the most part, members accepted the virtues of the speedy and comfortable Ariel-type high mount. To be sure, they favored rugged machines about five to ten pounds heavier than the racing variety, with somewhat lower driving wheels to facilitate hill climbing and a larger trailing wheel for greater stability. Even so, most amateurs adopted front wheels spanning at least forty-four inches, sufficiently large to require a mounting step and a running start—a daunting challenge that deterred many older and less athletic riders and effectively excluded women.

Club members quickly registered impressive results on their new-style bicycles. As early as 1871, three members of the Amateur Bicycle Club accomplished a hundred miles in a single day, a feat known as a century, notwithstanding a dally at Stonehenge where they triumphantly circled the "Druids." The following year, the Middlesex club retraced the inaugural run to Brighton of four years earlier, demonstrating the superiority of the new high wheeler. One member arrived in only five and a quarter hours, half the time it had taken John Mayall when a forty-four-inch wheel was "far greater than was ever thought of." In the summer of 1873, four members of the same club, riding wheels ranging from forty-five to fifty-two inches, rode from London to John O'Groats, the northernmost outpost in Scotland, covering seven hundred miles in two weeks.

Yet, while the high mount gained currency among racers and serious club members, independent riders—the "mainstay of bicycling" according to *The Field*—hesitated to mount the big wheel. Already numbering in the hundreds by 1872, these recreational

Four members of the Middlesex Bicycle Club en route from London to John O'Groats in the far north of Scotland, a jaunt of seven hundred miles that underscored the roadworthiness of the new bicycle and was illustrated here in *The Graphic* of 19 July 1873

riders were generally young urban males who held middle-class white-collar jobs. Although they perhaps lacked the time, means, or social status to join a club, they were nonetheless eager to practice the sport during their leisure hours. "I have often, after a close day of business mounted [a bicycle] with a dreadful headache," testified one clerk. "[Yet] however tired or low spirited, I have not been five minutes over the wheels before I was as jolly as a sand boy. In fact, I know of no other exercise so invigorating." Certainly, the trade could ill afford to wholly ignore the safety concerns of these weekend riders, since thousands of athletic males who earned a good living and longed for open-air excursions might conceivably invest in a bicycle.

One longtime rider outlined his objections in 1873, insisting that he represented a class "far more numerous [than] those who can do London to Brighton and back in ten hours." Four years earlier, he had purchased a velocipede that went "six miles an hour at the expense of aching arms and profuse perspiration." A few years later, when better machines appeared, he graduated to a still-manageable forty-two-inch bicycle that went "about eight miles an hour on a fair road without fatigue." He "quite enjoyed the machine when alone," but soon found himself lagging behind a friend who rode the latest Ariel. He thus bought a forty-eight-inch mount himself, which indeed accelerated his pace. But he struggled to control the oversized bicycle, protesting that "it appears to me much less safe" compared with his beloved but outdated forty-two-inch mount. In his estimation, "any invention which would enable the rider to stop altogether and still sit [on] the machine would do more to popularise bicycling than anything which has yet been done."

For some time, many recreational riders balked at driving wheels so high that they could not stop their machines simply by braking and touching their toes to the ground. One amateur insisted that many "timid" riders were "averse to mounting a thing like a giraffe, from which an impromptu descent offers unpleasant possibilities." He urged mechanics to create a treadle-drive bicycle with all the latest improvements. Another amateur was prepared to give up the bicycle altogether and settle for a tricycle. "Having personally learned and enjoyed to ride a modern 50-inch machine, I am convinced that such a vehicle is not the place for, say, a middle-aged *Paterfamilias,* or, in fact, for any man who has to work his brains during the principal portion of the day." He listed several factors that he felt would limit the appeal of the high mount to "any but a young man." These included "the tumbles one must go through to learn to ride," the "difficulty of mounting and dismounting," the "impossibility of resting when mounted," and the risk of "croppers," meaning head injuries suffered by airborne riders thrown from their machines.

In the aftermath of the craze, the Phantom Wheel Company mounted the most spirited campaign to promote an alternative—and presumably safer—design. It sought to re-

An unidentified New Zealander proudly poses with his Phantom bicycle, about 1871. The Phantom Wheel Company of London exported its distinctive bicycle with the unique pivoting frame around the world and won a small but devoted following. Nevertheless, the high wheel continued to gain favor and the company folded in the fall of 1872.

tain the seductively low profile of the original bicycle, while eliminating its technical flaws. In addition to lightweight metal wheels with rubber tires, and a flexible frame to facilitate steering while pedaling, the Phantom featured two small platforms between the wheels at the base of the frame on either side. These enabled the rider to mount and dismount without making acrobatic leaps. They also provided supports to stand on while the machine coasted, so that riders did not have to keep their feet on the spinning pedals or stretch their legs over the handlebars, potentially losing control of the machine.

Although the Phantom had failed to prolong the craze of 1869, the company still hoped it would attract a large number of would-be riders averse to the high mount. Its booklet *The Wheel and the Way*, published in 1871, insisted that improved low-mount bicycles were still destined to serve as a "universal, easy, and dependable method of locomotion." Yet for all the company's noble intentions, many riders found the Phantom difficult, if not impossible, to propel in a straight line. Some judged its wheels and tires inferior to those on other mounts. But perhaps the machine's greatest drawback was its excessively low gear that required vigorous pedaling, a problem inherent in a direct-drive machine with a small driving wheel.

With the demise of the Phantom in late 1872, the high mount had met its first serious challenge from an alternative bicycle design. A few makers continued to experiment with low mounts equipped with internal "speed gears," but the results were disappointing. Wrote one dissatisfied rider, "I have a geared bicycle, with wheel turning once and 3/4 to each turn of the cranks. But its unnecessary weight (66 lbs.) will compel me to get a new one." Meanwhile, recreational riders were increasingly willing to suppress their inhibitions and adopt larger wheels. After all, who could deny their functionality? By the end of 1873, one rider claimed to have ridden his Tension bicycle thirty thousand miles—equivalent to a trip around the globe. By the following year, entire groups regularly toured on high wheelers. "During the holiday months," noted the London correspondent for the *New York Times*, one often encountered "a dozen bicyclists, all in the uniform of their club, charging along the road on a pleasure trip."

The high mount was evidently destined to serve both racers and tourists, at least for the foreseeable future. Consequently, the trade lost any immediate incentive to develop a more manageable two-wheeler. To its many advocates, the high wheel represented nothing less than the ideal bicycle. One enthusiast who had toured all over England on his high mount declared in 1873, "I have passed some of the happiest hours of my life on my bicycle." Increasingly, sportsmen viewed its inherent dangers as an acceptable risk, given its unmatched economy, simplicity, and efficiency. Those who were unwilling or unable to put themselves in such a precarious position were encouraged to acquire a less intimidating machine with three or four wheels, such as the Edinburgh Tricycle. Introduced during the velocipede craze, this eighty-pound vehicle featured a single rear wheel driven by treadles and a seat with back support.

Ironically, while the new trade built directly on the original bicycle technology, it betrayed the popular utilitarian spirit that had characterized and driven the early movement. The Parisian pioneers, though mostly men of privilege, had insisted all along that their charming little vehicles were destined to serve as the poor man's horse, and that

The Edinburgh Tricycle, made by Mathew Brown and depicted here in *The Field* of 28 November 1874, was a wooden vehicle weighing about sixty pounds. In the first half of the 1870s, it offered a safer alternative to the daunting high wheeler, but it could not match the speed of a bicycle. The driver steers with a lever in the left hand and, as in the McCall bicycle of 1869, swings the feet, placed in stirrups, back and forth to move the treadles that power the rear wheel. The leather strap in front was for pulling the vehicle uphill.

one day, in the words of James Moore, they would be "as common in homes as umbrellas." The profusion of races at French civic festivals gave testament to the movement's democratic intentions. In the United States, the scores of indoor rinks that proliferated in the winter of 1868–69 ostensibly served to introduce the people to their future mount, even if they could not yet afford to buy one. In Britain, too, according to *The Field*, the masses of 1869 dreamed of traveling by bicycle in a "fabulously short time" with "an expenditure of wonderfully little energy." As a result, an army of crude bicycles "rattled over our streets, rolled along our by-ways, [and] pervaded our country lanes."

By adopting the high wheeler as its basic product, the specialty trade no longer proposed a practical "people's nag" but rather a highly refined and costly recreational tool, one that appealed almost exclusively to young middle- and upper-class males. To be sure, the original bicycles, when new, had cost a comparable sum. But the manufacture of those earlier machines drew heavily on traditional carriage-making skills and materials, so they could be built almost anywhere in great numbers, ensuring a lively secondhand market. And even more important, the low profile invited popular use, regardless of the rider's age or sex. Wary velocipedists knew they could always reconnect with mother earth simply by applying the brake and extending a leg downward. Obviously, that was not the case with the daunting high mount, which demanded considerable verve and athletic skill.

But why did the trade in the aftermath of the craze renounce any popular or practical aspirations, even as it vastly improved its technology? For one thing, makers realized that they simply could not deliver a cheap, durable, and practical bicycle using existing technology. In Britain, thousands of the original bicycles had passed into the hands of lower-class youths, only to fall apart. By 1872, few "boneshakers," as the press began to call them, were still to be seen. If the bicycle trade was to survive, noted *The Field*, it had to use the best technology, irrespective of cost, to overcome the bicycle's bone-jarring ride. "The difference between the best and the worst [bicycle] is really amazing," confirmed one amateur in 1871. "In one the weight is something like a mischievous urchin hanging on behind the machine, doing his best to hold you; in another it is like the same imp pushing you forward."

Yet given their high material cost and intimidating form, the new-style bicycles were evidently destined to serve an exclusive clientele who demanded of them, as *The Field* put it, "amusement, and nothing more." Moreover, their improved durability meant they were not as likely to pass into the hands of the less privileged, at least not for some time—and that suited many high-wheel riders just fine. Unlike the pioneers of the movement, they did not fancy themselves as trailblazers forging a new era of road travel. Rather, they relished their elitism, and were proud to be seen with their peers on machines of an unabashedly recreational nature. The secretary of the Amateur Bicycle Club, for one, declared that the mission of his organization was to promote the sport of bicycling among the "upper, middle, and higher classes of society."

Besides, the bicycle had already lost any semblance of a utilitarian machine, even if it occasionally facilitated practical services like delivery of the mail or small parcels. Nor could anyone imagine an alternative two-wheeler that might seriously challenge the conventional design. A compelling low-mount bicycle would evidently require a practical geared hub or some other indirect driving mechanism—inevitably adding cost and complexity. Few firms were willing to invest in such experiments without any guarantee that the product could ultimately displace cheaper tricycles that already offered a higher degree of safety. Moreover, the trade already had its hands full catering to the growing demand for high wheelers. It thus had little choice but to shift its pitch from popular utilitarian service to restrictive recreational use.

During the mid-1870s, as demand for the high mount continued to grow, makers simply concentrated on improving its construction. They pondered every detail, from spokes to the saddle spring, while adding such useful amenities as toe clips to secure the feet to the pedals and rigid "spoon" brakes that acted on the larger front wheel for better braking power. In 1874, the Coventry Machinists even improved the wheel itself, introducing a durable construction with individually tensioned spokes interlaced for greater strength. The weight of racing machines dropped to as little as thirty pounds, while touring models generally weighed a few pounds more. The refined high wheeler, in all its varieties, was now truly the king of the road.

The sport continued to thrive as well. On the professional race track, as many as ten thousand spectators watched such veterans as James Moore and John Keen take on newcomers such as David Stanton and Frederick Cooper. In the summer of 1874, Moore described the vibrant English racing scene in *Le Vélocipède*, a new French sporting review. "The bicycle in England is improving every day, thanks to races organized by a few energetic promoters. Indeed, these brilliant affairs promise to rival horse competitions. Our handicapped races are especially interesting. Imagine five or six racers arriving to the finish line separated by only a meter. What a treat for spectators! We are never without races or some sort of match, and thus never without some progress. Suffice it to say that a mile has been run in 2 minutes, 54 seconds. Isn't that wonderful?"

Moore was right: by the close of 1874, racers had set even more impressive marks. John Keen rode fifty miles in just three hours and nine minutes, nearly fifty minutes faster than Moore's original record. The amateur sport blossomed as well. In early 1875, the champion H. P. Whiting nipped a rising star, Ion Keith-Falconer, in a twenty-five-mile showdown at Lille Bridge, a popular track outside London. Whiting mounted a fifty-four-inch machine, while the six-foot-three Cambridge student rode a gigantic

By the mid-1870s, high-wheel racing was a popular spectator sport in England, as this illustration from the *Pictorial World* of 13 June 1874 suggests. A large crowd gathered to watch this six-mile race outside London, organized by the Surrey Bicycle Club, in which one competitor suffered an "awful cropper" that was dramatized here. "In truth bicycling is rather a dangerous amusement," conceded the journal, "but then it affords such capital exercise."

sixty-inch wheel. A few months later, Whiting successfully defended his amateur title atop a fifty-eight-inch bicycle built by Keen, his trainer. It was fully three inches taller than the one he had ridden the previous year in the same contest, and his time over the four-mile course improved by nearly a minute and a half, a pace approaching eighteen miles an hour.

Bicycling also became firmly established as bona fide university sport. By 1874, both Cambridge and Oxford boasted clubs, which gave a strong impulse to road racing. In the spring of that year, three racers from each school competed in the first annual Inter-University Championship. The course covered eighty miles between the two campuses. Eight hours after the sounding of the starting gun, the "Cantab" E. St. John Mildmay arrived at his college ahead of the field. Half an hour later, his teammate J. W. Plunkett followed. "Both winners" reported *The Field*, "were loudly cheered by the numerous spectators present, Mr. Mildmay being carried to his rooms by some enthusiastic [representatives of the] artisan class."

The following spring, the two clubs staged the second championship, this time covering fifty-two miles between Saint Albans and Oxford. Thirty miles into the contest, the two leaders from Cambridge, F. L. Dodds and Keith-Falconer, paused for a brief rest. Crofton, the leading Oxonian, shot past them, drawing wild cheers from the numerous bicyclists from Oxford who had pedaled over to watch the match. But "the Cantabs were soon in hot pursuit," reported *Bell's Life*. "Dodds caught [Crofton] about two miles further on," and Keith-Falconer soon eclipsed Crofton as well, making it a two-man race. Four miles from the finish line, the gentle giant overtook his teammate to finish in four hours and nine minutes, seemingly "fresh as paint."

Club members and professionals also took part in road races. Although the laws forbade "furious driving" on public roads, these colorful contests proved crowd-pleasing and helped underscore the roadworthiness of the high bicycle. In 1874, shortly after the first Inter-University run, seven members of the Middlesex Bicycle Club rode 106 miles between Bath and London to determine who would serve as the club's captain and sub-captain. The winner arrived at the clubhouse in about ten hours. A month later, David Stanton retraced the route on a fifty-seven-inch racing machine, taking only eight and a half hours. Villagers along the way turned out "en masse," and in London "a mob congregated to witness his arrival." But perhaps the most impressive road feat was registered two years later, when two members of the King's Lynn Bicycle Club accomplished an unprecedented "double century."

The continued success of bicycling in Great Britain in the mid-1870s, on the track and on the road, solidified the consensus in the cycling community that the high mount was indeed the ideal bicycle form, well worth the risk of an occasional fall. About such mishaps the newly founded *Bicycling News* informed readers in 1876: "Croppers . . . are

David Stanton arriving at the Three Tuns Hotel in London after leaving Bath the same morning and covering 106 miles in eight and a half hours. The feat, as seen here in the *Pictorial World* of 13 March 1874, seemed so incredible that some questioned the accuracy of Stanton's claims.

not an event of such importance as the over-cautious might suppose. Men who have learned how to 'ride for a fall' get through an astonishing number of tumbles without sustaining any appreciable injury." The thriving trade thus remained devoted to the high mount and continued to discount the possibility of safer bicycle designs.

As the high mount gradually emerged in the first half of the 1870s in Britain, the rest of the world did not remain entirely oblivious to the bicycle's improvement. Indeed, British cyclists gradually introduced the new bicycle to the kingdom's far-flung colonies. One who brought a forty-six-inch Ariel to India in the fall of 1872 related that he found it "highly amusing to watch the open-mouthed stare of the natives, and their frightened looks of astonishment." Europeans, in contrast, quickly became familiar with the high bicycle, since British bicyclists regularly toured the continent on their holidays. Clubs in particular promoted cycle tourism abroad. The Ariel Club, for one, organized rides throughout Europe. James Moore led one two-week excursion through northern France in the summer of 1874, escorting "very rich and honorable persons."

Nor had the Europeans themselves entirely neglected the bicycle in the aftermath of the velocipede craze. To be sure, continental cyclists were comparatively few in the early 1870s, and many, if not most, rode woefully outdated machines. Yet their lingering interest in the two-wheeler proves that, quite independent of the state of affairs in Britain, the bicycle had already established a foothold in the popular imagination and would never fall into a state of total neglect. That the bicycle had some sort of future was already settled. But whether it would ever amount to anything more than a pricey recreational tool for young athletic men remained to be seen.

Among the bicycle strongholds in Europe was the Belgian town of Mons, which held races in 1870 and 1871. In the Netherlands, at least three clubs were still active in 1872, including one in Rotterdam. The club of Deventer, named Immer Weiter (German for Ever Farther) had more than thirty members and sponsored an annual day of

A Hungarian caricature from *Ustökös* (The Comet) of 9 April 1869, invoking the velocipede as a symbol of progress being restrained by conservative forces in the church and the army. The caption read, "This velocipede would go along just fine, were it not for those who are trying to hold it back." (Translation by László Ottovay)

races. Geneva's club dwindled after 1869, but several years later it still included a few hearty amateurs. Several Italian clubs remained active as well. In the summer of 1872, forty-eight costumed members from Florence performed drills on stage atop their machines, raising money for flood victims. A few months later, in nearby Sesto Fiorentino, the club held outdoor races with rivals from Pistoia as the highlight of the town festival. In the spring of 1873, eight members of the Milanese club entertained a receptive crowd with processions and trick riding. By the following year, its members rode bicycles with the latest improvements, regularly visiting nearby towns.

France, however, remained the bicycling center of continental Europe. Remarkably, its velocipede industry rebounded shortly after the devastating war with Prussia. In 1871, *Le Vélocipède Illustré* reappeared for a spell, and Meyer, the leading maker before the war, resumed production of his spider wheels. A few more specialists emerged as well, notably LaGrange fils of Autun. Several clubs were revived and new ones founded, revitalizing the sport. Although most of the old champions were gone, some

Eight members of the Milan velocipede club as they entertained spectators during a fund-raiser for a memorial, portrayed in *Lo Spirito Folletto* (Elfin Spirit) on 22 May 1873. By British standards, their bicycles were already outdated.

killed in the war, new stars arose, such as Camille Thuillet. At first, French racing machines kept the same profile they had acquired just before the war, with driving wheels ranging from forty-two to forty-five inches. But in a curious switch, Moore and Keen brought oversized English bicycles to the championship races held in Lyon in May of 1873, prompting French makers to adopt English-style high wheelers.

These new and faster machines further energized the French cycling community. Racers undertook even longer road races, such as the grueling 170-mile route from Lyon to Chalon-sur-Saône and back. Bicycle tourism revived as well. In the fall of 1875, Albert Laumaillé of the Vélo-Club d'Angers rode a fifty-four-inch Coventry Machinist bicycle from Paris to Vienna, covering about seven hundred miles in twelve days. As the press duly noted, he beat the performance of a noted horseman by a few days, underscoring the superiority of the mechanical mount over long distances. Though it was no longer the leader of the international industry, France produced other notable cycling personalities in this period, including the racer Charles Terront, the industrialist Adolphe Clément, and Julles Truffault, a bicycle maker who introduced hollow forks and rims around 1876.

In 1874, French *bicycles immenses* were even put to some practical use. That spring, *Le Moniteur Universel,* the official newspaper of the empire, began to use bicyclists to convey reports from the National Assembly in Paris to the paper's press in Versailles. The couriers covered the ten miles in under an hour. Soon, bank agents at the stock market employed a cadre of some thirty couriers to deliver messages to the central telegraph office six miles away. The messages were then wired to the home office, which responded using the same relay system. The couriers earned up to twenty francs a day, potentially covering the cost of their vehicles after only a few weeks of service. The re-emergence of bicycles on city streets, however, triggered a new round of restrictions. Bicyclists were soon required to sound a bell to alert unsuspecting pedestrians of their approach, since their rubber tires and solid construction had all but eliminated the telltale rattle of the first bicycles.

Even Americans, though embittered by the velocipede fiasco, did not entirely ignore the bicycle in the aftermath of the craze. A handful of athletes occasionally competed on their old Pickerings and Demarests, notably William E. Harding, the sports editor of the *New York Daily News,* and the velocipede veteran William C. McClellan. On one such occasion in August 1871, McClellan beat Harding in a fifteen-mile race at the Empire Rink in New York, finishing in just under an hour. Still, the public showed little interest in a bicycle revival. In late 1872, in the midst of a "dearth of horses," the *New York Times* remarked that a few boneshakers had reappeared in shop windows "with seductively low prices affixed to them." Yet no one bought them.

The paper, however, attributed the lack of demand for bicycles not to any "inherent

Paris was perhaps the first city to host a fleet of bicycle couriers, some of whom are shown riding bicycles of the transitional form preceding high wheelers in a hectic scene outside the stock market from *Le Journal Illustré*, 5 July 1874

defect" in the machines themselves, as many supposed, but to "crude and unreasoning public opinion." It noted that a velocipedist simply could not appear in public without facing the unbridled "tyranny" of street boys who promptly gave chase. "Had the riders of bicycles gone forth in companies of fifty or a hundred, they would have mutually encouraged one another," the paper observed, "[and] we should now find the bicycle a general favorite [and] a possible means of . . . conveyance."

Still, as thousands in Britain took to the wheel in the mid-1870s, Americans could hardly continue to ignore the new bicycle. Already they were receiving a steady trickle of reports describing the progress of the high bicycle in England and the remarkable feats of both racers and tourists. Starting about 1873, a few individuals even imported European specimens to North America. And in the summer of 1874, a certain "Professor Brown" rode a high wheeler on a Boston stage. Some observers even began to clamor for a bicycle revival. "The velocipede is no longer a toy," declared the *Boston Sunday Herald* in the fall of 1875, "but a motor of men. Its merits must continue to advance it in public favor, and we do not doubt that it will soon secure its proper position on this side of the Atlantic."

As if to prove the point, a young Irishman had already accomplished a century on American soil atop the new-style bicycle. One October dawn in 1875, James M. Mason left his home in Hillsboro, Ohio, bound for London, Ohio. He aimed to complete the 106-mile round trip—the same distance David Stanton had covered the year before between Bath and London—within twelve hours, for a hundred-dollar wager. But the outbound journey did not go smoothly. He made a wrong turn and wound up on a "freshly graveled road" that "greatly impeded his progress," costing him half an hour. He also fell, spraining a leg. Nevertheless, he managed to get to London in less than six hours and, after a thirty-minute rest, he reversed directions. Eleven hours and forty minutes from the time of his departure and seven miles from his starting point, the exhausted cyclist dismounted and conceded his wager. Still, he had far surpassed any previous cycling performance in America.

That December, perhaps sensing an impending revival, the veteran racers A. P. Messinger and William Harding vied for the Long Distance Championship at the American Institute Building in New York. Whoever covered the most distance in twenty-six hours would earn the title. Messinger mounted a forty-six-inch Pickering, while Harding rode a forty-one-inch Demarest, receiving a 17-mile credit to compensate for his smaller wheels. Harding managed to rack up 104 miles before quitting after just over twenty-four hours, three times as long as it had taken Stanton to complete a comparable distance at Lille Bridge a year earlier. Harding was so lame by the end of the contest that he rested every two miles. Messinger, meanwhile, fared little better. He incurred several accidents en route to compiling 136 miles. Yet despite the modest results, the curious affair signaled that a new era was indeed at hand.

The following spring, the English champion David Stanton arrived in New York toting two high wheelers. He promptly called on the *New York Sportsman* to mobilize American challengers. The American Institute Building soon hosted the first highwheel competition ever held in the United States, pitting Stanton against William McClellan in a fifty-mile showdown. Stanton mounted a fifty-four-inch machine, while the American upstart rode a French-made bicycle two inches taller. Barely three minutes into the contest, at the mile mark, McClellan surged ahead. The crowd taunted, "Cheer up, Englishman!" and "Give the stranger a show!" but its euphoric outburst soon gave way to a humiliating hush. By the sixth mile, Stanton had lapped his overmatched opponent. McClellan's rear wheel began to squeak, forcing him to change machines. On the twentieth mile, he lost a pedal and his wheel collapsed, slamming him to the floor. Stanton cruised along alone, "exhibiting powers of endurance . . . never before seen in this country," and finishing in a record three hours and four minutes.

That spring, Stanton traveled to various venues to take on more challengers, including trotting horses. While in Philadelphia, he visited the Centennial Exhibition of

Extreme Indoor Racing

When some journalists openly doubted the reports that David Stanton had ridden a century between Bath and London in only eight and a half hours, the champion gamely set out to repeat the feat at the Lille Bridge track outside London. His bold bid in the fall of 1874 established endurance riding as a spectator sport. But it also underscored how grueling these affairs were, and how they demanded extensive training and proper racing techniques.

After sailing through the first forty miles in less than three hours, Stanton pulled aside for a snack. To the shock of the reporter on hand from *Land and Water*, the racer indulged in sponge cake soaked with brandy, which was decidedly "not the stuff we should give a man on such a task." Twenty minutes into his rest, Stanton nevertheless resumed his pedaling in fine form. But an hour later, he tired again, prompting another pause. At mile sixty-three, he stopped for yet another snack. This time, the fare consisting of mutton and tea, which was more to the reporter's approval since "a race of this sort requires solid food as well as stimulants." Stanton was nonetheless noticeably stiff when he took off, and his pace slowed considerably. Six hours into his duel with Father Time, at mile seventy-four, he stopped for a fourth time. Yet as he passed the ninety-mile mark, he still had almost an hour left to cover the remaining ten miles, giving his backers some hope. Stanton methodically churned the pedals as he sipped tea and brandy, but he was by then so exhausted that his attendant had to run alongside him and prop him up. Finally, Stanton's friends conceded the futility of the exercise and collected the groggy racer, carrying him back to the pavilion "where he at once fell asleep."

The reporter admonished Stanton to train better before the next contest, to eat good and plentiful food during the match, and to drink "champagne rather than brandy." Whether Stanton followed that advice is not known, but he did redeem himself a few weeks later in a match against John Keen at the same venue. Stanton completed 106 miles in a few minutes shy of eight hours, a cycling feat many regarded as the greatest on record. Yet only a year later, again at Lille Bridge, Stanton covered an astonishing 650 miles riding twelve hours a day for seven days in succession. To keep Sunday as a day of rest, the format was soon changed to eighteen hours a day for six straight days—the celebrated six-day race.

1876 and bicycled about the fairgrounds. But he had not crossed the Atlantic merely to race or to show off the bicycle—he had business on his mind. He placed an advertisement in the *New York Sportsman* offering Keen's Eclipse high-wheel bicycles for $150 to $175, whopping figures that included shipping but not the 35 percent import tariff. He assured his customers that he would personally attend to "the manufacture and shipping" upon his return to England. When he left in June, the *Sportsman* reported that he had amassed "quite a large number of orders." The journal wished him well and predicted success. "Through Mr. Stanton's endeavors, bicycling will be introduced in this country, as the pleasures of the pastime have been greatly enhanced by the new style of bicycle, a decided improvement on the old 'bone rattler.'"

In fact, English high wheelers were already on permanent display at the ongoing Centennial Exhibition—and drawing plenty of looks. They belonged to Timms and Lawford, a Baltimore agency with strong British connections that was "preparing to introduce [bicycles] largely in America." Its small fleet was composed of two varieties of Coventry-made machines, the Paragon and the Ariel. One of the four Ariels was a monstrous eighty-four-inch affair, built not for serious use but to underscore the strength of Starley's new Tangent wheel. Over the next few months, the firm sold about a dozen machines to courageous customers scattered about the country.

Meanwhile, the small American racing community made its own belated transition to high mounts. Two thousand spectators flocked to the American Institute Building that December to watch the Championship of America, pitting McClellan, on a fifty-three-inch machine, against William Du Noeille, who rode a wheel two inches taller. McClellan prevailed, winning two four-mile heats. His best time barely eclipsed fifteen minutes, nearly two more than the record at that time, held by Keith-Falconer. Still, the exciting affair proved that the high wheeler had finally arrived on the other side of the Atlantic, where it would soon vie for popular approval.

EIGHT *The Pinnacle of the High Wheeler*

In the late 1870s, the bicycle trade flourished in Britain and the ever-evolving high wheeler invaded Europe, North America, and—according to one trade journal—"every quarter of the world," notably "South America, Mexico, the West Indies, India, Japan, Australia and South Africa." The growing recreational interest in the sport even prompted a few makers to reconsider tricycles and lower, safer bicycles for the less athletic. Yet as trade insiders saw it, the bulky and pricey three-wheeler would merely complement—perhaps even promote—high-wheel sales. Few could have imagined that the standard bicycle would ever succumb to a more costly and complicated variety, however much safer it might be. The high wheeler, in fact, remained the approved bicycle pattern and the dominant cycle on the road—a paragon of simplicity, grace, and efficiency that called for little more than steady, incremental improvements.

facing page: By 1876, when Charles Spencer published *The Modern Bicycle,* the high mount had prevailed as the preferred bicycle configuration for both racing and touring. The train and the telegraph wires in the background offer other symbols of modernity.

182

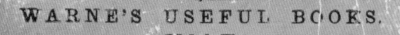

WARNE'S USEFUL BOOKS.

THE
MODERN BICYCLE

BY

CHARLES SPENCER

WITH PRACTICAL ILLUSTRATIONS

LONDON: FREDERICK WARNE &

The Importance of Bearings

When Albert Pope launched the Columbia make in 1878, he was eager to let Americans know that the high bicycle was nothing like the old discredited velocipede. Indeed, English mechanics were largely responsible for a most remarkable transformation, having implemented three key innovations. These were spider wheels with rubber tires, lightweight steel tubes, and improved bearings in the five principal moving parts of the front-drive bicycle: the steering column, the two pedals, and the two axles. These all-important fittings were what gave the high wheeler its seductively smooth yet solid feel.

The most important rotating part on the high wheeler was the front axle connected to the pedals. It acted much like the crank spindle inside the bottom bracket of a modern-day bicycle. Mechanics had to figure out how to secure the front axle safely within the fork ends, so that the wheel would not pop out, while still allowing the axle to spin freely. If the axle could not easily rotate, pedaling would be cumbersome. If the axle was too loose, pedaling would be inefficient and the bicycle would wobble. The ideal was a snug, easy rolling fit that required little attention.

The first boneshakers were usually fitted with what were called plain bearings. The front axle passed through round holes in the fork ends, the perimeters of which were surfaced with brass or steel for long wear. Nevertheless, the constant

The high mount was, after all, a mechanical wonder. Bicycle makers were constantly finding new ways to reduce the weight of the vehicle, introducing ever lighter steel backbones and even applying tubing to the front forks. At the same time, the bicycle gradually acquired a smoother and more solid feel, especially when trouble-free ball bearings appeared in Britain around 1878. These various improvements helped racers set new marks over distances ranging from a quarter mile to a hundred miles and more. In 1879, the professional F. Cooper set a new mile record, finishing in two minutes forty-eight seconds. John Keen covered a remarkable eighteen miles in a single hour. The amateur F. T. East set a new fifty-mile record, finishing in two hours and forty-seven minutes.

metal-on-metal contact between the axle ends and the bearings, even with a liberal application of oil, eventually wore away the surfaces and created excessive play. By the early 1870s, English bicycle makers had discovered that a conical surface fitted within a mated socket made for a snugger fit that could be adjusted for wear. Even though the increased area of contact created more friction, the idea proved advantageous, and these cone bearings were used in the first Columbia bicycles.

In the late 1870s, English inventors found an even better solution: ball bearings. By inserting a ring of loose, solid spheres within two circular cups fitted around both ends of the axle, the axle itself rotated smoothly without shifting, and the system was easily adjusted for proper play. Ball bearings were not entirely new; they had been used sporadically in other appliances for some years. The French mechanic Jules-Pierre Suriray had even applied them to bicycles as early as 1869, notably the one James Moore used to win the Paris-to-Rouen road race. But the first metallic spheres had to be made by hand, and they quickly ground down under pressure. The technology had to await the development of steel spheres with extremely hard surfaces that could be produced in series with great precision. American makers adopted ball bearings for the front wheel in the early 1880s, and they eventually found their way into every rotating part of the bicycle.

The public continued to frequent matches, especially six-day races engaging one or more contestants for up to eighteen hours a day, Sunday excepted. Although some denounced these grueling affairs as dangerous and inhumane, promoters insisted that they brought out the best in competitors without imposing serious health risks. Spectators took advantage of the long hours to drop in as their schedules permitted, increasing the take at the gate. In 1878, Stanton was the first to crack the one-thousand-mile mark, doubling the comparable pedestrian record for distance covered in six days. The following year, George Waller, a stonemason from Newcastle, rode more than fourteen hundred miles, beating out the new French champion, Charles Terront.

But perhaps the most vaunted high-wheel racer was the towering Ion Keith-Falconer. This "muscular Christian" of Scottish aristocratic stock eschewed such common vices as alcohol, swearing, and gambling. While still a student at Cambridge University, he even boycotted the 1876 Inter-University match to protest against alleged betting on the event. Although he was more devoted to his Arabic studies than to his athletic training, he nonetheless developed into a nearly invincible force on the amateur circuit following his graduation. On one memorable occasion in 1879, he even bested the professional John Keen, the "King of Bicyclists" himself, in a two-mile showdown in Cambridge. The prolonged participation of such a noble figure in the sport of cycling underscored its growing respectability and appeal.

Recreational riding thrived along with the competitive sport, as evidenced by the profusion of clubs. The first annual London-area meet in nearby Hampton, held in 1874, drew only forty cyclists from eight clubs. Two years later, the same event attracted about three hundred riders representing sixteen clubs. By 1878, this "monster meet" united nearly two thousand cyclists from more than seventy clubs; its procession stretched longer than a mile. Provincial clubs, over the same period, ballooned from barely ten to

The majesty of the annual Hampton Court gathering, as captured in the *Illustrated Sporting and Dramatic News* of 9 June 1877. These "monster meets," as they were called, held outside London attracted cyclists from across the kingdom and helped win public sympathy for the cycling cause.

well over one hundred. Though some counted only a few members, others, based in large cities or universities, had as many as several hundred.

Clubs were nonetheless exclusive entities. In general, a prospective member needed not only the means to cover the cost of a bicycle, uniform, and dues, he also had to be nominated by a current member and garner no more than one in five "black balls." Most clubs admitted only "gentlemen" who had never competed for monetary prizes. Tradesmen, deemed a bad influence, were generally barred as well. Some clubs even required a particularly elevated social standing, while others enforced a pet theme. The Tension Club, for example, admitted only riders of the Grout's make of bicycles. The Wanderers recruited men who preferred touring over racing. The Pickwick Club apparently sought only literati, since it required members to identify themselves with a character from *The Pickwick Papers* by Charles Dickens. One prankster, who happened to be among the club's fittest, competed under the deceptive alias "Fat Boy."

The largest and most accessible organization was the Bicycle Touring Club, formed in 1878 to help members plan trips, find cheap lodging, and cope with breakdowns. "In all the principal towns of this kingdom," explained one source, "they have their 'consuls,'" who provide members with "whatever help or direction they may need." The club also maintained a network of mechanics "officially appointed for setting right anything that may be amiss with the machines." In addition to a uniform, the club issued a badge, handbook, guide, and newsletter. Members enjoyed about a third off the price at designated hotels—as well as an open door. Noted one, "No matter how covered [wheelmen] may be with the mud and dust of the roads, their tickets of membership at once distinguish them from common tramps." The club also paved roads, posted "Dangerous" signs atop treacherous hills, and compelled city officials "to change the position of the sewer-grating."

Yet for all their diversity, clubs shared a common goal championed by their umbrella organization, the Bicycle Union: to make bicycling an ever more respectable gentleman's sport. Most also relied on weekend "club runs" from spring to fall to rally their membership. Typically, members met at the clubhouse on a Saturday afternoon, since riding on Sundays was discouraged. They started out in double file behind their captain, but contracted to a single line on busier roads when the bugler sounded the call. They usually headed to a country inn, where they enjoyed such traditional fare as eggs and tea, before "indulging in some harmony in the back parlour." In the evening, they lit their oil lamps and headed home under the moonlight, full of song. Most clubs also held regular social gatherings in the off-season to keep their group cohesive. Some sponsored grand "meets" that were open to other clubs and featured parades, picnics, and festivities.

Meanwhile, the number of unaffiliated riders was also on the rise. *The Times* estimated in 1877 that England had already produced some 30,000 new-style bicycles. A year later, it upped that figure to 50,000, and by 1879 the total had reportedly reached six figures. Evidently, the bicycling community far exceeded the collective number of racers and club members. Yet they all belonged to a certain elitist brotherhood, and all were expected to look the part. One commentator denounced the "vain or foolish men, who apparently forget that they are upon the queen's highway [and flaunt] freaks of ornamentation." In particular, he implored riders to "show their good sense" by avoiding circus-like costumes displaying "extraordinary combinations of colours."

Naturally, the British cycle industry grew to meet this demand. By 1880, more than a hundred bicycle firms operated across the kingdom, a dozen in Coventry alone. Coventry Machinists was the source of several spin-offs, including Starley's Ariel concern and the Singer Cycle Company headed by George Singer. The pioneer company itself had reemerged as the industry leader, producing 130 bicycles a week, compared with just 5 in 1873. The trade also acquired several journals and an annual exhibition, known as the Stanley Show after the club that sponsored it, which was itself named after the famous explorer then roaming Africa. For the most part, the public tolerated the invasion of bicycles on the roads, although some citizens still groused that the vehicles scared horses and endangered pedestrians.

The French bicycle industry also enjoyed a strong revival in the late 1870s. Racing was flourishing and touring was emerging as a popular activity for young males of privilege. A leading advocate of the recreational sport was Albert Laumaillé of Château-Gontier, in central France. As early as the spring of 1868, he had written Michaux to request a special velocipede "of the greatest solidity, capable of supporting the longest voyages without breaking down," assuring Michaux that he would gladly pay an extra hundred francs or more if necessary. That summer, Laumaillé toured Brittany on his Michaux bicycle. Seven years later, in 1875, he made his memorable twelve-day ride from Paris to Vienna on a fifty-four-inch English bicycle. But he accomplished his most sensational tour in 1878, when he and a fifteen-year-old companion spent a month touring central Europe on high wheelers. Their longest day ride was a hundred-mile stretch between Turin and Milan, accomplished in a mere nine hours.

Yet it was unclear at first whether American men of means would emulate their European counterparts and mount the high wheeler. Even after the introduction of a few new-style bicycles in 1876, the prospects for a bicycle revival on the order of the overseas movement seemed tenuous at best. Bitter memories of the dismal boneshaker still lingered in the public consciousness, giving bicycling a bad name. Moreover, across the country, anti-cycling measures were still on the books, just waiting to be enforced. Those Americans who were determined to mount the imposing beasts would have to brave both public opinion and the country's notoriously bad roads.

The masthead of Frank Weston's trade journal stressed that the new English bicycle was far fleeter than the old discredited velocipede. When the first issue appeared in December 1877 there were only a handful of bicyclists in the whole United States.

At least one thing was increasingly clear as 1877 unfolded: if there was to be an American bicycle renaissance, Boston would lead the way. That summer, as Timms and Lawford faded, two Bostonians vied for control of the emerging trade. One was Frank Weston, an architect and a native of England who was familiar with the new bicycle from periodic visits to his homeland. With the help of a few investors, he organized a bicycle import agency called Cunningham, Heath, and Company. In November, the firm received its first batch of bicycles from England and promptly opened a riding school. One journalist who dropped by pronounced the high bicycles "fearfully and wonderfully made . . . totally unlike the travelling tread-mills we had before under the same general name." He confidently predicted that "the bicycle, in its vastly improved construction, will soon come into extensive use in our country." In the meantime, Weston launched the modest *American Bicycling Journal* to promote the sport and his company's wares.

The other contender for the captaincy of the new industry was an ambitious thirty-three-year-old businessman named Albert A. Pope. This Civil War veteran, who had already amassed a small fortune making shoe parts and air pistols, had seen the high mounts in Philadelphia at the Centennial Exhibition. At the time, he wondered how anyone but an acrobat could manage such a thing. His interest was nonetheless rekindled the following spring when he chanced once again upon the giant creature. This time, he was riding his horse around his home in Newton, on the outskirts of Boston, when he saw a man fly by on wheels. The rider was a young lawyer named Alfred Chandler, who had recently acquired a Singer Challenger from Timms and Lawford. In vain, Pope struggled to catch up to the strange machine. Ever the entrepreneur, Pope immediately grasped the commercial possibilities of so fleet a mount that evidently consumed no oats.

Coincidentally, Pope was then hosting an English friend, John Harrington, who was well connected to the overseas bicycle trade. Harrington encouraged Pope's interest, assuring him that American gentlemen were indeed ready to take to the wheel. To prove his point, he commissioned a local mechanic to build a specimen. After Pope learned to ride that machine in the summer of 1877, he became so convinced about the prospects for an American trade that he arranged for Harrington to send him eight English-made bicycles upon his return to his homeland. On his end, Pope planned to test the market to see if the new vehicle could truly generate a significant demand.

A few months later, in January 1878, Pope received his first shipment of English bicycles. He was so pleased with them that he decided not only to import bicycles on a large scale but also to manufacture them. That spring, Pope took a train to Hartford with his Coventry-made Duplex Excelsior in tow. Upon his arrival, to the amazement of the locals, he bicycled from the station to the Weed Sewing Machine Company. There, Pope met with George Fairfield, Weed's president, and proposed that the Weed company reproduce his personal bicycle. That was no easy task, considering that it entailed the replication of some four hundred parts. Yet with business down, Fairfield could hardly afford to ignore Pope's proposition, however bizarre. Finally, the firm agreed to produce fifty copies of Pope's machine. At the same time, Pope boldly shifted the focus of his company to bicycles, drawing capital from his personal wealth. Pope also went to England that summer to study bicycle production firsthand.

Yet no sooner was a new bicycle business brewing when the royalty claims that had so crippled the earlier trade suddenly resurfaced. To tax a new generation of aspiring bicycle retailers, a shrewd Boston maker of children's carriages, the firm of Henry Richardson and George McKee, acquired the dormant Lallement patent, which defined the basic bicycle and still had six years of life left to it. To solidify its blanket claim, Richardson and McKee purchased several other velocipede patents. But after issuing licenses to Pope and Cunningham, Heath, the firm was itself sued by the Montpelier Manufacturing Company of Vermont. This competitor was making royalty demands of its own based on the MacKenzie rocking-horse patent, Smith's dubious weapon from 1869. Rather than settle their conflict in court, the firms agreed to pool their patents and collectively apply a fee of ten to fifteen dollars per bicycle.

A poster from about 1879, one of the first produced by the Pope Manufacturing Company, featuring numerous accessories pictured in the lower section. The rider is thought to be Albert A. Pope himself, who described the bicycle as "an ever-saddled horse which eats nothing."

Acting as administrators, Richardson and McKee promptly restructured Cunningham, Heath's import license, then turned its attention to the ambitious Pope. Reluctantly, Pope came to terms with the Boston firm, but he feared that its oppressive licensing fees would doom the fledgling trade. He then engaged in some tricky maneuvering of his own to purchase the patent pool for himself. He negotiated independently with the patent owners in Boston and Montpelier, and before either one knew of the deal the other had struck, Pope emerged with a controlling interest, which he leveraged to squeeze the others out. By the spring of 1879, Pope was already firmly in charge of the nascent trade. From then on, Pope continued to invest heavily in patents, snapping up all he could find that even remotely bore on bicycle production.

Patents in hand, Pope proceeded to rein in his growing number of competitors. He filed numerous lawsuits against those he claimed were infringing on his newly acquired rights. He then offered his rivals licenses to make or import bicycles at a relatively modest fee of ten dollars per unit. But Pope also restricted domestic production to inferior wooden machines and children's models, keeping the high-end adult market to himself. He knew that imported bicycles, after the hefty tariff and his own royalty fees, would sell for well over a hundred dollars, and he was confident that he could produce a comparable machine for less. And these were bound to sell—provided a healthy demand for bicycles materialized.

Indeed, banking on a bicycle revival was Pope's great gamble. During the boom of the 1890s, Pope delighted in painting himself as a visionary who championed the bicycle when the rest of the world disparaged it. Yet he was hardly a "lone pioneer." Before Pope made his first move, several others were already making plans to import English bicycles. And at least one mechanic, R. H. Hodgson of Newton, Massachusetts, had even initiated a small production. After all, there was hardly any mystery about the merits of the machine. English mechanics had been producing high mounts for years, and many thousands were already circulating in Europe. To anticipate a similar success in America required perhaps a leap of faith, but not a great deal of imagination.

Still, Pope's stance was not all bravado. Certainly no one threw himself more forcibly into such a tenuous and risky situation. For despite the proven appeal of the high-wheel bicycle abroad, the American public was not likely to welcome it with any great enthusiasm. On the contrary, so bitter was its lingering memory of the discredited boneshaker, and so limited was the market for this new machine, the public's reaction was bound to be subdued at best, if not outright hostile. To win over young American males and a measure of public acceptance, Pope faced an enormous and expensive marketing challenge. "Many of my old and valuable friends called me a fool," he later recalled, "and said I would be sure to lose my money and time."

As the first season got under way in 1878, some signs were encouraging. Although

Pope's own machines were not as yet available, a growing number of Bostonians purchased English imports. That February, Weston and thirteen others formed the Boston Bicycle Club, the first in the United States. The *Boston Transcript* described an early outing: "A gay scene was the meet of the bicyclists yesterday in the square opposite Trinity Church and the Art Museum. Attended by a semi-detached escort of ladies and gentlemen on horseback, with a few children on ponies, the jaunty riders of the lofty wheels sped easily around the noble square and off into the country with the speed of horseflesh, but apparently with no more exertion than that of walking. It was a novel

Members of the newly formed Boston Bicycle Club, including one on a solitary tricycle, as they gathered for an outing in the spring of 1878 in front of Trinity Church, the site now known as Copley Square. The first members rode English-built machines since Pope's Columbia bicycles were not yet on the market.

sight in old Boston, but one destined, no doubt, to become very common, as the advantage and charm of this form of out-door exercise get better known."

One adept promoter of the new vehicle was William R. Pitman, a twenty-seven-year old velocipede veteran and carpet salesman from Bangor, Maine. In early 1878, he became an instructor at Weston's rink. A few months later, he entered Pope's employ and began to demonstrate the new bicycle on the road. One March morning, he turned up in Haverhill, Massachusetts, atop a fifty-two-inch English-made bicycle. He proposed to cover the forty miles to Boston in about four and a half hours. A local newspaper reported that "boys flocked around [the bicycle] by the hundreds." Some two thousand citizens lined the route to catch a glimpse of Pitman as he sped by atop his majestic novelty. In April, Pitman staged a similar performance in Fitchburg, once again drawing a huge crowd.

Yet despite the public's evident interest in the large bicycle, the wisdom of Pope's venture was not yet evident. Though an undeniable improvement over the old bone-shaker, the new bicycle had yet to prove itself on inferior American roads. Pitman's initial ride, in fact, took an hour longer than he had predicted, and his average speed of eight miles an hour was hardly up to British standards. He fared little better over the second course, and an exhausted companion dropped out after barely twenty miles. A smattering of races that year in the Boston area also produced disappointing results, not to mention a few nasty spills. Meanwhile, Pope's bicycles were still not available, as the Weed company struggled to fill his order.

Even more troubling, many resented the bicycle's increasing presence on the road.

THE BICYCLE
FIEND IN THE PARK

In June, the Boston papers reported a disturbing incident involving a young man who was "carefully riding his bicycle on Boston Common" and a policeman who "violently forced over the machine." The reckless officer then tried to arrest the "prostrated rider," only to be deterred by the "indignation of the bystanders." Reception in New York was no more encouraging. "With park guards unfriendly, and policeman openly hostile," the

Caricature from the *New York Illustrated Times*, 4 October 1879. Many Americans feared the new bicycle would prove a menace to pedestrians and carriages, but Pope helped win over the public by launching a vigorous publicity campaign while staunchly defending the legal rights of cyclists.

New York Sun remarked in October, "the bicycle finds hard work in getting itself naturalized here." In a contest organized by the Manhattan Athletic Club that fall, the winning time for the mile was a woeful four minutes.

Still, the inaugural season of 1878 was largely a success. In all, some three hundred brave Americans acquired the art of cycling that year. Nearly a third bought a bicycle from Pope, whose sales were evenly divided between imports and his own make, the Columbia. And despite the latter's solid forks, inferior bearings, and relative bulk, it was widely considered equal to English roadsters—no small feat given the lengthy head start of the overseas trade. Some prospective buyers did balk at its ninety-dollar price tag, but it was a good twenty dollars cheaper than English imports. Meanwhile, there were other encouraging signs that the high bicycle would indeed take hold in the New World. Boston had already acquired a second club, and others were formed in Bangor, San Francisco, and Montreal.

The second season of 1879 proved that the American bicycle revival would flourish rather than fizzle. The city of Boston sponsored a successful race on the Fourth of July.

The Yale bicycle club in 1891, at the end of the high wheeler's reign. Harvard was the first American college to host a bicycle club, in 1879, but other Ivy League schools quickly followed suit.

Amateur vs. Professional

Until a generation ago, professional athletes were excluded from the Olympic games. The rationale was deeply rooted in nineteenth-century veneration of the amateur athlete who competed not for monetary reward but simply to cultivate physical and moral character. In England at that time, the promoters of sporting events were eager to attract upper-class competitors and spectators, and to distance themselves from popular sports like pedestrianism. Competitors in these lowbrow affairs often walked hundreds of miles with little food or rest, and were at times even compelled to perform bizarre acts such as carrying overweight individuals on their backs. Although the upper classes were often complicit, betting on the outcomes and putting up their own help to compete, these contests were strongly associated with working-class sorts who drank, cursed, and gambled.

The Amateur Athletic Club (AAC) was formed in England in 1866 to encourage and regulate physical contests among upscale males involving walking, running, swimming, and rowing. After 1869, the club also presided over bicycle competitions, until the Bicycle Union took over that task in 1878. At AAC-sponsored contests, no monetary prizes were awarded, and spectators were not allowed to bet on the outcomes. The club also banned or expelled any member known to

The bicycle began to infiltrate Ivy League schools, starting with Harvard College. The *Boston Globe* reported, "The 'steeds of steel' may be found reposing in the entries of all the principal dormitories." The club uniform consisted of a "gray jacket, cap, and knickerbockers." But in deference to lax student dressing habits, the club allowed "the color of stockings to be optional with each rider." Meanwhile, Pope established agencies in major cities nationwide, and his sales soared. Several dozen clubs sprouted up, notably in Washington, Philadelphia, Brooklyn, and Chicago.

The budding bicycle trade also made some progress in winning over the wary public. Pope published and distributed at cost five thousand copies of *The American Bicy-*

have competed for money at any point in his career, and even anyone who had knowingly competed against a professional without having secured beforehand the club's explicit permission. The club also refused to admit those it classified as "mechanics, artisans or labourers," ostensibly because their daily toil gave them an unfair physical advantage.

As the sport of cycling grew in the 1870s, however, the best professional and amateur racers were increasingly prone to intermingle. Many used false names and even disguises to participate in the other camp's events. Further complicating matters, the definition of an amateur varied from country to country. Some French amateurs, who were allowed in their own country to accept the patronage of bicycle makers, were branded professionals as soon as they crossed the channel, sparking heated controversy. In the mid-1880s, one conciliatory American association tried to find a middle ground, proposing an intermediate category it called "promateurs." Those who qualified would be permitted to accept equipment from industry sources without being labeled professionals. Still, the thorny issue of what constituted a true amateur simmered, with class-related tensions just below the surface.

cler, a primer on how to ride the high wheel by Charles E. Pratt, an enthusiast who soon became Pope's patent attorney. That fall, the energetic Pratt also organized a leisurely two-day bicycle tour around Boston and its south shore covering one hundred miles. Known as the Wheel Around the Hub, the tour engaged about forty riders, including Pratt and Pope, and highlighted the joys of traveling as a group atop new-style bicycles. Pratt's own illustrated account of the adventure in *Scribner's Monthly* helped promote the sport. Pratt also became editor of *Bicycling World,* a newsy weekly that replaced Weston's sporadic trade journal.

The close of the 1879 season also marked the debut of six-day racing in America.

Participants in the Wheel Around the Hub pose by the road in Readville, Massachusetts (now Hyde Park), in September 1879. At the far left is Charles E. Pratt, organizer of this inaugural tour and future patent lawyer for the Pope Manufacturing Company. To his side is Albert A. Pope.

Harry Etherington, a well-connected English cyclist and promoter, brought over three of Britain's brightest stars, Stanton, Keen, and William Cann, as well as the French champion Terront. Although the inexperienced Americans could as yet muster only token opposition, the European champions entertained enthusiastic crowds in Boston and Chicago. The inaugural affair took place under an enormous tent, with the support of Pope, who supplied the bicycles. The *Boston Globe,* for one, preferred the "light and graceful movements of the skilful riders" over the "painful staggering of dull and exhausted pedestrians." In its view, bicycling was a "rational substitute" for the professional pedestrian sport that had degenerated into a "senseless and even brutal" business based on "blind animal endurance."

In all, about twenty-five hundred Americans acquired bicycles in 1879, and many more learned to ride in schools. The high bicycle had obviously crossed the Atlantic, affirming the sport's international appeal. With an air of triumph, *Bicycling World* demanded to know why a certain American encyclopedia had as yet no entry for the word "bicycle." "Oh, the bicycle is a mere toy," replied an agent defensively, "and we only include practical and useful articles." Fuming, the editor pointed out that even the conser-

Pope's growing bicycle operation within the Weed plant of Hartford, from *Scientific American*, 20 March 1880. Over a ten-year period, Pope gradually acquired the firm and shifted its production to bicycles.

vative *Encyclopaedia Britannica* included the bicycle. To convince the agent of his "error and ignorance," the editor asked rhetorically, "Is the telephone a toy? Or the type-writer? Or the passenger-elevator?" To be sure, conceded the editor, bicycles are often used purely for pleasure. But that, he argued, does not make them toys. After all, "are railroad trains playthings [simply] because they carry picnic parties?" Indeed, to a growing number of advocates, the new bicycle was a true mechanical marvel.

NINE *Growing Safety Concerns*

The international bicycle community continued to flourish in the early 1880s, as manufacturers applied what amounted to the finishing touches to the vaunted high wheeler. Yet the more the sport developed among young men of privilege, the more the ranks of the would-be cyclists swelled. Many thousands of men and women of means longed to share in the joys of cycling without incurring the usual risks of serious bodily injury. A large number of cycling innovators answered their call. Suddenly, improved tricycles made surprising inroads, attracting legions of wealthy patrons of both sexes and of all ages. Several alternative bicycle designs also appeared, and these offered greater protection from the dreaded header. Still, the high wheeler appeared more than likely to hold its own in a vibrant market—until nagging safety concerns eventually caught up to it.

facing page: Aquarelle print by Hy Sandham, published about 1887, reflecting the dominance of the high mount in the early 1880s. The bulkier and more expensive tricycle did not at first pose a serious threat and seemed destined to serve only a select group of women and older men who sought to partake in the benefits of cycling without risking an unpleasant spill.

Throughout the early 1880s, British cycle makers focused on refining the high wheeler. They added improved seat springs, for greater comfort, and hollow rims to reduce weight still further. Some of the better models even featured ball bearings in the pedals and rear hubs. Most bicyclists abandoned the straight handlebar in favor of an elongated "moustache" bar, with a hump on either side to make room for the rider's knees at the height of their trajectory. The lower position of the bar ends enabled the rider to gain better control of the machine, and also to crouch down during sprints to reduce air resistance. Cyclists could also choose among a growing assortment of accessories, including wool outfits, oil lamps, tool kits, and cyclometers.

Naturally, results on the racing track improved as well. In 1882, the medical student H. L. Cortis set a new mile record from a standing start, finishing in 2:41 3/5. That same year, he became the first cyclist to cover 20 miles in one hour. A year later, Keith-Falconer rode 50 miles in just under two hours and forty-four minutes. Another amateur, F. R. Fry, rode a century in ten minutes shy of six hours—nearly two hours faster than Stanton's original mark set eight years earlier at Lille Bridge. Racers also set new records on the road. In the summer of 1882, Keith-Falconer covered nearly a thousand miles in thirteen days, riding from Land's End, the southern tip of Cornwall, to John O'Groats at the farthest end of Scotland. A year later, J. W. F. Sutton rode more than 260 miles over common roads inside twenty-four hours.

The sport and the industry, meanwhile, continued to develop elsewhere in the world. For in spite of its limited market, the towering direct-drive bicycle commanded a large and loyal following among athletic young males. Clubs flourished in every part of Europe, and even the French industry gradually regained a measure of its former prominence, thanks largely to Adolphe Clément and the brothers Eugène and Armand Peugeot, who headed major cycling concerns. Bicycling was also increasingly popular in the British colonies, and the high mount was even becoming a more familiar sight in Asia and the Americas.

In the United States, Pope continued to prosper. In 1880, he introduced several models built with lighter tubes and fitted with smooth ball bearings. George Bidwell, Pope's superintendent of agencies, demonstrated the improved Columbia bicycle in public squares from Denver to New Orleans. He later likened his eye-popping routine to that of "a tightrope walker, who stretches his rope from building to building." He recalled that "most everyone was interested, and greatly amused," even though "few could afford one." Still, the widespread publicity paid off. By 1882, Pope presided over the world's largest bicycle concern, capable of producing a thousand units a month. By Pope's own estimate, some twelve thousand adult machines were circulating in the United States in the spring of that year, about two-thirds of them from the Weed factory.

With the Lallement patent still in effect, Pope and his patent attorney Charles Pratt

High-Wheel Accessories

As high-wheel riding gained favor in the 1880s, the industry proposed an increasingly rich assortment of accessories, such as horns and warning bells. One of the more sophisticated add-ons was the Butcher Cyclometer, patented in 1883. Mounted on the front axle within the wheel, it kept a running score of miles pedaled. It came with a counterweight to keep the meter within the rider's view, but that could be replaced by another popular accessory, the oil-based hub lamp. Bicyclists were generally less enthusiastic about the head-mounted variety, since it made the bicycle more top-heavy and cast a more feeble light on the road. Other accessories included woolen suits with matching caps, portable wrenches, oilcans, and pocket-sized maps that highlighted the best roads. The Eastman Company of Rochester, New York, even suggested that cyclists take a Kodak box camera along for the ride.

The discerning cyclist could also modify the machine itself, installing a favorite handlebar grip or springy seat. In 1888, the Overman Wheel Company introduced a "handy carrier" weighing only six ounces. This front rack rested on the spoon brake, and featured adjustable straps to secure its cargo. The rider could instantly detach the entire load and carry it on foot as hand luggage. But perhaps the most imaginative proposal was the "Safety Handle Bar." Developed in several countries including Germany, the bar was sprung in such a way that it would instantly detach whenever an ejected rider's thighs brushed up against it. In theory, the rider could then hit the ground running, as opposed to the usual position, sprawled out on all fours. Alas, the innovation failed to eliminate the primary objection to the high mount.

An illustration by a Chinese artist of a high-wheel obstacle race, probably in Europe, from the Shanghai newspaper *Dianshizhai Huabao* (Dianshizhai's Pictorial Magazine) of May–August 1889. By the late 1880s the high wheeler was a familiar sight the world over. The article explained how competitors had to scoop up flags and ride over logs. "When the race is over," observed the writer, "the winner is awarded with bright flowers and good wine, while the injured riders keep doctors busy for a while." (Translation by Hsi-chu Bollick)

saw to it that they continued to dominate the trade. When McKee and Harrington of Lyndhurst, New Jersey, started manufacturing unauthorized bicycles in the spring of 1880, Pope won an injunction to suspend the company's production. Reluctantly, the New Jersey firm came to terms, but when it strayed back into the adult market Pope sued again. This time the defendants fought back fiercely and even grilled Lallement himself, but the stubborn Frenchman refused to renounce his claim to the invention. A triumphant Pope prevailed, whereupon he effectively expelled the insurgents from the tight-knit trade.

In the early going, Pope reaped a fortune from high-wheel sales and royalty fees. But he also continued to spend large sums to bolster the trade. In the spring of 1880, he helped launch the League of American Wheelmen to do for American cyclists what the

Bicycle Union and Bicycle Touring Club did for their British counterparts. As a lobbying force, the League fought for the right to cycle legally on roads and park paths. It also demanded a federal highway program, spearheading what soon became the powerful Good Roads Movement. As the central racing authority, it organized and regulated contests, setting policies such as amateur qualifications. For its growing membership, the League published tourist maps and a newsletter. Its flashy annual meets helped to win public favor. The second gathering in Boston in 1881 united some eight hundred members who paraded down Commonwealth Avenue before thousands of cheering spectators.

Pope himself paid for the legal defense of three men who gallantly defied Central Park's anti-cycling ordinance. Although the United States Supreme Court eventually upheld the five-dollar fines imposed by the city, the protracted legal battle garnered broad public sympathy. Pope also vigorously promoted the spectator sport, offering competitors numerous trophies and monetary prizes. Moreover, he spent lavish sums on advertising and cycling literature. In 1882, he launched *The Wheelman Illustrated,* an elegant cycling review. He even sponsored essay competitions to generate a steady stream of popular articles extolling the virtues of cycling.

But Pope was not the only apostle of the new sport. Starting in 1882, the bicycle club of Springfield, Massachusetts, led by Henry E. Ducker, hosted an annual meet at the Hampden Park racing track. The colorful affair drew the top professional and amateur racers from both sides of the Atlantic. The second tournament lasted three days and at times drew more than twenty thousand spectators to the field. The highlight was the twenty-five-mile amateur bicycle race, won in record time by a local youth and favorite son named George Hendee, who went on to manufacture bicycle parts and the Indian motorcycle. Within a few years, the Springfield event became so popular that the city virtually shut down for its duration.

Women's bicycle racing was also developing into a popular spectator sport. As early as 1879, eighteen-year-old Lizzie Balmer covered eighteen and a half miles in two hours at a tournament in San Francisco. Several female stars soon emerged to entertain large and supportive crowds across the country. The women competed among themselves and against male cyclists, pedestrians, and trotting horses. Though some denounced them as common showgirls, they were in fact highly trained and motivated athletes. In 1881, Elsa von Blumen of Rochester, New York, rode an incredible thousand miles during one six-day marathon in Pittsburgh, although toward the end she had to be propped up on her bicycle and given stimulants. The following year in Boston, Louise Armaindo took on John Prince, the American champion, receiving a five-mile head start in a fifty-mile race. The pair furiously traded positions, until at last Prince prevailed by barely a minute.

SPRINGFIELD BICYCLE CLUB.

BICYCLE CAMP-EXHIBITION & TOURNAMENT.
SPRINGFIELD, MASS. U.S.A. SEPT. 18. 19. 20. 1883.

A poster for the second annual cycling tournament held in Springfield, which attracted top competitors from both sides of the Atlantic and thousands of enthusiastic spectators. A local boy, George Hendee, became a star competitor. The 1883 meet included the first American cycle trade show, which introduced the Victor tricycle.

As the sport of cycling gained favor, some makers began to reconsider the theoretical merits of the three-wheeler. A well-made tricycle required no great skill to master, nor was it apt to catapult its driver over the handlebars, the peril that made bicycling so dangerous. Moreover, as *Popular Science News* noted once superior tricycles reached the market, they are "more comfortable for touring purposes" because "it is so much easier to stop when and where you choose, and enjoy the scenery." The tricycle could also carry "a larger amount of personal luggage," a capacity that lent itself to the

Ernestine Bernard of Paris in the midst of a "hotly-contested three mile race with a noted running horse" at a rink in Toronto, Ontario, from the *National Police Gazette,* 28 June 1879. According to the journal, the victorious French athlete "appeared in scant garments appropriate to the occasion." Within a few years, female high-wheel racers gained a large following in North America, although the machine depicted here looks as if it might have been of a transitional form.

The Lallement Patent Again

The emergence of a high-wheel trade in the United States in 1877 revived interest in the key Lallement patent, which was still potentially applicable for another six years. The patent fell into the hands of Richardson and McKee, a Boston maker of children's carriages, who promptly exacted royalty payments from the importers Cunningham, Heath, as well as the aspiring manufacturer Albert Pope. One of those two firms engaged the Boston patent lawyer Charles Pratt to assess the validity of the Lallement patent. Hoping to find evidence to undermine it, Pratt dashed off a letter to Brandon and Morgan-Brown, the Paris legal firm that had helped Calvin Witty purchase Lallement's share of the patent in 1869. David Brandon's response, however, was less than encouraging. "We give you the following information of this subject, which you can rely upon, as Lallement has been known to us for the past ten years. Lallement in the years prior to 1866 was employed in the making of perambulatory and children's coaches. The idea occurred to him of putting cranks on the ordinary two-wheeled velocipede and he succeeded in thus running a bicycle."

Pope eventually acquired the Lallement patent himself, and Pratt, as the company's new lawyer, assumed the job of enforcing it. Among their first targets were

delivery of goods and other practical applications. Finally, tricycles could more readily accommodate conventional women's wear, as well as a second rider.

For some time, the tricycle had been neglected. In the early 1870s, with the exception of a few French machines sporting spider wheels, the few three-wheelers still on the market were little more than boneshakers with a second wheel in back, or clumsy treadle-driven affairs with a second turning wheel in front. Many mechanics had written off the three-wheeler altogether as a weak sister to the bicycle. The two-wheeler was in fact faster, easier to steer, and cheaper to build. Moreover, as *Popular Science News* observed, bicycles offered distinct practical advantages. They could be easily stored "in an office, or almost anywhere," and should the rider suffer an accident, they "may be readily conveyed by any other light carriage to [the rider's] home or a rail-way station." Besides, for many, the act of balancing on two wheels provided a unique thrill.

the carriage makers McKee and Harrington of Lyndhurst, New Jersey, who were beginning to produce bicycles. In preparation for a showdown with Pope, one of the principals of that firm, Joseph McKee, reportedly traveled to Paris, where he "engaged the services of the Michaux brothers, who claimed to be the inventors of the bicycle." No doubt McKee's firm was also responsible for an advertisement that appeared in the leading French cycling journal in the fall of 1881. It promised a "healthy reward to whomever can prove, by a newspaper article or any other serious document, that the pedal system was applied to velocipedes before the year 1866." The following spring, when Pope's infringement suit went to trial in the Southern District of New York, the defense summoned Lallement himself, who had recently moved to Brooklyn. His interrogator prodded the Frenchman to reveal where he had first seen a bicycle. "I see the one that I made," he replied, "that is the one, first one. Before I made that velocipede, I did not see or hear anything about velocipedes with cranks." Pressed further about what he did with his bicycle, Lallement retorted: "I did not take that machine and put it in my pocket. I took it on the boulevard and all the people saw it."

But starting around 1876, a few bold mechanics set out to apply the latest bicycle technology to the three-wheeler. William Blood, a Dubliner, introduced a wire-wheeled tricycle with a large driving wheel in back, powered by treadles, and two parallel front wheels. At about the same time, James Starley introduced a novel configuration, the Coventry Lever Tricycle. On one side it sported a fifty-inch wheel driven by foot levers, and to the other side were two small wheels aligned with each other, both of which turned. The three wheels traced only two tracks rather than the usual three, thereby reducing the chances that one of them would find an unsettling rut somewhere on the road. Moreover, the extended span of the two smaller wheels made for a very stable ride. Starley's tricycle went on the market in the spring of 1877, and was manufactured under license by Haynes and Jefferis of Coventry, the same firm that made his Ariel bicycles.

Starley recognized, however, that the rotary pedals found on a bicycle would provide a more efficient and pleasant means of propulsion than the levers. But of course he could not simply attach pedals to the axle of the driving wheel, as was done on a bicycle. He could, however, adopt a pedal drive by means of a chain linking the cranks to the driving wheel. The idea of using a chain to power a bicycle or tricycle was not new; a number of patents dating back to the velocipede era had already called for its use to provide a more flexible gearing arrangement. But the poor quality of the chains available at that time made these schemes impractical. As it happened, Hans Renold, a Swiss engineer living in Manchester, England, had just patented a new type of chain with anti-friction bushings and rollers. Starley recognized that this type of chain could do the job nicely, and he engaged Renold to make chains for his tricycles. Starley then unveiled his revamped Coventry Rotary Tricycle, and it quickly became a hit, especially with society women.

Spurred by his success with three-wheelers, Starley developed the first two-seat tricycle, known as the Salvo Sociable. A variation of his Coventry Rotary, it featured two seats side by side and two large driving wheels at either side. Stability, however, was a problem with two drivers propelling two wheels at independent rates: the vehicle was prone to tip over, especially during turns. The resourceful Starley set out to resolve this problem as well, and he soon came up with what became known as the balance gear, or differential gear. This nifty mechanism incorporated a bevel-gear differential into the axle that connected the two driving wheels, so that the power from the two drives could be evenly distributed. It also allowed one wheel to rotate faster than the other during turns. The net effect was a much more stable double-drive tricycle.

Starley's new cycle technologies, the improved chain and the balance gear, eventually became fundamental to automotive design. But their immediate effect was to open up a wide range of possibilities for cycle makers. One or even two cyclists could now safely power two connected wheels, allowing for tricycles with a simpler single-wheel steering arrangement. Starley himself used the balance gear not only to improve his Sociable tricycle but also to create a line of single-passenger models with unprecedented functionality, and these became part of the Salvo family. The most popular design featured a small central guiding wheel in front, with rack-and-pinion steering, and two large driving wheels in the rear, connected by the balance gear and driven by rotary pedals and a chain.

By the late 1870s, the speed gap between two- and three-wheelers had narrowed to only about two or three miles an hour, and the fashionable circles of Britain took note. Under the headline "Tricycles Coming to the Front," *The World* of London reported in 1878: "There is quite a rage for tricycling this season at Brighton. Owing to the marvelous perfection attained in steel work, tricycles are now produced, combining great strength with extreme lightness. The mode of mechanical propulsion having also been

Starley's novel two-track Coventry Rotary Tricycle, introduced about 1878, featuring a large driving wheel on one side and two smaller guiding wheels aligned on the other, along with a chain, conventional rotary pedals, and tangential-spoke wheels. To steer, the rider twists the outer handle; on the other side, by the big wheel, is a handle for the other hand and a brake lever. Women's models came with a seat rather than a saddle. The design helped spark strong interest in tricycles among the British upper classes.

greatly improved, they have become a fascinating and exhilarating means of exercise and locomotion. Ladies have taken to them, doctors take their visits on them, and tradesmen circulate their goods by them."

Indeed, these improved tricycles promised to provide not only the exercise and amusement formerly confined to high-wheel riders, but also the utilitarian possibilities the conventional bicycle had thus far failed to deliver. To be sure, a few country doctors and postmen were using high wheelers to make calls and deliveries. But most individuals who pedaled for practical purposes opted for the more stable tricycle. Singer and Company, for one, introduced a "carrier" model with a large basket in front that could purportedly haul up to 150 pounds of goods.

Still, few observers initially expected the tricycle to challenge the high wheeler for market supremacy. With all its extra hardware, the three-wheeler was even more expensive than a bicycle. Moreover, no one tricycle design had as yet established itself as the industry standard, giving potential customers cause for hesitation. And conventional wisdom still held that the bicycle was the only sensible choice for any reasonably fit male who was out to derive maximum pleasure from the sport.

But the tricycle continued to advance. In 1881, Queen Victoria herself purchased a pair of Salvo tricycles, prompting Starley to add the descriptive "Royal" to its name. The noted American artist Joseph Pennell was among the growing number of tricycle enthusiasts. He made regular jaunts into the English countryside atop a tricycle laden with twenty-five pounds of gear, including two suits, an umbrella, sketchbooks, and a stool. In 1884, Pennell reflected on the rapid rise of the three-wheeler in Britain. "When the tricycle was first seen on the road in 1880, in competition with the bicycle, it was looked upon askance. It seemed like a resource of old age or timidity. But before long a few practical road-riding cyclers tried it, and did not find it wanting. Their example was speedily followed, with the result that in Great Britain, if not elsewhere, it has become a formidable rival of the bicycle, and is fast gaining ground."

The tricycle was indeed rapidly coming into its own, especially in Britain. The specialized literature included such manuals as "Tricycling for Ladies" and "Tips for Tricyclists," as well as two journals devoted to the sector. Tricyclists even formed their own clubs, as well as an umbrella organization called the Tricycle Association, which merged with the Bicycle Union in 1883 to form the National Cyclists' Union. The

facing page: A trade card from the mid-1880s showing a woman on what became the most popular tricycle design, a three-track machine with front-wheel steering and two rear driving wheels connected by an axle with a differential gear, powered by a chain and rotary pedals. Twisting one handle turns the front wheel, and twisting the other applies a rear brake.

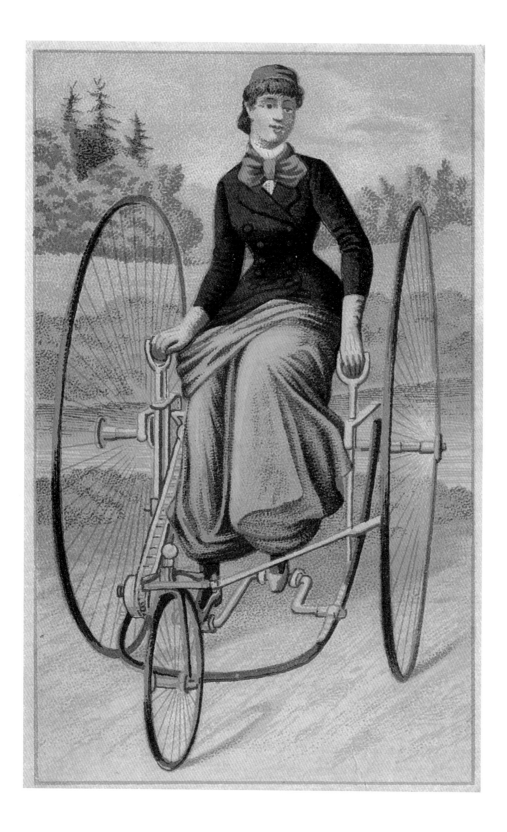

membership included both men and women, who tended to be older and even more upscale than their bicycle counterparts. Tricycle meets, in contrast with most bicycle-oriented affairs, stressed social intermingling rather than competition. At one gathering in the London suburb of Howe in 1883, some 160 riders sat down to a genteel tea after parading through the town. The biggest event of the year, however, was the annual London-area meet. The third reunion in 1883 took place in the suburb of Barnes and attracted around four hundred participants, evenly divided between club members and the "unattached."

Some tricyclists even clamored for a separate organization to cater to the more affluent cycle tourist. There were also those who demanded, among other concessions, exemption from ordinances that banned bicycle riding in parks, on the grounds that tricyclists constituted a more mature and refined lot. In general, tricyclists were eager to distance themselves from the run-of-the-mill bicyclist, whom they judged as being of lower social rank. In truth, as thousands of lower-class youths gradually acquired secondhand high mounts, bicycling was losing much of its snob appeal—a fact that might explain why some clubs were already in marked decline. Tricycles, in contrast, remained refreshingly elitist.

Although tricycles were primarily used for touring, makers were eager to demonstrate that three-wheelers were just as well made as bicycles, and could likewise achieve impressive results on the track and on the road. Cycling meets began to include a wide variety of tricycle events mirroring bicycle contests. The racers, most of whom also rode high mounts, used special lightweight models to register impressive results approaching those of the fastest bicycle. In 1882, A. Bird rode a Humber tricycle from Birmingham to Cambridge, covering 222 miles within twenty-four hours—only about twenty miles shy of the comparable bicycle record at that time.

As demand for tricycles continued to rise, the cycling community began to wonder if the tricycle might not make a run for market supremacy after all. "The general opinion here," affirmed one Coventry maker in 1881, "is that [the tricycle] will eventually supersede the bicycle. Many bicyclists have come to the conclusion that the additional two miles an hour in speed is not to be compared to the [added] comfort and safety of the tricycle." Nor was the popularity of the three-wheeler confined to Britain. Another Coventry firm boasted, "We have exported largely to Australia, New Zealand, and most European countries, and are doing a large trade with India."

The tricycle was even making inroads in the United States. In 1883, the Overman Wheel Company introduced the Victor, the first American-made three-wheeler of the high-wheel era, produced in Chicopee Falls, Massachusetts, outside Springfield. The lever drive on the first models soon gave way to the more popular rotary pedals. Despite the Victor's added expense, and the difficulty of riding such a broad vehicle over America's poor roads, it quickly gained favor. The following season, Pope scrambled to unveil a tricycle of his own. "The tricycle will gradually come into general use," Pope allowed, "until it will catch up and keep pace with the bicycle. Its future is certain. It meets a demand long felt by those who are too old, or heavy, or timid, to mount the bicycle; and it is also particularly adapted for the other sex." But as Pope saw it, tricycle sales would only "encourage and help the further introduction of the bicycle."

Tricycles, however, were not the only alternative cycles mounting a challenge to the high wheeler in the early 1880s. The idea of a lower and safer bicycle, which had also been languishing for some time, was finally beginning to show promise. Following the demise of the Phantom in 1872 and the geared Ariel shortly thereafter, prospective cyclists had little to chose from in the way of two-wheelers. Starley, for one, tried to change that. In 1874, he proposed yet another style of low-mount bicycle, this one targeted for

A man on a conventional high wheeler beside a woman on a Lady's Bicycle, about 1874. James Starley designed this unorthodox variation so that a woman could sit lower and farther back, an arrangement that facilitated mounting and dismounting and made for a more stable ride. It also allowed for a full dress and enabled the vehicle to stand on its own. Still, the design was complicated. Note how the left front fork blade is bent out and forward, to make room for the pedal drive connected to an extended front axle. The woman, Starley's niece, appears to be cramped by the backbone, and if she accidentally tipped to the side opposite the pedals she would have been unable to extend a leg to break the fall.

women. It was easier to get on and off than a conventional high wheeler, and a female cyclist was able to ride wearing a dress. Starley bent the backbone at two right angles in the center to form a foot-long perpendicular bar that held the seat-spring and seat, and he set the two wheels on separate tracks. The rider now sat closer to the center of the frame and in a lower position, to one side of the giant wheel rather than directly above it. Starley replaced the direct-action rotary pedals with foot levers that were connected to the extended front axle and traced an oval circuit. Whatever its technical merits, this design sacrificed the chief appeal of the conventional bicycle—its simplicity. The model was quickly abandoned, although it inspired Starley's more successful Coventry Lever Tricycle and Coventry Rotary Tricycle with their small wheels in an offset alignment.

In the late 1870s, as the tricycle began to advance, several inventors revisited the idea of a low-mount bicycle with a rear-wheel drive. When Thomas McCall and others originally proposed such a plan during the boneshaker era a decade earlier, it had seemed an appealing way to eliminate the awkward need to pedal and steer the same wheel. As the high mount developed and improved in the early 1870s, however, that perceived advantage became less compelling. Seated almost directly over the pedals, with the legs thrusting down and not forward, the high-wheel rider enjoyed much better control over the body and the bicycle, and needed only to angle the front wheel ever so slightly when turning. Moreover, the fork blades prevented the rider's legs from getting too close to the wheel, and rubber-tread pedals, often with toe clips, reduced the chances of the foot slipping into the spokes. Still, a bicycle with a rear-wheel drive retained some appeal as a means to resituate the bicyclist closer to the ground, so that the machine would be easier to mount and a spill would be less punishing to the rider, if not the bicycle.

In 1876, the British engineer Henry J. Lawson proposed a new rear-drive machine he called the Safety Bicycle. The rider sat nearly directly over the small front wheel, and shifting treadles back and forth propelled a driving wheel of standard size just behind the saddle. *Cycling* summed up its chief advantage: "The feet are always within easy reach of the ground, and the danger of falling is reduced to a minimum." Moreover, the journal observed, "you can mount by throwing your leg over—as over a pony—and start instantly. You can then go as slowly and steadily as you like, even in the most crowded thoroughfares, where high bicyclists must dismount." The journal even pronounced Lawson's machine "equal in speed to that of its more showy, though less safe, rival, the high bicycle."

Lawson induced Singer and Company to produce his new mount. In the summer of 1878, it gained a wide circulation among the fashionable set at Brighton, who were also beginning to ride tricycles. The Safety Bicycle soon fell from favor, however, perhaps on account of its rickety ride. Lawson nonetheless refused to give up on the rear-

The Bicyclette, introduced by Henry J. Lawson in 1879, anticipating the revolutionary Rover by some five years. Many historians believe that the Bicyclette failed to catch on not because it was inferior to the Rover but because the market at the time was less favorable to a radical change. Others have suggested that Lawson was perhaps not very effective as a promoter. The name "bicyclette" was nonetheless revived some years later and became the French term for the safety-style bicycle.

drive concept. The following year, 1879, he patented a revamped model that he named the Bicyclette. But this time he scrapped the treadle drive and used a chain and a sprocket instead, a more flexible system that had only recently appeared on Starley's tricycles. This choice of drive allowed Lawson to use not only rotary pedals but also a much smaller rear wheel. He could arbitrarily "gear up" the driving wheel simply by making the sprocket attached to it of a smaller circumference than that of the chain-wheel driven by the pedals, so that the rear wheel completed more than one revolution every time the cyclist brought the pedals around. Lawson also chose to use a larger front wheel for better stability, effectively reversing the order of the small and big wheels he had used in his earlier Safety Bicycle.

At about the same time, several other British inventors were likewise applying the new chain technology to bicycles, notably Henry Bate, a surgeon from Surrey. Still, prospective buyers showed little interest in these peculiar bicycles. Many found the rider's lowly position undignified. Others objected to their complicated appearance, and strongly suspected that their long chains would prove intolerably inefficient. The greater cost of these bicycles also presented a significant drawback to prospective

The Facile, one of the first safety bicycles to gain favor in the early 1880s, initially in Britain and then in the United States. The first models were ungeared, but its lever-driven pedals allowed riders to benefit from the largest manageable driving wheel.

manufacturers and purchasers. The chain in particular, despite improvements in its manufacture, was still an expensive proposition given its hundreds of movable parts. Although Lawson persuaded the Rudge company to produce a limited number of Bicyclettes, and a specimen caused a buzz at the 1880 Stanley Show, demand failed to materialize and production soon ceased.

The failure of the Bicyclette and similar low-mount bicycles spurred innovators to look for ways to modify, rather than supplant, the resilient high mount. At last, they achieved some success. The Facile, patented in 1879 by the British firm Beale and Straw, used lever extensions on the pedals to situate the rider closer to the center of the frame. The bicyclist pushed up and down on the reciprocating levers, tracing short arcs rather than full circles. Though almost as high up as before, the rider was purportedly less likely to suffer a header because the new seat position, along with the larger rear wheel, made for a better distribution of weight and hence a more stable vehicle. Before long the Facile began to prove itself in competition and attract a large following. In 1883, J. H. Adams rode one an astonishing 242 miles, setting a new twenty-four-hour record.

Americans, too, took a keen interest in the Facile, and several firms imported a large number of them. *Bicycling World,* for one, praised the design. Although it conceded that the new arrangement might not appeal to those "who have a passion for getting as high in the air as possible," the journal insisted that the Facile was safer than the high mount and did not make the rider "look awkward or undignified." American firms also imported another British safety model, Singer's Xtraordinary. Like the Facile, this modified high mount featured a lever drive, but it also adopted a raked front fork to shift the rider's weight even farther back, closer to the center of the frame. It, too, attracted a large following on both sides of the Atlantic.

Before long, a U.S. manufacturer introduced a safety model of its own. Known as the American Star, it reversed the standard configuration by placing a small wheel in front and a large driving wheel in the rear. It, too, used up-and-down levers to place the rider

Will Robertson of the Washington Bicycle Club riding a Star bicycle down the steps of the United States Capitol in 1885, a stunt he reportedly performed in the wee hours of the morning to avoid an arrest. The Star became a favorite among tourists and racers for its enhanced stability.

closer to the center of the frame. But the Star's levers acted independently, allowing the rider to push both down at once, a good technique for fast starts. Most important, the design eliminated the threat of the dreaded header: at worst, riders would fall off from the rear, landing on their behinds. George Pressey patented the design in 1880, and he licensed the H. B. Smith company of Smithville, New Jersey, to produce it. A few specimens appeared at the League of American Wheelmen meet in Boston in 1881, but several years passed before Pressey and Smith perfected the design and commenced large-scale production. Once the Star hit the market, however, it quickly claimed a following.

Although bicycle production was not a natural sideline for H. B. Smith, a maker of woodworking machinery, he was keenly interested in the vehicle's democratic potential. A man of socialist principles, he believed that the bicycle called for a complete overhaul so that more people could enjoy its benefits. And he was ready to fight for that cause. To highlight the Star's safety features, he hired performers to give exhibitions across the country, notably John Stout, a deaf mute from Chicago. Among other stunts, Stout rode his Star down the steps of the Michigan state capitol, a feat no sane high-wheel rider would ever contemplate. Smith also hired racers to compete against the high mount, proving that the Star was at least a competitive, if not superior, racing machine.

By 1883, it was becoming increasingly evident to the cycling community that the standard bicycle, now commonly called an Ordinary, would never regain the dominant presence on the road it had enjoyed in the late 1870s. Still, industry insiders confidently concluded that the cycle market was now sufficiently large and diverse that it could easily accommodate three distinct varieties. The purist would naturally remain true to the Ordinary. Couples, women, and the elderly would opt for the more stable tricycle. The aging or less adventurous male would ride some sort of "safety" bicycle.

The Graphic of 28 August 1880 included this scene of two British cyclists on a holiday tour in France, passing through a small town where the big wheel was evidently still a novelty

The state of cycle touring at that time seemed to support this vision. Tourists combed every part of Britain and the European continent on all varieties of cycles, prompting the Bicycle Touring Club to change its name to the more generic Cyclists' Touring Club. In Britain, as a result of this increased traffic, many struggling country inns and taverns enjoyed renewed business. Though bypassed by the railroad, and poorly served by the moribund coach, these rustic locales were well within the range of prosperous urban cyclists. As one source put it, cyclists could reach every hamlet, "in the most direct manner." Before long, reported Joseph Pennell, the Cyclists' Touring Club operated a "large and imposing" office in London with "many salaried officials." It established chapters around the world and its membership surged past the ten thousand mark. At the same time, lobbying groups, such as the National Cyclists' Union, founded as the Bicycle Union in 1878, scored significant legal victories to protect cyclists from hostile coachmen and overzealous policemen.

The international cycling industry was evidently poised to enjoy a prolonged period of prosperity as the mid-1880s approached. Yet despite the flurry of activity on both sides of the Atlantic to develop safer cycles, and the encouraging results, the future of the high bicycle still seemed reasonably secure. The Ordinary offered compelling advantages over the expensive and bulky tricycle, and several European armies were even contemplating the use of two-wheelers to relay messages or deploy troops. And while safety bicycles like the Facile had already attained a surprising measure of success, few observers expected these complicated affairs to gain anything more than a healthy market share. Conventional wisdom held that no costly and intricate safety bicycle could ever truly supplant the elegant, efficient, and economical high bicycle. Time, however, soon proved otherwise.

Part Four The "Safety" Era

TEN *The Rise of the Rover*

THE "NEW WOMAN."

The mid-1880s represents a volatile period in bicycle history. A vast variety of cycles flooded the market and a spirited struggle broke out to determine which ones would ultimately prevail. The high mount appeared to have reached a technical plateau, while its flaws were never more evident. Tricycles continued to gain momentum, and even began to outnumber two-wheelers at the annual Stanley Show. For the first time, an alternative bicycle, the Kangaroo, threatened to overtake the Ordinary as the most popular bicycle form. Before long, another rival arose: the Rover, a low-mount bicycle with two equally sized wheels and a chain drive. The intense competition stimulated technical development and attracted a new wave of men and women to the sport. By the late 1880s, it was evident to all that the high mount would never regain road supremacy. Yet many proponents clung to the mistaken belief that the vibrant market could indefinitely support a variety of machines, including the grand old Ordinary. But the Rover pattern rapidly improved, and it not only prevailed as the universal bicycle style, it also triggered an unprecedented worldwide demand that culminated in the great boom.

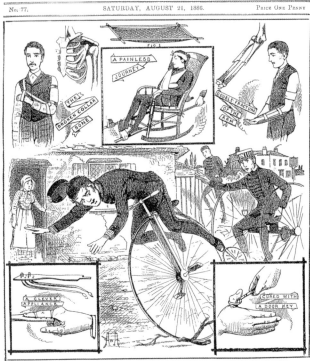

THE FAMILY DOCTOR

AND PEOPLE'S MEDICAL ADVISER

No. 77.   SATURDAY, AUGUST 21, 1886.   PRICE ONE PENNY

BICYCLING—ITS CASUALTIES & REMEDIES
(For Description see Next Page.)

No. 25.—VOL. III.

The *Family Doctor* of 21 August 1886 warned of the dangers associated with cycling, a growing concern in the mid-1880s. The journal offered tips on how to reset broken bones at home or how to transport the injured cyclist to a hospital.

By the mid-1880s the future of the once dominant Ordinary was increasingly less secure. The public was beginning to suspect that the high mount was far more dangerous than the trade had initially let on. Even *Bicycling World* acknowledged that "many a hardy and skillful bicyclist has been seriously and permanently injured by a forward fall off a high mount." It concluded, "This country needs safety bicycles for there is a large class of would-be riders who are deterred from enjoying the sport." The *Springfield Wheelmen's Gazette* echoed the sentiment, declaring, "It is better to make safe machines than to pooh-pooh the fears of people who don't want to get their craniums cracked." But whether any of the many alternative cycles crowding the market had any staying power remained to be seen.

To many, tricycles seemed the best solution, but even they came in a bewildering assortment of patterns. The single wheel was in back on some models, in front on others. Some were propelled by foot levers, while others featured conventional rotary pedals and a chain drive. Some offered two gears, others collapsed for easy storage. Tandem models were in vogue among such affluent couples as Arthur Conan Doyle, the creator of Sherlock Holmes, and his wife. Pennell and his partner, Elizabeth Robbins, took regular rides throughout Europe on a tricycle and published illustrated accounts of their adventures. But even two-seaters came in two distinct varieties: the original Sociable pattern sat two riders side by side, while most tandems placed one rider before the other.

By 1885 tricycles were increasingly in demand in America as well, especially among society women. In Washington, one of the nation's wealthiest and best-paved cities, some five hundred women combed the streets on their elegant three-wheelers. The *Sporting Journal* of Chicago asked local ladies why they had taken up tricycling. "I ride for both health and pleasure," replied one socialite, adding that she took fre-

A cycling couple posing in front of the White House, about 1885. Tandem three-and four-wheelers were then popular with affluent couples who were determined to cycle together. This one could be converted into a single tricycle by loosening bolts in the center and detaching either the front or the rear portion.

quent rides with her husband. Miss Florence Fuller revealed that she had ridden "a great many miles in the past two years," even taking "long and frequent rides alone" to enjoy "a certain feeling of independence." Frances E. Willard, president of the Chicago Ladies' Temperance League, explained that she rode regularly with her secretary "after several hours' hard work dictating correspondence." Added Willard, "I should like to see ladies take actively to tricycling, for I find it keeps me in excellent health."

The growing popularity of tricycles, most with chain drives, prompted some makers to reconsider how chains might be used to create safer bicycles. In 1884, Hillman, Herbert, and Cooper of Coventry introduced the dwarf Kangaroo. Its thirty-six-inch

The Kangaroo, one of the first successful dwarf bicycles, this one featuring foot rests extending toward the front. Because chain drives geared up the front wheel its size was reduced, but dangerous headers were still a possibility.

front wheel was geared up to the equivalent of sixty inches by means of two independent chain drives, one connecting each crank to its side of the front wheel. In the fall of that year, the company staged a one-hundred-mile road race restricted to Kangaroo riders. The professional George Smith broke the Ordinary record, finishing in just seven hours and eleven minutes. The *Springfield Wheelmen's Gazette* predicted that the Kangaroo would soon attract many would-be bicyclists and possibly even convert tricyclists, "if they can be persuaded that there is, as asserted, even less danger on it than on a three wheeler." Indeed, demand for Kangaroos surged, and a number of British firms took out licenses to produce their own variations.

Yet even as it faced growing competition, the high wheeler was not necessarily doomed. *Bicycling World* maintained that the vibrant market could continue to support all three basic types of cycles, but insisted that "the ordinary bicycle will still continue [as] the leading machine." True, it conceded, tricycles will "greatly increase in popularity," and the many alternative bicycles "will find a useful and profitable field." Yet, in its view, the only issue at hand was simply this: which safety bicycle will eventually emerge as the favorite alternative to the high wheeler, and possibly even erode the tricycle's healthy market share?

In fact, despite its evident flaws, the high mount was still in demand, especially in the United States. Although the American cycle trade remained small by British standards, it continued to prosper with Pope at the helm and the high mount as its mainstay. Following the expiration of the Lallement patent in the fall of 1883, Pope even relaxed his grip on high-wheel production and allowed several rivals to share in the lucrative high-end adult market. Gormully and Jeffery of Chicago and the Overman Wheel Company, no longer confined to tricycles, were among the firms that enjoyed a brisk business making high bicycles in the mid-1880s.

Pope, however, still ruled the roost. His competitors had little choice but to abide by his tradewide dictates governing production, pricing, and marketing. To maintain control, Pope continued to sue his rivals over alleged patent infringements, having amassed over the years legal rights covering virtually every aspect of bicycle production. A. H. Overman, however, gained some leverage of his own when he acquired a key ball-bearing patent. In 1886, *Bicycling World* complained that the endless litigation between the two leaders "has been a matter of annoyance and disturbance to many others in the trade." The journal sardonically labeled a recent truce the "Treaty of Springfield."

Although many in the trade resented Pope's continued clout, the industry itself appeared stronger than ever. The Ordinary still commanded the public's interest as a racing machine, as the ongoing success of the annual Springfield meet attested. Meanwhile, several high-profile tourists added to the mystique of the machine. One was Lyman Hotchkiss Bagg, a Yale graduate who began a two-year cross-country odyssey in the

Poster for the Overman Wheel Company of Chicopee Falls, Massachusetts, from about 1896. The company introduced the first American-made tricycle of the high-wheel era, known as the Victor, in 1883, and became a leading cycle producer during the great boom of the 1890s.

spring of 1884, which he detailed in his tome *Ten Thousand Miles on a Bicycle*. That same year, Thomas Stevens, a transplanted Englishman, rode his Columbia from San Francisco to New York. He then set sail for Europe, and for the next two and a half years he continued to pedal around the globe. He wrote periodic reports for *Outing Magazine,* his principal sponsor, later compiled in a book, *Around the World on a Bicycle*.

One of the many affluent males who continued to relish riding a high mount was the popular humorist Mark Twain. In an essay titled "Taming the Bicycle," he made light of his epic struggle to master the imposing beast.

> In place of [an instructor], I had some other support. This was a boy, who was perched on a gate-post, munching a hunk of maple sugar. He was full of interest and comment. The first time I failed and went down he said that if he was me he would dress up in pillows, that's what he would do. The next time I went down he advised me to go and learn to ride a tricycle first. The third time I collapsed he said he didn't believe I could stay on a horse-car. But next time I

THE
BOYS of NEW YORK
A PAPER FOR YOUNG AMERICANS

Vol. XII.   FRANK TOUSEY, Nos. 34 and 36 North Moore St.   NEW YORK, MARCH 5, 1887. $2.50 PER ANNUM, IN ADVANCE. $1.25 FOR SIX MONTHS.   No. 603

A cry of horror emanated from Ned's lips as he saw the locomotive dash into view and come rushing down upon him. But he did not pause an instant. His bicycle seemed to suddenly shoot forward along the single plank as though impelled by the impetus of a catapult.

AROUND
THE WORLD ON A BICYCLE.

A Story of Adventures in Many Lands.

By R. T. EMMET.

In the spring of 1887, the *Boys of New York* serialized the fictional adventures of a young man as he circled the globe on his high bicycle, a fanciful story no doubt inspired by Thomas Stevens's recently completed jaunt around the world

succeeded, and got clumsily under way in a weaving, tottering, uncertain fashion, and occupying pretty much all of the street. . . . A little girl passed by, balancing a wash-board on her head, giggled, and seemed about to make a remark, but the boy said, rebukingly, "Let him alone. He's going to a funeral."

Many of those who managed to tame the machine joined one of the many bicycle clubs across the country. Although some of these clubs admitted tricyclists, most still enjoyed a healthy patronage catering to high-wheel riders. In the spring of 1885, the Massachusetts Bicycle Club opened an elegant three-story clubhouse on Newbury Street, in Boston's newly created landfill known as the Back Bay. The ornate facade featured a roomy bay window protruding from the second story and a slab at the top announcing the name of the club. A ramp led from the sidewalk to the imposing front door, which was "wide enough to admit a Sociable tricycle."

The interior was even more lavish. Wheelmen returning from a ride entered into the spacious wheel room, where they could wash and store their bicycles. After proceeding up the central staircase to the second floor, riders could clean themselves off in the locker room. At last, they entered the parlor to enjoy a cigar or a drink while fraternizing with their fellow members. The room was finished in cherry with floors of polished oak. It featured a large rug and grand fireplace for a cozy "homelike appearance." The furniture included a piano, a mahogany table, and russet-colored leather chairs. The central chandelier sported gilded bicycle wheels with hubs of colored stone. On the walls hung numerous images of bicyclists. The adjacent "ladies' parlor" featured a library, devoted mainly to cycling. The third floor included a gymnasium and meeting room. The basement housed a furnace, bowling alley, and tables for billiards and pool.

In the winter of 1885, the club staged a "bicycle carnival" at the Mechanics' Fair Building in Boston. Billed as "the first public indoor cycling entertainment," the affair attracted some three thousand enthusiasts. At eight in the morning, as a band played, a hundred cyclists paraded into the building dressed as devils, counts, revolutionary soldiers, and even Santa Claus. Following the award ceremony for best costumes, a "bicycle drill squad" and a trick rider wowed the assembly. At nine, Pierre Lallement himself, now a Pope employee, appeared on his original 1865 velocipede. The champion William A. Rowe, meanwhile, rode the latest Columbia racer, on which he had recently eclipsed twenty miles in one hour. The crowd greeted this dramatic display of progress, spanning twenty years, with thunderous applause. The balance of the program included an obstacle race and a polo game on Star bicycles, followed by a sit-down lunch and a dance.

Few who witnessed this extravaganza could have imagined that the beloved high wheeler was about to make a hasty exit from the scene. True, certain safety models such

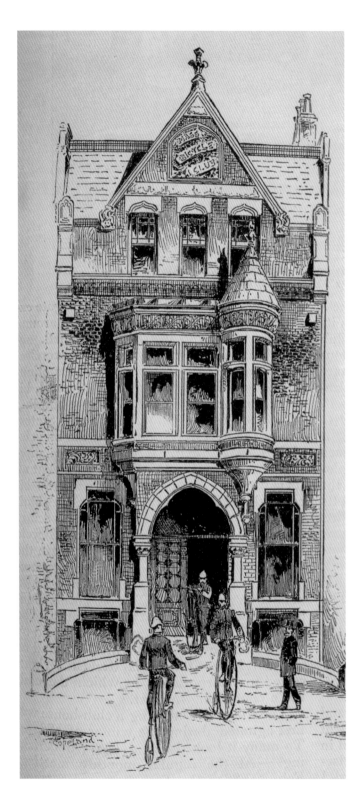

The Massachusetts Bicycle Club on Boston's fashionable Newbury Street, from *Outing Magazine* of March 1885. The well-connected club was closely associated with the Pope organization.

as the Facile and the Kangaroo had already attained a measure of technical and commercial success, but the venerable Ordinary seemed destined to withstand the effrontery. Nevertheless, the club's very programs that day contained a subtle omen of what was in store: a small advertisement announcing the arrival of the first Rover safety bicycles from England. In spite of its high price and complicated appearance, this diminutive upstart would soon accomplish what no alternative bicycle had done: entirely supplant the high wheeler.

The Kangaroo, despite its limited commercial success, had underscored a key technical point: a chain drive could indeed make for a practical safety bicycle. That revelation prompted several British makers to revisit yet again the seductive idea of a low-mount bicycle with a chain drive powering the rear wheel. From 1884 to 1885, a number of safety bicycles along these lines appeared at the Stanley Show, notably the Marvel, the Pioneer Safety, the Antelope, the BSA, and the Humber Safety. But unlike the Bicyclette displayed a few years earlier, these models all featured a small front wheel, less than thirty inches in diameter, connected to a long, sloping fork. This arrangement, already adopted by the American Star, allowed for direct steering by a handlebar placed within easy reach of the rider, eliminating the need to use rods to connect the steering handles to the steering column. But the small front wheel made for a harsh ride and none of these designs caught on.

At the 1885 Stanley Show, however, one safety bicycle stood out: the Rover. Its front wheel measured a full thirty-six inches, and its rear wheel, six inches smaller in diameter, was geared up to fifty inches by means of a chain and sprocket. Its low-mount frame was composed of curved tubes, and the entire bicycle weighed forty-five pounds. Priced at twenty-two pounds, it cost more than an Ordinary but less than a typical tricycle. Its creator, John Kemp Starley, was a nephew of the late James Starley. He later explained that he based his model on a tricycle he had built the previous year; his goal was to set the rider in "the right position in relation to the pedals" and "the proper distance from the ground." To accommodate individual physiques, he made the seat adjustable; it could be raised, lowered, and slid backward and forward. Starley also provided adjustable handlebars with ends that turned back toward the rear so the rider "could exert the greatest force upon the pedals with the least amount of fatigue." Finally, he used a chain and sprocket to power the rear wheel so that "gearing could be varied as desired," according to the size of the sprocket.

facing page: Pierre Lallement on a high wheeler in 1886, when he was working as a mechanic at Pope's office in Boston. A cycling journal reported that "the original inventor is circulating among his friends photographs of himself and his original velocipede, with another view showing him on his new Expert Columbia."

The Humber Safety Bicycle of 1884, introduced at about the same time as the Rover. It was one of the first frames to abandon a single-tube backbone in favor of the stiffer and more compact diamond pattern. A step was fitted just below the rear hub on the side opposite the chain to enable the rider to get a running start before stepping up into the saddle. Footrests were included at the base of the steering column, near the coil-spring suspension system.

Although many traditionalists found the Rover's low profile undignified, it actually gave the machine a significant advantage over the high mount. Thanks to its lower, more aerodynamic form, the Rover was fundamentally faster despite its greater weight. Curiously, reducing air resistance does not appear to have been one of Starley's primary objectives. Yet at least one contemporary astutely recognized that wind provides the greatest impediment to bicycle riding, and that "little machines" such as the Rover offer "practically no resistance." Some riders even claimed yet another advantage for the Rover. Front-drive low mounts like the Kangaroo were supposedly prone to lurching to the side on slippery roads when the cyclist thrust downward on the pedals. The rear-drive Rover purportedly alleviated that problem by achieving a better distribution of weight.

Still, many who saw the original Rover on display at the Stanley Show came away unconvinced of its technical merits. The curious-looking machine was not only significantly heavier than an Ordinary, it was decidedly more complicated in appearance. In particular, it suffered from a glaring flaw. Like the old Bicyclette it resembled, it used a complicated indirect steering mechanism terminating at the center of the top tube.

THE ROVER SAFETY
BICYCLE (PATENTED).

Safer than any Tricycle, faster and easier than any Bicycle ever made. Fitted with handles to turn for convenience in storing or shipping. Far and away the best hill-climber in the market.

MANUFACTURED BY

STARLEY & SUTTON,
METEOR WORKS, WEST ORCHARD, COVENTRY, ENGLAND.

An advertisement for the original Rover in *The Graphic*, March 1885, showing the indirect steering mechanism at the center of the top tube, soon to be replaced with handlebars attached directly to a raked front fork

Caught Off Guard

THE "NEW WOMAN."

The captains of the international bicycle industry evidently failed to anticipate the extraordinary appeal of the Rover-style bicycle. For years, British cycle makers ignored Lawson's Bicyclette, and the American trade was even slower to adopt the chain-driven low mount. Even Starley himself, it appears, did not anticipate that the Rover would "set the fashion to the world," as his advertisements later boasted. In several articles and interviews during and after the boom, Starley affirmed his initial faith in his design and his confidence that it would eventually supplant all others. He also expressed great satisfaction that his firm was the first to ship Rovers around the world. But he did not actually claim

Caricature from *Puck*, 19 June 1895. The "New Woman's" passion for the safety bicycle surprised the bicycle industry and helped trigger the great boom of the 1890s.

to have foreseen its enormous appeal among people of all social and economic classes. That, evidently, was a happy surprise.

Some historians have suggested nonetheless that the British bicycle industry made a deliberate decision in the mid-1880s to throw open the doors of the cycling kingdom to admit a wider public. Certainly, manufacturers were eager to develop safer bicycles with broader appeal, but they do not appear to have identified, let alone targeted, a vast potential market of lower-rung cyclists. On the contrary, the first makers of Rover-style bicycles were probably looking up, not down, the social ladder, at upscale tricyclists who longed to ride a sporty but safe vehicle. An affluent clientele would not have been put off by the Rover's high price —in fact, they may have found it reassuring, knowing that they would never be mistaken on that machine for one of the growing numbers of lower-class cyclists who were riding secondhand Ordinaries.

But why, then, were industry insiders so blind for such a long time to the vast potential market for Rover-style bicycles? For one thing, no one could have foreseen the timely introduction of the pneumatic tire, which largely eliminated technical objections to the low mount. Starley himself was intrigued when he first heard of inflatable tires, but questioned whether they would prove practical. Second, few could have imagined that the Rover could ever be produced at a widely affordable price. After all, nearly a decade after its introduction, the much simpler Ordinary still fetched a sizable sum. But perhaps the industry's greatest oversight was its failure to anticipate that the low-mount bicycle would greatly appeal to women of all classes.

Moreover, many observers assumed that its long chain would prove intolerably ineffi-cient, as friction dissipated the rider's pedaling power.

But at least one French reviewer, who tested a specimen a few months after the Stan-ley Show closed, was full of enthusiasm. He found the Rover "easy to steer, absolutely safe, and very easy going, even on cobblestone." He cruised almost effortlessly at eleven or twelve miles an hour, a speed "hardly inferior to the ordinary bicycle." Ascents pre-sented no more than the usual challenge, yet he could descend "without any danger, even at a great speed." In his view, the Rover was the "desideratum" of tricyclists who had spurned the bicycle. On a Rover, they can "go full speed ahead, even at night or in tight spots, because, with only one track, [the Rover] can pass virtually anywhere. More-over, its center of gravity, being at the rear wheel, precludes it from tipping forward, even after the strongest of jolts." The Rover, declared the writer, "is the only 'Safety,' up to this point, that has any chance of dethroning the ordinary bicycle."

The Rover was not quite ready for that Herculean task, however. As Henry Sturmey of *The Cyclist* observed, its "long frame and connecting bars gave it a heavy and compli-cated appearance, which militated against its commercial success." Although the origi-nal model "went easily enough," its steering "was neither firm nor direct." Fortunately, Steven Golder, Sturmey's editorial assistant, had a solution. He had recently ridden Lawson's latest creation, which likewise employed a chain drive. He found that particu-lar frame—essentially a single curved tube—overly flexible, but he liked the machine's direct steering, made possible by a "slightly sloping fork" that brought the handlebars within reach of the rider. Golder urged Starley to adapt a similar steering system to his Rover and, after some experimentation, Starley complied.

The revamped Rover proved a great success. In September 1885, George Smith rode one a hundred miles in the record time of seven hours and five minutes, six minutes faster than the mark he had set the year before riding a Kangaroo. The next year, Starley further modified the Rover, giving it two wheels of equal size, each thirty inches in di-ameter. The new profile was now eerily reminiscent of the old boneshaker, an irony that did not escape some astute observers. But British makers were nonetheless satisfied that the design was now practical and marketable, and they began to shift production in favor of the new-style bicycle.

Americans, too, began to give the Rover a closer look. *The Cycle* of Boston reported: "The new Rover looks like a better machine than the earlier ones. The frame appears more rigid and decidedly stronger [and] also lighter, and it seems a trifle less sensitive. If it will stand the strain of steady work, it ought to become popular." Indeed, a speci-men exhibited at a League of American Wheelmen meeting on Martha's Vineyard in the summer of 1886 stirred considerable interest. "I was greatly impressed and gave the

'Safety' a good tryout," recalled George Bidwell, the former Pope showman who now ran his own shop in New York, "and the more I rode the wheel, the more I liked it."

The leading American manufacturers nonetheless quickly dismissed any talk that the upstart Rover would ever displace the venerable Ordinary. After touring English cycle factories in the summer of 1886, where Rover-style safeties now abounded, a defiant Pope declared: "One thing I am now satisfied, and that is we in this country have nothing to learn from the Englishmen as to how to build a bicycle." As Bidwell recalled, "Colonel Pope and the rest of the Pope Company turned thumbs down [on the Rover]." Overman likewise "refused to see any chance" that the Rover would prove "anything more than a passing fancy." Bidwell told Pope himself "that he was wrong in his opinion of the thing," but the colonel "only looked at me in a patronizing way as much to say: 'Poor boy, it is too bad you haven't had the experience of us older men.'" As far as the Pope leadership was concerned, such naive "youngsters" as Bidwell were "carried away by every new toy that comes along."

In Britain, however, Rover-style bicycles were already giving the trade an enormous boost, attracting scores of new recruits from both sexes. London's *Daily News* marveled at how far the English cycling business had come in just a few years. "Most of us who can look back twenty years can remember the first bicyclist wobble by on his precarious-looking perch. Practically within fifteen years a new industry has sprung up, affording occupation, it is now computed, for not much less than 50,000 people in one way or another. It is believed that there are now not less than half a million bicycles and tricycles in the United Kingdom, and there are somewhere about two hundred manufacturers of them."

As the newspaper's account suggests, the bicycle business was no longer a cozy, shop-based trade catering exclusively to wealthy young men. Rather, it had developed into an impersonal international industry with bustling factories serving the demands of a broader population that looked toward the bicycle not only for recreation but also for utility. A nostalgic Joseph Pennell could only reminisce about the early 1880s when the master Thomas Humber personally patrolled his works, eager to "build a bicycle to suit you." From the public's perspective, however, the transformation was welcome progress. At last, the bicycle was beginning to fulfill its original promise as the "people's nag."

In Britain, Rover-style bicycles continued to prove their advantages in competitions against Ordinaries, erasing any lingering doubts about their technical superiority. Yet even as the high mount was rapidly becoming obsolete in the land that gave rise to it, the leaders of the American trade continued to buck the Rover trend. At the onset of the 1887 season, all the principal American makers were still committed to the Ordi-

Trade card issued by the Pope Manufacturing Company for Valentine's Day, 1885, showing cycling during three different times of the day. The firm initially dismissed the Rover bicycle as a passing fad and continued to stress the romantic qualities of the high wheeler.

Silver trophy awarded to
George Hendee for winning
a high-wheel competition in
1886, by which time the British
trade was already shifting to
Rover-style safeties

nary as their principal product. None of them, in fact, had yet introduced a Rover-style bicycle of their own.

Bidwell nevertheless remained partial to the Rover he had seen the previous summer. After he returned to New York, he "never ordered another high wheel." Instead, he made arrangements with the Rudge Company of Coventry to import its Rover-style safety, a revamped Bicyclette, for the 1887 season. Thanks to the "shortsightedness" of others in the trade, Bidwell reaped an enormous profit that year when he single-handedly supplied the entire New York market with his highly coveted safeties. In Boston, the agents for the Rover and the Bicyclette likewise enjoyed a bonanza. American makers finally began to awaken to the demand. Before the season closed, the Overman Wheel Company rushed out a Rover-style safety. The following year, many more firms followed suit. Even Pope finally relented, unveiling his first low-mount safety, the Veloce Columbia.

Many in the American trade nevertheless viewed the new safety bicycle with deep suspicion. Some thought that demand for the Rover, like the initial burst of interest in tricycles some years before, would eventually level off once its novelty wore thin, establishing a modest niche to complement the main markets for the Ordinary and the tricycle. The safety bicycle might attract a few newcomers to the sport, they reasoned, and even prod aging high-wheel riders to switch mounts. But at a standard price of $150, about $50 more than an Ordinary, prospective buyers would surely think twice before choosing a Rover-style safety.

Yet a surprisingly strong demand quickly emerged from a most unexpected source: society women. Increasingly, they ditched their trusty tricycles in favor of the sleeker low-mount bicycle. Explained one female contemporary, "A sudden desire awoke in the feminine mind to ascertain for itself, by personal experience, those joys of the two-wheeler which they had so often heard vaunted as superior, a thousand times, to the more sober delights of the staid tricycle."

Mrs. Harriette H. Mills of Washington, D.C., formed the country's first women's bicycle club in the spring of 1888. It quickly attracted some fifty members, who wore "a close fitting waist, a plain loose skirt, walking length, riding hat and gloves." The pioneers rode the newly introduced Ladies' Dart Bicycle with a "drop" frame, made by the local Smith National Cycle Company. When that firm failed to keep pace with surging demand, newcomers adopted the Psycho ladies' bicycle imported from England. The club made regular excursions covering up to forty miles. That summer, several members rode in the League of American Wheelmen parade in Baltimore, the first time women appeared on bicycles at the annual meet.

The local press took due notice of the novel club. That fall, the *Washington Critic* confirmed that "some of the more venturesome" of the many female tricyclists in the area had been spotted on the new bicycles. Another journal counted as many as 150 defectors, nearly a third of the original tricycle contingent. And it soon became apparent that Washington was not unique. *Bicycling World* noted "frequent allusions to ladies' safeties in the various papers throughout the country." It predicted "the number of lady riders will be greater than most of us have anticipated." Indeed, the *American Athlete* confirmed in the spring of 1889, "cycling for ladies is rapidly gaining ground." By the end of that season, another writer observed that "ladies' bicycle clubs are being formed in many of the largest towns throughout the United States." Nor were female bicyclists confining their jaunts to cautious circuits around the park. In June of 1890, three women completed a century run between Newark and Philadelphia, outdistancing many of the male participants.

One by one, makers added women's models to their catalogs, even as a fierce national debate brewed over the propriety of women cycling. Indeed, the prospect of the

New Woman on wheels did not pass without controversy. Some social guardians insisted that bicycling was physically and morally harmful to women. One prominent minister, Rev. A. Cleveland Coxe of western New York, even likened the female cyclist to "an old woman on a broomstick." But others disagreed. "It is refreshing to see the independent young creature scorn other people's 'thinks,'" declared one cycling advocate, "and strike out for health and happiness on this machine." And as more women took to the wheel, attitudes began to change. One female bicyclist happily reported in 1891 that her riding no longer drew "remarks calculated to disturb the equilibrium" but rather "smiles and admiring comments."

Many in the cycling community even began to ask the unthinkable: would the safety bicycle totally supplant the high wheeler? "The English papers, during the past few months," *Bicycling Word* reported in 1889, "have been filled with bitter discussion as to the relative merits of the ordinary and the rear-driving safety. It all started in a very gentle manner by a champion of the safety type assuring us that the ordinary was doomed, that it would soon be relegated to the place where all obsolete machines go, and that the machine of the future was the new safety." For its part, *Bicycling World* con-

The Pickwick Club on an expedition in France that included a tandem tricycle, several hard-tired safeties, and a number of Ordinaries, from *The Graphic* of 15 September 1888. At the time it was unclear which models would ultimately prevail in the marketplace.

ceded that the high mount would no longer "hold indisputable sway, as *the* only machine." But it also insisted that the new design had a limited appeal. "The element of safety is rather distasteful to a good many riders that prefer to run some risk, as it gives zest to the sport." Its conclusion: "The ordinary has a future, and will never be an obsolete pattern; it has far too many splendid qualities for that."

Nevertheless, several timely improvements to the safety bicycle removed its weak point—its harsh ride—and finally sealed the fate of the old Ordinary. The first was the development of the rigid and linear diamond-shaped frame, which endures to this day as the basic bicycle design. At first, makers explored ways to make the safety frame more flexible without compromising its strength. The Rover's original curved tubes soon gave way to straight ones, but bicycle designers still struggled to find an optimal arrangement. One early favorite was the "cross frame," featuring a long diagonal main tube descending from the steering column to the rear hub. By 1890, however, most builders settled on the sturdier diamond pattern. Yet many designers still felt compelled to add various anti-vibration devices. The Overman Wheel Company, for one, offered an elaborate fork spring. In England, the popular Whippet incorporated a series of external springs suspending the entire frame.

The second key innovation, a true breakthrough that rendered sprung frames superfluous, was the pneumatic tire. As the jittery low mount gained favor in the late 1880s, makers began to consider more forgiving tires as a means to deaden vibration at the rims. The Overman Wheel Company introduced the popular "cushion tire" with a hollow core, but a Scottish veterinarian living in Belfast soon trumped that idea. Tinkering with his ten-year-old son's tricycle in 1888, John Dunlop discovered that a tire with an inner-tube filled with compressed air not only cushioned the ride, it also increased speed by about a third. The following year, an unheralded racer adopted the new tire and won several contests in Belfast. Impressed with the product, Harvey Du Cros, an Irish financier, persuaded Dunlop to sell him marketing rights. Together they launched the Pneumatic Tyre Company to supply inflatable tires to the entire British cycle trade.

Skeptics at the 1890 Stanley Show ridiculed the first pneumatic tires, calling them "steamrollers." Others dismissed the tire as puncture-prone. The company responded by vulcanizing a "stout canvas" to the inside of the outer case, while making the inner tube "stronger and thicker." In the course of that year, British and Irish racers on safety bicycles proved the merit of the inflatable tire. T. A. Edge rode a century in only five hours and twenty-seven minutes, smashing all existing records. W. C. Jones lowered the longstanding mile record by nearly ten seconds, to 2:20. The Irish crack racer R. J. Mecredy, editor of the *Irish Cyclist* and a partner in the Dunlop affair, ran away with four safety championships, topping all existing records. In his view, the inflatable tire

The Whippet bicycle's variety of springs helped absorb the increased road shock resulting from the use of smaller wheels. It was designed to keep the body stationary relative to the pedals and handlebars while the rest of the frame offered considerable give over rocky terrain. The arrival of the pneumatic tire shortly afterward largely did away with such elaborate anti-vibration frames.

was "undoubtedly the tyre of the future, [throwing] a vast field open which the makers of the present day can hardly realize."

Although the pneumatic tire was as yet too costly and too impractical for general use, it promised well for the future of the new safety bicycle. Meanwhile, demand for the hard-tired variety continued to swell. By the end of the 1890 season, Britain was home to about half a million bicyclists. Germany followed with about two hundred thousand, and France had roughly half that number. Italy, too, was rapidly emerging as a leading bicycle nation, as were Belgium, Denmark, and the Netherlands. In fact, the Rover bicycle was quickly making its way around the world, stirring far more popular interest than the Ordinary ever had.

The Memorial Controversy

In 1891, on the cusp of the great boom, German cyclists proudly proclaimed Drais the father of the bicycle. With great fanfare, they reburied the forgotten baron forty years after his death. Indignant French cyclists demanded a memorial of their own to honor Pierre Michaux. Since the early 1880s, the French cycling literature maintained that the blacksmith had conceived the true bicycle in 1855, building a few specimens here and there over the next dozen years before the public finally took note. Henry Michaux, a surviving son, promptly gave his blessings to the project as he busily prepared to revive the Michaux cycle brand. Aimé Olivier, back in his homeland after a long sojourn in Africa, likewise took a keen interest in the affair. Here at last was an opportunity to gain recognition, if not for himself, at least for his beloved brother René, who had died in a carriage accident. The two parties, however, offered conflicting accounts about the original bicycle company, sparking a heated controversy that eventually reshaped prevailing bicycle history.

For his part, Aimé insisted that the application of the pedal was a trivial contribution and that the true glory belonged to René and himself for having introduced a functional bicycle under the Michaux name. But Henry would have none of that. Dispelling the notion of a slow start to the bicycle affair, he declared that his father not only applied pedals to the two-wheeler, he also made more than a thousand bicycles on his own before 1867, effectively denying the Oliviers any credit for early development. As far as the French press was concerned, Henry was evidently the authority. In the spring of 1893, a committee of journalists made plans to place a bust of the lamented blacksmith in his native city of Bar-le-Duc, about 140 miles east of Paris.

The project appeared to be heading for a swift conclusion, when Aimé suddenly went on the offensive. He planted several sensational articles in the Parisian press asserting that Michaux's deceased son Ernest, not the blacksmith, had conceived the pedal. Moreover, he alleged that the elder Michaux was feeble-minded, had never in fact ridden a bicycle, and had even tried to steer his gifted son away from the two-wheeler. Caught off guard, Henry countered that his brother "had nothing to do with the invention." But the cycling press spearheading the memorial project began to debate which Michaux—father or son—deserved the credit for the bicycle invention. Cracked one irreverent wit: "It's a pity there wasn't a little 'holy spirit' in the family."

But the mayor of Bar-le-Duc was not amused. He summoned Henry Michaux to his office and demanded a clarification. Put on the defensive, Henry suddenly recalled that his brother Ernest had indeed affixed pedals to a broken draisine, but he was only following his father's instructions. Moreover, he added, the year of discovery was 1861, not 1855 as previously reported. Henry in fact distinctly remembered the events of that fruitful day in March, when he was seven years of age. Henry's new account satisfied the mayor and the steering committee, which promptly scrapped the proposed bust of the blacksmith in favor of a joint memorial that would recognize both Pierre and Ernest Michaux as the original inventors and developers of the bicycle. Much to Aimé's disappointment, the Michaux memorial was dedicated in the fall of 1894.

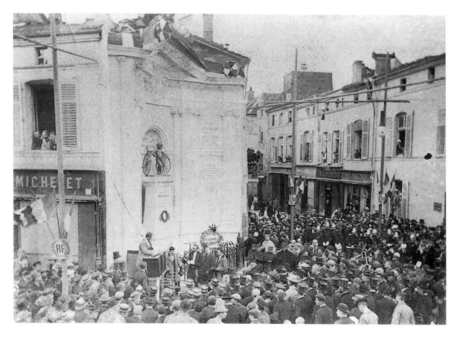

Dedication of the monument to Pierre and Ernest Michaux in Bar-le-Duc, September 1894. Several surviving sons of Pierre Michaux attended the festivities, which lasted for several days and included the finish of a bicycle race from Paris.

The growth of the American trade was especially pronounced. Between the start of the Rover era in 1887 and the beginnings of the boom three years later, the number of firms making or importing bicycles rose from barely a dozen to about seventy-five. Pope, although slow to accept the safety bicycle, was vigorously expanding his work-force and production capacity by 1890. He bought out the Weed Sewing Machine Company and dedicated it exclusively to production of safety bicycles. He also launched the Hartford Cycle Company to market a more economical line of safeties that would not compromise the Columbia name or price. Meanwhile, in the same three-year pe-riod, the number of cyclists doubled, reaching 150,000 nationally. The vast majority of new purchasers, many of whom were female, favored the new-style safety bicycle.

By 1890, the excitement surrounding the safety had reached new heights. "It is the cleanest, most strengthening and healthful sport ever invented," declared one American enthusiast. "Men women and children alike can and do enjoy it. It is not expensive when compared with boating, gunning or even fishing." In France, where the safety be-came known as the bicyclette, the journalist Pierre Giffard dubbed it the "little queen," and declared that bicycling was now more than a sport, it was a social benefactor. Two recent graduates of Washington University in Saint Louis, Thomas G. Allen, Jr., and William Sachtleben, gamely set off on what would be the first transworld journey atop new-style bicycles. Even the competitive sport was preparing to make the switch. In late 1890, the English amateur champion, F. J. Osmond, made the startling announcement that he would ride a safety the following season.

As the 1890s dawned, there was obviously a new king of the road, and that machine was the Rover-style safety. At last, the bicycle was on the verge of fulfilling the original promise of a practical and efficient machine that any able-bodied person could manage. As one observer put it, the new bicycle was rapidly shaping up to be not only the "rich man's recreation" but also the long coveted "poor man's horse," a role it would in-evitably fill once its elevated price declined. But few could have anticipated just how profound and pervasive its influence would become. Unbeknownst even to industry in-siders, a great boom was about to explode.

ELEVEN *The Bicycle Boom*

In the early 1890s, the Rover-style bicycle overtook all other cycles on the road. Earlier safety designs, including the once popular Kangaroo, quickly faded away. A new wave of alternative cycles followed in their wake, but by the spring of 1891 a London journal could already detect the unmistakable trend. "The safety is becoming more popular every day," it reported, "and is displacing both the Ordinary and the tricycle." The international cycle industry greatly expanded in both size and output, focusing almost exclusively on Rover-style safeties. In the course of 1891, Americans alone purchased a staggering 150,000 bicycles, effectively doubling the country's cycling population. As the low mount rapidly improved, and as more men and women around the world began to appreciate its vast and varied possibilities, a veritable boom exploded.

Some bicycle makers nonetheless resisted the chain drive at first, giving one last push to establish an alternative bicycle of their own. Several British firms proposed "rational" Ordinaries said to guard against headers by virtue of their raked front forks and larger rear wheels. The Crypto-Bantam revived the idea of a front-drive bicycle with a speed-gear hub enabling the wheel to make nearly three revolutions for every turn of the pedals. The American Eagle borrowed the Star pattern but used rotary cranks rather than levers. But none of these proposals succeeded in mounting a serious challenge. The Rover, as its advertisements boasted, had truly "set the fashion to the world."

A key factor driving demand for Rover-style safeties was the pneumatic tire. Racers had already shown its merit by 1890, and in principle it was ideally suited for the Rover's two small wheels of equal size. But the first specimens, single units that incorporated the tire and inner tube, were expensive, prone to leak or burst, and had to be glued in place and repaired by a specialist. That changed in 1891, when Edouard Michelin of Clermont-Ferrand in France introduced a detachable tire. The outer casing was affixed to the wheel by means of a series of clamps bolted below the rim. This eliminated the need for glue and, most important, in the event of a puncture the cyclist could now repair or replace the independent inner tube with the help of a few simple tools and spare materials.

Race results helped confirm the practicality of the detachable pneumatic tire. The veteran Charles Terront overcame five flats while winning the grueling race from Paris to Brest and back in 1891. The following year, the Michelin company organized a race from Paris to its headquarters in Clermont-Ferrand, a distance of 260 miles. Operatives sprinkled nails along the course so that the public could observe firsthand how easily mechanics mended the inevitable flats. Tire technology developed quickly, leading to the now-familiar clincher tire. The outer casing featured a wire bead that "clinched" into the lips inside of the rim, eliminating the need for any hardware to hold the tire in place. At the same time, manufacturers also developed more practical single-unit pneumatic tires that, though harder to repair, were easily replaced.

As the pneumatic-tire safety gained popularity, the sport generated unprecedented popular interest. In the United States, tracks proliferated and soon hosted hundreds of amateur and professional races. College cycling clubs, once confined to a handful of Ivy League schools, were now commonplace. Safety riders also gradually took over road races founded in the late 1880s for high-wheel competitors, notably the annual twenty-five-mile run in New Jersey between Irvington and Millburn and the similar Pullman race in Chicago. Other American cities, particularly Boston, St. Louis, and Cincinnati, soon established annual road races for safety riders. The new sport gave rise to celebrity cyclists, such as Arthur A. Zimmerman of New Jersey, a former Star racer. By 1894, he reportedly made a staggering forty thousand dollars a year while touring the United States and Europe.

The low-mount pneumatic-tire safety even proved itself the fastest cycle on the road, effectively turning the vaunted old Ordinary into a ridiculed relic. By the end of 1893, track racers on the new-style safeties surpassed twenty-five miles an hour. Meanwhile,

facing page: The Michelin company's famous mascot, the tire man, known as Bibendum in France, was introduced in 1898 to promote its clincher bicycle tire featuring a detachable inner tube for easier repairs and an installation free of glue or attaching hardware. By the time this poster was issued in 1910 the company was focusing on automobile tires.

for the first time, the mile record from a standing start dipped below two minutes. At last, the bicycle had eclipsed the best performance by a trotting horse, proving that the mechanical variety was now the faster of the two even over short hauls. "Only two or three years ago," marveled the *National Magazine,* "it seemed impossible for the crack wheelmen to approach the trotting records."

But the safety was even more impressive over long distances. As early as 1891, at London's Herne Hill velodrome, A. Holbein set a twenty-four-hour track record, covering 326 miles. Yet three years later at the same venue, Frank Shorland topped that mark by a full hundred miles, underscoring the rapid improvement in safety construction. The safety also enabled six-day racers to set new marks. Starting in 1891, New York's newly constructed Madison Square Garden hosted these popular spectacles, offering up to two thousand dollars in prizes. At first, racers rode Ordinaries, but within two years they had all switched to safeties. In 1893, Albert Schock, who had set an American record of 1,400 miles on an Ordinary seven years before, surpassed that mark by 200 miles.

In France, safety racing in velodromes also became popular, but the new bicycle figured most prominently as a road racer. Organizers were particularly keen to demonstrate just how far and fast sleep-deprived racers could travel with the help of "pacemakers," allied cyclists in for the short haul to break the wind and push their man on. In May of 1891, the *Vélo-Club* of Bordeaux held the inaugural safety road race from that city to Paris, a distance of 360 miles. Of the thirty-eight starters, the Englishman George Pilkington Mills prevailed in twenty-six and a half hours. That fall, *Le Petit Journal* of Paris sponsored the even more arduous Paris–Brest–Paris race—the marathon that established the Michelin clincher tire. The veteran Terront beat out a field of two hundred, covering 750 miles in three days. Other city-to-city races soon followed, and many became long-established traditions. Indeed, the road race proved a powerful promotional tool not only for the bicycle itself but also for race sponsors.

A French caricature poking fun at the instability of the high mount, from *La Bicyclette,* 18 March 1897. Although it had only recently been abandoned, the high wheeler evoked much irreverence during the boom.

Frank Lenz in China, during his ill-fated quest to circle the globe on a bicycle. He took the photograph himself using an extended cable trigger of his own design, and it appeared in the *Pall Mall Budget* of 1 June 1893. Lenz was among the first to bring a safety bicycle to China, a country that today has nearly half a billion bicycles.

The safety bicycle likewise supplanted the high mount for touring purposes, as several high-profile adventurers underscored. In the summer of 1893, three years after setting forth from Saint Louis, Thomas G. Allen, Jr., and William Sachtleben successfully completed their celebrated world tour. Along the way they called on the prime minister of China, who wondered why anyone would want to travel under his own power if he could rely on someone else's. In the meantime, Frank Lenz, a young man from Pittsburgh, set off on his Victor safety for a solo trip around the world, carrying a camera in a knapsack strapped to his back. Like Thomas Stevens a few years before, Lenz secured support from *Outing Magazine,* which published his periodic progress reports. Although the Lenz story ended tragically when he disappeared in Armenia two years into his journey, the apparent victim of an assault, he nonetheless opened the public's mind to the romance of touring atop the new safety bicycle.

One who needed no such enlightenment was Frank A. Elwell, of Portland, Maine. In the mid-1880s he had organized several high-wheel tours in Maine and Quebec for parties of about thirty. In 1889, he led the first of his many European cycle tours, through

The Memorial That Wasn't

In the spring of 1894, as the proposal for a Michaux memorial languished, Aimé Olivier vied for a monument of his own. He appealed to his former classmates at the Ecole Centrale to support an alternative memorial that would recognize his brother and himself as the true industrial pioneers who had introduced the original bicycle. At Aimé's thirtieth-reunion banquet, a sympathizer arose to toast his fellow alumnus, amidst wild cheers: "To comrade Olivier, the true creator of the useful and practical velocipede. To him is due our grateful recognition for the innumerable interests that the bicycle movement serves every day in our modern life. To Olivier, who by his powerful initiative and his generous character has honored the science of engineering while giving French industry yet another triumph."

But Aimé knew that he could not prevail in the arena of public opinion without first discrediting his nemesis, Henry Michaux, who still denied the Oliviers any substantial role in early bicycle development. Aimé in fact possessed the company books to prove that he and his brother had founded and directed the original bicycle operation. But he also knew that if he were to destroy Henry's credibility and establish the Oliviers' role as developers, he would inevitably reopen the thorny question of the invention, which, after all, was the focus of the drive for a French memorial. Aimé wrestled with this dilemma in a letter he wrote to René's son Louis to explain his project.

Dear Louis,
I am going to try to have a statue built to honor your father as the inventor of the modern velocipede. . . . To achieve my goals, I will have to at-

tribute to your father all the merit [of the invention], without giving the slightest hint of a second thought. If anyone senses room for doubt, rivals will arise. And so will jealousies, under the pretext of fairness, of information that needs to be discussed to the effect that your father—so active, so intelligent, so likable—merely executed the ideas and plans that were brought to him, but was not in fact the inventor. These objections will jeopardize my negotiations with public opinion. . . . I urge you to maintain the utmost discretion, until all negotiations are far enough along that they cannot be stopped. If any outsiders talk to you about all this, respond vaguely, as if you were on the moon. Say only that in your family we all recognize that your father richly deserves a statue, as would many others, had their work been sufficiently useful to merit this honor.

The identities of these "rivals" are unclear. Certainly, Aimé may have been concerned about Georges de la Bouglise, who was evidently entitled to a healthy share of the credit as a developer. Aimé might also have had Lallement in mind as a possible claimant to the invention itself, perhaps not realizing that the patentee had died some years before in Boston. In any event, following Henry Michaux's revisions, which had largely satisfied the public, Aimé apparently concluded that pursuing his own monument might yield as much embarrassment as glory. He quietly abandoned his project and Henry's dubious account passed into the history books.

England and France, advising participants to use the new low mounts. The trips lasted several months, and all the arrangements were first-class, including the steamship passages. A London journal reported that Elwell had taken care of the "business arrangements and the route." His entourage of two dozen men, aged between sixteen and fifty, came "from all over the United States" and included "a parson, two doctors, a real live American politician, [and] several businessmen." They "all breakfast together, start when they please, cover the day's distance as they wish, and dine together in the evening. Lunch is arranged for at some convenient place on the way, and the men drop in and take it as they pass." In this manner, "friendships are formed, men pick out their fellow riders, and the country is seen most delightfully and independently." In 1892, Elwell added a Ladies Tour limited to twenty riders, with no male participants "unless accompanied by a lady."

The newfound practicality of the bicycle also suggested specialized uses ranging from postal to police work. One of the most promising markets was the military cycle. Although several armies had considered adopting high wheelers during the 1880s, these massive structures were obviously poorly suited for combat missions. But by the end of that decade the new low-profile safety was drawing second looks. In 1890, one enthusiastic Russian lieutenant rode a sixty-pound hard-tire safety over two thousand miles from Saint Petersburg to London. He averaged about seventy miles a day, arriving in just over a month. As construction of the safety rapidly improved, various European armies began to seriously consider bicycle use, notably those of Britain, France, Germany, and Italy. Some even created bicycle regiments.

In the United States, Albert A. Pope led a vigorous campaign to induce the army to adopt safety bicycles. In the summer of 1891, to prove their practicality, he provided about forty Hartford cycles to the First Signal Corps of the Connecticut National Guard. The following year, the Corps adopted a cushion-tired Columbia with two special clamps on the top tube to hold a rifle. The soldier kept his ammunition and kit in a large leather pouch suspended under the seat. The Corps confirmed that bicycles could "bring reinforcements into the field quickly and silently" and convey messages when "signaling or other means of communications are impractical." Moreover, it found that the bicycle scout can "cover more ground in a day than a foot man could in three." While the army mulled over bicycle use, the prospects for vast military sales appeared solid.

Even more promising was the likelihood that average citizens would soon use bicycles for everyday errands. Conceivably, they could cycle from surrounding areas to the city center and, once there, to points of interest. Although electric trolleys were beginning to shuffle urbanites around at clips approaching fifteen miles an hour, they were often crowded and noisy, and required a fare. The silent bicycle, in contrast, could go

Two members of the Connecticut National Guard at pistol practice in 1892, with military bicycles produced by the Pope Manufacturing Company. In spite of Pope's promotional efforts, the military bicycle gained little circulation in the United States.

whenever and wherever the rider wanted, at no extra cost. Predicted one writer in 1892, "The effect [of bicycles] upon the development of cities will be nothing short of revolutionary." In particular, he asserted that bicycle use would reduce "the filth incessantly deposited in the city streets [by] animals." More important, the silent steed would all but eliminate "the exasperating noise and confusion of city life" and thus "the main source of nervousness that so universally afflicts city dwellers."

As the safety bicycle began to capture the public's imagination, Pope's company expanded rapidly. By 1891, the Hartford workforce had swelled to more than a thousand. Pope soon purchased and expanded the nearby Hartford Rubber Works to supply the entire trade with pneumatic tires. He also launched a new factory to produce "fine seamless steel tubing," formerly available only from Great Britain. Pope's elegant new headquarters in Boston featured a showroom on the first floor, beneath "one of the largest and best equipped offices in the country." About fifty employees worked behind a polished bank counter, including correspondents, bookkeepers, stenographers, mail and

advertising personnel, and a dozen officers who sat at rolltop desks. Along the perimeter were the legal department, the reception room, and Pope's posh private office. By the mere touch of an "electric keyboard," the president could instantly query "any man in the office." The third and fourth stories contained stockrooms and a repair shop, while the top floor featured "the most complete riding school in existence."

The new bicycle, widely celebrated as one of the great inventions of the age, figured prominently in the World's Columbian Exposition in Chicago. The opening ceremonies in the fall of 1892 featured military cadets from Toledo, Ohio, parading on bicycles. The following spring, to prove the superiority of the mechanical mount, several newspapers organized a bicycle relay race. The nation's supreme commander General Nelson A. Miles, a proponent of the military bicycle, consigned a message from the fairgrounds to be delivered to a subordinate in New York. Wheelmen rode segments of eight to thirty-five miles over poor roads and delivered the message within five days.

A few months later, the League of American Wheelmen, whose membership now numbered in the tens of thousands, held its eleventh annual meet in conjunction with the Columbian exhibition. The affair included the first world championships, which were dominated by Zimmerman. The grand Transportation Building at the Chicago exposition featured elaborate stands with scores of bicycles from leading American and European firms. The Pope Manufacturing Company mounted a historical exhibition as well, featuring Lallement's original 1865 bicycle, which Pope had obtained to bolster his patent claims when he first went into the bicycle business.

As the year 1893 drew to a close, the trade was poised for even more remarkable growth. In just three years makers had significantly improved the pneumatic-tire safety, reducing its typical weight from about fifty to thirty-five pounds. The public was now largely persuaded that the bicycle, if not quite perfected, had at least reached a compelling state of practicality. At the same time, it was also becoming more affordable. Pope reduced his base price from $150 to $125, while other makes sold for even less. At a time when the annual per capita income was about $1,000, however, the bicycle was still a costly proposition, but makers eased the burden by offering installment plans. Moreover, a large secondhand market was beginning to materialize as more affluent riders traded in their old machines for the latest models.

Demand for bicycles exploded in the United States in 1894, despite an economy plagued by a deepening depression and widespread labor unrest. By the following season, the weight of the typical bicycle had been reduced to only about twenty-seven

facing page: "The Spirit of the Wheel," one of the many images celebrating the bicycle's liberating qualities produced during the boom, from New York's *Truth,* 22 August 1896

pounds, earning the handle "featherweight." Meanwhile, Pope lowered his base price yet again by another twenty-five dollars, to $100. Makers also offered improved accessories, such as carbide lamps. Still, many speed-conscious riders preferred to travel with a minimum of gear to keep their mounts as light as possible. American cyclists generally preferred wooden rims over the steel variety to save weight, and some even adopted wooden handlebars for the same reason. Spoon brakes acting on the tire tread were available, but many cyclists went without them to avoid unnecessary weight. To stop, they simply pedaled backward to keep the cranks from spinning, braking the rear wheel.

Many now considered the pneumatic-tire safety bicycle a paragon of mechanical perfection. Few who had the means and inclination to buy one saw any cause to defer their purchase. Adding further incentive to buy, dealers now offered a great variety of models for men and women, including tandems of the sort celebrated in Harry C. Dacre's immensely popular ditty "Daisy Bell." In 1895 another million riders joined the bicycle movement from a broad cross-section of American society. Even as the automo-

"The Unrestrained Demon of the Wheel," from *The Judge*, 23 September 1893. Many citizens complained of the irresponsible "scorchers" who sped through city streets on their lightweight bicycles, alarming pedestrians and horses.

Racial Restrictions

During the boom, the bicycle was widely praised as a democratic vehicle. At the onset of the boom, in 1892, the League of American Wheelmen bravely declared that men of all races were eligible for membership, despite pressure from southerners to ban blacks, and "fierce opposition" in California to Chinese members. Satirical journals like *Puck, Judge,* and *Life,* however, regularly featured racially charged caricatures of cyclists, especially black ones. The champion Marshall "Major" Taylor was persecuted on the racing circuit on account of his race. But the greatest blow to black cyclists was no doubt the decision by the League of American Wheelmen in 1894 to bar blacks. For several years, the lawyer William W. Watts of Louisville, Kentucky, had been lobbying unsuccessfully for a color line, arguing that the increasing number of black members would stunt the growth of the organization in the South. When the annual convention came to his hometown, Watts at last prevailed despite strenuous objections from some northerners.

The League's action nonetheless drew widespread condemnation from members and nonmembers alike. Robert T. Teamoh, the only black member of the Massachusetts House of Representatives, implored his colleagues to censure the League for condoning "baseless and obsolete prejudice." But while the legislature was sympathetic to his arguments, it had no authority to rectify the injustice. The policy thus remained in force until the League itself disintegrated in the early part of the twentieth century.

bile age dawned, few could imagine anything but prolonged prosperity for the burgeoning bicycle trade, which appeared poised for indefinite growth, at least until the advent of a personal flying machine.

In the mid-1890s, as the author Stephen Crane put it, "Everything is bicycle." Hardware and department stores added bicycles to their inventories, and membership in the League of American Wheelmen shot past the one hundred thousand mark. Scores of repair shops dotted the country. Scrambling to meet the extraordinary demand for bicycles were some three hundred firms, including many already known for their arms and sewing machines. Scores more produced accessories from tires to toolkits. The competitive sport also thrived. From among thousands of participants, about a dozen top-notch professionals stood out, including Walter C. Sanger, E. C. Bald, and Tom Cooper. For the most part, they were sponsored by bicycle makers eager to gain publicity. Popular events such as the International Bicycle Tournament, held at Madison Square Garden in 1894, attracted top racers from the United States, Britain, France, Germany, and Italy.

Nor was bicycle use confined to sport and recreation. Although military demand was slow to develop, other specialized utilitarian markets were emerging. Some postal workers and deliverymen adopted bicycles, as did many municipal workers. New York City's commissioner of street cleaning provided the fifty or so foremen under his command with bicycles so they could conduct their inspections more regularly. Formerly, noted the commissioner, "every workman could feel reasonably sure that, when the foreman had once passed him, he had gotten rid of him for the day." Mounted on a bicycle, however, there was no telling when the dreaded foreman might pop back.

But perhaps the most important specialized use of the bicycle was for police work. In 1896, New York City assigned bicycles to five officers who patrolled Central Park. The experiment proved so successful that the squad was soon expanded, and other cities, including Chicago and Buffalo, followed suit. Theodore Roosevelt, then a New York police commissioner, recalled the "extraordinary proficiency" of the cyclist officers who reined in runaway horses and chased down speed demons known as "scorchers." One officer even managed to catch up with a carriage as it fled a crime scene. To the great surprise of its occupant, the policeman vaulted from his bicycle into the vehicle and promptly made an arrest.

Above all, however, the bicycle was appealing as a personal vehicle. To youths it gave speed; to women, freedom; and to many ordinary citizens it was simply a source of great pleasure and utility. To all, it offered exercise and adventure. For the new breed of cyclist was an independent sort, even if he or she belonged to a club. Atop a safety bicycle, one could flee the commotion of the city and take refuge in the countryside. The bicycle was, in effect, an antidote to the many tensions brought on by incessant innovation—even though, ironically, it was itself a product of that day's high technology. One source declared in 1895: "The bicycle has done more to foster love of out-of-door life than any other invention."

On the open road, cyclists found tranquillity, fresh air, good exercise, and even fellowship. For many, the bicycle was truly an eye-opener. Whether used alone or in conjunction with the local train network, it enabled the rider to reach and experience new landscapes, towns, and watering holes. Some communities even discussed the possibility of constructing special paths restricted to cyclists. In 1895, Brooklyn set an example,

COLLIER'S WEEKLY

AN ILLUSTRATED JOURNAL

Vol. XVII.—No. 3.
Copyright, 1896, by Peter Fenelon Collier.
All rights reserved.

NEW YORK, APRIL 23, 1896.

PRICE TEN CENTS.

A New York City bicycle policeman seizing a runaway horse, from *Collier's Weekly*, 23 April 1896. For officers on foot patrol, this feat would have been impossible.

opening such a route from Prospect Park to Coney Island. About ten thousand cyclists participated in the inaugural parade. Some idea of the bicycle's extraordinary appeal during the boom is rendered by this glowing report from Indianapolis, dated 1895:

> Cycling is a furore here. Thousands of riders are on the streets, at all hours of the day. A colored woman who would weigh over 200 pounds has just wheeled gaily past. Lawyers, doctors, professors, clergymen and teachers ride bicycles —in fact, everyone rides, except ragmen and banana peddlers. We scarcely see a carriage on this street. Every evening it is lined with cyclers of all descriptions —old and young, black and white. Women in bloomers are numerous. Five years ago, four ladies rode the first bicycles here, to the deep disgust of the men of the town and the deeper disgust of the women. Now the women who ride are legion and their number is increasing every day.

The massive influx of women cyclists—making up at least a third of the total market —was perhaps the most striking and profound social consequence of the boom. Although the new bicycle had appealed immediately to a few society women, its impact would have been modest had it not attracted a greater cross-section of the female population. Yet it soon became apparent that many of the privileged pioneer women bicyclists had not taken up the sport as an idle pastime. Rather, they saw cycling as a noble cause to be promoted among all women as a means to improve the general female condition. Not only would cycling encourage healthy outdoor exercise, they reasoned, it would hasten long-overdue dress reform. To feminists, the bicycle affirmed nothing less than the dignity and equality of women.

The bicycle's celebrated role as an "agent of reform": the man who formerly spent his Sundays reading trashy newspapers, in this cartoon from *Puck* of 1 July 1896, now rides his bicycle into the countryside where he instead contemplates "Nature's book"

Their message clearly struck a chord, as thousands of women from all classes took to the wheel in the mid-1890s. One young lady, Margaret LeLong, even cycled alone from Chicago to San Francisco in 1896, packing a powder-box and a pistol. Yet some observers questioned feminine dedication to the sport. One matron complained in the ladies' column of *Bicycling World* that the new female bicyclist lacked the sincerity that had characterized her predecessors in the early days of tricycles and hard-tired safeties. "Most cycling women seem to spend more time beside their bicycles than on them," she groused. "I never see these girls ride more than a quarter of a mile [whereupon] they get off their machines and hold long conversations. They want to show their smart costumes and excite admiration from the public, not enjoy a healthy exercise. It's just an excuse for gossip, that's all."

Other critics insisted that women should not be bicycling in the first place, even casually. The Woman's Rescue League of Washington, D.C., claimed that the activity prevented women from having children, promoted immodest attire, and encouraged improper liaisons with the opposite sex. Others charged that bicycling led "young and innocent girls into ruin and disgrace" and subjected them to improper remarks from the "depraved and immoral." Some even hinted that friction between a woman and her saddle caused illicit sexual arousal. But such rants held little sway with the public. And medical authorities were virtually unanimous in recommending moderate cycling to both men and women as a healthy exercise.

The question of what a proper woman should wear while bicycling, however, sparked genuine controversy. On a horse, she could ride sidesaddle and thus retain the long flowing dresses that were then the norm. But on a bicycle, she had to sit squarely on the saddle and wear clothing that neither constricted her ability to pedal nor interfered with the bicycle's working mechanisms. Designing a garment that satisfied these objectives and still met with general approval was no easy task, given the rigid Victorian dress code in force at that time.

Since the 1850s, dress reformers had promoted baggy "Turkish pants," or "bloomers," as an alternative to ankle-length dresses. Some women of privilege did in fact adopt less restrictive garb, at least when engaging in such approved outdoor activities as archery and lawn tennis. Yet for the most part, women were still covered from head to toe and were expected to wear constrictive accoutrements like the corset. Such garb was clearly incompatible with cycling, which demanded form-fitting outfits that would not interfere with the moving parts and nothing that might restrict breathing. With thousands of women taking to the wheel, bicycling would thus force the issue of rational dress as had no other recreational pursuit before it. "Dress reform talked of for a generation or two," noted one admirer of the bicycle in 1896, "has suddenly become a reality."

To alleviate the dress problem, bicycle makers introduced the women's "drop

A woman cyclist in her bloomer outfit preparing for an outing, leaving her beleaguered husband in charge of the children, from *Puck*, 7 July 1897. The bicycle did enable many women to strike out on their own, a frightening proposition to some social guardians.

frame," reminiscent of Denis Johnson's plan from 1819. Lacking a horizontal top tube between the saddle and the handlebar, this style of bicycle was somewhat more tolerant of superfluous garb. Yet it still required sensible attire that was comparatively skimpy and form-fitting. The female cyclist had three basic dress options, at least in theory. She could don either straight-legged trousers like a man's, or fuller and presumably more feminine bloomers. Alternatively, she could wear a skirt modified for cycling that was either heightened or divided in such a way that the legs were largely unencumbered when she pedaled, though off the bicycle it would maintain the appearance of a full-length garment.

Trousers were no doubt the most practical solution, but they were also the most controversial since they blurred the physical distinction between the sexes. One avant-garde proponent was Mrs. Angeline Allen of Newark, New Jersey. She gained notoriety in the summer of 1893, when she appeared in a nearby Asbury Park resort wearing a shockingly skimpy costume that one journalist branded an "apology for a bathing suit." So outraged were her fellow beachgoers, they confronted her with "jests and innuendo,"

The Chalet of the Bicycle in the Bois de Boulogne, by Jean Béraud, 1890s. Wealthy Parisian women took up cycling and adopted bloomers in 1893, and the Bois de Boulogne became a favorite rendezvous for upscale cyclists.

prompting officers to escort her back to the bathing house. That fall in Newark, the provocative Mrs. Allen ruffled more feathers when she appeared on her safety bicycle wearing a "natty uniform as near like that worn by men as possible." Her lower limbs were all but exposed, covered only by "knee high leggings." For many, even in the bicycle community, that was simply going too far. The *American Athlete* denounced Mrs. Allen's masculine attire, insisting on a "continuance of chastity." It advised wheelwomen to "abstain from anything that will attract censure."

Bloomers were somewhat more acceptable than trousers because they retained what some considered a feminine look. In the summer of 1893, scores of bloomer-clad Parisian women invaded the public parks on their bicycles, helping to popularize the costume. But in some places these puffy pants were slow to catch on, or even banned

THE NATIONAL POLICE GAZETTE

THE LEADING ILLUSTRATED SPORTING JOURNAL IN AMERICA.

Copyrighted for 1893 by the Proprietor, RICHARD K. FOX, Franklin Square Publishing, Printing and Engraving House, New York City.

RICHARD K. FOX,
Editor and Proprietor

NEW YORK, SATURDAY, OCTOBER 28, 1893.

VOLUME LXIII.—No. 843
Price Ten Cents.

Angeline Allen, the bold dress reformer from Newark, as portrayed on the cover of the *National Police Gazette* of 28 October 1893. "She Wore Trousers," blared the caption, while the article branded her "eccentric" and recounted how her costume had shocked the good people of society.

outright. In 1895, the police of Victoria, British Columbia, decreed that "bloomers are not suitable for ladies' street wear, even when worn as a bicycling costume." A defiant— or possibly naive—Miss Ethel Delmont nonetheless appeared on her bicycle clad in the forbidden garb. "The sensation could not have been greater," reported *The Wheel,* had she been "Lady Godiva herself." Stunned townspeople "came forth to gaze" and even the police were at first "petrified with amazement." Finally, they "aroused to action" and issued a stern warning that "a repetition of her appearance in *that* costume would mean a court summons."

To resolve the pressing problem of what a proper female cyclist should wear, many American newspapers sponsored design competitions. The general consensus favored short or divided skirts, with stockings to cover any exposed leg. That such costumes would inevitably reveal a woman's contours from her knees down did not trouble the more progressive reformers. The time had passed, asserted one, "when a woman would faint if a strange man so much as caught glimpse of her well-turned ankle." The revelation "that women have legs like any one else, and that they are made for use," declared another, "marks the beginning of a new era." In that writer's view, the bicycle would contribute to the "final emancipation of woman from the discomfort of that most sense-less of all garments—the skirt." Others predicted the bicycle would ultimately enable women to wear not only bloomers but also masculine trousers.

Yet as animated as the dress debate was, it was not the only social controversy sur-rounding the great boom. Many moralists were concerned about the newfound freedom of young men and women to roam about the countryside on their bicycles without the benefit of a chaperone with the stamina to keep up with them. Nor was it clear how the usual rules of chivalry applied to cyclists on the road. Should a man, for example, tip his hat when passing a lady, even at the risk of losing control of his machine? Should he offer to push her wheel if she appeared exhausted? Should he stop to repair her flat tire? And should she even accept such propositions from a perfect stranger? One expert sug-gested the matter was perhaps a bit academic, since women appeared surprisingly less receptive to conventional male courtesies while they were on their wheels as opposed to exercising on a golf course or the tennis court.

The widespread practice of Sunday riding was another grave concern, at least to many religious leaders; by some accounts, it had led to a marked decline in church at-tendance. Others decried the reckless young "scorchers" who tore through city streets at a breakneck pace in defiance of the speed limit. Still others linked excessive riding to a variety of conventional and bicycle-specific disorders. The "bicycle stoop," for exam-ple, allegedly resulted when racers arched their backs for long periods. Riders were also said to acquire the "bicycle face," a contorted appearance supposedly brought on by

A vision of a bicycle hell, from *Puck*, 21 July 1897, contemplating the fate of nonobservant bicyclists who spent their Sundays in the saddle rather than in a pew

their incessant struggle to keep their vehicle in balance. But an army of bicycle defenders held firm, insisting that moderate and sensible cycling was both moral and healthy.

By the mid-1890s, high society helped ease these various objections to the sport by lending its wholehearted approval. Although a few affluent citizens were among the first to adopt the safety bicycle, some years passed before such icons as John D. Rockefeller took to the wheel. Parisian celebrities led the way in the summer of 1893, invading the park in the Bois de Boulogne as the pioneer velocipedists had done a generation before. A year later, the fad hit the fashionable resort of Newport, Rhode Island. Society ladies regularly took morning spins wearing shockingly simple costumes. "It is hard to believe," marveled one observer, "that they were the same women who went out in the afternoon for the formal carriage parade."

By the summer of 1895, cycling had become a veritable fad among the "smart set." In New York, the exclusive Michaux Club rented out an old armory on upper Broadway where its four hundred members could ride two evenings a week while a band played. The club also sponsored rides along Riverside Drive, and excursions to Staten Island and the suburbs. Other elitist clubs held dances and teas with bicycle themes, as

The smart set of New York City taking a spin on Riverside Drive at the peak of the boom, in a drawing by W. A. Rogers, 1895

well as contests for the best flower-decorated bicycle. The famous jeweler Tiffany and Company offered a full-size "Tiffany-ized" Columbia valued at more than three thousand dollars. Its lugs sported "eighteen karat gold mountings," its spokes had gold-covered nipples, and its ivory handlebar grips were "tipped with gold." The handlebar was gold-frosted and supported a "massive sapphire," while the steering column featured "a row of semi-precious stones." Diamond Jim Brady, a notorious spendthrift, reportedly bought a specimen for the actress Lillian Russell.

In London, too, a craze raged among the upper classes. A few fashionable cyclists, including women, led the way. These prominent trendsetters rambled through Battersea Park and, before long, hundreds of their peers, including many leading citizens, filled Hyde Park. Bicycle makers like Humber began to publish long lists of distinguished patrons, citing many members of the royal family. Numerous kings and queens across Europe, in fact, were photographed on their bicycles, thereby lending their seal of approval to the popular sport. And at least one, Tsar Nicholas II of Russia, really was an avid participant in the sport. His passion for cycling reportedly gave bodyguards "the greatest trouble," for they found it "impossible to follow him."

Yet the rich and powerful were by no means the only ones taking to the wheel. In spite of the high cost of a bicycle, the sport already included numerous representatives of the middle class, and even some from the lower classes. In the United States, "hundreds of thousands" purportedly saved "every spare penny" to buy a wheel, to the detriment of other businesses. In London, a Mrs. Fawcett urged readers of *The Wheelwoman* to donate their old machines to "working girls' clubs." The editor heartily endorsed the idea, adding: "The working girls who labour in hot stuffy rooms day after day would welcome the chance of borrowing a cycle for an hour's ride." She even encouraged readers to reach out to "their poorer sisters" and teach them the art.

A loose-knit socialist organization called the Clarion, based in Birmingham, England, strongly encouraged its working-class membership to adopt the bicycle. It even organized a cycling club composed of volunteer "cycling scouts" of both sexes. They were to use their wheels, supplied by their clubs at a discount, to spread the gospel of proletarian revolution among "agricultural labourers and the rural population generally." Thanks to their increased mobility, these propagandists could more easily reach remote villages. Upon their arrival, they were expected to distribute literature and engage the locals in "friendly conversation" to explain to them the ideals of Socialism. Ideally, the cyclist scout would also hold a preannounced village meeting to convey the basic Socialist message in "ten or fifteen minutes."

What the President's hand-shaking receptions will soon develop into, at the rate the bicycle craze is growing.

President William McKinley in a reception line imagined in *Puck*, 28 April 1897, as the bicycle continued to work as a social equalizer

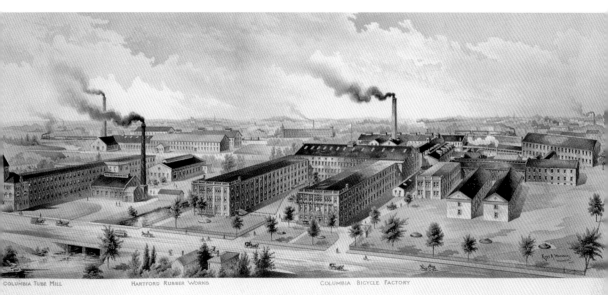

COLUMBIA TUBE MILL   HARTFORD RUBBER WORKS   COLUMBIA BICYCLE FACTORY

FACTORIES OF POPE MFG. CO. HARTFORD. CONN.

The Pope Manufacturing Company's bustling factories in Hartford, in a lithograph from 1896, at the peak of the boom. Pope's operation was truly immense, although the artist exaggerated its expanse.

Not all cyclists welcomed the less privileged to their ranks, however. *Brooklyn Life* alleged that certain "tramps" on bicycles threatened the security of country life. Some pundits warned that cycling "will die out altogether with the fashionable element [given] the extent to which the sport has been taken up by the *hoi polloi*." But others insisted that the bicycle was truly "the great leveler," one that fostered a kindred spirit. After all, cyclists traveled on the same roads, faced the same conditions, and even frequented the same locales. And even if one cyclist had spent twice as much as another on a wheel, chances were it went no faster. "There was a real democracy in the cult of the wheel," one writer reminisced a generation later. This "comradeship born of the road" included "a readiness to help in times of trouble [and] a never failing willingness to discuss the various makes of wheels [in] every detail."

As early as 1892, Thomas Stevens, the original cyclist globetrotter, outlined how the new safety had already narrowed class divisions within his native England:

Heretofore when Lord Willoughby met young Tompkins the trademan's son on the road, the former was on horseback and the latter afoot. Tompkins looked inferior and felt it, whilst Willoughby looked down on him as naturally in one respect as in another. By and by, however, both Willoughby and Tompkins

An Interview with Albert A. Pope

From the *Cycling World* of London, 22 July 1896

Hearing that Colonel Pope was in London, I sought him out in order to discover what he intended doing in England. I found him at the Savoy Hotel seated amidst a throng of business callers, but quite willing to give an interview. "What am I going to do in England?" repeated the Colonel, as I put the question to him. "Well, I'm afraid that's just about the one thing I can't tell you. I can tell you one piece of news, though—I shan't set up a factory in England, for the very good reason that I fancy I can make the machines at my present factory and send them over here for less than it would cost to manufacture them in England."

Q.: "Colonel, will you tell me something about the Columbia machines?"

A.: "Well, as an Englishman accustomed to English-made bicycles, I suppose you will be interested to hear that the weight of our machines is only 25 lbs 'all on.' We are enabled to make a good bicycle of this weight because of the exceptionally fine materials that we use. A great deal of the tubing is nickel-steel, which is fifty per cent stronger than any other tubing, inasmuch as it contains fifty per cent. of the carbon. So far as we know we are the only manufacturers in the world who can draw any quantity of nickel steel tubing."

Q.: "By the way, Colonel, what do you think of the boom? Is it going to last?"

A.: "Yes, it is. I don't think it has reached its height yet. Of course, after a time, the craze may subside a little, but I think there'll be a steady increase in the demand for cycles."

Q.: "I should like to have a few particulars concerning the construction of your machines, if I may?"

A.: "Certainly. In the first place let me tell you that we show our works to anybody who likes to see them, and we have a man who does nothing else but attend to visitors. Of course we should be careful about showing everything to a rival manufacturer, and we don't allow anyone to see certain parts of the works. No other manufacturer can have such machinery. I can't give you any particulars, but I may tell you that one of those machines, with two men to look after it, will do the work of eighteen men. But to come to the cycles. Every bicycle we make is subjected to the closest inspection before it is allowed to leave the works. You may not know that a bicycle contains over 800 separate pieces, and each one is examined thoroughly before it is put into the machine. This vigilance system is expensive, but I am confident that it is a good one. Another special feature of our business is our employment of expert cyclists whose work simply consists in riding about on machines of almost every make. These men test the machines in every conceivable way, their one idea being to think out a perfect bicycle."

Q.: "One more question, Colonel. Would you mind satisfying the public curiosity by letting me have a few facts and figures about the cycle works?"

A.: "You can get some idea of the extent of the place when I tell you that we have 17 acres of floorage. Then we employ 200 clerks who are stationed in a large building all to themselves, and over 2,000 workmen. We have our own rubber works, steel-tube works, printing works, telegraph office, &c, &c. In fact, we make quite a little town by ourselves."

bought bicycles, and both happened to alight for refreshments at the same way-side inn. They were naturally interested in each other's mounts, for they rode rival types, and were curious to learn something from each other's experiences. From being interested in Tompkins's wheel, Willoughby, after meeting him several times on the road, gradually became interested in Tompkins himself. He was agreeably surprised to find that he was not half a bad fellow, and much better worth knowing than he had been brought up to suppose.

Even age was no longer a barrier to cycling. By the mid-1890s, citizens were thoroughly accustomed to seeing older men and women spinning along on their wheels. Children, too, routinely dashed about on their bicycles. And unlike the toy tricycles of an earlier generation, or the miniature high wheelers confined to privileged boys of the 1880s, these vehicles provided genuine service. Even boys and girls of modest means could ride something that resembled an adult machine. As early as 1891, the John P. Lovell Arms Company of Boston offered a twenty-six-inch hard-tire safety for children between eight and fourteen, priced at only thirty-five dollars. Within four years, many firms offered juvenile pneumatic-tire safeties for about fifty dollars. As there were still few opportunities to participate in organized sports, cycling became a favorite activity among children who could afford to buy a machine.

As a result of the bicycle's extraordinary appeal, the American cycle trade developed into one of the largest industries in the country. Its immense output was even beginning to yield a large surplus destined for worldwide exportation. Tool companies such as Brown and Sharpe of Providence, Rhode Island, helped to develop highly specialized machinery for the mass production of bicycles. These included—for wheel-making alone—special tools to shape and drill wood or steel rims and to thread and cut spokes, as well as truing stands to facilitate manual lacing. Also needed were special equipment to grind ball bearings, to manufacture chains, and to shape every part of the bicycle. The entire process required a vast assortment of lathes, jigs, milling machines, drill presses, and metal polishing equipment.

The astonishing prowess of the American cycle industry became the envy of the world. Following the Columbian exposition of 1893, one of the leading French bicycle makers, Adolphe Clément, embarked on an extended tour of American plants. As he explained in his 1895 catalog, he wanted to observe firsthand "the marvelous machinery that has already enabled American mechanics to compete successfully against the Old World" and to purchase the best equipment for his own production.

Perhaps the most impressive bicycle operation of all was that belonging to Pope, widely acclaimed as the "father of the American cycle industry." Using the most advanced technology, including an electrified assembly line, Pope's Hartford works pro-

A cover in the Art Nouveau style, which was just then coming into vogue as the art of illustration flowered, from
The Judge, 9 May 1896

duced a complete machine every minute of the working day. But even more striking were its progressive labor policies. Every employee was provided with a locker and sink, and all were assigned a private stall to keep their bicycles during working hours. Off the clock, workers could visit the large library and reading room stocked with the latest general and mechanical literature. At noontime, the kitchen served coffee and soup for pennies. Pope even purchased a tract of land near the factory where he built dozens of single houses "according to the latest ideas of convenience and health," and he then sold them at cost to his workers. One contemporary heralded these measures as nothing short of "revolutionary," pronouncing Pope's operation as a shining "model of its kind."

To sell all the bicycles streaming from the factories, the international trade spent enormous sums on art and advertising. As it happened, the bicycle boom coincided with what became known as the "golden age of illustration." Cycle makers commissioned scores of works to advertise their products in magazines, on billboards, and behind shop windows. A favorite medium was the large colorful poster, made possible by recent advances in lithography. In the summer of 1896, Pope held a competition to create a new wave of Columbia posters. The illustrators, including some of the best-known names in the art world, submitted over a thousand images. Pope's committee selected half of them for a traveling exhibition that drew "immense crowds." A young Maxfield Parrish won first prize, collecting $250 and a Columbia bicycle.

Meanwhile, the campaign for better roads was finally beginning to yield results. Some states had already initiated highway programs, and a few had even begun to enlist convict labor to build roads. For his part, Pope continued his relentless personal campaign. He gave six thousand dollars to the Massachusetts Institute of Technology to establish a department of road engineering, and he even paved a stretch of Boston's Columbus Avenue at his own expense to showcase the benefits of asphalt. Pope presented the federal government with a massive petition demanding a road department, prompting the formation of a commission to study a national network. He won sympathy from many powerful figures, including railroad magnates and President Benjamin Harrison. In 1896, one writer credited "the vast road improvement going on all over the country" to Pope's remarkable "energy and persistence."

Yet Pope, for all his fame, was but one of the trade's top five magnates. The illustrious cadre included two fellow veterans of the high-wheel trade, A. H. Overman and R. Phillip Gormully, and two newcomers, R. L. Coleman and H. A. Lozier. The firms associated with the first two, the Overman Wheel Company and Gormully and Jeffery, like Pope's plant, rapidly expanded after taking up safety production in the late 1880s. Coleman, shortly thereafter, assumed control of the massive Western Wheel Works of Chicago, makers of the famed Crescent bicycle. Lozier's factory in Toledo, Ohio, started

Poster for Cleveland Cycles, by Jean de Paleologue, printed in Paris in 1897. The cycle manufacturer was at the time one of the largest of its kind in the Midwest, and like many other American brands its machines were widely advertised and sold abroad.

producing children's safeties in 1890 and at its peak six years later produced a hundred Cleveland bicycles every working day. In fact, the center of the American industry had by then shifted to the Midwest. Chicago alone had twenty-five bicycle makers, including the newcomer Arnold, Schwinn and Company. Other bicycle companies in Ohio, Indiana, and Illinois were experiencing tremendous growth. Some eastern cities were also major bicycle producers, notably Syracuse, Buffalo, and Erie, Pennsylvania.

Still, as the boom began to fade in late 1896, the long-term prospects of this vibrant industry looked increasingly tenuous. Many observers warned that the industry faced dire consequences following years of massive overexposure and overproduction. Some people began to wonder openly just how much longer the bicycle could maintain its grip on the public's fancy, insisting that Americans would not continue to buy millions of machines year after year. Evidently, at least some industry leaders agreed. Pope and many of his rivals were already dabbling in automobile production, looking ahead to a new era when motorized vehicles would rule the road.

Yet some industry insiders confidently predicted many more years of growth and prosperity. "Some say that next year will be the climax in the cycle trade—that after 1896 business will keep about so," admitted the *American Cyclist,* one of the many trade publications. "[But] we do not think so. High water marks won't be touched next year, the year after, or the year after that—unless we are very poor at guessing." Alas, they were. The boom came to crashing halt in 1897, casting a dark cloud over the future of the once glamorous and lucrative bicycle business.

TWELVE

Legacy of the Boom

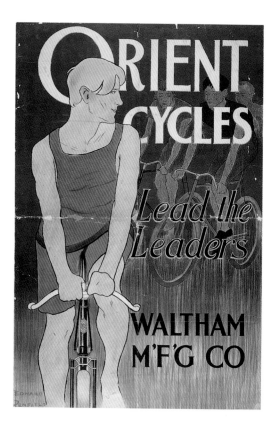

As the 1897 season approached, the American bicycle trade prepared for what it hoped would be another banner year. One encouraging sign was the continued popularity of professional racing, which ran from spring through Christmas at tracks throughout the country. The leading competitors were now national celebrities on a par with baseball stars. One captivating new personality was Marshall "Major" Taylor, a young black man from Indiana. In December 1896, he distinguished himself during a six-day race at Madison Square Garden before a record crowd of fifteen thousand. The following season, he developed into a formidable force, regularly giving his opponents "all and more than they wanted."

Nevertheless, as the season unfolded, domestic demand plummeted. The leading makers, who had long held to a base price of one hundred dollars, suddenly slashed it by one-quarter in a desperate bid to stimulate sales. Still they found themselves saddled with unsold stock. In the course of 1897, the American trade would manage to produce another million bicycles. But as one industry insider acknowledged twenty years later, "many thousands were of the cheapest variety, thrown together by irresponsible makers,

The Overman Wheel Company, promoted in a poster by Will H. Bradley from 1896, was one of the oldest and most respected names in the American bicycle business until its sudden collapse that shocked industry insiders and signaled trouble ahead

and dumped on the British market." As a result of this "short-sighted policy," American bicycles, which had once enjoyed a worldwide reputation for lightness and solidity, "suffered irreparable injury." Moreover, the dwindling demand at home signaled trouble ahead.

More shock waves rippled through the troubled trade at the close of 1897 when the pioneer Overman Wheel Company announced it had shut its doors. The previous season, the company had cleared half a million dollars in profits; now it was awash in debt. The firm assigned all its property to a local bank to protect itself from hungry creditors. A game A. H. Overman, president of the company, insisted that "the outlook for the future is excellent provided the present difficulty can be overcome." Alas, the company never recovered. Some blamed its sudden demise on its ill-advised venture into sporting goods. But others feared for the future of the industry itself, openly suggesting that perhaps the appeal of the bicycle was ephemeral after all.

facing page: This poster by the noted artist Will H. Bradley promoted the annual Springfield meet. Even as the boom waned in 1897, racing continued to attract a large following.

The industry was already reeling from Pope's stunning announcement that he would supply department stores with bicycles starting in the 1898 season. Pope had long disdained chain stores, selling the bulk of his bicycles through independent agents at his set prices. But now he needed the stores' marketing clout to move as much stock as possible. The *Cycle Age* lamented that "high class cycles have gained a foot-hold in the department stores," and questioned whether "customers of the bargain counter" were really prepared to pay "higher prices for better goods." The trade journal warned that if the experiment failed, and the stores unloaded top-quality bicycles for a song, the maker's "reputation and price will go."

Yet even as Pope desperately dumped his bicycles, he initiated a bold plan to reclaim control of the trade. Pope bet that a radically revamped bicycle would set a new design standard, revive demand, and boost the base price back over a hundred dollars. His innovation, the so-called chainless bicycle, replaced the chain with a shaft drive featuring beveled gears at either end, all contained inside an oil-filled tube stretching from the crank hanger to the rear sprocket. The enclosed drive offered a cleaner appearance and was easier to keep lubricated. The shaft drive also made for a smooth ride and even earned the approval of some racers. Most important, it eliminated the possibility that the chain would soil the rider's clothing, a feature that presumably appealed to the all-important women's market. Moreover, according to company literature, the shaft drive was more efficient than the standard chain. One journalist predicted a swift return to boom-level sales as he teased his readers: "How are you going to resist a chainless wheel?"

The idea of a shaft-driven bicycle was actually not particularly novel. The League Cycle Company of Hartford had made one as early as 1893, before Pope absorbed the

A schematic drawing of the Acatène chainless drive by Métropole of Paris, published in the *American Cyclist* of 25 September 1896, showing the beveled gears at both ends of the shaft and the hardware enclosures that kept the oil inside, away from the cyclist

operation in preparation for his own chainless production. Shortly thereafter, a French company, Métropole, marketed a model known as the Acatène. But the chainless had yet to catch on. For one thing, compared to a standard bicycle, the chainless variety was more difficult and costly to produce since it required a higher degree of precision machining. Making it work properly was also a challenge. Pope's own model was delayed for several years while his engineers struggled to work out its kinks.

In late 1897, Pope finally unveiled his advanced chainless model that purportedly surpassed all previous entries. For some time, the cycling press had been trumpeting its arrival. *Cycling Life* declared that if one were to compare the chainless bicycle with the newly discovered X-rays, based on publicity alone, "it would be hard to decide [which] is of greater importance to humanity." Yet for all the marketing hype, Pope's initiative proved a disappointment. Although his chainless bicycle performed reasonably well, it failed to demonstrate compelling advantages over the standard mount, despite its higher cost.

A poster for Humber Cycles of Beeston, Nottinghamshire, from about 1906, celebrating its elitist clientele with Windsor Castle looming in the background, while at the same time suggesting that bicycles serve all of humanity. The man leading the procession is King Edward VII, who assumed the throne in 1901 following the death of his mother, Queen Victoria.

The Next Revolutionizer

The *American Cyclist* observed in 1897 that the first Rover-style safeties introduced a decade earlier had halted and reversed what had been a modest but
steady decline in the price of a bicycle. And just when the price of the low mount
itself began to fall a few years later, the pneumatic tire came along to boost prices
right back up. With prices on the downswing once again, the journal wondered
what "revolutionizer" would serve as the next "price-sustainer." Some in the industry, it noted, "have faith in chainless wheels," while others looked toward
"some new-fangled and as yet unheard of frame arrangement or other sweeping
variation from the conventional model."

For some time, in fact, inventors had been scrambling to identify some sort of
sensational breakthrough with only limited success. Several firms proposed light
and economical bamboo bicycles, but they proved too flexible. In 1894, the Saint
Louis Refrigerator Company introduced a lightweight bicycle with an aluminum
alloy frame it called the Lum-Mi-Num, imploring the public to disregard "cause-
less suits" brought by unscrupulous rivals who aimed to "frighten our customers."
By 1898, even such established firms as Iver Johnson and Humber Cycles offered
bicycles of aluminum alloy that weighed little more than twenty pounds, though
some riders complained that they lacked sufficient rigidity.

Other innovators explored novel frame configurations. A Frenchman introduced a lightweight folding bicycle designed for military use. A Danish engineer,
Mikael Pedersen, devised a distinctive suspension bicycle built with multiple thin-
gauge tubes and equipped with a comfortable hammock seat. Even after the pneumatic tire largely solved the problem of frame vibration, the Pedersen commanded
a loyal following, but never caught on in a big way. An American proposed a
model called the Easy Chair, an early recumbent design, which was evidently of
short duration. "It looks very pretty and appears to run very well," wrote one reviewer, adding that a rider could load it up with "all the comforts of home" while
"distancing creditors."

Still others dreamed up novel accessories. In England, William S. Simpson
introduced the distinctive "lever chain," claiming that it gave the cyclist greater
leverage to power the rear wheel. It was composed of triangular links and a chainring and a compatible sprocket having grooves rather than teeth. Several Euro-

pean makers adopted it, as did many racers, but it failed to endure. The Eagle Bicycle Company of Torrington, Connecticut, marketed aluminum wheel rims, but Americans remained partial to the wooden variety. Several English firms proposed variable gear devices that shifted the chain over a block of three or four escalating sprockets, but these early derailleurs failed to catch on.

Despite hundreds of imaginative initiatives, the standard bicycle changed little during the boom. For its part, the *American Cyclist* confessed it was not sure if the chainless bicycle truly possessed the "revolutionizing qualities" required to create yet another, higher-priced standard. But, it conceded, "nothing else appears to be in sight." As it turned out, neither the chainless bicycle nor any other novelty boosted prices back up to boom levels. On the contrary, the price of a standard bicycle continued to decline for several more years until it stabilized at about twenty-five dollars.

One of Mikael Pedersen's unusual bicycles weighing less than twenty pounds; this one from about 1898 featured a woven hammock seat for an especially comfortable ride. The rider could adjust a leather strap at the front of the seat to make it tighter or slacker according to taste. Even after the pneumatic tire greatly reduced road shock on conventional bicycles, there was still a modest demand for this model.

In fact, Professor R. C. Carpenter of Cornell University conducted extensive experiments in 1897 proving that even a well-worn chain is up to 99 percent efficient—a higher rating than the shaft drive. The trade's relentless "chain-bashing" was thus largely self-defeating. After all, makers had profited handsomely over the years by selling millions of chain-driven bicycles. To denounce that device now, at a time when many cyclists already resented how much their initial investments had depreciated, merely reinforced the growing perception that the bicycle had been overvalued all along. Nor did the chainless bicycle succeed in rekindling demand. Although the trade continued to offer the shaft drive for many years to come, it never generated much enthusiasm.

In proposing the chainless bicycle for $125, almost twice the going price for a standard mount, Pope evidently hoped to induce wealthier riders to adopt a new status symbol inaccessible to the average citizen. But by the time high society took up cycling in 1895, the sport had already achieved a strong measure of popular success. The socialite who purchased an up-to-date bicycle that year gained the opportunity to participate in the craze then sweeping the nation, and to be seen with the right crowd, wearing the latest fashions. But with so many bicycles already on the road, the mere ownership of a bicycle, even the most expensive chrome-plated variety, offered little cachet. Nor was the bicycle destined to retain its cutting-edge appeal—not with motorized vehicles well on their way. All told, it was highly unlikely that a revamped bicycle, however clever or attractive, would force a new wave of passion among the upper crust once the initial fashion had died out.

So the bicycle business continued its downward spiral. By the end of 1898, department stores were selling serviceable bicycles for less than fifty dollars. Profit margins evaporated, forcing many firms and retail stores out of business. The *Youth's Companion* blamed the trade's predicament on the "regime of high prices" that had reigned during the boom, when shortsighted managers spent lavish sums on such extravagances as "expensive agencies" and "ornamental advertising." Their bloated profits, in turn, attracted "hundreds of new factories" that soon glutted the market with bicycles. The leaders compounded the crisis by clinging to artificially high prices, a stall tactic that only attracted more competitors while delaying the inevitable downward adjustment. When that finally came, it was not only drastic, it was downright demoralizing. Concluded the magazine, "The makers who have survived the 'golden age' are coming down to a hard business level."

facing page: A poster for the newly introduced Columbia Chainless from about 1898, by A. Romes, adapted from an earlier poster showing a conventional bicycle that won third prize in Pope's contest. The box at the bottom was reserved for a dealer's address.

A Military Bid

James A. Moss, a lieutenant stationed at Fort Missoula, Montana, was one of the most prominent champions of the military bicycle during the boom. In 1896, with the blessings of General Nelson A. Miles, he formed the 25th Infantry Bicycle Corps, consisting of himself and eight Buffalo Soldiers—black army volunteers. The men strapped rifles to their backs and rode rugged bicycles with steel rims specially built to Moss's specifications by A. G. Spalding and Brothers of Chicago. Their daily workouts involved cycling between fifteen and forty miles, and scaling fences and crossing streams with their loaded bicycles in tow. The corps made several inaugural excursions including an eight-hundred-mile trek to Yellowstone Park. Moss noted that even when his men proceeded on foot over impassable terrain the bicycles served to transport forty pounds of gear, which included tents, food, and water.

But the true test of the bicycle took place in the summer of 1897, when Moss led an expanded group of twenty soldiers aged between twenty-four and thirty-nine, including a bugler and a bicycle mechanic, to Saint Louis, Missouri—a distance of nearly two thousand miles. Joining them were a surgeon and a journalist. The route crossed five states and entailed steep hills, poor roads, mosquitoes, rain, sleet, and even snow. On several occasions, the black men faced hostile locals. Finally, after covering over forty miles a day for forty-one days, all but one of the original party reached Saint Louis. Some ten thousand citizens cheered their arrival, and the local press heralded their performance as a resounding triumph for man and machine.

But some diehard bicycle producers were determined to restore the old regime that had generated such fat profits. One of the surviving leaders, A. G. Spalding, organized a bicycle trust known as the American Bicycle Company. He persuaded many of his peers, including Pope, to sell their stock and manufacturing facilities to the conglomerate, in exchange for a share of ownership and a voice in management. The new company's collective production power, coupled with diminished competition, would pre-

Alas, the brass thought otherwise. No army officials were on hand to greet the weary cyclists, and General Miles, despite heaping praise on Moss and his men, ordered them to return to Montana by train. The corps was disbanded the following spring, and the bicycle saw little action in the Spanish-American War later in 1898. The increasingly embattled cycle industry never secured the lucrative government contracts that Pope and other leaders had coveted. Perhaps the military concluded that bicycle technology was not a worthwhile investment, given that motorized vehicles were already on the way.

Lieutenant Moss and his 25th U.S. Infantry Bicycle Corps practicing near Fort Missoula in 1897

sumably ensure profitability. After prolonged negotiations, the trust absorbed some forty companies that made up about three-quarters of the American trade, and it began operations in 1899.

That same year, the racer Charles M. Murphy made headlines by riding a specially designed racing bicycle just behind an express train along a three-mile stretch of the Long Island railroad, following wooden planks that had been laid between the rails. By the second mile, he had worked up his speed to an incredible sixty miles an hour—a pace equal to that of the fastest motorcycle. This feat immortalized "Mile-a-Minute" Murphy and validated his theories about the importance of aerodynamics in bicycle design. But Murphy's work did not appear to have important practical implications with regard to the bicycle itself, and his exploits failed to sustain popular interest in the lowly two-wheeler. The bicycle's tenure as a sensational vehicle had evidently passed.

By this time, the competitive sport was also losing much of its former allure. Many of the boom-era stars were no longer competing, including the great Arthur A. Zimmerman and the diminutive Jimmy Michaels of Wales, who had dominated middle-distance competitions. "Racing has been shorn of much of its popularity," acknowledged *Bicycling World* in the spring of 1899. The national circuit of velodromes was now reduced to only a few hotbeds, notably Newark, New Jersey, and Salt Lake City, Utah. Meanwhile, the recreational sport had all but died out, and very little demand for high-grade bicycles remained.

The American Bicycle Company proved powerless to halt the drastic decline in the bicycle business, and sales quickly sank to levels not seen since the high-wheel era. By the time the trust itself collapsed in 1902, national production had fallen from 1.2 million bicycles a year to about a quarter of that figure. In roughly the same period, membership in the League of American Wheelmen plunged from more than one hundred thousand to barely ten thousand, leaving little hope for even a modest recovery in the near future. Thousands of discarded bicycles, many with flat tires and broken spokes, were relegated to cellars, attics, woodsheds and barns. What was left of the once powerful industry faced a grim struggle for survival.

Why was the collapse of a once prominent industry so sudden and catastrophic? Some historians have pointed to the arrival of the motor bicycle and the automobile, vehicles that offered far greater speed and mobility. But that alone does not adequately explain the implosion of the American bicycle industry. After all, motorized vehicles were still scarce at the turn of the century and did not become truly practical and affordable for at least another decade. Many Americans still relied on bicycles for basic transportation. *Good Roads Magazine* pointed out in 1902, "There are many bicycles sold today and there are many bicycles on the road." But, it added: "Riders are using bicycles for utilitarian purposes almost altogether. For the most part, the cycler is going to and from his business, or is upon an errand. The fraternal element, the touring spirit, have about gone out."

Evidently, although the bicycle remained in general use in America, the army of commuters alone could not sustain boom-era demand or prosperity. After all, cyclists who rode primarily for economy were not likely to spend large sums on their mounts, nor were they inclined to change models every year simply to keep up with fashion. At

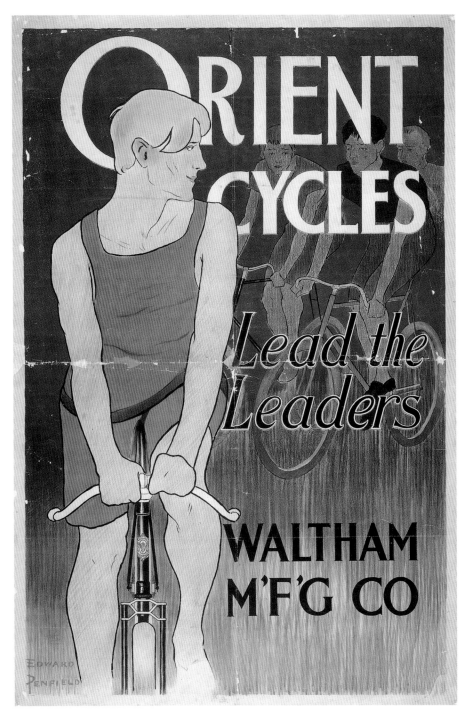

Poster by Edward Penfield, about 1897, for the Waltham Manufacturing Company, one of several firms that took up motorcycle production once the boom petered out. In 1898 the company introduced the first successful American production motorbike with a four-cycle engine.

the heart of the crisis, therefore, was the near total loss of the lucrative recreational market. But why had so many abandoned a sport that had once commanded such popular appeal? That nagging question would haunt the downsized American bicycle industry for years to come as it struggled to redefine its mission.

No doubt a crisis of some sort was inevitable once the fad faded, prices plummeted, and the automobile emerged. Even those who continued to cycle to work were wont to turn to other, more fashionable sports for their outdoor exercise, such as golf and lawn tennis. Meanwhile, as one source observed, the low cost of a bicycle, while a boon to the commuter, "removed the cachet of exclusiveness and, with it, half the charm of ownership." And the advent of motorized vehicles did indeed obliterate the bicycle's appeal as cutting-edge technology. Wealthier riders, who had once spent lavish sums on bicycles, were prone to abandon cycling once they procured motor bicycles or automobiles.

Still, the near total collapse of the American recreational market after 1897 seems surprisingly drastic from a contemporary perspective. After all, many citizens had taken up cycling during the boom not merely for the sake of fashion, but also to enjoy good exercise and fellowship—things the bicycle could presumably still deliver. In Europe, in fact, the recreational sport endured even though the trade likewise suffered a sharp decline in demand. Clearly, the American bicycle industry itself bore some responsibility for its glaring failure to sustain even a modest recreational demand. Had its leaders

Century runs of a hundred miles or more were popular during the boom, a trend satirized in *Puck* on 15 January 1896 and criticized by some pundits who warned that overindulgence would doom the bicycle trade

exercised greater technological foresight, they might well have engineered a smoother and more successful transition to the motorized age.

In retrospect, the American industry's focus on chainless technology was ill advised in that it did not address the most pressing needs of the average cyclist. The industry surely would have done far better to develop and apply genuine improvements to the touring bicycle, which despite great advances still suffered from two major shortcomings. First, its lack of a freewheel compelled riders to either pedal at all times, even when they lost the will, or to shuffle their feet back and forth between the pedals and the footrests. Second, riders had no means to adjust gearing as the terrain varied. These twin oversights severely curtailed the versatility of the vehicle and the pleasure it could provide.

Had industry leaders introduced a practical freewheel or a variable gearing system during the boom, ideally as accessories that could be easily retrofitted to the existing army of bicycles, they might well have sustained a more robust recreational interest. By 1899, American manufacturers did introduce the handy "coaster brake," which provided not only a freewheel mechanism but also a brake activated by pedaling backward. But by that time many riders had already abandoned the sport. And whereas Europeans had already developed rudimentary variable gears, the American trade had largely dismissed that possibility. At the peak of the boom, both Pope and Overman had insisted that any "hill climbing" device offering an assortment of gears would prove overly costly and cumbersome. The first variable gear systems, two-speed hubs, were likewise introduced only belatedly, shortly after the boom.

But regardless of what American makers might have done to mitigate or delay the post-boom crisis, its effects were felt worldwide. Even the British trade, though not quite as devastated as its American counterpart, faced a protracted struggle. Joseph Pennell called 1899 "as bad a year as the trade has ever seen." Largely in response to the flood of cheap American imports, makers had cut their prices in half, forcing many to either merge or fold altogether. Such industry stalwarts as Singer and Humber posted record losses. The national trade shows drew fewer spectators, and motorized vehicles dominated the floor space—a sure sign that the day of the bicycle had passed in Britain as well. Elsewhere in Europe, the decline of the bicycle industry was not as pronounced, but its golden age had come and gone.

The international bicycle industry, diminished and depressed, clearly faced a difficult road ahead. Yet it had registered three significant achievements during the boom that provided a solid foundation for its future. First and foremost, the bicycle had proved itself a remarkably practical and versatile machine providing both recreational and utilitarian services. Second, mass production had brought the price of a new bicycle within reach of the general population. Finally, after a long struggle, the bicycle had won broad

"The 'new' Mother-in-Law, arriving for a long visit," from *Puck*, 19 June 1895, spoofing the "new woman." The popularity of the bicycle enabled people irrespective of age and sex to cycle without drawing second looks from the citizenry.

social acceptance. "Only a few years ago," *Bicycling World* noted in 1896, "[the bicycle] was an object of curious interest. To-day who thinks of turning his head to look after a bicycle? No one." Indeed, even women and the elderly could now safely cycle in public without having "all the street gamins hoot" as if they were "unclassified freaks."

The low-mount bicycle, in fact, had secured more than a mere measure of public tolerance. It had earned broad popular sympathy and appreciation for its substantial and profound contributions to the emerging modern way of life. In the United States, the bicycle was widely recognized as the chief catalyst behind the increasingly success-ful campaign for better roads, which was soon to culminate in a great national network of highways destined to serve as the country's transportation backbone. "Whatever may come afterwards," declared one bicycle maker in 1902, "the bicycle must go down in his-tory as the pioneer of road improvements."

Many also insisted that the bicycle had exerted a profound social influence not only by instilling a greater appreciation for outdoor exercise but also by improving the con-dition of women. In 1897, Mrs. Alice Lee Moqué, one of the first female bicyclists in America, recalled how she had worn long cycling dresses when she first took up the sport in the nation's capital some seven years earlier. "How I ever escaped a broken neck I do not know," she mused. "[But] I would have been absolutely ostracized socially had I dared to appear on the wheel in such cycling garb as I now wear. The bloomered and short-skirted women of to-day, who merrily ride away in freedom and comfort, do not dream of what we of earlier days went through. I feel a sense of thankfulness that times have changed."

Even automotive pioneers praised the humble bicycle for its catalytic role in sparking their own industry. Hiram Percy Maxim, who created the Columbia electric car in 1895, insisted that the bicycle had inspired the relentless quest for a practical and affordable automobile. "The reason we did not build mechanical road vehicles before 1895, in my opinion, was because the bicycle had not yet come in numbers and had not directed men's minds to the possibilities of independent, long-distance travel over the ordinary highway. We thought the railroad was good enough. The bicycle created a new demand beyond the ability of the railroad to supply. Then it came about that the bicycle could not satisfy the demand which it had created. A mechanically propelled vehicle was wanted instead of a foot-propelled one, and we now know that the automobile was the answer."

The bicycle, in fact, provided the emerging automotive industry with more than mere inspiration. The American Automobile Association, founded in 1902, took its lead

A poster by Edward Penfield from 1896 evoking the sense of freedom many Victorian women experienced while cycling. Stearns was a popular brand based in Syracuse, New York.

from the League of American Wheelmen, even attracting many of its former members. The numerous bicycle repair shops helped provide the foundation for a nationwide network of service stations. Many of the pioneer automobile makers, such as Charles Duryea and Henry Ford, were themselves former bicycle mechanics. They drew heavily on that experience, adopting numerous cycle innovations to automobiles, including pneumatic tires, wire spokes, steel tubing, differential gears, ball bearings, and chain and shaft drives. And once they undertook large-scale production, they used many of the manufacturing and assembly techniques originally developed for the bicycle industry.

Bicycle production also assisted other emerging technologies, notably motorcycles and aviation. As a former bicycle mechanic, Glenn Curtiss went on to develop motorcycles, the first practical seaplane, and the first combat planes, which were used in World War I. Orville and Wilbur Wright, in particular, were experienced bicycle mechanics who built the first successful airplane using the metal- and wood-working skills they had developed in the cycle trade—as well as familiar bicycle tools and parts like chains, ball bearings, and wire wheels. From the start, they realized that any practical aircraft, like the bicycle itself, would require precision manufacturing as well as a skillful pilot who had acquired an intuitive feel for the machine and its motion.

In December 1892, exactly eleven years before their first flights at Kitty Hawk, the brothers opened a modest shop in Dayton, Ohio, where they sold and repaired bicycles. Three years later, as their business began to suffer from heightened local competition, they began to handcraft their own bicycles for a wider market, acquiring in the process an intimate knowledge of bicycle construction and technology. They even made their own hubs, which they claimed needed oiling only once every two years. Their modest profits from this activity enabled them to pursue another passion on the sideline: the quest for a powered airplane.

Starting in 1899, the brothers traveled regularly to the windswept dunes of North Carolina's Outer Banks, where they tested their specially designed kites and gliders. These devices failed, however, to fly as high or as far as the brothers had anticipated based on their calculations. In 1901, they turned to the bicycle to develop more accurate mathematical models defining the principles of flight. They attached a miniature wing and drag plate to the front wheel of a bicycle, then raced the vehicle through a wind tunnel, carefully measuring the lift and drag. These extensive tests yielded data unprecedented in scope and detail, which guided the brothers as they designed the wings and propellers for the Wright Flyer. With the help of an assistant, they built the craft itself, including the motor, in their own bicycle workshop.

Still, despite the impressive technical and social achievements registered during the boom, the bicycle industry would evidently need to adapt the two-wheeler to the needs of the motorized age. In particular, whereas it had relied on a single dominant design during the boom, the one-speed featherweight with a minimum of accessories, it would need to develop more specialized models in the twentieth century to suit a variety of tastes and budgets. That challenge, though difficult, was far from hopeless. The bicycle boom had defined three broad applications that begged for development: utilitarian, recreational, and competitive cycling.

As the price of a bicycle fell rapidly, a vast utilitarian market loomed ahead. From the start, the boneshaker had promised a swift and economical means to transport small loads and to shuttle people to and from their place of work. As one customer explained to Michaux in 1868, he wanted a velocipede to avoid having to walk a mile to and from his place of business every day. A Boston review from the same period observed: "In every city there are large numbers of business men who live in the suburbs and who pay for transportation to and fro, all the way from $50 to $150 or $200 per year. By securing a velocipede and learning to ride it, they can not only save money but at the same time derive much benefit from the exercise." Now, at last, the safety bicycle was in a position to fulfill these useful services on a worldwide scale.

The recreational market likewise offered strong possibilities, despite the passing of the boom. Even in its crudest form, the bicycle engendered a loyal following among men and women who sought agreeable outdoor exercise, adventure, and camaraderie. As early as 1869, a Parisian who had taken part in club rides marveled at "a strange effect of velocipede touring; in the morning, when we start out, we're perfect strangers. Yet, after only a few hours on the road, we part as the best of friends—promising to meet again." The well crafted high wheeler fully established the joys of cycling, and the safety design largely eliminated the risk of a serious accident. Surely, the marvelous low mount would prove a perennial attraction that would never completely pass from favor.

The third principal area for development was competitive cycling. In spite of the limited demand for delicate, lightweight machines, racing had proven an effective catalyst for technical innovation. More important, as Aimé Olivier recognized as early as 1869, cultivating the spectator sport offered the trade an important means to sustain the public's appreciation for the bicycle by playing on its passion for speed. As the inaugural road race, Paris-to-Rouen, approached, Aimé wrote to the director of the French post office to predict that the results would confirm "that the velocipede is not merely an instrument of luxury but rather a rapid and little-tiring carriage, useful on any surfaces, anywhere." A lingering public interest in racing, in fact, helped the trade through some lean years in the early 1870s, and again in the aftermath of the boom. The *Bicycling World* affirmed in 1899, despite the general downturn, "Race meets are still going and large numbers of people frequently attend them." Moreover, the journal asserted,

The Motorcycle Spin-off

In 1818, a French caricaturist whimsically depicted a draisine with a steam engine, not realizing that a motorized two-wheeler was a genuine possibility. "It might have been funny then," observed the *Brooklyn Daily Eagle* in 1869, "but it is practical now." As soon as the mechanized two-wheeler appeared, in fact, mechanics began to add engines to achieve speeds of up to forty miles an hour. S. H. Roper of Roxbury, Massachusetts, was one of the first to build a steam-powered bicycle, which is now at the Museum of American History in Washington, D.C. In Chattanooga, Tennessee, a half dozen engineers built a three-wheeler designed to go forty miles with a supply of oil, although the driver had to periodically add water. These early machines did not prove practical, however. "The rider is half roasted by the boiler," complained one critic in 1869, "and [is] liable to be blown off at a tangent without a moment's notice." In the high-wheel era, the Copeland brothers of Phoenix, Arizona, introduced a Star bicycle with a detachable steam engine weighing twenty pounds, fuel included. Reportedly, the bicycle could run for an hour without a refill of water or gasoline. Although it was a decided improvement over early motorcycles, it likewise failed to catch on.

As the bicycle progressed rapidly during the boom, mechanics revisited the idea of adding a motor. In 1894, E. J. Pennington of Cleveland introduced the Motor Cycle, a two-wheeler with a ten-pound kerosene engine and oversized pneumatic tires. It caused a buzz at trade shows, but proved impractical on the road. A few years later, another American proposed something called the Gun Powder Bike. Purportedly, it could reach one hundred miles once lit, "if it does not blow wheel and rider sky high." More practical motorcycles with small gasoline engines soon appeared in Europe, thanks to the pioneer work of Germany's Gottlieb Daimler. In 1898, the Waltham Manufacturing Company of Massachusetts, mak-

facing page: The happy owner of a new motorcycle produced in about 1906 by Glenn Curtiss, one of the pioneer makers of motorized two-wheelers. The first models retained a crank and pedal drive as a means to start the engine and also as a backup source of power, but these accessories were eventually discarded once motorcycles became more advanced.

ers of the Orient bicycle, introduced the first successful line of American motorcycles. Many other bicycle makers followed suit, producing motorized bicycles as a sideline.

Several pioneer firms emerged shortly after the boom, including Harley-Davidson of Milwaukee and the Hendee Manufacturing Company of Springfield, Massachusetts, makers of the Indian. Oscar Hedstrom, a transplanted Swede, designed the original model, and George Hendee, the former high-wheel racer, provided the capital. Some early machines approached sixty miles an hour, but they were loud and dangerous. One of the casualties was Frank A. Elwell, the pioneer bicycle tourist, who suffered a fatal road accident when his forks collapsed in 1902. Within a few years, however, manufacturers made vast improvements to the motorcycle, and it soon came into extensive use and evolved into a distinct industry of its own.

"The feats of the competitors frequently put to blush those of bygone years," suggesting that bicycle racing still offered promising possibilities for development.

In sum, the boneshaker of the 1860s introduced the basic idea of the bicycle and its ideal—a compact pedal-powered two-wheeler anyone could master. For the next two decades the high wheeler, while straying from that original objective, nonetheless inspired the technology necessary to make the two-wheeler a truly roadworthy vehicle. Finally, the pneumatic-tire safety of the 1890s made good on the original idea, drawing on existing technology and spawning some of its own. Even as the public eagerly awaited affordable automobiles, it rightly regarded the safety bicycle as one of the great technical and social contributions of the Victorian age. And although the humble bicycle would never again rule the road as it had in the last quarter of the nineteenth century, it offered new and compelling opportunities for technical and commercial development.

facing page: A poster by Francisco Tamagno from about 1910 for Cycles Automoto of Saint-Etienne, a company that was established in 1902 and produced bicycles and motorcycles until it closed in 1965. In contrast with the United States, demand for bicycles remained strong in Europe in the early twentieth century.

Part Five The Twentieth Century

THIRTEEN

Utilitarian Cycling

The pneumatic-tire safety bicycle of the 1890s was, in effect, the long-coveted mechanical horse that provided, above all, practical transportation. As its price fell rapidly by the end of that decade, the bicycle finally emerged as a compelling "people's nag." Indeed, largely obscured by the calamitous fallout from the boom were newfound opportunities to market the utilitarian bicycle. As *Bicycling World* observed in 1902, nearly everyone could make use of the two-wheeler, especially those who lived in rural communities where no trolleys circulated. "As an economical and ever ready vehicle to convey the boy to school or the man to work," the journal confidently predicted, "the bicycle probably will forever remain without a peer." In the twentieth century, the two-wheeler did in fact become the world's most popular vehicle for personal transportation.

The emerging market for cheap bicycles—clunkers, as we call them today—at the onset of the twentieth century was, however, largely devoid of the glamour that had permeated the boom. Nor did it entail the fat profit margins the trade had come to expect from a vibrant recreational market. Still, the vast potential demand for cheap, serviceable bicycles was an alluring prospect that the depressed industry could ill afford to

車行自跑海上刻新

Cyclists in Shanghai around 1902. The bicycle was still an expensive novelty in China, but many Westerners were already eyeing a vast potential market for cycles.

ignore. In Europe, bicycle commuters were already commonplace. The president of the Touring Club of France confirmed that legions of cyclists were "pottering about" from one destination to another. In Denmark and the Netherlands routine riding was fast becoming a way of life. Demand for bicycles was also growing elsewhere in the world, including some potentially enormous markets like India and Japan. China, noted *Bicycling World,* "with its countless millions of population may prove the best foreign market on the globe."

Certain improvements in construction, meanwhile, continued to make the bicycle ever more practical. Of primary importance was the freewheel, an idea that had been frequently proposed for direct-drive bicycles but only sporadically applied. By the turn of the century, several bicycle makers in the United States and Europe, notably Ernst Sachs of Germany, had introduced freewheels incorporated within the rear sprocket of the safety bicycle. These enabled cyclists to adjust their pedaling cadence at will, and even keep their feet at rest on the pedals while coasting. They could also dismount at any time without having to fuss with moving pedals. *The Engineer* of London noted in 1900 that the freewheel was fast becoming "almost as universal as the pneumatic tire," and predicted it would give "a much-needed fillip to the cycle industry."

Use of the freewheel also mandated the addition of a brake, since backpedaling would no longer stop the rear wheel from spinning. In the United States, the freewheel was generally incorporated into a unit that included a coaster brake activated by pedaling backward. The British trade, in contrast, favored the hand or rim brake, usually affixed to the frame just above the rear wheel. By squeezing a lever mounted to the handlebar, the rider tensioned a Bowden cable and compressed a spring in the brake, forcing its calipers to close and apply hard rubber surfaces against the sidewalls of the rim. In contrast with earlier spoon brakes that plunged a hard surface against the top of the tire, both the rim and coaster brakes spared the tire treads. Their additional weight was a small price to pay for a convenient and reliable braking system.

In spite of the evident advantages of brakes and freewheels, some purists like Joseph Pennell denounced these additions. They prided themselves on their ability to control the brakeless safety bicycle, and insisted that freewheels detracted from the vehicle's "charm of simplicity." As Pennell saw it, freewheels offered no advantage to recreational riders, and served only those mundane cyclists "who wish to loiter about at the rate of six or seven miles an hour in the grease among the traffic." Yet that was precisely the objective of the urban commuter who had to navigate through narrow spaces while frequently adjusting direction and pace. Moreover, it soon became apparent that the freewheel was in fact a boon to all classes of cyclists.

British cycle manufacturers in the early part of the twentieth century also introduced other practical accessories that made the bicycle more serviceable, if somewhat heavier. Basic low-cost models acquired wide, cushy seats supported by springs to absorb road shock, and swept-back handlebars to allow the rider to sit in a comfortable upright position. Heavy-duty models featured fenders, a waterproof case to shield the chain from the elements, and a thick enamel finish to guard against rust. Meanwhile, a number of firms made handy accessories for cyclists. Brooks Limited, of Birmingham, for one, made an assortment of leather products, including tool bags and saddles that became standard equipment on all styles of bicycles.

The Raleigh Cycle Company of Nottingham, England, reigned as the industry's leader, a position it maintained for virtually the entire twentieth century. It grew out of a small cycle shop purchased in 1888 by Frank Bowden, a prosperous lawyer and cycling advocate who was committed to bringing more practical and affordable bicycles to an ever-wider public. During the boom, the company grew into the largest bicycle factory in Britain and gained international fame as the sponsor of Arthur A. Zimmerman. When business began to slide at the turn of the century, Bowden vigorously pursued factory innovations to cut operational costs and regain long-term profitability. In the late 1890s, he sent the factory foreman George Pilkington Mills, the winner of the historic Paris-to-Bordeaux race of 1891 and a university-trained engineer, to the United States to study and acquire the most advanced labor-saving machinery.

Bowden had long recognized the need to offer the cyclist a range of gears to handle

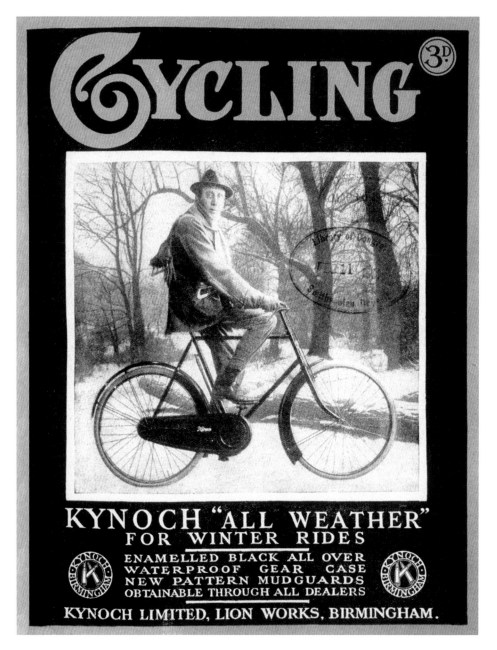

After the boom, the British trade focused on making bicycles even more practical. This bicycle, designed for year-round use in all kinds of weather, adorned the cover of *Cycling*, 24 February 1921.

diverse terrain. Although a number of variable-gear systems from derailleurs to two-speed hubs had been proposed over the years, few had shown much commercial promise. Around 1902, however, Bowden began to see some three-speed hubs to his liking, conveniently operated by cable-connected thumb shifters affixed to the top tube or handlebar and offering a wide range of gears. The middle speed was direct—it rotated the wheel at the same rate as the external sprocket. But the high speed increased the gear by about 25 percent, while the low speed decreased it by about 20 percent. The hub gear also required little maintenance and was well protected from the elements. And unlike derailleur systems, it did not displace the chain. As a result the rider could change gears at any time even without pedaling.

In 1902, Bowden hired Henry Sturmey and James Archer to oversee production of three-speed hubs, giving rise to the celebrated Sturmey-Archer label. By the following year, the division was marketing an improved model, designed by William Reilly, that allowed freewheeling in all three speeds. Manufacturing it was no simple task, however. The hub gear is by far the most complicated component on a bicycle, made of dozens of tiny parts. It works on the principle known as "planetary gearing." The "sun" gear (rigidly attached to the rear axle) is surrounded by three or four identical "planet" gears, which are in turn encircled by an internally toothed "gear ring." By selecting a speed, the cyclist determines how these elements interact and the speed with which the rear wheel turns relative to the chain-driven sprocket. In the middle gear, the sprocket and wheel rotate at the same speed. The high and low gears use the planetary gear train in opposite directions, causing the wheel to turn either faster or slower than the sprocket, usually in a 3:4 ratio.

A cutaway view of a 1902 Sturmey-Archer three-speed hub, drawn by Jim Gill, showing its complicated internal elliptical gears. Hub gears offered the first practical way to give a bicycle multiple speeds that could be changed on the fly, and many people at the time anticipated that three gears would prove more than adequate.

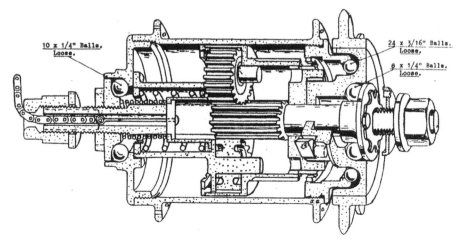

Portable Bicycles

Compactness and portability have always been coveted features in a bicycle. Even in the prime of the massive high wheeler, W. H. J. Grout of London recognized the desirability of a portable model. He proposed a variation with a front wheel that collapsed into four sections, allowing the entire machine to fit into one large but luggable bag. Happily, the standard bicycle of the 1890s already had a far more practical profile, even without special folding provisions. Yet a few inventors still felt compelled to devise even more portable designs. During the boom, several proposed foldable small-wheeled bicycles for military use. Others recognized the need for compact "city bicycles" that riders could take indoors with them, eliminating the need to find a parking spot outdoors and reducing the risk of theft. The owner could also easily transport such a compact mount in an elevator, a car, a bus, a train, a boat, or even an airplane.

In 1919, C. H. Clark proposed a city bicycle with a tall vertical frame and two small wheels barely a foot high and a foot apart. He brought the curiosity to the Manhattan office of *Scientific American,* where he pointed out to the startled editors: "I did not have to leave the wheel at the curb and invite you down to the street to see it. I brought the machine up with me, not in the freight lift, but in a crowded passenger elevator, and neither the starter nor the operator offered the slightest objection." The enterprising inventor even took his miniature machine to the Newark Velodrome where he gave credible chase to the hunched racers as they whizzed around the wooden track—to little avail.

Although hub gears were originally intended for the high-end recreational market, they gained wide diffusion over the next few years as the price gradually came down from a lofty three pounds to roughly a third of that figure. One popular model, introduced in 1908, included a coaster brake. The racer Harry Green used it that year to cycle 866 miles from Land's End to John O'Groats, covering the course in less than three days—a record that stood for more than twenty years. By 1913 the company was producing its cheapest model to the tune of 100,000 units a year. Over the years, the

From 1963 to 1967, the British engineer Alex Moulton produced the Stow-away, a separable version of his novel city bike with small wheels and a distinctive dual-suspension frame. It helped establish a demand in Britain for small-wheeled bikes with frames that either fold or detach into two pieces. For the past thirty years, the foldable Brompton has evolved while claiming a large following. Since 1983, Moulton himself has offered a new generation of separable models. A more recent entry is the Strida, featuring a foldable aluminum frame and a greaseless belt drive.

C. H. Clark's portable "city bicycle," in *Scientific American*, December 1919. The photograph on the right illustrates the inventor's confidence that his design would become the next evolutionary stage of the bicycle.

Sturmey-Archer hub gear served as an integral part of the classic British three-speed bicycle, a high-end utilitarian vehicle that was sold the world over. By the jubilee year of 1952, production had surpassed two million a year.

The persistent efforts of the British bicycle industry to develop cheaper and more practical bicycles at the start of the twentieth century paid off quickly. By the fall of 1905, *The Field* was already speaking of a second boom "due largely to the adoption of the wheel by those of the lower classes" who had not been able to afford bicycles "in the days of high prices." The journal observed, "The bicycle is being pressed more and more into the service of everyday life. The great majority of the machines are of the cheapest grade, but, even so, when made by the more responsible firms, they are strong and serviceable." So popular was the basic machine, in fact, that "it is now practically impossible to escape the ubiquitous bicycle even in the most remote and secluded highways."

British workers were also using bicycles to transport goods. In 1906 *Bicycling World* reported that, "every other butcher, baker and candlestick maker in the Kingdom finds use for the cycle." The British trade, it continued, offered an "astonishing" number of delivery cycles, notably "'man-killing' carrier tricycles and quadricycles with parcels or burdens of some sort stowed in the big box. . . . They are to be seen even in the very thick of London traffic, and the 'galley slaves' who do the pedaling seem unconcerned about their safety." In addition, scores of "cycling newsboys" combed the streets of London, and the British post office had purchased "many hundreds" of bicycles to deliver mail.

The bicycle trade was in fact prospering throughout Europe. By 1910, the German industry had overtaken its British counterpart to become the world's leading exporter of cycle goods. Domestic demand rose as well, especially among the working class. Whereas few German workers could afford a bicycle during the boom, they made up about half the country's cycling population by 1906. Two years later, Solidarity, a national association of working-class cyclists, counted more than a hundred thousand members—four times the number it had just four years earlier. France also emerged as a leading exporter. Among its leaders was the Manufacture Française d'Armes of Saint-Etienne, which made both weapons and bicycles depending on the season. Its popular Hirondelle (Swallow) offered two speeds, and pedaling backward engaged the low gear for hill-climbing.

In Asia, demand for utilitarian bicycles was also on the rise, especially in Japan. In 1910, the American vice consul in Yokohama confirmed, "Bicycles are in general use throughout the Empire." Moreover, Japan, once a heavy importer of Western bicycles, was progressively supplying its own demand for the machines. Only fifteen years earlier, during the boom, the *American Cyclist* had dismissed as "absurd" the "bare notion that the Japanese will ever be able to produce high-class wheels for their own use." Yet now Japanese cycle makers were even threatening to erode the West's bustling export trade throughout the Far East.

The American industry, however, continued to struggle. In the spring of 1903, a gallant Albert A. Pope, who four years earlier had sold off his bicycle concern to embark on automobile production, set out to restore the country's devastated bicycle business. The sixty-year-old colonel left his comfortable retirement home in Cohasset, Massachusetts, to return to Hartford, where he reclaimed his bicycle factory from the ashes of the failed American Bicycle Company. Eight hundred past and future employees gathered to give him a hero's welcome, cheering and waving flags while a band played in the background. "I am back to lead to victory," declared an emotional Pope over the din. "As Sheridan turned the tide of battle in the Shenandoah Valley, I hope to turn it here." He expressed his heartfelt conviction that the Hartford bicycle plant would soon be running "to its utmost capacity again."

Pope evidently detected lingering opportunities in the bicycle trade. He knew, of course, that conditions had changed, and that he would have to offer more affordable models to tap the large contingent of cyclists who rode simply to get somewhere. Still, he believed a new-style "high grade" bicycle could appeal to wealthier sorts inclined to cycle simply for pleasure and convenience. Among the elite who remained faithful to the wheel were the financier John D. Rockefeller and the diplomat A. A. Adee. Harvard's septuagenarian president, Charles W. Eliot, was another prominent cyclist. He routinely covered several miles between his home on Brattle Street and his office in Harvard Yard, often accompanied by his cyclist wife. "Every clear morning," reported *Bicycling World* in 1908, Eliot "jumps on his bicycle . . . like a boy in his teens."

The trade journal likewise held out hope for a British-style revival. One encouraging sign, it noted, was the expansion of the Emblem Manufacturing Company of Angola, New York, outside Buffalo. In 1906 it became the first American bicycle company in nearly a decade to open a new factory. Yet prosperity proved elusive. In 1909, annual production sank below a quarter million units, a new post-boom low. The anticipated upscale market was slow to materialize, and the once lucrative export business had all but evaporated. A certain domestic demand for economical bicycles persisted, but even that was modest by European standards.

To encourage greater use of the bicycle, American manufacturers began to promote London-style delivery vehicles. In 1909, the year that Colonel Pope died, the Pope Manufacturing Company, now operating exclusively in Westfield, Massachusetts, unveiled its heavy-gauged Daily Service Bicycle. It was designed for letter carriers, policemen, firemen, messengers, and linesmen. According to advertisements, it answered "a heavy demand during the past three years for a bicycle possessing greater strength and durability [to] stand up day in and day out." Other firms quickly followed suit. The Excelsior Supply Company of Chicago, for one, offered a delivery bicycle with integrated front and rear racks and a motorcycle-style spring fork and rear stand.

At last, a small American market for serviceable bicycles did materialize, and production inched upward. According to *Bicycling World*, "a few butchers and bakers" began to transport their goods in "handle bar baskets." And even though the postal service had not formally adopted the bicycle, an occasional postman "employed his

Specialized Services

The cycle industry has felt compelled from time to time to identify and promote specialized applications to boost overall demand. One early proposal calculated to drum up new business was the military bicycle, designed to transport soldiers and equipment. Yet for all the hoopla this concept received in the 1890s, it has yet to prove of great tactical value. The bicycles that have probably played the greatest role in a conflict to date were not special military models at all, but rather mundane clunkers: during the Vietnam War, the forces of the North Vietnamese successfully used standard bicycles to shuttle supplies along the Ho Chi Minh trail under the cover of thick brush.

The police bicycle is another recurrent proposition that has fluctuated in and out of favor. Such vehicles were commonly used for patrols in the early twentieth century before they gave way to cars and motorcycles. Nevertheless, since the introduction of the mountain bike, police bicycles have regained favor. Seattle was among the first cities to form a mountain-bike squad in 1987. Since then, numerous urban communities have assigned bicycles to police officers so that they can patrol city centers discreetly and navigate through crowds. Recently, emergency medical technicians have also employed mountain bikes to cover large outdoor events.

Another resurgent role is that of the bicycle messenger. In the first half of the twentieth century, the bicycle-equipped "telegraph boy" combed cities worldwide, but began to disappear once the agencies began reading messages over the telephone. "Errand boys" who delivered small packages from the pharmacy or market were also once familiar figures, but they, too, have been lost in the automo-

own bicycle to assist in collecting mail." Moreover, many cities opted to supply bicycles to police officers. These vehicles were not only cheaper than horses and motorcycles, they also proved effective as urban patrol vehicles. Of the eleven thousand arrests made in Indianapolis in 1908, the bicycle squad of a dozen officers took credit for nearly a quarter.

tive age. Until recently, newspaper boys and girls on their trusty bicycles were still part of the American suburban landscape, but adult motorists have largely taken their place. Nevertheless, over the past twenty years, a new breed of bicycle carrier has appeared: the bicycle courier. These highly fit men and women shuttle time-sensitive documents from one urban business to another, and they have earned a wide reputation for their dazzling speed, traffic-weaving skills, and outlandish appearances.

Bicycle couriers passing by the White House. Over the past thirty years bicycle delivery services have developed into a significant industry.

Still, the modest domestic demand stemmed chiefly from juveniles, who favored models resembling the latest motorcycles. Sold chiefly through department stores, these bicycles featured heavier tires, extended handlebars, and fake gas tanks that sometimes held batteries to power the headlight. Though these machines weighed a hefty forty to fifty pounds, children were drawn to their flashy styling and seductive gadgetry. More-

Bicycle police in Stamford, Connecticut, in about 1910. The large gears on these bicycles suggest that these po-licemen were serious about chasing down offenders, though it would have taken some effort to work up speed.

over, parents appreciated their robust, almost indestructible, design. Although some children sought bicycles purely for amusement, many had practical goals in mind, like riding to school or making a few dollars by shuttling small packages and groceries for pharmacies and markets. Companies that employed young people insisted that they were not exploiting children but simply providing a character-building experience.

Perhaps the most prominent urban cyclist in the first half of the twentieth century was the telegraph boy. One of the largest firms, Western Union, bought some five thou-sand bicycles a year, then resold them to its messengers nationwide at a discount. The boys, who were as young as ten years old, were usually part of a fleet ranging from one to three dozen or more. Every morning they reported to the central office in uniform and awaited their assignments, receiving payment by the mile. Though some went by foot, most relied on the bicycle to deliver messages to distant destinations. John Dickson of Dallas, Texas, for one, racked up more than 16,000 miles between April and September 1915, covering 85 to 120 miles every day.

The life of a messenger boy was often full of adventure. The *Western Union News* of September 1915 reported this heroic performance in Philadelphia:

1917 Arrow

Great Bicycle Offer!

An advertisement from *Boys' Life* in February 1917 emphasizing the many similarities between a kids' "moto cycle" and a motorized two-wheeler, although none of the various gadgets included on the bicycle really enhanced its roadworthiness

A few days ago, Messenger Salvatore Stanie was given a rush message for a passenger on one of the ocean steamships. As he sped down Delaware Avenue on his trusty bike, he saw that the ship had cast off, a couple of tug-boats turning her in the river preparatory to her dash for the open sea. Salvatore grasped the situation, slowed up and grabbed a potato from a basket on the sidewalk without even stopping to apologize. He then sped on to the end of the pier, and yelling to the ship "Is Mr. Blank aboard" and received an affirmative response from the man along the rail. Salvatore wrapped the message and delivery sheet around the spud and, securing both by a rubber band taken from his cap, wound up and made a second base throw to one of the deck officers, who made a fine catch and turned over the message and sheet to Mr. Blank. The latter signed the sheet and made a perfect return throw to Stanie, who came on back and turned in his sheet as nonchalantly as if delivering messages to steamships a la baseball was an everyday occurrence. Next?

Bicycle messenger boys at the American District Telegraph Company (ADT) headquarters in Indianapolis in 1908. The boys bought their own bicycles but received a discount through the company.

But few topped the experience of Robert Crawford, a young messenger in the nation's capital. In the fall of 1913, he drew national attention after he collided with an automobile carrying Woodrow Wilson, the president of the United States. Coincidentally Wilson himself was an ardent cyclist. Before assuming office the previous year, he had gone on a relaxing cycle tour of Bermuda, where he reportedly did "a lot of thinking in the saddle." So concerned was the president for Crawford's health, he assigned his personal physician to oversee his recovery. A few days later, Wilson paid a visit to the hospital and presented the stunned lad with a new bicycle. "I did not know it was the President's car that I ran into," stammered the boy from his bed. A smiling Wilson replied, "I rather thought it was the President's car that ran into you."

Yet, other than the occasional collegiate cyclist, American adults showed little inclination to remount the neglected two-wheeler. "It is difficult to understand," lamented *Bicycling World,* "why the bicycle as a means of utility should be in such comparatively restricted use in this country." Nor were American bicycles in high demand abroad. In the estimation of many Europeans, the trade that had once led the world had failed to keep pace. American machines, in fact, had arguably regressed. Although they generally offered the convenience of coaster brakes, they weighed a good ten to fifteen pounds more than the typical twenty-five-pound featherweights of the boom era. Many now featured the so-called cushion frame, with a secondary top tube that supposedly softened the ride. But whatever its technical merits, it made the American machines even heavier.

In Europe, by contrast, demand for utilitarian adult bicycles continued to grow. The Hercules Cycle and Motor Company of Birmingham, England, founded in 1910, focused on delivering reliable and affordable bicycles to the masses. The firm pointedly eschewed novel accessories until they had proved their merit and could be offered at little additional cost. The company's popular pitch proved so successful that it soon became Raleigh's chief rival. In France, meanwhile, demand for serviceable bicycles was also on the rise. In 1913, *Scientific American* marveled that nearly three million bicycles circulated in that country alone, compared with only about one hundred thousand motorcycles and even fewer automobiles. The journal noted that one out of every thirteen French citizens owned a bicycle, up from one in thirty ten years earlier.

The bustling European trade nonetheless suffered a setback of its own when World War I broke out in 1914. With metal and rubber diverted to the war effort, bicycle firms shifted to arms production. Yet demand for bicycles actually intensified. In the summer of 1917 London's *Weekly Dispatch* reported that the city was in the throes of a "famine in bicycles." With train service reduced and packed buses charging higher fares, scores of frustrated commuters demanded bicycles. "Manufacturers are making the machines out of the old stock of parts they happen to have on hand," reported the newspaper. "When that stock is exhausted, as it soon will be, they will not be able to obtain any more." The Germans likewise suffered from a shortage of bicycle parts. Resourceful cyclists fashioned makeshift tires out of wood, rope, canvas, and even cork.

The war gave the long-suffering American trade a new crack at prosperity. For the first time in years, U.S. companies began to export large numbers of bicycles to Europe. Meanwhile, some hopeful signs pointed to a possible revival at home. Domestic demand continued to nudge forward and the public showed a renewed interest in recreational and competitive cycling. And after the United States entered the war in 1917, the government commissioned American cycle firms to produce ten thousand Liberty bicycles for its troops. It also encouraged bicycle use at home as a way to conserve scarce supplies of petroleum.

The conflict itself, according to *Bicycle News,* a new trade journal, reaffirmed the practical value of the bicycle. Thousands of soldiers on both sides rode bicycles. About half of these were conventional models, and the rest were folding bicycles that had been especially designed for military use. "The cyclist soldier is an important arm of practically every one of the contending armies," asserted the journal. "[The bicycle] has proven an invaluable aid time and time again. [It] enables large bodies of infantry to quickly and quietly approach within striking distance of the enemy. For scouting work

... the inconspicuous and noiseless bicycle goes unseen and unheard where the horse or motorcycle would be immediately detected."

After the war ended in the fall of 1918, the rejuvenated American industry appeared poised at last to mount a sustained recovery. Production had climbed back to the half-million mark. The Cycle Trades of America (CTA), a newly formed trade association, launched the "Ride a Bicycle" promotional campaign, confident that Americans were at last ready to adopt the bicycle on a far greater scale. According to a survey it conducted, fully three-quarters of the American adults who purchased bicycles were seeking a means of cheap transportation rather than a source of recreation. The CTA concluded that the utilitarian market offered the best prospects for growth, if more urbanites could be per-

An advertisement from the Cycle Trades of America's "Ride a Bicycle" campaign, in *Printer's Ink*, 19 February 1920, promoting the bicycle's advantages for commuting and short-distance trips

suaded to abandon the trolley in favor of the wheel. The CTA advertisements implored adults to cycle "to and from work," stressing a savings of "time, money, and temper" as compared with riding a trolley.

Unfortunately, the resurgence of the American cycle industry proved short-lived. The mass migration to the bicycle never materialized, and once European demand evaporated, domestic production resumed a downward trend. In 1921, annual production once again receded to below a quarter million. Frank Bowden, the head of the Raleigh Cycle Company, said, "It is remarkable that with a population of 110 millions, the output of [American] bicycles is not greater than in England." He attributed the weak demand to the "astounding" prominence of the increasingly affordable American automobile. "Everyone's ambition in the States," he concluded, "seems to be to have a motorcar." Indeed, by 1920 annual sales of Henry Ford's Model T, introduced in 1908, had reached about three-quarter million. Priced at about four hundred dollars, it was rapidly fulfilling Ford's dream of an "automobile for the great multitude" and undercutting a greater role for the bicycle in American life as a means of personal transportation.

Conceding defeat, the CTA shifted its focus back to the faithful juvenile market. In 1923, it produced a short promotional movie titled "How Dreams Come True." The group insisted it was not advertising but rather "a gripping picture of a boy's life," depicting "how badly he wants a bicycle and what he does to get one." The CTA promised "plenty of laughs and a few tears," and added, "the kiddies love it, and so do the grownups." The group supplied the film at no charge to any dealer who made arrangements to show it at a local theater. It advised dealers to distribute tickets free of charge to neighborhood children, asking them to record their addresses on the stubs for follow-up contacts.

Juvenile sales remained strong throughout the 1920s. After all, unlike adults, children had little opportunity to graduate to motorized machines. Moreover, despite some safety concerns, many parents were pleased to satisfy their children's demands for shiny new bicycles. For all its gaudy ornamentation, the child's bicycle provided a genuine service. Well before "soccer moms" shuttled children about in minivans, youngsters made their own rounds atop their trusty two-wheelers. Bicycles offered a cheap, convenient, and independent means to get to school, perform errands, or simply reconnoiter with friends. American makers sold the majority of their wares over the Christmas holidays, though some lucky children received bicycles on their birthdays.

Elsewhere around the globe, however, bicycles continued to provide serious adult transportation, especially in Europe. When the president of the Packard Motor Car Company toured European auto factories in 1924, he was amazed to see no automobiles on the premises, except for "those in charge of chauffeurs waiting in front of the general offices." What he saw instead were "long double rows of bicycles" under "pergola-like

Cover of *Open Road for Boys,* April 1939, underscoring how children used bicycles to carry light loads

structures," their rear wheels secured in bike racks. It reminded him of American parking lots fifteen years earlier, before the automobile became so commonplace. Even the Soviet Union launched a bicycle production program in 1928, and the country reached an annual output of half a million by 1937.

Although the bicycle played a relatively modest role in American life, the cycle industry nonetheless mounted an impressive comeback in the 1930s, thanks in large part to a heightened recreational interest. In addition many citizens, hit by the Great Depression and unable to maintain an automobile, turned to the bicycle for cheap transportation. The industry mainstay, however, remained children's bicycles, which gained even greater favor following the introduction of the "balloon" tire. Resembling the automotive variety, these fat tires on smaller wheels fired an adolescent's imagination. They also offered practical advantages over the narrow-gauge, single-unit standard: the heavy outer tread guarded against punctures, while the independent inner tube simplified repairs. The balloon tire could certainly tolerate much greater abuse than thinner varieties, an undeniable asset for a child's model. As *Consumers Union Reports* pointed out, "jumping curbs, hurdling ditches, and speeding over bumpy surfaces is part of the joy of cycling." Moreover, the rugged construction enabled children to ride off the pavement and explore nearby woods or head to the local lake for a dip.

Schwinn presented a trendsetting model in 1933 called the Aerocycle. It addition to balloon tires, it featured an imitation gas tank and curving "streamlined" tubes patterned after the latest airplanes, autos, and locomotives. Top models sported an assortment of battery-powered gadgets, such as speedometers, clocks, and horns. Some even included the celebrated "cyclelock," a key-operated lock built into the fork crown that prevented the steering column from moving. According to Schwinn, the device was the long-awaited "final solution of the bicycle theft problem." The success of the Aerocycle spawned a number of similar models, notably the Shelby Air-Flow and Monark's aluminum-alloy Silver King.

In 1936, American production finally broke one million cycles per year for the first time since the boom. The Homer P. Snyder Manufacturing Company of Little Falls, New York, was the leading producer, selling a variety of brands through department stores and mail order catalogs. Its chief rival, the Westfield Manufacturing Company, successor to Pope's bicycle company, continued to exploit the Columbia trademark. Rounding out the top four were two holdovers from the boom period, the Schwinn company of Chicago and the Iver Johnson Arms and Cycle Works of Fitchburg, Massachusetts. A newcomer was the Huffman Manufacturing Company of Dayton, Ohio, later known simply as Huffy. Its president, Horace M. Huffman, was encouraged by what he saw as a "change of attitude" on the part of adults who were increasingly inclined not only to let their children ride bicycles but also to ride one themselves.

The number of bicycles circulating in the United States climbed to about two or three million by the mid-1930s, but that figure paled in comparison to the European fleets. Germany, which had half the American population, counted fifteen million bicycles. Great Britain and France each had about seven million cycles, followed by Italy with four million. Even the tiny Netherlands had three million: one for almost every other citizen. Every working day, some 400,000 cyclists commuted in and out of Amsterdam alone. One visitor observed that the Dutch cyclist, freed from noise and the smell of gasoline, took time to notice "things like birds and flowers," which the American motorist "leaves in the roar and dust." Affirmed another traveler: "All Hollanders are accomplished bicyclists from the princess down to the most humble scrubwoman." To the Dutch, the observer asserted, a bicycle "becomes a matter of individual expression, almost a part of the body." Another hypothesized that if there was anything to the theory of evolution, another century should see Dutch babies "coming into this world on tiny bicycles."

In many parts of Europe, the bicycle had become the most popular form of transportation. A study of Copenhagen traffic in 1930 found that bicycles carried fully a third of the populace; 29 percent of the people used street railways, 21 percent walked, and the rest rode in automobiles or some other vehicle. In 1933, *Fortune* observed how sharply the European reliance on the bicycle contrasted with the American scene: "On the [European] continent, 95 percent of all bicycles are bought by hard-working people who think them too luxurious for children." The magazine marveled that, while Americans owned seventeen autos for every bicycle, Europeans had seven bicycles for every car.

Naturally, with such a robust demand, the European trade continued to thrive. By the late 1930s, the British industry produced about two million bicycles a year. About a fifth went overseas, mostly to colonies and former colonies, including India and South Africa. Raleigh, which had swallowed up Humber Cycles and modernized its plant, produced about half a million machines a year, fully ten times its typical output in the early 1920s. The German industry produced over two million bicycles a year in the 1930s, before it was consumed by the war. In France, Saint-Etienne emerged as the "Capitale du Cycle," with more than a hundred bicycle-related firms that together produced 80 percent of the country's cycle output. Italy's fascist government strongly encouraged bicycle use, equipping dozens of regiments with bicycles.

Demand for the economical vehicle was also rising throughout the world, espe-

facing page: The Schwinn Streamline Aerocycle, in an ad from June 1934 in *Toy World and Bicycle World*, with its modernistic design that spoke to children's tastes and heavy-duty balloon tires that let them ramble off the paved roads with little fear of punctures

Arnold, Schwinn & Co.

Introduces The Streamline Aerocycle

WITH THE NEW WELDED FRAME — BUILT LIKE AN AEROPLANE FUSELAGE

Another basic and radical improvement—in strength, beauty, and modern streamlined appearance.

It's a greater sales stimulator than the revolutionary balloon tire introduced last year by this leader of the industry.

WRITE AT ONCE FOR THE NAME OF YOUR NEAREST JOBBER

ARNOLD, SCHWINN & CO.

1718 NORTH KILDARE AVENUE, CHICAGO
7 EAST 17th STREET, NEW YORK CITY

cially in Asia. Japan remained a major producer of bicycles and parts, and it was a growing force in the export market thanks to its highly competitive prices. Japan itself, though not quite as bicycle-saturated as Europe, nonetheless hosted some six million machines, two or three times the number in the United States despite having only half as many people. China, too, had a growing fleet of bicycles, mostly imported from Germany, Japan, and Great Britain. Peasants were gradually giving up the traditional donkey and using a bicycle instead to get to and from their fields.

With the outbreak of World War II, the utilitarian bicycle assumed an even greater presence on both sides of the Atlantic. In 1941, a committee representing the American industry petitioned the Office of Production Management, the government's industrial regulatory agency, for permission to continue operations, arguing that bicycles could serve commuters at home as they did in Europe. It asserted that forty-pound bicycles could, in many situations, replace Chevrolets weighing over a ton. The agency agreed to allocate the industry sufficient rubber and steel to produce 750,000 bicycles in 1942. In return, the trade agreed to limit its line to two utilitarian adult models, one for each

A street in Shanghai in the 1930s filled with a great variety of human-powered vehicles, notably traditional rickshaws loaded with goods and passengers, as well as a number of bicycles

facing page: Along with the Netherlands and Sweden, Denmark has long been one of the world's most bicycle-friendly nations, a tradition reflected in this poster from 1949 for the National Travel Association of Denmark

Leon Henderson, administrator of the Office of Production Management, and Betty Barrett, his stenographer, riding around Washington in March 1942 to commemorate the first lot of Victory carrier bicycles, intended to facilitate domestic deliveries as an oil-conservation measure for the war effort

sex. These Spartan "Victory bicycles" were stripped of all the customary gadgetry and weighed only about thirty-four pounds, approaching the lightness of a typical British bicycle. Moreover, priced at about a dollar a pound, they were within the means of working people.

With automobile production suspended during the war, and the existing fleet shrinking daily in the midst of a shortage of spare parts and tires, the American public relied increasingly on the bicycle for everyday transport. In Chicago, dealers quadrupled their sales. Across the nation, bicycle racks sprang up "for the convenience of suburbanites who are using bicycles instead of their cars for local transportation." Cities and utility companies sharply curtailed motorized travel and encouraged their workers to make their rounds on bicycles. Even the armament workers who churned out tanks and airplanes dutifully cycled to work. Many offices allowed female workers to wear slacks if they rode in on a bicycle. Some three hundred communities initiated bicycle registrations to foster safe cycling skills and reduce bicycle thefts. Los Angeles reported

A happy Kevin Ryan collecting a school prize, a shiny new Schwinn, in 1956

that the recovery rate of stolen bicycles rose from about 15 percent in 1934, when the program began, to 90 percent eight years later.

In Europe as well, bicycle traffic rose during the war years. An extreme example was Sweden, which overtook Denmark and the Netherlands to become the world's leading bicycle nation. By the end of the war, Sweden's fleet had ballooned to some three million cycles, one for every other citizen—even though a basic bicycle cost the equivalent of the average worker's monthly salary. More than forty thousand cyclists crossed Stockholm's major bridge every day, ten times the typical flow twenty years earlier. Moreover, a study revealed that "the use of the bicycle in Sweden is not confined to any age group or class. It is utilized almost equally for going to school and work and for recreation."

After the war, bicycle commuting subsided in the United States, though a mild recreational interest continued. The American industry once again turned its attention

Workers streaming out of the Morris automobile factory near Oxford, England, at the end of the day, from *Fortune,* July 1946. One deft cyclist in the center steers with one hand while focusing on his reading material.

Bicycle Offshoots

Over the years, a number of specialized cycles have been proposed to facilitate a variety of services. One towering model from the boom period was designed to help lamplighters make their rounds without ever having to descend from their bicycles. Other specialized models from that time included ambulances and fire-fighting vehicles. Most of these ideas were short-lived, but at least one has enjoyed a long life: the delivery cycle with two or three wheels, heavy-duty tires, and built-in racks to carry a generous supply of goods. Such vehicles were common in Europe before the 1950s, and are still widely used today in developing countries where motorized vehicles are luxuries.

Another specialized cycle that has been around for decades, especially in Asia, is the tricycle rickshaw. On some models, the driver sits in front and one or two passengers sit on a bench between the two rear wheels, facing either forward or backward. On others, the passengers sit between the two front wheels facing forward while the operator pedals from behind. Pedal-powered rickshaws are still a common sight in much of the developing world.

A number of companies in Europe and North America now run fleets composed of comfortable models known as pedicabs—Manhattan alone boasts two such services. Pedicabs are usually slower and more expensive than conventional cabs, but they offer certain advantages—they are more maneuverable in heavy traffic and can travel where motorized traffic is prohibited. They are especially popular with tourists who want to better experience their host city. The drivers often double as tour guides, though that service often entails a supplementary fee. Pedicabs have also proven to be a highly effective advertising medium.

One of the Manhattan Rickshaw Company's pedicabs carrying a passenger in SoHo. The company has been shuttling people across town for more than a decade in these vehicles, which typically carry advertisements, and their drivers often provide commentary for tourists.

to the youth market, then teeming with baby boomers. A pent-up demand for stream-lined fat-tired models propelled annual output to nearly three million units. Through-out the 1950s, largely on the strength of the juvenile demand, domestic production hov-ered around two million. Some of the most highly prized models were those that evoked popular cartoon and television figures like Donald Duck, Howdy Doody, and Hopalong Cassidy.

In Europe, bicycle commuting remained popular for a few more years. In 1946, *Fortune* found it ironic that the vast majority of workmen at the Morris automotive plant outside Oxford, England, cycled to work, since they could not afford to purchase the very vehicles they produced. Two years later, the Italian director Vittorio De Sica im-mortalized the worker cyclist in the award-winning movie *The Bicycle Thief* (titled *Bicy-cle Thieves* for its U.K. release). Yet as the 1950s progressed, motorized vehicles became increasingly affordable to Europeans and they gradually displaced bicycles as the most popular means of transportation. The growing volume of motorized traffic, in turn, dis-couraged those still inclined to cycle. The once ubiquitous bicycle commuter was fast becoming an endangered species throughout the developed world.

While demand for the utilitarian bicycle declined sharply in Western countries after the war, it continued to rise throughout the developing world, giving Raleigh and other industry leaders a new mandate. In 1949, *The Economist* noted that the British cycle industry was exporting large numbers of bicycles to India, Pakistan, Malaya, and Africa, adding that "a good number of machines go to the Middle East and South Amer-ica." Raleigh in particular kept its enormous plant busy throughout the 1950s by export-ing up to half its output. The postwar Japanese and German bicycle industries also reestablished a healthy export trade with developing countries. But homegrown com-petition intensified as well. The Indian bicycle industry in particular developed into a major global producer with the help of a protectionist government. More recently, Brazil has become an important regional producer.

The declining domestic demand for bicycles in the postwar period, followed by an invasion of cheap imports from Taiwan and the Far East, caused considerable upheaval in the international bicycle industry. In the United States, the Columbia brand stag-gered on for several decades, and even enjoyed an upswing in demand during the bi-cycle revival of the early 1970s, but the century-old bicycle name was finally retired in the 1980s. The Schwinn concern survived long enough to celebrate its centennial in 1995, but the company filed for bankruptcy shortly thereafter. In Europe, venerable cycle producers like Hercules and Motobécane of France were either swallowed up or dismantled. Even Raleigh, after a long struggle, eventually succumbed to bankruptcy. Some brand names live on, but only because new companies have acquired the associ-

British poster for *Bicycle Thieves*, Vittorio De Sica's masterpiece from 1948 (released in the United States the following year as *The Bicycle Thief*). In impoverished Rome in the aftermath of the war, the unemployed hero finally finds a delivery job that requires a bicycle, but when his is stolen, his life falls apart. In the famous closing sequence he is tempted to fill the void by stealing someone else's bike.

ated rights. The industry is now a globalized operation, with the vast majority of frames and accessories produced in the Far East and merely assembled in the country of sale.

In spite of the travails of the cycle industry following World War II, and humanity's growing reliance on the automobile, bicycles continue to provide essential transportation in much of the world. In the 1980s, more than a million Japanese cyclists rode to and from commuter rail stations every day, and the number has risen sharply since then. Bicycle parking became such a problem, in fact, that the Construction Ministry has built multifloored computer-operated storage facilities. When cyclists arrive at one of these giant "parking garages," they hang their bicycles by the handlebars on suspended arms, turn a key to lock them in place, and off go their bikes to some predetermined location on high. On the cyclist's return, the system retrieves the right machine in less than a minute. Other cities, such as Muenster, Germany, operate downtown garages specially designed for bicycles.

But of course the country with the most bicycles, as *Bicycling World* astutely predicted at the turn of the century, is the People's Republic of China. By 1980, cycle facto-

This parking facility near the train station in downtown Muenster, completed in 1999, holds up to thirty-five hundred bicycles. Rates are by the day, the month, or the year and a cycle shop in the facility rents and repairs bicycles. Germans are far more likely than Americans to use bicycles for short-distance errands or commutes.

Bicycle commuters in Shanghai, clearly not fair-weather riders, in 2001. China remains heavily dependent on bicycle travel despite the government's recent campaign to promote automobile production and sales.

ries were operating in virtually every province and the country had amassed some hundred million machines. Ten years later, China had tripled its bicycle fleet, claiming about a third of the world's total, which approached a billion bicycles. Over the same period, the government built vast multilane bicycle highways in all its major cities to accommodate the extraordinary two-wheeled traffic. China has also become, like its neighbor Taiwan, a major global exporter of bicycles and parts.

In recent years, many developing countries like China have begun to encourage domestic automobile production as part of its economic development plan. Conceivably, over time, bicycle use could decline sharply as more people turn to motorized vehicles for everyday transportation. Still, in much of the world, automobiles remain a luxury well beyond the means of average citizens and account for only a small fraction of the total number of vehicles in circulation. The commuting bicycle is thus likely to remain a fixture the world over for some time to come.

Ironically, at the same time some developing countries have taken steps to encourage automobile use, European officials have championed a return to the bicycle to alleviate urban congestion and pollution. Commuters themselves have a strong economic incentive to take up bicycle riding, since gasoline in Europe costs three or four times what it does in the United States. In recent years, France and Germany have been particularly active in building urban bicycle paths, many even featuring their own stoplights. An increasing number of European cities have closed their historic centers to motorized traffic while inviting bicycle use. Some cities even offer a fleet of readily identifiable rental bicycles, available to the tourist for little or no cost.

Even the well-known American car culture has shown cracks in recent years. The energy crisis of 1973 prompted many citizens to reconsider the merits of the humble bicycle, and ever since then the two-wheeler has enjoyed a certain ecological cachet. A number of college towns like Davis, California, and Madison, Wisconsin, have long enjoyed special bicycle lanes alongside major thoroughfares. Some urban planners and concerned citizens have prodded other cities to create similar lanes, with some success. Since the 1990s, several federal initiatives have explicitly endorsed bicycling as a viable means of transportation and have even allocated modest funds to develop and maintain bicycle paths. Many employers have installed bike racks at the workplace, and some provide bicycle commuters with showering and changing facilities. A few even offer their workers financial incentives to abandon their cars and commute by bicycle.

Even so, compared with Europeans, Americans make little use of pedal power. Recent figures show that they make less than 1 percent of all urban trips by bicycle, compared with European rates ranging from 5 percent in Italy to 30 percent in the Netherlands. Still, the German experience suggests that the rate of urban bicycle use can rise significantly if communities establish special bicycle lanes, provide parking facilities,

Like many European cities, Muenster's historic center is packed with bicycles

and discourage motorized traffic. In 1972, the rate of urban bicycle use in what was then West Germany stood at about 8 percent; by 1995, following an aggressive campaign to promote cycling, it had risen to 12 percent.

New designs and accessories have also facilitated urban cycling. Many commuters now ride variations of the rugged and popular mountain bike, sometimes called hybrids or city bikes. Like the old three-speeds and balloon-tire bicycles, these styles carry the rider in a comfortable upright position and feature wide tires that are well suited for poor roads. Unlike the older designs, however, they also offer lightweight frames, alloy components, and a wide selection of gears. Shifting is usually effortless, requiring only a slight turn of the handlebar grips until they click into position. New-style helmets are lightweight and comfortable, offering vital protection from potential spills, and a variety of robust cycle locks have been introduced.

In short, the bicycle continues to offer cheap, speedy, and efficient personal transportation, and the most advanced models even provide a sporty and satisfying ride.

Still, to what extent the bicycle will continue to serve as a people conveyer is an open question. In developing countries, motorized traffic is likely to grow, while in others the pedal-powered bicycle faces growing competition from other attractive transportation options, including scooters, rollerblades, and various small motorized and electrical vehicles. Ironically, the greatest competition may come from the increasingly practical and affordable electric bicycle. But whatever lies in store, the conventional bicycle is likely to remain a compelling choice for personal transportation for some time to come, given its inherent economy, efficiency, and charm.

Recreational Cycling

Recreational cycling declined in the years immediately following the boom. Bicycle touring in particular lost much of its mystique, as motorized vehicles offered a faster and less taxing means to see the world. Whereas the press had once eagerly followed the exploits of daring cyclists who pedaled their way across Europe, America, and Asia, it now told similar tales of intrepid motorists who covered great expanses in astonishingly little time. Even those who were still inclined to bicycle for pleasure were often deterred by the growing presence of loud and menacing motorized vehicles. "The automobile has divided society into two classes," cracked one wit in 1912. "Those who ride in their own automobiles, and those who ride in their friends' automobiles." Nevertheless, over the course of the twentieth century, the bicycle would repeatedly reassert its compelling recreational value.

Even with the passing of the boom, recreational cycling retained a certain appeal, at least in Europe. In 1903, the Cyclists' Touring Club, though struggling, still counted almost fifty thousand members throughout Great Britain. The Touring Club of France had nearly eighty thousand members, while the Italian equivalent, the Touring Club d'Italia, had thirty-four thousand—and both organizations grew markedly in the decade that followed. These clubs did cater increasingly to motorists, but they also continued to promote bicycle touring. Indeed, the trusty bicycle still offered certain advantages over motorized travel, especially in the early going, when automobiles were expensive and unreliable.

To tour with an automobile in Britain, explained Joseph Pennell in 1900, "one must be more or less of a mechanic, as competent repairers are rare. One must carry, if touring, a large supply of petrol, because the average grocer or oilman has not the sense, as on the Continent, to stock it." Of course, everyone expected the situation to improve over time, although the prospective pace and direction of automobile development remained uncertain. Pennell, for one, proclaimed "the steam carriage is coming, and will simplify matters." Yet, like many of his contemporaries, he fully expected steam- and gasoline-powered engines to yield to the electric automobile, "the cleanest and quietest, the simplest and the fastest." As for the "self-propelled bicycle," he affirmed it was still "a thing of the future, but it too is coming."

In time, the automotive industry settled on the internal combustion engine and did indeed develop more practical and affordable models. Motorcycles also gained great popularity in the first decade of the new century. Yet many Europeans continued to value the humble bicycle as a means to explore the outdoors. In addition to its well-known "health-giving" qualities, mused one British writer in 1906, the bicycle exerts "a good influence on the youth and manhood of the nation." Outwardly, he asserted, the cyclist becomes "more generous and more social" and even acquires a greater "love of nature and attachment to his native land." Inwardly, the sport "teaches [the cyclist] caution and gives him presence of mind in emergencies," and even reveals hidden "mechanical or inventive genius." Moreover, the practice makes a person more "self-reliant" and teaches "temperance and self control."

Even the royal family continued to lend its approval to the sport, and its members were occasionally spotted riding their bicycles on the pristine grounds of Cambridge University or the country paths surrounding their favorite retreats, like Balmoral Castle in Scotland. Both King Edward VII, who ruled from 1901 to 1910, and the son who succeeded him to the throne, George V, were known to be cyclists, as was George's eldest son, the future king Edward VIII. Further proof of the bicycle's enduring appeal among the British upper class in the early twentieth century was the thriving business of the master builder John Marston. For years, he produced in his modest shop in Wolverhampton exquisite pleasure cycles designed for a discriminating and affluent clientele willing to pay up to five times the norm. His legendary Golden Sunbeam, introduced in 1900, featured an oil-bath chain case and a two-speed gear inside the bottom bracket.

But recreational cycling in Britain was by no means confined to the upper classes.

facing page: A Raleigh advertisement in *Cycling* from 30 September 1920 evoking the lingering recreational appeal of the bicycle. A British motorist stops to gaze nostalgically at a Raleigh bicycle parked outside a pub and "wonders if he was wise to ever part with his Raleigh." Although Americans had largely given up recreational riding by this time, Europeans continued to favor the sport.

3D

CYCLING

TEAS & LUNCHEON BEDS

OCT 21 1920

MEMORIES
REVIVED

When he remembers the real care-free enjoyment he used to get out of his old cycle, the love for his new car weakens, and he wonders if he was wise to ever part with his

RALEIGH
THE ALL-STEEL BICYCLE

which, fitted with Dunlop tyres and Sturmey-Archer 3-speed gear, is the finest private carriage a man could hope for.

Write for "The Book of the Raleigh," showing all the latest models, post free from the Raleigh Agent in your town, or direct from

Raleigh Cycle Company, Ltd., Nottingham.

The growing diffusion of utilitarian bicycles among the masses stoked a keen popular interest in the sport. In 1905, *The Field* detected unprecedented "streams of riders who may be seen wending their way out of the towns for a day in the country, thus making their bicycles minister to pleasure as well as to business." The Clarion Cycling Club still counted thousands of members and encouraged the working class to participate in the pastime. Although the club had softened its political edge, it continued to offer bicycles at a discount to its membership. It also operated a network of clubhouses that, before the advent of youth hostels, provided cyclists with low-cost overnight accommodations.

In France, too, cycling remained a popular recreation that transcended class lines. Mechanics were already hard at work developing a new style of touring bicycle to include a wide range of variable gears so that the cyclist could climb the steepest hills without having to dismount. As prescribed by the Touring Club of France, this so-called mountain bicycle was to combine the ruggedness and practicality of the utilitarian mount with the elegance and lightness of a racer. To oversee development of this dream machine, the club appointed a blue-ribbon committee. True, conceded the club correspondent, "not one in a thousand cyclists has any special need" for a mountain

A German caricature of a "mountain bicycle," from *Fliegende Blätter* (Flying Leaves) in 1896. Some mechanics were already considering how to build a bicycle for mountain climbs.

climber. Yet, the club reasoned, if a bicycle can be made to handle the steepest ascents it should satisfy the needs of the most demanding tourist.

In the fall of 1902, the club conducted an initial series of tests in the Pyrenees, where it evaluated forty-eight machines by twenty-four makers. The judges quickly determined that nearly half lacked sufficient clearance between the frame and the front wheel to allow for such essential touring accessories as heavy tires, racks, and mudguards. The judges also concluded that, for touring purposes, British-style caliper brakes were preferable to the American coaster variety. But they devoted the greatest scrutiny to the various gearing systems. Only those that offered at least three gears, accessible on the fly, received a nod. The gold medal went to the Terrot company of Dijon, for a bicycle with a chain on either side, which collectively yielded a staggering four gears.

The impressive revival of the recreational sport in Europe did not spread to America, however. Ironically, the bicycle's very success as a utilitarian tool seems to have diminished its appeal as a recreational vehicle, at least in the eyes of the upper classes. For the most part, the old guard that had developed the high-wheel sport in the United States a generation earlier looked with disdain on the common cyclist who had displaced the privileged recreational rider. In 1902, Frank Weston, whose credentials as a cycling pioneer were second only to those of Albert A. Pope, spoke disparagingly of those who cycled "as a mere matter of convenience." In his view, the utilitarian rider "is a cyclist in name only. We can—in a cycling sense—part company from him without regret and without dignifying his 'passing' by connecting him even remotely with cycling as we know it."

The *New York Journal* lamented that the renewed European enthusiasm for the recreational sport had not caught on at home. "Will somebody kindly start a bicycle boom over here?" it pleaded in 1905. "A bicycle revival would take hundreds of thousands of young men from the city street corner on Sunday out into the fresh air. Nothing could be more charming than the great crowds of young women with knickerbockers and rubber-soled boots pumping their way out toward the green country." It noted that Colonel Pope had promised to revive the sport, and it wished him every success. It also urged President Theodore Roosevelt to "ride a wheel for a while, write one or two articles and deliver one or two speeches . . . to start the bicycle business all over again."

Bicycling World likewise yearned for an American cycling renaissance. But it cautioned that "the bicycle trade does not want a boom" like the last one, which had left a sour taste "in the mouths of the survivors." What *was* needed, it insisted, was simply a "healthy revival" without "the hysteria of the fad," driven by "the calm force of a rational demand." The pastime would thrive again, it predicted, if only the industry could win back two critical constituencies: young adults and women. Although juvenile sales were flourishing, it reported, and some boom veterans still rode for pleasure, few between the ages of eighteen and thirty were active riders. Equally pressing, in its view, was the need to bring back women so that "mankind will follow."

Still, the prospects for an American recreational revival seemed dim at best. "The touring side of cycling, so keen in Great Britain, is very much undeveloped in America," lamented *Bicycling World*. Many people still traveled abroad for a cycling holiday, it noted, yet they gave little thought to exploring their own country by bicycle. The journal blamed the moribund League of American Wheelmen for not having done more during its heyday to promote cycle touring at home. "In the days of the boom we were so full of racing and century runs and the like that we gave [touring] small thought," it continued. "And now that the bicycle has 'settled down' it is too generally viewed as a conveyance of utility and economy or for an afternoon's outing. To use it as a means of going far afield and viewing all that nature holds and that history has hallowed is foreign to the average cyclist."

Compounding the problem, according to *Bicycling World,* were popular misconceptions about the nature of cycle touring. Many tourists, it asserted, dispensed with such common-sense accessories as the coaster brake, for fear that it might "induce a disposition to loaf." Yet those same cyclists thought nothing of carrying along a "miniature repair shop" so as to "change sprockets en route." A tourist should not feel compelled to perform hard work, it insisted, or to cover ninety miles a day—that was not touring but merely "scorching" or "plugging." The "real tourist," it declared, does not care about accomplishing impressive speeds or distances but is simply out for "one grand, care-free, enjoyable loaf."

Yet American bicycles were generally ill-suited even for such casual meandering. The leftovers from the boom were admirably light and fleet, but not particularly roadworthy. They also generally lacked a freewheel, an absence that made coasting down steep hills more of a chore than a pleasure. Moreover, the cyclist's customary stoop on those machines was hardly conducive to soaking up the scenery. Newer bicycles, in contrast, generally provided the convenience of a freewheel and coaster brake and usually sat the rider upright. However, they were designed primarily for utilitarian use and were unduly heavy for touring purposes. Furthermore, few bicycles offered any provision to facilitate hill climbing.

Like the Touring Club of France, *Bicycling World* recognized the pressing need for technical improvement if the pastime was to revive and prosper. "After the first flush of enthusiasm and novelty has worn off," it conceded, "the fact that cycling entails manual labor forces itself home." It, too, called for the addition of variable gears to increase the pleasure of cycle touring. "The next big improvement," it affirmed in 1902, "is the application of some simple method of altering the gearing to suit the varying conditions."

But, parting from the French consensus, the journal predicted that the newly introduced two-speed hub would prove satisfactory. Indeed, in its judgment, "three [gears] and over are not wanted and will never meet with any demand."

In spite of *Bicycling World*'s professed optimism, the American industry continued to struggle and the recreational sport made little headway. A faint hope flickered in 1907, when a few energetic New Yorkers formed a new type of cycling club that encouraged members to tour the countryside "without racing their heads off." The club, the Purely Pleasure Pedalers, admitted both male and female cyclists—in fact, its president was herself a woman. Members would meet on Sunday mornings to head for "unfrequented places free from the dust of hundreds of automobiles." *Bicycling World* welcomed the concept, asserting that many individuals had given up recreational riding precisely because they had no one to cycle with.

Yet despite a mild upswing in American bicycle sales after the nadir of 1909, the recreational sport still floundered. To be sure, a few enthusiasts continued to preach the gospel of cycle touring. *Bicycling World* explained how one could strap a tent to a bicycle and enjoy the "pleasures of cycle camping." A correspondent to the *New York Tribune* vouched in 1913, "As a wheelman still active, of twenty-five years, I have roamed over the United States, Canada and Europe, always with a bicycle, and in no other way can the 'common touch' be so well found." In the fall of 1916, a new trade journal called *Bicycle News* even detected a faint growth in the recreational sport. The number of clubs nationwide had doubled in recent years to more than one hundred, the vast majority dedicated to the noncompetitive cyclist. Moreover, both the Boy Scouts and the YMCA had recently formed cycling groups that were meant to undertake trips of moderate distances.

Still, bicycle touring in America remained, as one observer tactfully put it, a "lost art." Some were quick to pin the demise of the sport on the rapid rise of the motorcycle and the automobile. But Abbott Bassett, a veteran of the high-wheel era, faulted the bicycle industry itself. As he saw it, leaders had taken "no steps to bring back touring, no steps to encourage the formation of clubs [or] to promote the fraternal spirit which sent riders to the wheel in groups." Lamented Bassett, "Makers are content to produce and sell a cheaper grade of wheel than that of the old-time club and touring days." In his view, the trade's newfound emphasis on economy rather than quality precluded a revival. Not only were present-day utilitarian bicycles unsatisfactory from a tourist's perspective, their slim profit margins offered "no encouragement for the inventor to improve the wheel. He is working on the auto and the motorcycle."

A contributor to *Outing Magazine* seemed to back up Bassett's claim. He described how he had embarked on a leisurely tour of New England in the fall of 1912, after a dozen-year hiatus from the saddle. "You experience a rebirth of that forgotten sense of

kinship with the birds," he reported. "You wonder why you ever gave up cycling, and resolve that hereafter you will ride a certain distance every day, if not farther." Yet he found that the nostalgic rush "lasts for a mile or two, provided the wind favors you and there are no hills. Then you thoughtfully slow down and find, to your surprise, that your heart is laboring like a ship's engine in a storm. It has known nothing like this since the last time you ran for a train. You recall that [the bicycle] is, after all, a fallible contraption."

The stagnant state of the American bicycle took its toll on the industry. In 1913, after struggling for years to revive an upscale market, the resurrected Pope Manufacturing Company sold off its plant in Westfield, Massachusetts, and finally folded for good. Although the trade itself enjoyed a modest growth in the 1910s, thanks mostly to the juvenile demand, adult recreational interest remained minimal. Frank Bowden of Raleigh Cycles observed in 1920, "There is very little pleasure riding in the United States—no bicycle journeys undertaken for long distances. There does not appear to be the same desire for exercise among young people in America as in England. The principal idea of sport in America appears to resemble that of the football follower in England—that is, to be quite satisfied with looking on at games played by paid experts."

In Europe, by contrast, the recreational sport flourished in the 1920s and 1930s along with the utilitarian culture. A popular weekend program was to bicycle to the countryside and camp overnight. Touring clubs abounded, especially in France, where the Fédération Française de Cyclotourisme, founded in 1923, served as the new umbrella organization, displacing the increasingly automobile-focused Touring Club of France. Cycle tourists also benefited from a growing number of youth hostels across Europe. These low-cost shelters, often in rustic or historic buildings, offered male and female cyclists cheap and comfortable overnight accommodations, hearty meals, and good company. The house parents were also sympathetic to their needs and knowledgeable about touring in the surrounding region.

European tourists were increasingly adopting bicycles that were specifically designed for long-distance touring. The best ones were reasonably lightweight, pleasurable to ride, and equipped with an assortment of gears to facilitate hill climbing. Improved British-style three-speed hubs were commonly used, and French-style derailleurs were gaining popularity. These external mechanisms did just what the name implies—they derailed the chain in order to shift it from one size sprocket to another that offered a

facing page: A French poster from 1925 promoting De Dion-Bouton bicycles and presenting cycling as a means to commune with nature. Cycle touring developed rapidly in the 1920s and 1930s in Europe, where many people went on overnight trips, bringing tents or lodging in a youth hostel.

The Founding of International Youth Hostels

The founder of the international youth hostel movement was a modest German schoolteacher named Richard Schirrmann who began his career in the early part of the twentieth century. He sought to expose his pent-up pupils to the beauty of nature, taking them on long walks in the woods surrounding a nearby twelfth-century castle. It occurred to him that if his children could pass the night in that castle, they would have more time to spend outdoors and could also learn about their cultural heritage. In 1910, the local government granted him permission to set up cots in the castle. The hostel proved so successful that several more promptly appeared in the vicinity. Supportive citizens soon offered furniture and contributions to cover maintenance, and some even volunteered their own homes to serve as additional venues. Before long, a growing number of hostels provided not only cheap overnight accommodations but also inexpensive meals. Guests were expected to arrive under their own speed, either on foot or by bicycle, and to participate in house chores.

By 1913, about twenty German hostels had banded together into an association headed by Schirrmann. The schoolteacher dreamed of expanding the network beyond Germany, but World War I intervened. Schirrmann managed nonetheless to rebuild the program in the 1920s, and the youth hostel movement eventually spread throughout Europe, including Great Britain. In 1932, hostel directors from a dozen countries met in Germany to create an international alliance.

better gear for the given terrain. Compared with hub gears, derailleurs were lighter and offered a wider selection of gears.

The first primitive derailleurs were developed in England during the boom, but they were largely improved in France, thanks in large part to Paul de Vivie, a cycle merchant who resided in hilly Saint-Etienne. Since 1887, he had also been the publisher of *Le Cycliste*, a trade review dedicated to the bicycle tourist. "Velocio," as his readers knew him from his nom de plume, was an early champion of many and varied gears. He participated in the first tests by the Touring Club of France, and he even presented sev-

Shortly thereafter, the Nazi government took over the German association, removing Schirrmann from the helm. Not until the fall of the Third Reich in 1945 did the seventy-one-year-old founder regain control of the hostel organization. Desperate to rebuild the decimated program, he sent the following emotional plea to his friend Monroe Smith, co-founder of the American chapter:

My dear Monroe:

Here I have been in the hospital for almost fourteen days as the result of a bad fall from my bicycle. The doctor has put me together as well he could. But all this doesn't matter much for terrible events have taken place in the last six years in Europe, especially in Germany and in the neighboring countries: [we face] a devastated world filled with ruin and death. Germany's last resistance was broken by the bomb carpets of the Allies. Her once teeming and prosperous cities are reduced to rubble and ashes. You know how we feared the coming of this war. We in the International Youth Hostel tried to work against it by bringing together the youths of all nations. Our efforts, we hoped, would build a peaceful world. Sadly enough, the beast of war broke its chains too soon. We must begin anew our work of reconciliation. Can you help so that the German Youth Hostel organization will again be separated from the State and again serve its original purpose? I have the energy and am eager to rebuild it.

eral innovative systems of his own. Over the years, after trying every conceivable solution, he settled on the derailleur as his favorite mechanism.

In 1914, with Velocio's blessings, a local mechanic named Joanny Panel began to offer a rudimentary derailleur on his hand-built frames. Panel's initiative inspired another mechanic, Albert Raimond, to launch Le Cyclo, which became the first commercially successful derailleur. The company's first shifter, introduced in 1924, bolted onto the rear stay of a generic bicycle, and worked in conjunction with a two-sprocket freewheel. Despite its limited range, Raimond's system drew high praise from the Touring

Evelyn Hamilton arriving in London to a boisterous reception in September 1935 after riding from John O'Groats in northern Scotland. She covered the seven hundred miles in just over four days on a bicycle, a Claud Butler mounted with a Cyclo derailleur, that was the state of the art at the time.

Club of France. He soon introduced a more advanced three-speed system, followed by a front derailleur that worked with a double chainring. By using front and rear derailleurs, the cyclist benefited from as many as six gears.

In the early 1930s, Cyclo introduced a freewheel with four sprockets and lighter derailleurs made with aluminum alloy rather than the heavier steel—exploiting new materials that had been developed for aviation. A few years later, Cyclo came out with a triple chainring, which together with the four sprockets in the rear gave the rider as many as twelve gears. Even British tourists began to demand Cyclo products, prompting Raimond to set up a small factory in Birmingham. In the meantime, rival firms arose in France, notably Simplex and Huret. Other companies began to use aluminum alloys for different components, like the cranks made by Stronglight of Saint-Etienne. Several innovative frame makers, notably René Herse and Alex Singer of Paris, made high-end custom-designed touring bicycles. They used the latest in butted steel tubing, and adjusted the frame geometry to create a more comfortable ride. They also devised creative ways to accommodate useful accessories such as racks and lights. A few firms, such as Caminade, even produced alloy frames. The coveted "mountain bicycle" was at last a reality.

Americans, however, remained largely oblivious to these promising technical developments in Europe. For years, the recreational sport was largely confined to a few women's educational institutions, such as Smith College in Northampton, Massachusetts. Nevertheless, by the early 1930s, conditions were ripe for a recreational revival. The bicycles then on the market, if little improved, stood out nonetheless on account of their eye-catching accessories, including coaster brakes, mudguards, and electric lights. And a fully loaded machine cost as little as twenty-five dollars. Many citizens, pinched by the depression, were inclined to buy a bicycle anyway for basic transportation. Moreover, dress codes had relaxed considerably since the boom days, allowing both men and women to wear comfortable cycling outfits, including shorts.

In 1932, yet another cycling craze broke out, this time in California. The Hollywood couple Joan Crawford and Douglas Fairbanks, Jr., took up cycling to keep trim—and set a fashion. Other socialites who had vacationed in Bermuda, where cars were banned, returned to act as "missionaries to cycling." Before long, department stores in Los Angeles and San Francisco pushed the latest cycling fashions in their storefronts. College students took up the sport, and clubs sprang into being. Tandems came back into style; even road races revived. Bicycle shops scrambled to meet the soaring demand. One observer described the fad as a "psychological revolt against a highly mechanized age."

The Californian craze quickly swept across the country. "Rent-a-Bike" stands appeared in cities and college towns, booking weekend rentals months in advance. Numerous cities sponsored "bicycle days." In 1935, with great fanfare, Atlantic City opened up its famous boardwalks to cyclists. That fall, the Boston and Maine Railroad carried scores of Boston-area cyclists and their mounts to New Hampshire's scenic White Mountains. The following spring, the New York, New Haven and Hartford line organized similar runs to rustic Canaan, Connecticut, as part of a program dubbed Bike to Nature. The "cycle train" left Manhattan at eight in the morning and returned in the late evening. The roundtrip fare was $2, plus $1.50 for a bicycle rental. Tourists could take morning and evening meals in the dining car; at midday, they could procure a fifty-cent box lunch, or patronize a roadside establishment. On the inaugural ride, more than two hundred enthusiasts filled seven railroad cars.

Adults soon accounted for nearly a third of the total American demand for bicycles. The primary force behind the revival, by most accounts, was the renewed feminine in-

Urban residents headed for a day of cycling in the countryside with the Bike to Nature program, which was supported by department stores eager to sell bicycling outfits. The "Cycle Train" ran from New York City to Canaan in northwestern Connecticut. This photograph appeared in *Railway Age*, 2 May 1936.

terest in the sport. The Cycle Trades of America was generally credited with having orchestrated a shrewd marketing campaign to win back women. It had deduced that women were reluctant to ride because of safety concerns stemming from the rising tide of motorists. Mothers were also disinclined to let their children ride under such harrowing conditions. In fact, despite the immense appeal of balloon-tire bicycles to juveniles, only a decided minority actually owned one. For years, the trade chose to ignore parental safety concerns, reasoning that any discussion of danger would only fan fears. But at last the CTA decided to tackle the issue head-on, launching a radio and magazine advertising blitz to stress how cycling is fun, healthy, and safe. It also revived the League of American Wheelmen, pushed for cycling lanes, and initiated numerous programs to teach safe cycling habits to younger riders. The new pitch struck a chord, and children's sales promptly shot up.

The CTA also successfully persuaded women themselves to buy bicycles. It pushed a full line of cycling gear, including blouses, hats, gloves, shoes, and divided skirts imported from France known as coulottes. It even organized a series of fashion

facing page: Actress Joan Crawford, shown on the cover of *Toy World and Bicycle World* for July 1934, riding an exercise bicycle

Toy World and **Bicycle World**

742 Market Street, San Francisco, Calif.

Official Organ of the Western Bicycle and Toy Vehicle Industries

JULY, 1934

Jaunty Joan

Bewitching Joan Crawford, Hollywood film luminary, is making the wheels go 'round on this man's bicycle exerciser. The barrels, a la treadmill, are what make it real exercise.

While most industries suffered in the Great Depression, bicycle sales actually rose to levels that hadn't been seen in years. This cartoon in the May 1933 issue of the trade journal *Toy World* suggested that the industry's continued success could help propel the economy back to prosperity.

shows, hiring models to wear the new cycling garb while posing atop shiny bicycles. In Atlantic City, one athletic beauty earned the vaunted title of Miss Cyclist. Department stores, though hesitant at first, gradually adopted the line, sparking a fashion sensation. Suddenly women, who had accounted for no more than ten percent of the adult market, were now buying more than a third of all adult bicycles.

Bicycle manufacturers were even optimistic that feminine enthusiasm for cycling would endure this time around. The new-style bicycles, though heavy, offered women distinct advantages over their grandmothers' mounts. The freewheel and coaster brake facilitated the ride and enhanced safety. The wide, spring-supported seats and fat tires added comfort. Moreover, women were now free to adopt the most comfortable wear for cycling, choosing among divided skirts, trousers, and even leg-exposing shorts, popularized during a recent fad for sun bathing. Three girls who cycled up a beach in San Diego one night, however, went a little too far—they decided they needed nothing more than the cover of darkness. The police promptly intervened, and cloaked the free spirits in actual blankets.

The founding of American Youth Hostels, primarily dedicated to cyclists, further stimulated interest in bicycle touring. Social activists Isabel and Monroe Smith opened the first American hostel in 1934 in Northfield, Massachusetts. Within two years, New

England boasted thirty-three hostels, most of them in farmhouses, and by 1940, the organization was running similar establishments across the country. One enthusiastic supporter was President Franklin Roosevelt. "I was brought up on this sort of thing," he affirmed, "and realize the need for hosteling. From the time I was nine until I was seventeen I spent most of my holidays bicycling on the continent. This was the best education I ever had; far better than schools. The more one circulates in his travels the better citizen he becomes, not only of his own country, but of the world."

Suddenly, young Americans began to take to the roads on bicycles in an effort to see the world. One of the more extreme examples was Fred A. Birchmore, who set out from his native Athens, Georgia, to circle the globe in 1935, at the age of twenty-five. In what

Two teenagers, William Fay and Bob Drake, embarking on a six-hundred-mile bicycle trip through northern Minnesota in about 1935. The secondary top tubes on their bike frames were said to cushion the ride, and each of these bicycles probably weighed at least fifty pounds—without the gear.

was then Nazi Germany, he purchased a special touring bike marked Reinhardt, which he later donated to the Smithsonian Institution. The entire trip, through Europe, Asia, and the United States, west to east, covered forty thousand miles, of which he pedaled about twenty-five thousand, and the rest was by boat. He wore out four saddle covers and seven sets of tires; he bought the last set of tires (the ones that are still on the bike) in Calcutta, India.

Planners began to talk seriously about creating European-style bicycle lanes in city parks and alongside scenic highways. In 1935, a petition demanding more bicycle paths in Chicago collected 165,000 signatures. In response, the city created 40 miles of trails in forest preserves. In 1936, New York City opened a cycle path in Central Park, celebrating the event with a parade and a pageant. One of the honored guests was the great boom-era racer Arthur A. Zimmerman. Some even talked of reclaiming the old Coney Island path—long since taken over by horseback riders—for cyclists. Over the next few years, New York City's parks commissioner Robert Moses paved over 20 more miles of inner-city bicycle paths, while promising to add another 140 miles. Pundits specu-

Two young ladies in Washington, D.C., head out to claim their bicycles in 1942. Rental services became so popular that patrons often had to book their bikes days or even weeks in advance.

lated that the national health would greatly improve thanks to the renewed popularity of bicycling.

Still, some experts warned that the weight of the standard American behemoth would inevitably quash the budding adult recreational interest. Some adults, to be sure, had acquired lightweight European-style bicycles with thin tires and three-speed hubs, such as those exhibited at the Chicago World's Fair of 1934. But they were the fortunate few. One female enthusiast recounted how she was sailing along one day on her twenty-three-pound English roadster when she came across two women pushing their American mounts, each of which weighed easily double her own. The sympathetic tourist stopped and engaged the dispirited pair in conversation. She suggested they test ride her bicycle, just to see how much fun cycling should be. They accepted her offer, and discovered, to their great surprise, that they were no longer fighting pedals but rather blissfully "floating through air."

"The immediate creating of a lightweight bicycle," asserted one source in 1934, "would do more right now to benefit the entire cycling movement as nothing else could possibly do." A few American companies, including Shelby and Schwinn, heard such pleas and scrambled to unveil lightweight models of their own. Yet, despite their billing, most of these bicycles weighed well over thirty pounds, hardly up to European standards. Nor were gears commonly available. A few dealers offered English-style three-speed hubs for an extra ten dollars, but French-style derailleurs were still a rarity. For the most part, the enhanced pleasures of riding a truly lightweight machine were not available to American cyclists.

The outbreak of World War II put a damper on the budding recreational sport, forcing popular, gadget-laden bicycles off the market. The approved Victory bicycles were nonetheless refreshingly lightweight by comparison and gave many Americans their first taste of what it was like to ride a higher-quality bicycle. Moreover, as *Time* reported in 1954, many of the five million U.S. servicemen stationed in Britain during the war brought home an appreciation for the lightweight British bicycles they had used for their daily routines. American youngsters, too, the magazine observed, coveted such British refinements as generator-operated lights, hand brakes, and three-speed gears. Demand for quality bicycles grew steadily, spurred by such prominent cycling advocates as Dr. Paul Dudley White, President Dwight D. Eisenhower's personal physician. When Eisenhower suffered a heart attack in 1957, he took up cycling at White's behest.

As American adults became more discerning about their bicycles, shunning forty- or fifty-pound balloon-tire roadsters, manufacturers like Schwinn and Columbia began to offer lighter models with British-made three-speed hubs. They also introduced a new category called the middleweight, said to combine the ruggedness of a juvenile machine with the riding pleasure of a European lightweight. Many Americans, however, took ad-

The Stewart-Warner bike speedometer, advertised in *Boys' Life* of July 1947, recorded speeds up to fifty miles per hour, an improbable pace even for the fleetest riders on the lightest machines at the time, but it demonstrated the seductive allure of automotive-style gadgets for kids

vantage of the weak pound to purchase British-made machines. The American industry fought unsuccessfully to raise import tariffs from 7.5 percent to 15 percent, and European cycle makers captured 40 percent of the American adult market, with the lion's share going to the three big British producers: Raleigh, Hercules, and BSA Cycles.

In Europe, sales of all varieties of bicycles flourished in the aftermath of the war. Various cycling magazines, often featuring exquisite drawings by the Frenchman Daniel Rebour, helped sustain a general interest in the sport. But bicycle sales began to dip by the late 1950s as motorized vehicles proliferated. Not only were utilitarian cyclists fast disappearing, pleasure cycling likewise went into a marked decline. Both the Cyclists' Touring Club in Britain and the Fédération Française de Cyclotourisme were rapidly losing members. Youths in particular were increasingly averse to participating in a sport they deemed outdated, creating a crisis in the cycling community and casting a cloud over the future of the industry and the recreational sport.

The United States, by contrast, experienced a modest cycling revival in the 1960s, thanks to the introduction of European-style ten-speed bicycles with modern derailleur gears. By 1965, Schwinn was offering three popular models priced from $70 to $130. At about forty pounds, though, these mid-priced bicycles were still oppressively heavy by European standards. Only the top-of-line Schwinn Paramount, costing a whopping $240, was truly a first-class machine. Nevertheless, Schwinn's bold initiative helped fan adult interest in the recreational sport. Demand for the more expensive imported variety began to pick up as well. In California especially, an increasing number of discriminating cyclists sought top-quality European racing models. At about the same time, the League of American Wheelmen sprang back to life yet again in preparation for another full-scale revival.

Meanwhile, a new juvenile craze broke out and propelled domestic bicycle sales past the four million mark for the first time. This time around, the demand was for newfangled "high-risers" like Schwinn's Sting-Ray. These distinctive bicycles, with wheels only twenty inches in diameter, came in bright metallic colors and featured "long horn" handlebars that rose to about shoulder height and then curved back toward the rider. They also had an elongated "banana" seat shaped like an ironing board with "sissy bars" in back to provide a backrest—also helpful for carrying a passenger or popping a wheelie. Most had coaster brakes with two-speed hubs, but top-of-the-line models sported rear derailleurs with massive stick shifts protruding from the sloping top tube. Children loved the rebel chopper look and clamored for one of their own. Parents usually acceded to their demands, hoping to encourage outdoor exercise. After all, medical authorities were increasingly bemoaning the slothful habits of a "boob tube" generation glued to the television.

In the early 1970s, yet another bicycle boom erupted in the United States—but this time adults, not children, were the driving force behind it. And what they wanted were those European-style ten-speed bicycles. Many had only recently ridden high-risers, and they were ready to graduate to more roadworthy vehicles. Others had not cycled in years, but welcomed the opportunity to engage in healthy outdoor exercise. Cycling clubs proliferated, and even touring revived. During the banner years from 1972 to 1974, Americans purchased a staggering forty million bicycles.

For the first time in years, American-made adult bicycles were in high demand, notably Schwinn's forty-pound Varsity, equipped with a hodgepodge of low-end European parts. But European imports were also widely coveted, and dozens of brands were

A proud collector showing off his mint-condition Schwinn Sting-Ray, a chopper-style bike that sparked a major American fad in the mid-1960s, featuring short chrome fenders and a vinyl-covered "banana" seat. By the early 1970s, millions of American teenagers were poised to graduate to European-style ten-speeds.

introduced. Mid-priced bicycles from France like Motobécane and Peugeot were popular. They usually weighed less than thirty pounds and came with derailleurs by Simplex or Huret, brakes by Mafac, and freewheels by Maillard. British bicycles like Raleigh, Holdsworth, and Dawes were also selling well and offered a wide range of prices and models. Italian bicycles likewise came in great variety, from midrange brands like Chiorda and Atala to custom-made frames that were among the most expensive and usually featured sturdy but elegant racing components by Campagnolo and Cinelli. The Spanish parts maker Zeus gained a certain following selling Campagnolo knockoffs at a reduced cost, and also marketed complete bicycles.

But perhaps the most surprising development in the cycle market was the sudden flood of competitively priced Japanese imports with previously unknown cycle brands like Fuji, Nishiki, Panasonic, and Bridgestone. These ten-speeds came equipped with Shimano or Suntour derailleurs, Sugino cranks, and Dia-Compe brakes. Some parts even showed important innovations, such as the Suntour "barcons," handlebar-end shifters formerly used only in cyclo-cross. Suntour also introduced the so-called slant parallelogram derailleur. Whereas standard European derailleurs were pivoted just below the right rear dropout, Japanese derailleurs were arched back so that the cage was placed farther away from the freewheel, which allowed the chain to shift more smoothly onto the sprockets. This design has since become standard on all derailleurs.

Dealers scurried to find bicycles wherever they could find them, and then sold them as fast as they came in the store. Even the long-suffering American cycle industry enjoyed a brisk business, although most of its bicycles still weighed a hefty forty pounds or so. When an energy crisis broke out in late 1973, the boom even received an unexpected boost. The Arab oil embargo in the wake of the Yom Kippur War sent petroleum prices soaring and caused long lines of cars at the gas pumps. Many citizens began to seriously consider using their bicycles for routine errands. Sales returned to a pre-boom level in 1975, but managed to climb up again in the late 1970s.

A rest stop for a group of cyclists who rode in the Bikecentennial in 1976, many of whose participants traversed the United States on bikes following the designated Transamerica route. Most riders traveled in groups of about a dozen, starting in either Oregon or Virginia and at times crossing one another's paths.

A Touring Revival

Greg Siple and Dan Burden are not your ordinary cycle tourists. The touring bug bit Greg in particular at an early age while he was growing up in Columbus, Ohio, in the 1950s. While other kids rode hefty balloon-tire bikes, Greg rode a svelte Hercules three-speed. As a young teenager in the early 1960s, he graduated to a Sears eight-speed bicycle, one of the first derailleur-equipped bikes sold in the United States. In 1962, Greg and his dad, a former six-day racer, made a two-day, two-hundred-mile trip from Columbus to Portsmouth, Ohio, and back. For Greg, it became an annual ritual, and with the help of his friend Dan and other local cycling enthusiasts like Charlie Pace of the American Youth Hostels the affair blossomed into the TOSRV (Tour of the Scioto River Valley). By the late 1960s, hundreds were participating in what has become the longest-running mass ride in America.

But Dan, for one, was not about to confine his cycle touring to Ohio. He conceived the idea of bicycling from the northern tip of Alaska to the base of South America—nearly twenty thousand miles. He enlisted his wife, Lys, and Greg and his wife, June. He dubbed the adventure the Hemistour and secured support from *National Geographic,* which published a partial account of their journey. In June 1972, the quartet set off from Anchorage, Alaska, on their ten-speed bikes—each laden with about fifty pounds of gear. Knowing that stores would be few and far between, they stocked a week's supply of canned food in their panniers, and stopped at post offices along the way to collect new supplies they had mailed to themselves before departure. As Dan put it, this was one way to promote the joys of cycle touring.

Unfortunately, after the quartet reached Mexico in 1973, Dan became ill with hepatitis, and he and Lys had to return to their base in Missoula, Montana. Still, Greg and June gamely carried on, reaching Chile in February 1975. But the group's missionary work did not end there—they were already working on another plan, to organize mass rides across the United States as part of the bicentennial festivities to take place in 1976. Bikecentennial was born, staffed by hundreds of volunteers. More than four thousand men and women eventually participated in the various rides, nearly half opting for the cross-country route covering forty-two hundred miles from Virginia to Oregon. Most cyclists traveled in small groups of about a dozen, with an experienced leader, and slept either in camps or in sleeping bags laid out on the floors of participating institutions.

Both couples remain active participants in cycling causes. Greg and June still work for the Bikecentennial organization, headquartered in Missoula and now known as Adventure Cycling Association. It continues to promote cycle touring as a healthy and educational recreational outlet, although its focus is now on shorter tours. Dan served as the pedestrian and bicycle coordinator for the state of Florida and is now an independent urban design consultant advising cities and towns on how to promote cycling and walking as alternatives to driving. Lys has helped develop bike trails and is actively involved in bicycling events near their home in White Springs, Florida.

American cycle tourist June Siple riding through a village in the Peruvian Andes under heavy escort, in a photograph taken by her husband, Greg, in 1974. The Siples had left Anchorage two years earlier bound for the tip of South America, and they completed the journey a year later. *National Geographic* covered their adventure, billed as the Hemistour, and the publicity helped rekindle American interest in cycle touring.

The boom of the 1970s proved to be something of a letdown, however. As in the 1890s, an eager public armed themselves with the latest cycling guides and repair books and plucked their shiny bicycles off the showroom floors; they then gallantly mounted their wheels and sailed off into the great outdoors. Once again, however, their bicycles were often inadequate for the assignment. Despite the profusion of derailleurs, many machines had heavy frames and outdated components like steel rims, and their total weight was hardly any less than the discarded balloon-tire heavyweights from a generation before, making pedaling something of a chore. And the parts on the cheaper models were often unreliable; low-end derailleurs in particular were prone to malfunctioning, sometimes causing damage to the rear wheel or even the frame.

Nevertheless, the second boom helped reestablish cycling as a healthy and rewarding adult activity. Americans would no longer consider the bicycle a mere child's toy, and would gladly spend several hundred dollars or more on a well-made machine. Even after the downturn in sales in 1975, the ten-speed bicycle remained the industry's principal product. In the late 1970s, the market proved highly receptive to innovative American bicycle companies. Trek bicycles of Waterloo, Wisconsin, for one, gained a wide reputation for quality touring bicycles with steel frames. Other firms, meanwhile, were beginning to experiment with new frame materials. Gary Klein, an MIT alumnus who founded Klein bicycles (maker of the mountain bike that never left Jerry Seinfeld's TV-show apartment), introduced an aluminum alloy racing frame that was lighter and more flex-resistant than the conventional steel variety. By the early 1980s, Litespeed and Merlin Cycles were developing lightweight titanium frames, an idea that dated back several decades but had yet to come to fruition.

Before long, new designs and materials were making their way to the general market at more affordable prices. In the early 1980s, another American firm, Cannondale Corporation, launched what it called "aluminum for the masses." Cannondale introduced several styles of aluminum-alloy frames for road and off-road, including an early mountain bike, priced for the general market. Cannondale has since gained a strong presence worldwide for its wide range of cycling products. By the late 1980s, Trek had shifted its focus to mountain bicycles, featuring bonded aluminum frames, and in the early 1990s it introduced a variety of bonded carbon-fiber frames. The road model used by Lance Armstrong and the U.S. Postal Service team weighs a scant two and a half pounds. Although steel frames still offer many beneficial qualities, these alternative materials have become increasingly popular with racers and high-end recreational riders.

The revival of the sport of cycling in the 1970s also highlighted the need for greater safety. Racers had occasionally used leather helmets, but head protection for the recreational rider was virtually unknown. In 1975, Bell Helmets of California, long known for its motorcycle helmets, introduced the celebrated Bell Biker with a thick Styrofoam-like

A couple cycling through Missouri in the early morning on their way across the country in 1976. Cycle touring, long a tradition in Europe, has gained popularity in the United States since the mid-1970s thanks partly to the promotional efforts of Bikecentennial and its successor organization, Adventure Cycling. Many private companies now offer guided tours.

shell and red straps. Over the years, cycling helmets have become much lighter and more resilient, and they are now standard equipment. In 1974, traffic engineer John Forrester published the first edition of *Effective Cycling*, the first of many books to offer safe-riding tips. The revived League of American Wheelmen, now renamed the League of American Bicyclists, has carried on the fight to defend the legal rights of cyclists to share the road with motorists, and it has also sponsored numerous programs to teach safe riding techniques to children and adults.

The ten-speed boom also created a greater demand for recreational cycling paths free of automobiles. The idea of converting the country's many miles of abandoned railroad beds into car-free bicycle and pedestrian paths was introduced in the mid-1960s and gained considerable momentum during the ten-speed boom. Since 1986, the Rails-to-Trails Conservancy, with headquarters in Washington, D.C., and offices in six states, has spearheaded the national movement. More than twelve thousand miles of bicycle paths have been created in the past forty years, some of them as long as forty miles. The group aims not only to expand the number of paths but also to interconnect them wher-

A bicycle path that has been converted from an abandoned railway in Savannah, Georgia. The Rails-to-Trails Conservancy has been promoting the creation of paths like this since 1986.

ever possible. Many of these paths are along highly scenic routes, and they are popular with families who want to cycle together without having to brush with automobiles.

But by far the most profound development in the cycling world since the 1970s has been the meteoric rise of the rugged but lightweight mountain bike. Though originally conceived strictly for off-road use—literally for barreling down a mountainside—these small-wheeled machines with fat knobby tires and a plethora of gears have come into wide general use: in fact, they have sparked a new surge in bicycle sales and now claim the lion's share of the adult market. Their popularity is understandable; the rider can go just about anywhere in style and comfort, thanks to puncture-resistant tires, effortless shifters that offer twenty-four speeds or more, responsive cantilever brakes, and even hydraulic front and rear shocks that cushion the ride. Like the original mountain bicycle envisioned by the Touring Club of France a century ago, these bicycles are conducive to exotic expeditions. Yet, like an updated Raleigh three-speed, their rugged nature is also well suited for city use.

The mountain bike also answers a long-felt desire to extend the range of the bicycle beyond the confines of the road. The soldiers under Lieutenant Moss bicycled across the wilderness of the American West in 1897. A year later, during the Klondike gold rush, a few ambitious prospectors cycled across the Alaskan tundra. In Australia, adventurers explored the rugged outback on bicycles. One early proponent of off-road cycling was the British statesman Winston Churchill, who recommended in 1908 that jungle explorers in Africa use bicycles. He reckoned they could average seven miles an hour over narrow paths with dense brush, even if they had to periodically get off and travel on foot over "sharp rocks, loose stones, a water course, or a steep hill." After a visit to Uganda, Churchill affirmed that "nearly all the British officers I met already possessed and used bicycles, and even native chiefs are beginning to acquire them."

It was nonetheless a recreational, rather than utilitarian, impulse that sparked the development and commercialization of a bicycle especially designed for off-road use. In the 1930s, *Le Cycliste* ran a column about cycling over *muletiers* (mule paths). In the early 1950s, some twenty young men formed the Vélo Cross Club Parisien. They revamped traditional French touring bicycles to create something rugged enough to race on the dirt courses used by off-road motorcyclists. By building bicycles that could handle steep descents and sharp turns without forcing the rider to dismount, these rough-riders in effect anticipated the contemporary mountain bike. But they made no attempt to market the idea, and their activities sparked no commercial demand for an all-terrain bicycle.

Starting in the early 1970s, several cliques of young Californians with a countercultural bent took up a similar activity in the hills around Cupertino and Marin County, sixty miles to the north. These cyclists, who were mostly men in their early twenties, regularly got together in remote areas to charge downhill on beat-up old Schwinns with balloon tires. One steep two-mile descent down Pine Mountain in Marin County became affectionately known to participants as the Repack, since their coaster brakes became so overheated by the time they reached the bottom that the internal grease had all but evaporated and the bearings needed to be repacked. A few began to modify their vehicles to better handle the demands of the sport, adding drum brakes and derailleur gears so that they could ride uphill as well as down. Some soon recognized that the mountain bike had distinct commercial possibilities.

In 1979, three of these veteran hill chargers, Gary Fisher, Charlie Kelly, and frame builder Tom Ritchey, formed MountainBikes, the first company dedicated to the production of off-road bicycles. Another frame builder who was part of the scene, Joe Breeze, also began making and selling mountain bikes. In 1981 the cycle supplier Specialized of Morgan Hill, California, introduced the Stumpjumper, the first mountain bike to gain a wide circulation. Japanese parts makers like Shimano and Araya quickly recognized the commercial possibilities, rushing out a series of specialized parts for the emerging market, including high-range derailleurs and twenty-six-inch aluminum alloy rims with fat, knobby tires to match. In 1987, after his fellow Americans had already purchased some three million mountain bikes, Paul Turner developed a full-suspension mountain bike with front and rear hydraulic shocks. These systems were soon sold and

Offbeat Recreation

Some cyclists, not content with merely riding around, have found other ways to derive pleasure or profit from their bicycles. One of the more offbeat uses is in a game of polo, with bicycles taking the place of ponies. Practiced in the United States on Star bicycles in the mid-1880s, the sport gained a small but enthusiastic following in Britain during the boom. At first, players used their front wheels to hit the ball, but eventually they adopted sticks as in the conventional game.

Since the 1930s, the sport has developed a small following in both Britain and France. The introduction of the mountain bike, with its small wheels and fat tires, has apparently given the sport a boost (although the bicycles must be stripped of brakes, derailleurs, and any unnecessary equipment). Six International Bicycle Polo Championships have been held since 1996 in India, New Zealand, the United Kingdom, France, the United States, and Canada.

But perhaps the most time-honored unconventional use of the bicycle is as an acrobatic instrument, which dates back to the Hanlon Brothers in 1868. The following year, a certain Dr. Jenkins rode a bizarre bicycle across Niagara Falls on a

Acrobats and entertainers have long used bicycles to enthrall spectators with stunning balancing acts. Here ten Chinese performers ride on one bicycle, no doubt some sort of record, outside Paris in 1966.

high-wire. Trick riding on high wheelers—not to mention unicycles—became popular in the 1870s and 1880s. After all, as one journalist reminisced in 1896, on an Ordinary "every rider was, in a degree, a trick rider. If you could do a few simple feats, in addition to staying on, the wonder at the staying-on part increased to such an extent that people would pay money to see you." Nevertheless, he allowed, some acts were more sensational than others, such as one rider carrying three or four people on the shoulders, or "taking your wheel to pieces and riding on less and less, until you had nothing left under you that would come off."

But when the safety arrived, the journalist explained, it was "difficult to find anything hard enough to do." The number of performers dwindled, and many began to rely on specially built props like spiraling ramps. "A more thrilling exhibition can scarcely be devised," affirmed *Cosmopolitan* in 1902, "than that of the bicycler plunging down a long decline at speed so great as to make of him and his machine but an indistinguishable flash of color, with death on the side always." Cyclists also defied gravity by circling loops. One boom-era performer, Charley Kilpatrick, bounced his way down a high, steep, and narrow flight of stairs—the kicker being that he only had one leg.

Some resourceful performers, however, developed new tricks using the safety bicycle itself. One young man from Milwaukee, Lee Richardson, devised a memorable closing act in 1896. While gliding on his bicycle on stage, he brought both legs to one side of the frame, then slipped his inner foot under the frame's top tube and onto the other pedal, bringing the bicycle to a stop. He then slowly stuffed his body through the frame's central triangle and, upon reaching the other side, swung his inner leg back over the bar, and sped off again. Even today, a handful of professionally trained performers still dazzle crowds with amazing bicycle tricks like those of Justin Case. This Australian's repertoire includes riding a bicycle while standing upside-down with his head on the saddle, and pedaling a bicycle six inches tall (yes, pedaling it) through a flaming hoop of fire.

The mountain bike also makes for a practical city bike, as demonstrated by the many police forces that have adopted them for patrolling congested urban areas

popularized under the trademark RockShox, and today they are considered must-have equipment for any serious mountain biker.

As legions of mountain bikers invaded public parklands in the late 1980s and early 1990s, however, controversy erupted. Many traditional trail users—such as hikers, bird-watchers, and equestrians—rebelled, charging that these newfangled bicycles were disrupting the serenity, causing accidents, and even harming the ecosystem. In 1988, the International Mountain Bicycling Association was formed in California to serve as an advocacy group. The debate over the rights of cyclists to use trails continues, but tensions have eased somewhat in recent years. Representatives of the various camps and parkland officials have worked out a series of guidelines and restrictions to make certain trails available to cyclists while preserving the rights of other groups to use trails safely and without unwarranted intrusions.

But of course, not everyone who rides this rugged style of bicycle regularly hits the mountainside or disappears into the wilderness. Like the balloon-tire bicycles of the 1930s, much of the mountain bike's appeal is whimsical, playing on the urbanite's pent-up desire to escape into the countryside or to enjoy romps in the mud reminiscent of childhood. The enduring popularity of the mountain bike probably has more to do with its practical side: on such a machine, one can ride over rough city streets in a comfortable upright position and easily change gears to suit any terrain.

Whatever might be the secrets of its success, the mountain bike has done much to revive popular interest and participation in the sport of cycling. It has also helped make the bicycle better answer the transportation needs of the twenty-first century. Yet at the same time, the proliferation of mountain bikes in recent years has reaffirmed the fundamental and enduring value of the basic bicycle itself. The pedal-powered machine, in all its forms, still provides a healthy and enjoyable recreational outlet for people of all ages and backgrounds.

FIFTEEN *Competitive Cycling*

Early bicycle racing helped generate much of the basic technology that has made cycling so pleasurable and efficient. For most of the twentieth century, however, racing bicycles had a comparatively modest impact on the makeup of the great army of bicycles. In fact, during the 1920s and 1930s, cycle tourists were primarily responsible for introducing such important innovations as butted frame tubing, derailleurs, and aluminum-alloy parts. Some say that the competitive sport has even obstructed progress by its longstanding ban on low-slung recumbent bicycles and other radical designs. Still, in recent years, the sport has helped introduce a number of innovations like clipless pedals that have strongly influenced the high-end recreational market. And most important, despite chronic allegations of drug abuse, the spectator sport has continued to serve as a powerful promotional tool for the industry, staging such time-honored pageantry as the annual Tour de France. Arguably, as an American source put it in 1917, "Racing has been the most potent force behind the progress of cycling and the growth of the trade."

By the early years of the twentieth century, competitive cycling had already developed into the three distinct branches that still characterize the sport today: track, road, and off-road. Early track racing took place along oval circuits ranging in length from about an eighth to a quarter of a mile, in indoor and outdoor facilities known as velo-

Arthur A. Zimmerman, rear, on a tandem racing bicycle in about 1891. Racing during the boom helped develop bicycle technology and also engendered a loyal following.

dromes. Events ranged from short sprints to grueling six-day marathons. Road racing failed to develop in North America, but it continued to gain popularity in Europe, creating legendary figures and providing free entertainment to the masses. Off-road racing, now generally practiced with mountain bikes, was originally introduced as the sport of cyclo-cross, which involved cycling through the woods on conventional racing bicycles, and running on foot over the roughest terrain, carrying the bicycle on one's shoulder.

In the United States, track racing retained a large following in the first few decades of the twentieth century, and was highly attractive to bettors. The standard track bicycle, apart from the tandem variety, resembled boom-era featherweights. It had a fixed gear and no brake or freewheel, and weighed little more than twenty pounds. The preferred track surface was composed of thin wooden planks parallel with the contours of the track and steeply banked at the corners. Some outdoor tracks, however, were entirely flat and made of dirt or concrete. Though the racing circuit diminished after the boom, a few outdoor velodromes continued to draw well, notably one in Newark, New Jersey, and another in Salt Lake City, Utah. Madison Square Garden in New York also

The start of a bicycle race at an outdoor velodrome in Toronto about 1900. Racing kept a loyal fan base even in the years immediately following the boom.

continued to host an annual six-day tournament, which drew thousands of fans and a competitive international field.

The top American sprinter at the onset of the twentieth century was Marshall "Major" Taylor, a worthy successor to Arthur A. Zimmerman. This outstanding black athlete, of medium stature but powerful build, was a popular figure on both sides of the Atlantic. One of the most exciting contests in the annals of the American sport took place in 1900 at the Newark Velodrome before ten thousand screaming fans. Taylor, who had won the world championship in Montreal the previous year, took on a rising star, Frank L. Kramer. The first to win two one-mile heats, six laps around the oval, would collect the purse and earn the national championship. Taylor nipped his hapless rival down the stretch in two straight sprints.

The following year, Taylor embarked on a European tour after promoters reluctantly agreed to release the devout Baptist from Sunday competitions. Taylor drew immense crowds while visiting sixteen cities in Belgium, Denmark, France, Germany, Italy, and Switzerland. He won more than forty races, besting numerous national champions including the legendary French sprinter Edmond Jacquelin. The two met twice at

Major Taylor adorned the cover of *La Vie au Grand Air* of 10 March 1901. The European cycling world was abuzz with the anticipated arrival of the American champion described here as the "famous black sprinter."

the Parc des Princes velodrome in Paris, before as many as thirty thousand spectators. Taylor lost the first set, but in the second he prevailed convincingly in two straight heats, making good on his claim to be the fastest racer in the world. This international celebrity revisited Europe on numerous occasions and in 1904 he competed in Australia and New Zealand.

In 1905, *Bicycling World* articulated why track racing continued to "hold the attention of the sporting world," despite the growing prominence of motorized racing. The colorful spectacle drew "all who love a good sprint, terminating in a hot and exciting finish." Long-distance indoor races were particularly exciting, as they usually featured "a bunch of riders spinning lightly round the boards" and becoming "almost horizontal" at the steeply banked turns. As the racers went round and round, the crowd fell into a mesmerized state. Meanwhile, each competitor kept "a jealous eye on the others to anticipate any sprinting tactics." Finally, when the bell sounded at the last lap, the lull was shattered and each racer let out "all that is in him." The pack raced for the finish, inches apart, as the fans sprung to their feet, erupting in "a pandemonium of cheering."

One of the most popular spectacles was the six-day race at Madison Square Garden, an annual event since 1891. Although New York state law prohibited racers from cycling more than twelve hours a day in 1898, in response to humanitarian protests, the resourceful organizers hastily concocted a new formula to salvage the event. From then on, contestants competed as part of a two-man team: while one rode, the other relaxed on the infield where he could eat, drink, sleep, or mingle with fans. The affair became more popular than ever, attracting competitors from as far away as Europe and Australia eager to share in the seductive prize monies. Before long, numerous indoor venues across the country regularly hosted six-day races on makeshift wooden tracks.

Fans enjoyed the carnival-like atmosphere, the flexibility to pop in at leisure, and the opportunity to socialize or even bet. Not only were racers themselves approachable during their rests, some even conducted conversations with fans while still in the saddle. One competitor claimed he kept two conversations going at once—on opposite sides of the tracks. Indeed, racers were constantly fighting monotony as they pedaled for hours on end, sometimes without even changing position in the pack. This routine was periodically interrupted, however, by scheduled sprints, each with its own prize. But the most exciting event, the one that kept everyone on their toes, was the "jam." Without warning, a racer might suddenly swoop above the pack and begin a mad sprint trying to "steal" a lap. Ultimately, a team's fate hinged on its ability to execute, or thwart, these surprise attacks.

Yet another popular form of bicycle racing was the so-called motorpace. By drafting behind a motorbike that set the pace, a cyclist could achieve and maintain speeds exceeding fifty miles an hour. One who excelled in this exhilarating but dangerous competition against time was Bobby Walthour, Sr., a Georgian nicknamed the Dixie Flyer. Like his contemporaries Taylor and Kramer, he became an international celebrity who regularly competed abroad. And despite suffering numerous bone fractures and other serious injuries—tires were prone to burst at high speeds—he consistently prevailed over his rivals. Walthour was also a perennial six-day champion.

In the 1910s, as the American bicycle industry enjoyed a modest resurgence, the sport prospered. Taylor and Walthour retired, but the veteran Frank L. Kramer carried on. Indeed, after losing to Taylor in 1900, Kramer was nearly invincible. Famed for his "clean living and careful training," he collected fifteen straight national sprint championships. Along the way he won several six-day races and the 1912 world championship in Newark. In 1915, the manager of the Newark velodrome signed Kramer to a long-term contract. Although he would not reveal the details, he crowed: "Kramer's earnings for the next three years will make Ty Cobb and his yearly stipend look like a jitney bus alongside a limousine." Kramer did not disappoint. Even after his string was broken in 1916, he switched to a larger gear and won two more national championships. He finally retired in 1922 at the age of forty-one, but not before he beat his own record covering a sixth of a mile. Twenty thousand fans gathered that evening to bid an emotional farewell to the ageless champion.

Bobby Walthour in 1909 riding at the Newark velodrome, a banked wooden oval similar to ones used for indoor six-day races

Six-day races also continued to draw well, producing a new star in Alf Goullet. In 1914, this transplanted Australian and a partner set a new record of 2,759 miles. Meanwhile, the atmosphere at these events became even more charged, with live bands providing additional entertainment at all hours. A professional cook fed the racers, who consumed as many as ten meals at each outing. On a typical day in 1917, one contestant reportedly ate "two dozen soft boiled eggs, six undercut tenderloin steaks, fifty slices of buttered toast, ten cups of hot meat broth, and thirty side dishes of vegetables." The men generally gained between three and four pounds in the course of the week, yet they consistently rode as fast on the sixth day as they had on the first. In racking up more than a thousand miles, each rider went through four or five tires.

The 1920s were the golden era of track racing in America, before the sport declined during the depression years. Velodromes proliferated in major cities across the country, including one in Los Angeles patterned after an automobile race course. Some six hundred professionals made the rounds, using trains to shuttle themselves and their bicycles from one venue to another. Regular standouts included the longtime holder of the hour record, the Swiss racer Oscar Egg. Madison Square Garden added a second annual six-day race, and an increasing number of cities hosted similar spectacles. As many as twenty thousand fans came to watch at a given time, making cycling one of the most popular American spectator sports along with baseball. Although critics considered the affair decidedly "low brow," it attracted a cross-cultural mix. "Coal-heavers, mechanics, cab drivers, and clerks," noted one source, took their seats beside "sportsmen, white shirt-fronts, and low-cut gowns."

In Europe, bicycle racing also remained popular after the boom. Velodromes operated in a number of major cities, including London, Paris, and Berlin. In 1900, representatives of several European racing associations met in Geneva and formed the Union Cycliste Internationale (UCI) to govern the professional and amateur sport worldwide, track and road. It established and oversaw several annual events, notably the world sprint and road championships. The International Olympic Committee, which had already introduced cycling at the first Olympic games in Athens in 1896, took on the responsibility for organizing bicycle races at future Olympics and at other regional games.

But road racing soon became the most prominent and popular manifestation of the competitive sport in Europe, especially in France. For no admission, the public could gather along the roadside of the announced route and catch a close-up glimpse of the racers as they streaked by. The tradition of city-to-city races was particularly strong in France, which had hosted the inaugural Paris-to-Rouen race in 1869. France also took the lead in the safety era, introducing both the Paris-to-Bordeaux and the Paris–Brest–Paris races in 1891. Within a decade, numerous point-to-point races had become popular annual rituals, attracting the best racers from France and beyond. Each race developed its own distinct character, based on the distance, terrain, and time of year. The springtime Paris-to-Roubaix event, for one, has taken racers over the punishing cobblestones of the north country almost every year since 1896. To this day, it announces the opening of a new season and budding aspirations for glory.

The most important event on the European cycling calendar has long been the legendary Tour de France, which has also spawned such notable imitations as the Giro d'Italia (Tour of Italy), run since 1909, and the Vuelta a España (Tour of Spain), since 1935. The Tour de France is one of the most grueling—and widely reported—endurance tests in all of sports. Georges Lefevre, the cycling editor of *L'Auto-Vélo*, a sporting daily, hatched the concept a century ago to upstage his paper's chief rival, *Le Vélo*. Headed by the tireless promoter Pierre Giffard, *Le Vélo* was already running two races, Paris–Bordeaux and Paris–Brest–Paris. As Giffard had discovered, the buildup to and coverage of the races themselves provided an excellent means to sell newspapers. Lefevre's boss, Henri Desgrange, agreed to try out the idea of a grand "stage race" that would last several weeks and attract the top racers.

The inaugural race of 1903 brought together some sixty professional racers for the start in Villeneuve-Saint-Georges, just outside Paris. Although some riders were sponsored by various cycle makers, and thus associated with a team, the contest was essentially every man for himself. The racers were to complete a fifteen-hundred-mile loop in six stages over eighteen days, riding even at night. They had to keep the same bicycle throughout the race and make any necessary repairs themselves. Lefevre followed the entire affair by train and on a bicycle. He not only served as the official timekeeper, he also wrote the daily reports for *L'Auto-Vélo*. In all, twenty riders completed the entire course, headed by thirty-two-year-old Maurice Garin. He won three of the six stages, averaging more than sixteen miles an hour, and his total time of ninety-five and a half hours was nearly three hours better than the runner-up. The formula proved an immense success, as townspeople came out in droves along the route and Parisians gathered en masse to witness the champion's triumphant arrival.

The Tour was evidently off to a good start, but the second edition was rife with scandal. Contestants allegedly sneaked onto trains in the dead of night to reach the next checkpoint. On the road, they sprinkled nails in their wake to puncture the tires of their rivals. A few were even attacked en route by hired thugs. The organizers conducted an investigation and sent a stern message to the racers that no more shenanigans would be tolerated: three riders were banned for life, and the top four finishers were disqualified. Garin, who had won again, received a two-year ban for the seemingly minor infraction of accepting food from a motorist during the competition. In 1953, he was finally honored in ceremonies marking the fiftieth anniversary of the Tour, but his second victory was never reinstated despite his lifelong protests that he done nothing wrong.

Maurice Garin, winner of
the first Tour de France the
previous year, pictured on the
cover of *La Vie au Grand Air*,
28 July 1904. After winning
the second Tour as well, Garin
was stripped of his title and
suspended for two years for
alleged infractions that he
vigorously denied.

Suddenly, it appeared that the grand race was doomed to a short existence. After careful reflection, however, Desgrange decided to go ahead with a third Tour in 1905, taking several measures to curtail cheating and sabotage by racers or non-racers. In particular, Desgrange did away with nighttime riding so that the racers no longer disappeared into the darkness. He also expanded the format to eleven stages that were shorter, and thus presumably easier to monitor. The public, not particularly bothered by the hint of a scandal in the first place, continued to show its wholehearted approval of the spectacle, lining up to see the racers when they came by and buying newspapers to keep up with the action.

Over time, the Tour became ever grander, with more racers riding more stages over more varied terrain. Increasingly, the contest became an international affair. In 1909, François Faber of Luxembourg became the first non-Frenchman to win the Tour, and in the ensuing years a number of Belgian racers took highest honors. In 1910, the Tour entered the great passes of the Pyrenees, and the following year it headed into the Alps.

From then on, racing over forbidding mountains became a routine part of the Tour and a mandatory test of character for any would-be champion. In the early years, racers had only two speeds, with a high and a low gear mounted on either side of their rear wheels. The only way to switch gears in preparation for a climb was to get off the bicycle, remove the rear wheel, flip it to the other side, reattach the chain to the sprocket, and tighten the wheel before hopping back into the saddle.

Tales of heroic cyclists in the mountaintops, fighting off their rivals and the elements, quickly became part of popular lore. The cyclists faced extreme weather conditions, from heat waves to snowstorms. They suffered bloody accidents, at times falling at breakneck speeds while trying to make hairpin turns. When their bicycles were so damaged that they could not proceed, they improvised repairs. One of the most famous misadventures occurred during the 1913 Tour when Eugène Christophe broke a fork blade while careening down a mountain pass. He ran on foot to the nearest village, toting his broken bicycle over his shoulder; finding a forge, he personally mended his machine as Desgrange reportedly guarded against unwarranted assistance. He then gallantly rejoined the race, though he had lost any chance of winning.

World War I forced Tour organizers to impose a hiatus that lasted four years. The bloody conflict also claimed the lives of many top performers. Among the casualties was the French ace Octave Lapize, whose combat airplane was shot down over Pont-à-Mousson, Lallement's hometown. The Tour nonetheless resumed in 1919, when the tradition of the yellow jersey was established: ever since, the overall leader at the start of each day wears the hallowed shirt with a color matching the yellow pages of the original sponsoring journal. The Tour continued to grow in popularity, as towns clamored to be included in the official race route, often paying large sums for the privilege.

A contributor to the *New York World* described the aura of excitement in Orleans as the locals anxiously awaited the passing of their heroes in the 1924 Tour. "Two hours before 'they' are to pass, all find excuses to be at the turn of the road, to view their faces as they pass us. Forerunning the show by a mile are three big cars, floured from spokes to windscreen with white dust, with flags on their radiators, bearing initials—referees and journalists. They scan us; some shout news, most stare ahead with assured importance." At last the racers arrive, with "haggard lines under their eyes, and smudges around their mouths where they have brushed the dust away. In front of each in a box on the handle-bars are two bottles, one for water, one for cold tea. Round their shoulders are two spare inner tubes. Their caps are reversed, with the peak to keep the sun off their necks. They lift their faces together to read the red twill strip above the road that sets them the direction. Then they are gone round the bend, too tired and set to notice our cheers."

Road racing, like track racing, quickly developed into a sophisticated sport. In the

French cycle tourists charging up a hill in the annual races outside Paris called the Poly de Chanteloup, in 1948. In the 1920s, touring cyclists used this event to showcase the need for derailleurs, and sometimes even outpaced those professionals who chose to race without multiple gears.

early days, noted the *World* correspondent, the winner rode hard from start to finish. But "nowadays the racers are so equal that it needs brains to win. They play a waiting game, choosing the moment for the *démarrage,* the sprint. When rivals of the squad are in difficulties; when there is a puncture or a tumble, the rest put on as many miles at top speed as they can. Or a cunning hand, like Francis Pelissier, this year's conqueror, will judge the moment for a sprint when the others are nodding." The winners, the correspondent continued, became national heroes, and bicycle makers used their triumphs for advertising fodder. "Every laborer in France," he explained, "remembers the name of the winning make when he has to buy a new machine."

In the first three decades of the twentieth century, while the touring bicycle developed, the racing bicycle remained largely unchanged, save for an occasional incremental improvement such as lightweight tubular tires. Henri Desgrange, in fact, banned the most radical accessory, derailleurs, from the Tour until his reign ended in 1937. At first, racers generally spurned the lightweight alloy components that tourists were beginning to use by the early 1930s. For the most part, the competitive community resisted any new devices or materials that might detract from the purity of the sport by favoring gadgetry over individual valor.

Nevertheless, by the mid-1930s, the racing bicycle finally began to develop. Racers adopted alloy components and other useful improvements like the quick-release hubskewer, introduced by Tullio Campagnolo of Vicenza, Italy, who went on to become the most coveted name in the racing parts business. In 1934, a French company named Mavic introduced an aluminum-alloy rim that weighed about one and a half pounds—a full pound lighter than the conventional steel variety. The racer Antonin Magne reportedly tested them in the 1934 Tour with great success, but had to paint them to look like wood because they were banned by the rules. Racers even began to adopt derailleurs offering three or four gears, despite the Tour ban. In France, Simplex of Dijon produced cable-operated derailleurs especially designed for racers. They employed one or two jockey wheels to maintain proper chain tension.

In Italy, the Nieddu brothers of Turin introduced the novel Vittoria racing derailleur, with a stick shift that swung through the base of the frame's central triangle, sandwiched between two arched metal bridges. The lever moved a long extension arm with a single jockey wheel at the end, which forced the chain to dip as low as a few inches off the ground to maintain proper chain tension. On the first models, the rider did the actual shifting manually, reaching down to tap one side of the chain while pedaling backward. On later models, however, the rider only had to twist a small handle at the end of the shift stick; this operated two levers fixed to the end of the chain stay that shifted the chain to the desired gear. Oscar Egg developed a cable-operated variation of

The Hour of the Recumbent

Shortly after the introduction of the pneumatic safety bicycle, racing officials began to keep track of hour records set on indoor tracks. The first official title-holder in 1893 was none other than Henri Desgranges—who would preside over the first Tour de France a decade later. He registered just over 35 kilometers (about 22 miles), but within five years racers had pushed the record over the 40-kilometer mark. In 1907, the French racer Marcel Berthet set a new record of 41.5 kilometers at the velodrome of Paris. For the next seven years, he and the veteran Swiss racer Oscar Egg engaged in a protracted game of one-upmanship. Finally, Egg set a seemingly untouchable mark of 44.245 kilometers (27.4 miles)—which endured for nearly twenty years as one of the most vaunted records in cycling.

Both Berthet and Egg knew, however, that they could readily increase their distances simply by adopting more streamlined bicycles. Both men successfully experimented with front and rear aerodynamic shields, known as fairings, but restricted their rivalry to conventional track bicycles in deference to tradition. By the early 1930s, however, the conservative sport was beginning to show a greater receptiveness for technical experimentation, and several French mechanics explored radically different designs. One was Charles Mochet, who built a recumbent bicycle he called the Vélocar, an idea first suggested during the bicycle boom. In July 1933, a little-known racer named Francis Faure brought the low-slung vehicle to the Vélodrome d'Hiver of Paris, where he boldly set out to challenge Egg's long-standing hour mark. Much to the amazement of onlookers, Faure smashed the record by nearly half a mile, throwing the racing world into a tizzy.

Shortly afterward, Berthet—now a forty-seven-year-old ex-racer—set out to top Faure's mark with a radically revamped bicycle of his own. Drawing on his earlier experiments, he added full fairings to a conventional bicycle, and promptly registered a record distance of nearly 50 kilometers. In 1934, however, the UCI voted by a narrow margin to disallow any record not set with a conventional bicycle, and even banned such designs from future competition. Undaunted, Mochet's son Georges created a new version of the Vélocar that retained the recum-

Francis Faure racing the original Vélocar at the Vélodrome d'Hiver of Paris in early 1934, about six months after he had smashed Oscar Egg's twenty-year-old hour record at the same venue and on the same bicycle. His success against conventional racers like Henri Lemoines, right, prompted the UCI to ban recumbents from sanctioned competitions.

bent position while adding fairings. This happy marriage of technologies led to yet another unofficial record in 1938, set once again by Faure. Riding the new Vélocar, the veteran became the first cyclist to crack 50 kilometers (over 30 miles) in an hour. That mark was not matched on a conventional bicycle until 1984, when the Italian racer Francesco Moser covered 51.151 kilometers. And even then, Moser benefited from special aerodynamic disc wheels and the thin air of Mexico City.

Over the past twenty years, the hour record has been broken several times, most recently in 1996 by the British racer Chris Boardman, who covered 56.375 kilometers—about 35 miles. But exactly what constitutes a bicycle remains a contentious issue as hour racers become increasingly reliant on high-tech designs, materials, and gadgetry like aerodynamic helmets, special handlebars, and carbon-fiber frames. To level the playing field the UCI has now established a new hour category, called the Conventional Hour Race, restricted to bicycles frozen in the Merckx era. But the UCI has yet to rescind its ban on recumbents, a policy that still rankles proponents of these low-slung vehicles who passionately believe that they represent the bicycles of the future.

the Vittoria derailleur, produced from about 1933 by the French firm Super Champion and sold in the United Kingdom under the trademark Osgears.

One of the most popular racing derailleurs before the war was Campagnolo's Cambio Corsa (race changer). To operate it, the rider reached back with the right hand to move two levers, one just above the other, both of which were connected to rods that paralleled the right seat stay. The rider flicked the first lever to release the hub skewer, then pushed the second to guide a forklike device that shifted the chain over the range of three or four sprockets on the freewheel. As the rider positioned the chain over the desired gear, the unhinged wheel naturally shifted within the elongated serrated drop-outs (forward when shifting to larger gears, and vice versa) until the chain regained normal tension, at which point the rider tightened the quick-release mechanism to secure it. The entire operation took some skill to execute smoothly. Gino Bartali, who used this system in the mountain stages of his triumphant 1938 Tour, was said to be a master at it.

All the while, the Tour was gaining in popularity until it was derailed by the outbreak of World War II, which forced a suspension from 1940 to 1946. When contests finally resumed, the sport reached what was perhaps its peak of popularity. War-weary citizens, many of whom still relied on a bicycle simply to get around, were eager for diversion. And no other sport created larger heroes or more epic battles. Older French people still talk about the 1947 Tour and the "Miracle de Bonsecours." It was on that hill in Normandy that the Frenchman Jean Robic began an improbable spurt toward Paris, overtaking the leaders to finish in first place. In so doing, he became the first racer to overtake the rider wearing the yellow jersey during the final stage of the race.

The following year, however, was perhaps the most dramatic performance of all. One evening midway through the contest, while resting in his hotel room, the aging Gino Bartali received a telephone call from his friend Alcide De Gasperi, a deputy in the ruling Christian Democratic Party of Italy. Their homeland was on the verge of civil war, following an unsuccessful attempt on the life of Palmiro Togliatti, the leader of the Communist party. De Gasperi begged Bartali to win a stage to help Italians feel a sense of national unity and take their minds off the political turmoil. Bartali promised he would do that and more—he would win his second Tour. In dramatic fashion, he gradually overtook his rivals and entered Paris alone to the delight of the cheering throngs. Bartali did indeed give his fellow Italians something to cherish. No one else has ever won two Tours ten years apart.

Yet Bartali was but one of two giants who dominated Italian cycling in the postwar period. The other was Fausto Coppi, who won the Tours of 1949 and 1952 as well as five Giros between 1940 and 1953. Despite certain similarities—both had brothers who died in bicycle racing accidents—the two champions could hardly have had more contrasting personas. About half of Italy rooted for the gruff, hardworking, and deeply religious

Bartali, known as Gino the Pious. The rest favored the flamboyant Coppi with the movie star looks. He was even rumored to have a mistress, the notorious "dama bianca" (woman in white). Whenever these rivals met, the atmosphere was charged with excitement. The contests often came down to a mano-a-mano battle, capped by an electrifying sprint.

As motorized vehicles finally became widely affordable in the postwar period, Europeans largely abandoned their bicycles as a means of transportation, and even recreational use suffered. Nevertheless, road racing continued to capture the popular imagination. Every July, some thirty million French citizens—over half the population —observed the Tour at some point in its trajectory. Many gathered along country roads, hours in advance, packing provisions for a picnic. As the entourage approached, the spectators dutifully took their positions by the roadside, often leaving just enough space for the cyclists to slither through. When the racers finally arrived, fans barked out encouragement, splashed cold water on their heads, and even reached out to pat them on the back. All this continues as part of a cherished tradition, one that gives fans a unique opportunity to connect with their idols.

The 1950s spawned a new generation of superstars, starting with Louison Bobet, France's answer to Coppi. In 1955 this plucky Breton, considered a master strategist, survived a heat wave to win a record-tying third Tour. The mantle soon passed, however, to Jacques Anquetil, who became the first ever to win five Tours (in 1957 and 1961–64) and always seemed to edge out his archrival, Raymond Poulidor. Yet many consider the next Tour standout the greatest racer of all time: Eddy Merckx of Belgium, nicknamed "the Cannibal." Starting in 1967, when he won his first professional race, he utterly dominated the sport for almost a decade. He too won five Tours (in 1969–72 and 1974), as well as three Giros and countless other classics. He even found time to set an hour record that lasted for twelve years. Whereas most contemporary racers pace themselves during the long season, targeting a few select victories and even then expending only as much energy as necessary, Merckx went all out in every race he entered. Inevitably, his hapless opponents could only watch his rear wheel.

Meanwhile, the racing bicycle was achieving an extraordinary degree of refinement. Even before the war, British craftsmen were building extremely lightweight frames from special butted tubing by the Reynolds Tube Company of Birmingham, founded in 1889 by William Reynolds. In 1934, the company introduced double-butted Reynolds 531 tubing, which set the standard for decades. The thin-walled tubing gradually thickened toward the ends, at the points of stress where they were fitted into lugs and brazed into place. Master builders like Horace Bates and Hyman Hetchins were among the leaders of the famed British lightweight school of the 1930s. By the 1950s, Vitus of France supplied special tubing to celebrated French firms like Mercier and Gitane,

During the 1960 Tour de France, an exhausted Fernando Manzaneque of Spain receives vociferous boosting from a spectator, an honorable French tradition

while Columbus of Italy did the same for prestigious makes like Legnano, Bianchi, and Frejus. And just as the French cycle industry was famed for its touring bicycles, its Italian counterpart became known for its exquisite racing frames built by masters like Faliero Masi.

The French cycle industry maintained a strong presence in the postwar racing scene. Joining the older names were some new ones like T.A. (cranks), Mafac (brakes), and Lyotard (pedals). Italian component makers like Regina (freewheels and chains) were also highly prized by racers. But the most legendary name of all was Campagnolo of Vicenza, Italy, founded by Tullio Campagnolo in 1933. In 1951 the company introduced the Gran Sport rear derailleur, the first to combine the principal features of the modern parallel design with dual jockey wheels in a compact, elegant form. In the 1960s, more often than not, the winner of the Tour de France crossed the finish line with a bicycle sporting the full line of "Campy" components known as the Nuovo Record. In the mid-1970s, the company sold annually about twenty thousand of its upgraded Super Record group, the vast majority going to high-end recreational riders.

Another Italian who went from racing to parts manufacturing was Cino Cinelli. A

A special-edition rear derailleur from Campagnolo's famed Super Record component group, issued for the vaunted Italian maker's fiftieth anniversary in 1983

close friend of Campagnolo, he made everything in his factory in Turin that the Vicenza firm didn't, including stems and bars. Up until the 1950s, these vital parts were generally made of steel, since alloys were not considered sufficiently strong to withstand the rider's pressure. But eventually even these became made of alloy, shaving off another pound or two. Cinelli was also an early proponent of the lightweight plastic-shell seat, which gradually replaced the traditional leather saddle. Known as an innovator, Cinelli proposed a clipless pedal years before they came into style. Also highly coveted were

Cinelli frames, with a sleek sloping fork crown and distinctive seat stays converging behind the top of the seat tube.

The recreational boom of the late 1960s and early 1970s rekindled American interest and participation in the competitive sport. Youths began to take up cycling as a modest racing network developed, producing national road cycling champions like John Howard and John Allis. For the first time in many years, American cyclists began to appear on the international circuit. In 1971, Howard won a gold medal in the Pan American Games road race in Cali, Columbia. In 1973, the Amateur Bicycle League of America, founded in 1921 and since renamed the U.S. Cycling Federation, organized its first national road and track teams with seven members each. At the 1976 Olympics in Montreal, George Mount became the first American in sixty-four years to place in an Olympic cycling event. In the early 1980s, Mount competed in the Giro d'Italia while his compatriot Jonathan Boyer rode in the Tour de France—becoming the first Americans ever to enter those prestigious classics.

But the pioneer American road champion was Greg LeMond, who in 1986 became the first non-European rider to win the Tour de France. The following year, he suffered a nearly fatal hunting accident. Yet he came back to win again in 1989, when he raced with a new aerodynamically shaped helmet and a clip-on bar extension that projected out over the front wheel. The add-on allowed LeMond to stretch out his arms and crouch down, increasing his lung capacity and also enhancing his aerodynamic advantage. His dramatic victory that year, overcoming the commanding lead of Laurent Fignon in the race's final stage to win by a mere eight seconds, was the closest finish ever. LeMond won his third and final Tour the following year, but he was forced to retire a few years later after having contracted a rare cellular disease. His French teammate and rival, Bernard Hinault, was another dominant professional in the 1980s. He won five Tours in all (in 1978–79, 1981–82, and 1985), matching the record then held jointly by Anquetil and Merckx.

In the 1990s, the towering Spaniard Miguel Indurain was virtually untouchable. He became the fourth man to win five Tours, but the first to win them consecutively, from 1991 to 1995. By the end of the decade, however, a new American champion emerged, Lance Armstrong. In 2003, this former triathlete from Plano, Texas, matched Indurain's record with his fifth straight victory, and in 2004 he claimed an unprecedented sixth straight title and even hinted that he might try for more. Armstrong's stellar career is all the more remarkable given that he underwent surgery and treatment for testicular cancer in 1996, an inspirational story he has recounted in two best-selling biographies. Thanks to the collective efforts of LeMond and Armstrong, Americans have taken a much greater interest in the professional sport.

The Tour de France today commands global attention. Much has changed, of

Women's Racing

Women have participated in competitive cycling since its inception. In the late 1890s and early 1900s, women even competed in a modified six-day format, with evening competitions. Still, it was not until the second half of the twentieth century that official annual track and road titles were established. Whereas men have competed for the world sprint championship since 1893, when Arthur Zimmerman prevailed in Chicago, the women's equivalent was not inaugurated until 1958. The Olympics have included a track sprint for men since the first modern games of 1896, but the first such race for women had to await the 1988 games in Seoul. Women's road racing was equally slow to develop. Since the 1920s, men have competed for the world road championship covering about 150 miles; a similar event for women began only in 1958. And while the Olympic games have always had a road race for men, the women's counterpart dates only from the Los Angeles games of 1984—also the year of the first women's version of the Tour de France.

Nevertheless, in the past thirty years, women's racing has made up for lost time. An American, Sue Novara-Reber, was a perennial sprint champion in the 1970s, winning seven consecutive world championship medals, including two golds. She was followed by a number of outstanding American female racers. Some, like Connie Paraskevin-Young and Beth Heiden, were already noted speed skaters. Connie Carpenter-Phinney was a dominant road racer, while Rebecca Twigg distinguished herself on both road and track. Two outstanding European female cyclists are Maria Canins of Italy and Jeannie Longo of France. Canins has won the women's Tour de France twice and is also an accomplished mountain bike racer. Longo won five world championship road races between 1985 and 1995 and three women's Tours de France. In 2000, she set a women's hour record of just over twenty-eight miles—and is still racing in her forties.

Women did not have to wait, however, to join the two recent branches of the sport, triathlons and mountain biking. In fact, women's races have been a part of the official calendars of both sports from the start. The Hawaiian Ironman, despite its name, has included a women's race since the inaugural year of 1978. The original mountain bike championship, known as NORBA, had included women's competitions since its first series in 1987. Among the pioneer champions were Jacquie Phelan and Julie Furtado, and a professional women's circuit is now fully established.

Lance Armstrong, wearing the leader's yellow jersey, on his way to winning the centennial edition of the Tour de France in 2003

course. In 1999 Mario Cipollini of Italy finished a 120-mile stage averaging more than twenty-five miles an hour—almost ten miles more than the winning pace in 1903. The course now covers more than three thousand miles in at least twenty stages and lasts a good three weeks. The formula for individual time classification has also grown more complex, taking into consideration results in the time trials and various bonuses and penalties. Teamwork has assumed an increasingly important role in determining the outcome. Teams are often built around one superstar, with teammates chosen for their specialties in hill climbing, time trials, and other facets of the race, to maximize the leader's chances of victory.

Still, the essence of the Tour remains the same: to test just how far and how fast one rider can travel on the strength of muscle and will, with the help of a bicycle. And the racers still trace the hexagonal perimeter of France, although the route often strays into neighboring countries. Since the 1950s, noncontiguous segments in foreign countries have also become regular attractions, including a start in Dublin, Ireland, in 1988. And while the number of racers has grown to about two hundred and the publicity caravan of motorized vehicles is now a traveling city, this colorful event still brings the citizenry to the roadside, eager to voice their sentiments. They appreciate that bicycle racing is the most demanding and grueling of all sports.

In spite of the enduring popularity of the sport, race organizers, and the racers themselves, continue to battle allegations of rampant drug abuse. Many past champions were indeed notorious dopers who sought to gain a competitive edge or suppress their agonizing pain through drugs. One of the darkest days in the history of the Tour de France was the sudden demise of Tommy Simpson in 1967. As the top British racer, he was under enormous pressure to be the first rider from the United Kingdom to win the Tour. To boost his chances, he took amphetamines. He collapsed under the scorching summer sun while climbing a mountain road near Marseille. A fan helped him back on his bike, but Simpson fell again a few yards down the road and never revived. A small monument marks the spot where he died, and cyclists regularly visit that shrine to pay their respects.

Simpson's tragic death underscored the magnitude of the drug problem in the professional ranks and prodded Tour organizers to institute the first drug control program in any sport. Yet as recently as 1998 a major bust involving several teams and their trainers marred the Tour. One team was expelled and several withdrew, reducing the field by nearly half. The hundred or so racers who participated complained bitterly that the press and organizers were treating them as criminals. They organized a sit-down strike that delayed the start of one stage by two hours. Another stage was nullified altogether when the racers crossed the finish line together holding hands. The organizers have since implemented new tests and insist that the drug problem is under control. The current crop of champions, headed by Lance Armstrong, likewise insists it is clean.

The third branch of competitive cycling, off-road racing, was first developed in France in the early twentieth century as the sport known as cyclo-cross. Using modified racing bicycles, competitors tore for miles through woods and over streams, running with their vehicles draped over their shoulders whenever the going got too rough for pedaling. Championed by Daniel Gousseau, a French army private, cyclo-cross quickly gained a small but enthusiastic following in Europe. By 1908, organizers in Turin, Italy, staged an annual cross-country race over a five-mile course open to both cyclists and pedestrians. The terrain was "up hill and down dale, over stone walls and through shallow streams." The champion cyclist, despite having to make frequent dismounts, completed the course in about fifteen minutes—beating the top pedestrian by two and half minutes.

But it was not until 1910 that the sport gained widespread attention. Octave Lapize attributed his victory in the Tour de France that year to his participation in the sport during the off-season. In 1924, Paris hosted the first international competitions. Starting in 1950, the UCI oversaw an official annual world championship, which attracted many of the top road racers eager to keep in shape over the winter months. Belgium's

An early cyclo-cross race through the woods near Paris, as shown on the cover of *La Vie au Grand Air,* 17 January 1903. Since the 1950s, the sport has been a popular off-season activity for professional racers.

Eric de Vlaeminck became to cyclo-cross what his countryman and contemporary Eddy Merckx was to road racing. Vlaeminck won the championship in 1966 and then each year from 1968 to 1973. In the mid-1980s, Bernard Hinault was another prominent figure in cyclo-cross competitions. Over the years, the cyclo-cross bicycle has become more specialized. Frames are built with more relaxed angles than the typical road bicycle for optimal handling. Equipment varies as well, from wider tires to bar-end shifters that allow the racer to shift without moving the hands from the handlebars.

Since the late 1970s, however, mountain bike racing has become the most prominent form of off-road racing, and it has developed its own constituencies of racers and fans. Unlike cyclo-cross racers, mountain bikers stay on their more rugged machines even on the roughest terrain, making the contests a true test of cycling skills. In 1983, the newly formed National Off-Road Bicycle Association (NORBA) organized an annual national championship with categories for men and women in the United States. Since 1990, the UCI has overseen the annual world championships, and since the Atlanta games of 1996, the sport has had an Olympic event all its own.

Arguably, competitive cycling, in all its varieties, still succeeds in its twin missions to promote technical innovation and to keep the bicycle in the public eye. On the tech-

Barbara Kreisle, a professional mountain biker who specializes in marathons (races from sixty to a hundred miles) and twenty-four-hour team relay races, training near Lake Mead, Nevada

nical front, road racing in particular has helped spawn a new wave of design innovations, though the bike's basic configuration has changed little. Leading high-end component manufacturers, such as Shimano of Japan, have rethought and revamped many conventional parts, notably gear changers, which are now indexed and operated from the handlebars or brake levers. A French manufacturer of ski equipment, Look, introduced clip-on pedals in the 1980s, and they have since supplanted the old system of cleats and toe clips. Road racing frames are now being made of alternative materials such as aluminum, titanium, and carbon-fiber composites, and they have adopted a new generation of lightweight high-pressure clincher tires in place of the old tubular tires that were glued in place.

Even the track sport has done its part to spawn design innovations. In 1984, Francesco Moser of Italy broke Eddy Merckx's longstanding hour record, riding a shade over

The BMX Bicycle

The American recreational boom of the early 1970s helped spawn a popular new class of juvenile two-wheelers: the Bicycle Moto Cross or BMX bicycle. Inspired by motorcycles specially designed for off-road competition, these small, lightweight, single-geared machines first became popular with Californian teenagers in the mid-1970s. The young competitors used them to tear around rugged outdoor courses, deftly handling the steep drops and sharp turns. At first, BMX racers simply stripped down their old Sting-Rays, but before long some enterprising individuals began to offer kits to add striking features like simulated gas tanks.

By the late 1970s, dealers nationwide were offering specially designed BMX bicycles to a booming market. These retained the twenty-inch wheels of the Sting-Ray, but featured lighter and more maneuverable frames and strong wheels made of injection-molded plastic. BMX bicycles also featured special handlebars and sturdy handgrips, and an extremely low gear to help the wheels work their way over loose terrain. Naturally, this peculiar style of bicycle is not conducive to road use. But that is of little concern to the legions of youngsters worldwide who train and compete on official BMX courses.

The sport demands its own specialized skills. Contestants learn to jump off steep wooden ramps and land rear wheel first so they can make a speedy getaway. They also execute difficult turns that require them to brake the rear wheel while they skid around tight corners. Some use variations of the BMX bicycles to perform dazzling acrobatic feats. Much like skateboarders, these young cyclists streak down an incline and then somersault into the air while miraculously clinging to their machines.

A rider on a BMX bike successfully clears the bar during a "bunny hop." Competitors learn how to pick up speed and maneuver their bicycles to get a maximum lift as they go airborne.

thirty-one miles using ceramic disc wheels to gain an aerodynamic advantage. Since then, a number of alternatives to the spoke wheel have invaded the high-end recreational market, such as no-maintenance bladed wheels made from carbon-fiber composites. Mountain biking has also spawned new technology of its own, much of it borrowed from motorcycles, such as hydraulic disc brakes and fork suspension systems. Even road racers have experimented with variations of these suspension forks for more rugged courses, with some success.

But beyond its technical contributions, the competitive sport continues to keep the bicycle in the public eye and has developed significantly over the past twenty-five years. Not only have mountain bike competitions gained popularity, road racing has also enjoyed a remarkable growth and diversification. One annual event, introduced in 1982, is the three-thousand-mile Race Across America. The men's record stands at just over eight days, the women's a shade over nine. Since the late 1970s, triathlon competitions for men and women—involving running, swimming, and cycling—have also given road racing greater exposure and a stronger amateur base. One of the longest running and most prominent events of this kind is the Ironman Triathlon World Championship, held in Kailua-Kona, Hawaii. Every October, about 1,500 cyclists participate in the 112-mile bike race around the island of Oahu. Women's road racing has also made notable progress.

Even track racing continues to attract world-class athletes and an enthusiastic, if widely dispersed, fan base. Dozens of velodromes still operate, mostly in Europe and North America, but also in Australia, New Zealand, and elsewhere. In Japan, a variation of the track sport has thrived for over half a century. Known as Keirin, it has long been a major source of gambling revenue. Specially-trained professional cyclists start out behind a motorized vehicle, working their speed up, lap after lap, to about thirty miles an hour. Then the vehicle leaves the track, and the racers cover the last few laps on their own, amid wild cheers from thousands of spectators. Evidently, even in the twenty-first century the bicycle in all its varieties retains an inherent appeal as a speed machine.

CONCLUSION *Cycling into the Future*

Let it be remembered, too, that America shares with France the distinction of having introduced the bicycle to the world. And with France and England the credit of improving its crude form toward perfection, and of developing and throwing about its uses the social and other attractions which make it a perennial delight.

—Charles E. Pratt's tribute to Pierre Lallement, the original bicycle patentee,

published in the *Wheelman Illustrated,* October 1883

The safety bicycle of the 1890s fulfilled the centuries-old dream of a useful and enjoyable human-powered vehicle. Even after Drais had narrowed the objective to a personal mechanical horse, in 1817, it proved an elusive creature. Nearly half a century passed before the French bicycle provided the foundation for sustained development of the two-wheeler—an intense, international process that culminated in the bicycle as we know it. Yet most histories present the short-lived draisine as the absolute starting point to a clear-cut, if slow, convergence toward the modern bicycle based on steady, incremental improvements. And to prove that the draisine was in fact discreetly developing behind the scenes all those years, these traditional accounts usually rely on alleged stepping-stones like the MacMillan bicycle of about 1840. Meanwhile, they ignore or downplay the work of Willard Sawyer and other known velocipede makers of that period, on the ground that these unfortunates were on the "wrong track."

403

Poster for Cycles Gladiator, circa 1895

In truth, Drais failed to validate the concept of the mechanical horse, let alone establish the two-wheeler. What drove subsequent velocipede experimentation, among the few who persisted, was a stubborn conviction that some sort of vehicle would ultimately make better use of human power for personal transportation than the legs alone, and thus the mechanical horse was worthy of pursuit, whatever the form it would ultimately assume. That the most appealing and practical solution should have but two wheels, after all, was the boneshaker's surprising revelation. Among those responsible for the initial bicycle breakthrough in Paris between 1863 and 1865 were Pierre Lallement, René and Aimé Olivier, Georges de la Bouglise, and the Michaux family.

By demonstrating and establishing the full principle of the bicycle, the boneshaker quickly gave rise to the fleet and refined high wheeler. Incorporating a variety of improvements developed primarily in France, the United States, and England, this towering machine gave great delight to scores of athletic young males of certain means throughout the 1870s and 1880s. But the high mount also reneged on the boneshaker's original promise: a practical vehicle any able-bodied person could master. The low-mount safety bicycle, developed in England and then equipped with pneumatic tires, finally delivered the people's nag. The end result deservedly ranks among the great contributions of the Victorian age.

Naturally, the enormous success of the safety bicycle during the boom confirmed the vision of those who had fervently believed in the future of the primitive pedal-powered two-wheeler. But, in a larger sense, the bicycle of the boom also honored Drais, Johnson, Sawyer, and all those noble mechanics who had struggled over the years to devise a practical human-powered vehicle. For it was their work, their ideas, their conviction, that kept the search for the mechanical horse alive. And to the extent that they all believed in the possibility of improving on the natural human means of walking through the use of some mechanical contrivance, they, too, were vindicated.

Still, despite the impressive state of the bicycle at the onset of the twentieth century, there was much more work to be done. Further advances, including the freewheel, caliper or coaster brakes, and the three-speed hub gear, soon made the bicycle even more practical. At the same time, thanks largely to improvements in manufacturing, the price of a reliable bicycle fell to a level the masses could afford. Further refinements later in the twentieth century included reduced weight, greater comfort, a vast selection of gears, and effortless shifting. Around the world, this mechanical marvel has provided not only broad utilitarian service but also healthy outdoor exercise for people of all ages.

Developing countries in particular rely heavily on the bicycle for everyday transportation. And while many governments are now banking on motorized vehicles as a

An Austrian caricature from the boneshaker era already envisioned a practical role for the bicycle in everyday life, published in *Kikeriki,* 22 April 1869

means to greater prosperity, automobiles are unlikely to become widely affordable for some time to come. The bicycle itself is still a luxury for many residents of the Third World, especially Africans. A number of nonprofit organizations, notably Bikes Not Bombs, have organized successful programs to export discarded bicycles from affluent countries to less developed ones where they are eagerly put into use. Even in China, many more citizens would presumably buy a bicycle if it were more affordable. All told, bicycle use in the Third World could well go up before it goes down.

As a recreational pastime, cycling appears to be firmly established in developed countries and likely to hold its own against other attractive outdoor activities competing for leisure time, such as skateboarding and in-line skating. Cycling could even become more popular with an expanded network of bike-friendly suburban paths and scenic off-road trails. In time, the recreational sport will also likely take hold in developing regions where bicycle use has been largely confined to mundane transportation. Even as some countries lessen their dependency on the bicycle for everyday service, a wealthier population might well adopt the recreational sport for health and pleasure.

But where might the basic bicycle go from here—what changes might we expect in form or function? We have seen that the timely introduction of a compelling new bicycle design, such as the Rover or the mountain bike, can greatly stimulate popular interest, expand the cycling population, and even open new cycling opportunities. Conceivably, a further enhanced, or radically revamped, bicycle could reignite the popular imagination and unleash yet another wave of enthusiasm and development. But where might such opportunities lie?

The utilitarian realm would appear to offer the greatest chances for growth in the near future. In many highly developed countries, especially the United States, the bicycle is woefully underused. Nearly a third of the gasoline pumped at American service stations goes for trips of three miles or less, more often than not to transport a single passenger. Clearly, despite its limitations in inclement weather, the bicycle could accomplish many of these routine errands and save a vast amount of fossil fuel. A number of bike activists in recent years have called attention to the cycling cause on ecological grounds. But whether more people can be pried away from the steering wheel is unclear. Drivers will cite safety concerns as a prime reason not to cycle. Indeed, many social scientists doubt that there will be any mass migration to the bicycle unless cycling facilities improve greatly and the price of gasoline rises substantially.

Whether or not the bicycle ultimately assumes an even larger presence around the world probably hinges more on such extraneous factors as median income, the price of gasoline, and the creation of cycling paths rather than on any fundamental change to the bicycle itself. After all, the conventional design is already remarkably affordable and serviceable, offering great economy and swift door-to-door transportation as well as satisfying recreation. Nevertheless, it is worth considering whether further technical refinement or development could make the bicycle even more compelling for daily service or outdoor exercise. There are essentially four factors involved: cost, convenience, comfort, and performance.

One of the oldest ideas for making the bicycle as cheap as possible is to slash labor costs by using a material conducive to serial production in molds. This was apparently René Olivier's objective in the mid-1860s when he selected malleable cast iron over forged iron for the first production bicycles. Interest in this approach abated with the introduction of the steel high wheeler, a relatively simple design. But the general diffusion of the more complicated safety frame has revived the incentive to find an alternative material that lends itself to production in molds. Ideally, from the utilitarian point of view, it would also be lightweight and offer greater resistance to corrosion produced by exposure to the elements.

One notable attempt to revolutionize frame construction was the futuristic Bowden Spacelander, made of fiberglass. It was designed by the British engineer Benjamin Bowden in 1956 and produced in limited quantities a few years later. During the boom of the early 1970s, a company called the Original Plastic Bike offered a seventeen-pound ten-speed with frame and components made of Lexan. The idea was to provide the performance of a fancy Italian racer at a fraction of the cost. A few years later, Swedish engineers who had been working on a Volvo minicar developed the Itera bicycle, made of corrosion-resistant injection-molded plastic. The process virtually eliminated labor—a complete wheel could be made in under a minute. In 1982, the company presented two models, a standard bicycle weighing about thirty-two pounds and a trimmed-down sports model. Both were billed as maintenance-free and even featured a built-in lock.

Unfortunately, the plastic bicycles flopped, as critics judged them overly flexible. The possibility nonetheless remains that a high-tech, weather-resistant material produced in labor-saving molds will eventually replace conventional steel in the standard bicycle. One promising possibility is the monocoque frame of carbon fiber, of the sort developed by the British engineer Mike Burrows for Lotus engineering and ridden by Chris Boardman in the 1992 Olympics. This material has already been successfully used on racing bicycles and high-end recreational models, but it does not as yet offer any economic advantages. Nevertheless, with advances in material processing, monocoque frames could one day yield affordable, lightweight, and weather-resistant bicycles.

But even the conventional frame composed of tubes conceivably invites the use of a high-tech material that might better withstand the elements or rider abuse. Aluminum, titanium, and lugged carbon-fiber frames, which have already earned a strong following among recreational cyclists, do in fact offer lightweight, noncorrodible materials. But steel frames are quite resilient in their own right and still significantly cheaper. More-

A fiberglass-frame Bowden Spacelander from 1960 manufactured by Bomard Industries of Kansas City, Missouri

over, it does not appear likely that the use of a high-tech frame material alone would substantially increase the practicality or appeal of the low-end bicycle. After all, a new material would not eliminate a chief objection to greater bicycle use: namely, the rider's own exposure to the elements.

A recurring idea to negate the effects of nasty weather is to enclose the cyclist inside a lightweight shell. This addition also allows for improved aerodynamics and hence faster speeds with less effort. As early as 1914, the French cyclist Marcel Berthet easily beat various indoor records from one to five kilometers using a fish-shaped windshield inspired by recent advances in aviation. Berthet continued his experiments in the 1930s, devising a hood that included a side door for climbing in and out of the vehicle. In the first Human Powered Vehicle race in 1974, the winning bicycle was also a conventional racer with a faired enclosure, and it surpassed forty miles an hour. But shells on standard bicycles have proved impractical because they make the craft dangerously top-heavy.

One design that does conceivably allow for a shell, on account of its lower center of gravity, is the recumbent bicycle, ridden in a reclining position. A number of engineering students have proposed recumbent models that call for lightweight plastic shells, or some other external structure, to provide at least partial protection from the elements. But it is not clear if an enclosed recumbent could ever displace the standard utilitarian bicycle. The conventional design, with a much shorter wheelbase, offers easier maneuverability in traffic. And, in truth, it can be operated even in highly unfavorable weather. If conditions are truly intolerable, the commuter might do best to drive or take public transportation.

Still, with or without a shell, the recumbent offers distinct advantages. For one thing, it is significantly faster than a conventional bicycle, with drag reduced by as much as 50 percent. Since the 1970s, the International Human Powered Vehicle Association has brought renewed attention to recumbents by organizing no-holds-barred design competitions and races to showcase the superior speed of the low-slung bicycle. From the start, recumbent racers were already flirting with the fifty-mile-per-hour mark. In 2002, at the annual international races in Battle Mountain, Nevada, Sam Whittingham reached an incredible eighty miles an hour riding the state-of-the-art Varna Diablo, which features advanced materials and a fiberglass shell.

Even proponents, however, admit that the most advanced racing recumbents, which place the cyclist's back just inches off the ground, are not practical for everyday use. The rider's peripheral vision is greatly limited, and motorists can easily overlook such a low-profile vehicle. Still, advocates maintain that this technology can be applied to create faster and more comfortable bicycles for recreation and for everyday use. One

The Varna Diablo competing in the 2003 World Human Powered Speed Challenge in Battle Mountain, Nevada, where pilot Sam Whittingham eclipsed eighty miles an hour with the same vehicle the previous year

intriguing design that mitigates the chief objections to the racing model is the "semi-reclined" recumbent, in which the cyclist sits up straight but fully extends the legs. This arrangement still offers significant aerodynamic advantages, and hence greater speed, as well as greater comfort, without severely compromising the rider's vision or visibility.

Nevertheless, it appears unlikely that recumbents of any style will win road supremacy, at least in the near future. Besides being more expensive, the stretched-out models require more storage space than conventional bicycles, a significant drawback for cramped urbanites. Recumbents are also more difficult to maneuver in traffic, and their superior speed on the open road does not offer a great advantage for short hauls in the city. But even if recumbents do not replace the conventional bicycle as a utilitarian vehicle, they could conceivably gain a much larger share of the recreational market. After all, their superior speed allows the tourist to cover more ground with less effort.

To be sure, some maintain that recumbents lose much of their advantage when riding over hilly terrain, for climbs can be more challenging. But there's no denying that the addition of a backrest is a compelling plus for recreational cyclists who want to tour long distances in comfort. In the early 1980s, in fact, when the first recumbents reached the market, some makers confidently predicted that they would capture up to half the adult cycling population within a decade. Obviously, that has not happened. Conceivably, the mountain-bike vogue in the interim staved off a massive defection to the recumbent. Or perhaps a mass conversion of this sort demands more time. In any case, in the years to come, more recreational riders might well gravitate toward the low-slung vehicle for greater comfort, if not speed.

Another design with revolutionary possibilities is the electric bicycle, or "ebike," which is already gaining prominence in Asia and Europe. While most retain the conventional bicycle form, ebikes radically alter the cycling experience by enabling speeds up to thirty miles an hour with much less physical effort. They also offer great convenience, because they are recharged in a matter of hours using standard electrical outlets at little cost. Priced at about a thousand dollars, the ebike compares favorably to other compact high-tech urban vehicles, such as the Segway scooter. But it appears far too expensive to threaten the clunker, though of course the price could come down considerably over time if the idea catches on.

But will electric bicycles prove a boon or a bane to traditional cycling? On one hand, electric bicycles could encourage more people to leave their cars behind and head out on the road with a two-wheeler, buoyed by the assurance that they can use the auxiliary means of power whenever their will to pedal wanes. Moreover, ebikes retain the bicycle's ecological cachet as compact, quiet, unobtrusive vehicles. On the other hand, the presence of an onboard electric motor arguably undermines the spirit of cycling and detracts from the bicycle's charm and simplicity. Purists are more apt to see the ebike as

A semi-reclining recumbent with front fairing for streamlining. Proponents predict this style will become more popular with tourists looking to travel long distances in comfort.

an aberration of the bicycle rather than a respectable adaptation—one that threatens to curtail cycling rather than promote it.

The cycle industry itself has long frowned on the addition of a motor to the bicycle. One reporter, after visiting Pope's Hartford plant in 1896, found "many advocates of the power bicycle" who anticipated that the article would come into demand. Yet he also found that industry leaders did "not believe that the great army of bicycle riders throughout the country will take kindly to the idea of sitting idly in the saddle, and merely balancing the machine while the motor does the work." In their view, "the chief element in the popularity of bicycling is the enjoyment the rider gets from the wholesome exercise of his muscles. If a person were too indolent or feeble to pedal himself along, he would probably discard the bicycle altogether in favor of a motor vehicle on three or four wheels, where he would be relieved even from the exertion of balancing.

Ebikes, however, are not entirely at odds with the spirit of cycling, since they are in fact functional bicycles despite the added weight of the motor. One popular variety, the so-called pedelec, even rewards the cyclist by providing a greater boost the harder he or she pedals. The other variety, the "twist and go," is admittedly less conducive to pedaling, since it allows the idle rider to accelerate simply by turning a throttle, as if driving

The TidalForce M-750 by WaveCrest Laboratories, designed for military use, is a high-performance, all-terrain, folding bicycle with an electric motor in the rear hub. A more economical recreational version weighs sixty-four pounds and reaches a top speed of twenty miles an hour with a range of twenty miles.

a motorcycle. Nevertheless, both varieties provide an economic incentive to pedal, since human power can extend the range of the vehicle up to forty miles. Ebikes would seem particularly attractive to the commuter who faces steep hills or is looking for only an occasional workout. Their recreational value, however, is probably more limited, because ebikes provide less pedaling enjoyment and less incentive to exercise.

Perhaps the most promising cycling innovations, at least in the short run, are not revolutionary makeovers but rather incremental improvements that enhance the appeal or functionality of conventional cycles. After all, the resurgence of recreational cycling over the past few decades is no doubt due in large part to the prevalence of better-quality equipment at cheaper prices, on a wider assortment of models. If the trend toward greater value for the cycling dollar continues, more cyclists will likely enjoy a zippier ride thanks to high-tech materials like titanium and carbon fiber applied to the frame, wheel rims, and other parts. Utilitarian cyclists could also benefit from lighter, stronger, or more weather-resistant materials, or even handy accessories. The new generation of hub gears offering seven or more speeds, for example, might gain popularity with those who want high performance but a minimum of maintenance. More effective antitheft devices might ease security concerns and even induce people to invest more freely in their bicycles and to ride them more. One promising initiative is a GPS tracking device recently installed on a fleet of clunkers by the city of Amsterdam to counter a rash of thefts.

However the bicycle may yet evolve in form or function, it will no doubt endure as a popular, well-loved vehicle for people of all ages and backgrounds. These thoughts expressed by the editor of *Brooklyn Life* in 1895 ring as true today as they did during the great boom. "Many call the interest taken in bicycling a fad. But they are wrong. A fad has no substance; it is ephemeral and has no real foundation. On the other hand, bicycling is very real . . . it has brought a degree of perfection never before reached in vehicular construction. It is hard to imagine wherein the safety of to-day can be improved. A ride in its saddle is the perfection of motion and the acme of gentle exercise. Once there, a man or woman wants to be there most of their time. The desire grows. And this is the reason why bicycling is not a fad, but something that is going to last so long as men and women have legs."

"Queen of the Wheel," copyrighted in 1897 by the Rose Studio of Princeton, New Jersey

Notes

Introduction

p. 3 "The proudest triumph": *Monthly Magazine,* 1 November 1819.

p. 3 "Never before in the history": *New York Times,* 10 January 1869.

p. 3 "impossible to calculate": *Cosmopolitan,* August 1895.

p. 3 "she needs a man's opportunities": *Ladies' World,* June 1898.

p. 3 "demands a radical change in costume": *Cosmopolitan,* August 1895.

p. 5 bicycle repair shops evolved: *Social Forces,* vol. 30, no. 3, 1952.

p. 5 bicycles produced by motorcycle makers: *Bicycle News,* February 1917.

p. 8 soldiers returning from Britain: *Time,* 5 July 1954.

p. 10 producing some forty million bicycles: *Business Week,* 10 October 1977.

p. 11 John Howard's mark: John Howard with Peter Nye, *Pushing the Limits* (Waco, Texas: WRS Publishing, 1993), p. 225.

CHAPTER ONE *The Elusive Mechanical Horse*

p. 15 problems Ozanam identified: J. Ozanam, *Récréations Mathématiques et Physiques* (Paris: Jean Jombert, 1696), p. 291. All translations, unless otherwise indicated, are by the author.

p. 16 Ovenden's carriage: *Universal Magazine* (London), vol. 55, December 1774.

pp. 16–17 Blanchard's carriage and exhibitions: *Journal de Paris,* 27 July and 17 August 1779.

pp. 17–18 Bolton's patent: *Velocipede* (Washington: United States Patent Office, 29 September 1804).

p. 19 "A machine of this kind will afford a salutary recreation": W. Hooper, *Rational Recreations* (London: B. Law & Son, 1794), p. 197.

p. 19 Drais's four-wheeled vehicle: *Badisches Magazin,* 22 December 1813.

p. 19 accolades of the Russian tsar: Ibid.

p. 19 patent applications rejected: The state of Baden rejected Drais's petition on 24 February 1814; Austria declined on 4 September 1816.

p. 19 Tulla's evaluation of Drais's four-wheeled vehicle: Dated 17 December 1813. Held by the Badisches Generallandesarchiv, Karlsruhe, Germany.

p. 19 to the embarrassment of his colleagues: In a letter dated 17 September 1814, Baden officials warned Drais that he would "greatly risk compromising the honor of the delegation" if he demonstrated his carriage in Vienna. Held by the Badisches Generallandesarchiv.

p. 19 Vienna exhibition: Drais reportedly exhibited his carriage in the Burgplatz. Hans-Erhard Lessing, *Automobilität: Karl Drais und die unglaublichen Anfänge* (Leipzig: Maxime, 2003), pp. 126-29.

p. 21 Drais shifted to other scientific endeavors: Ibid., pp. 132–37.

p. 22 "pushes the wheels along": *Village Record* (Westchester, Pennsylvania), 19 May 1819.

p. 22 extra ground with every "step": *Gentleman's Magazine,* June 1819.

p. 22 "facilitator" and "accelerator": Karl von Drais, *Le Vélocipède du Baron Charles de Drais* (Paris, ca. 1818; French translation of original German prospectus).

p. 22 when running atop a velocipede: *Union, United States Gazette, and True American* (Philadelphia), 18 May 1819.

p. 24 letter to royal patron: Letter from Drais to Princess Stephanie, the grand-duchess of Baden, dated 21 August 1817. Held by the Badisches Generallandesarchiv.

p. 24 "strange invention": *Baltimore Morning Chronicle*, 20 May 1819.

p. 24 "Nothing of the Day": *Alloa Journal* (Scotland), 26 June 1869.

p. 24 "every species of transatlantic nonsense": *Berks and Schuylkill Journal* (Reading, Pennsylvania), 22 May 1819.

p. 24 "towing the boat": *Northern Whig* (Hudson, New York), 1 June 1819.

pp. 24–25 one skeptic in Philadelphia: *Union, United States Gazette, and True American*, 18 May 1819.

p. 25 "Velocity is the fashionable mania": *Evening Star* (London), 1 May 1819.

pp. 25–26 "We teach the dumb to speak": *Easton Gazette* (Easton, Maryland), 24 May 1819.

p. 26 "calculated for much amusement": *Western Spy* (Cincinnati), 14 August 1819.

p. 26 "There are multitudes who go to the grave": *Cincinnati Inquisitor Advertiser*, 10 August 1819.

p. 26 editor in Westchester: *Village Record* (Westchester, Pennsylvania), 19 May 1819.

p. 26 Drais's demonstrations in Germany: *Badwochenblatt zum Nutzen und Vergnügen der Badegäste in der Stadt Baden*, 12 June and 28 July 1817.

p. 26 draisine knockoffs in Germany: One imitation from Dresden is described in *Miscellen zur Belehrung und Unterhaltung*, 28 November 1817.

pp. 26–27 Drais setting liberal patent terms: Drais, *Le Vélocipède du Baron Charles de Drais*.

p. 27 Drais's Baden patent: Awarded 12 January 1818.

p. 27 Tulla's assessment of the running machine: Dated 30 December 1817. Held by the Badisches Generallandesarchiv.

p. 27 Drais secured a French patent: Dated 17 February 1818.

pp. 27–28 Drais's prestige grew: For example, the Society for the Encouragement of Useful Arts in Frankfurt issued Drais a diploma on 1 September 1817. Held by the Badisches Generallandesarchiv.

p. 28 sorry performance in the Luxembourg Gardens: *Journal de Paris*, 6 April 1818.

p. 28 "Drais deserves the gratitude of cobblers": *Journal Général de France* (Paris), 6 April 1818.

p. 28 Lagrange in Dijon: *Journal de la Côte d'Or* (Dijon), 25 August 1818; *Journal d'Annonces* (Beaune), 27 August 1818.

p. 29 Mannheim to Frankfurt and back: *Frankfurter Ober-Postamts-Zeitung*, 12 April and 23 April 1818.

p. 29 Drais in Nancy: *Journal de la Meurthe* (Nancy), 6 October 1818.

p. 29 Drais in Paris: *Moniteur Universel* (Paris), 21 October 1818.

pp. 29–30 "providing healthy exercise": *Journal de Paris*, 21 October 1818.

p. 30 Monceaux Park rentals: Garcin's rental service was regularly advertised in the *Journal de Paris* from 11 July to 8 August, 1818.

p. 30 Burg in Vienna: *Briefe aus neu angekommenen Eipeldauers* (Vienna), vol. 7, 1818.

BOXED INSET   *Why Not a "Bicycle"?*

p. 23 "words made for French and English": Testimony of Charles Pratt given 12 December 1884 in *Pope Manufacturing Company v. T. G. Jeffery*, Northern District of Illinois. Held by the National Archives, Great Lakes Region, Chicago.

p. 23 "*Velocipede* (velox pedis, swift of foot)": *Portobello Advertiser* (Scotland), 18 June 1869.

CHAPTER TWO *The Draisine Abroad*

p. 31 Johnson announced he would market: *Courier* (London), 11 December 1818.

pp. 31–33 Johnson's hobbyhorse design: Johnson outlined his design philosophy in his patent specification, dated 22 December 1818 (no. 4321). A detailed technical discussion of the Johnson machine appears in Roger Street, *The Pedestrian Hobby-Horse at the Dawn of Cycling* (London: Artesius, 1998), chapter 3, "Denis Johnson and His Pedestrian Curricle."

pp. 33–34 Johnson's riding school: *Literary Gazette and Journal of the Belles Lettres, Arts, Sciences, &c*, 27 February 1819.

p. 34 "fear of ill success": *New Times* (London), 8 April 1819.

p. 34 "velocipeder" surrounded by a hostile mob: *Evening Star* (London), 25 March 1819.

p. 34 Hyde Park riders: *Birmingham Commercial Herald*, 3 April 1819.

pp. 34–35 numerous exhibitions announced across England: Two other localities where races were falsely announced in local newspapers were Blandford (*Salisbury and Winchester Journal*, 5 April 1819) and Worthing (*Sussex Weekly Advertiser*, 5 April 1819).

p. 35 Canterbury race: *Kentish Gazette* (Canterbury), 6 April 1819.

p. 35 "charger" in Liverpool endured censures: *Kaleidoscope* (Liverpool), 5 April 1819.

p. 35 apprehended on Leather Lane: *London Packet*, 15 May 1819.

p. 35 "the general topic of conversation": *Norwich Mercury*, 20 February 1819.

p. 35 "forty and fifty miles distant": *Salisbury and Winchester Journal*, 31 May 1819.

p. 35 "now exhibiting in the Cloth-Hall": *Leeds Mercury*, 8 May 1819.

p. 35 Johnson at the Stork Hotel: *Aris's Birmingham Gazette*, 10 May 1819.

p. 35 "we had no conception": *Liverpool Mercury*, 28 May 1819.

p. 35 Johnson's production soon reached: Although the exact figures are unknown, Johnson appears to have numbered each machine sequentially, giving a rough idea of production.

p. 36 "spurious imitations": *Liverpool Mercury*, 21 May 1819.

p. 36 between Brighton and London: *Berrow's Worcester Journal*, 17 June 1819.

p. 36 "sensible and modest enough": *Yorkshire Gazette*, 15 May 1819.

p. 36 "We have again to remark": *Hull Advertiser*, 2 June and 9 June 1819.

p. 36 dandy charger against opponent on jackass: *Yorkshire Gazette*, 12 June 1819.

p. 36 "disgrace and odium of Dandyism": *Sussex Weekly Journal* (Lewes), 31 May 1819.

p. 37 "So great was the eagerness": *Ipswich Journal*, 10 July 1819.

p. 37 event set for York: *Yorkshire Gazette*, 26 May 1819.

p. 37 "better worthy a dandy striving": *Lincoln, Rutland, and Stamford Mercury*, 18 June 1819.

pp. 37–38 Johnson's velocipede for ladies: *Liverpool Mercury*, 11 June 1819.

p. 38 London College of Surgeons: *Sussex Weekly Advertiser*, 16 August 1819.

p. 39 *Savannah* left New York: *Eastern Argus* (Portland, Maine), 6 April 1819.

p. 39 New York to Philadelphia: *Columbian* (New York), 25 May 1819.

p. 39 Benjamin Dearborn of Boston: *American Watchman* (Wilmington, Delaware), 14 April 1819.

p. 39 Stewart displayed his Tracena: *Baltimore American*, 10 February 1819.

p. 39 "The constructor feels very confident": *Federal Gazette and Baltimore Daily Advertiser*, 6 February 1819.

p. 39 "the gaze of the crowd": *Boston Intelligencer*, 24 April 1819.

p. 39 Salisbury invited the public: *New England Palladium* (Boston), 21 May 1819.

p. 39 "Boston folks are always fond": *Franklin Gazette* (Philadelphia), 7 May 1819.

p. 40   "indifferent blacksmith": Letter from Charles Willson Peale to his son Rembrandt dated 22 May 1819. All Peale letters cited are held by the American Philosophical Society in Philadelphia.

p. 40   "a few pounds additional": Ibid.

p. 40   "heavier than it might have been": Letter from Charles Willson Peale to his son Titian dated 20 July 1819.

p. 40   "very little of the original machine": Letters from Charles Willson Peale to his son Rembrandt dated 31 July 1819 and 26 September 1819.

p. 40   "a very considerable profit": Letter from Charles Willson Peale to his son Rembrandt dated 22 May 1819.

p. 40   Chambers hired out velocipedes: *Poole's American Daily Advertiser* (Philadelphia), 14 May 1819.

p. 40   handiwork of J. Stewart: Letter from Charles Willson Peale to his son Rembrandt dated 22 May 1819.

p. 40   Franklin's machine made of wood: Letter from Charles Willson Peale to his son Titian dated 20 July 1819.

p. 40   both Peale machines in action: *Union, United States Gazette, and True American* (Philadelphia), 18 May 1819.

pp. 40–42   Franklin tore around the square: Letter from Charles Willson Peale to Charles P. Polk dated 16 May 1819.

p. 42   "It seems to differ entirely": *Union, United States Gazette, and True American,* 18 May 1819.

p. 42   elder Peale noted that Franklin: Letter from Peale to his son Titian dated 20 July 1819.

p. 42   one rider fined three dollars: *National Messenger* (Georgetown), 5 June 1819.

p. 42   "salubrious air" of his garden: Rubens Peale, "Memorandum and Events of His Life" (undated manuscript held by the American Philosophical Society).

p. 42   Peale also encouraged his family: Letter from Charles Willson Peale to his son Rembrandt dated 31 July 1819.

p. 42   "swiftness that dazzles the sight": Ibid.

p. 42   "down hill like the very devil": Letter from Charles L. Peale to his brother Titian dated 10 May 1819.

p. 42   "was exhibited yesterday" in New York: *Mercantile Adviser* (New York), 23 May 1819. Some have suggested that the Englishman was Denis Johnson himself, but that does not appear possible given reports that he was exhibiting in Liverpool at about this time.

p. 43   "without charging the moderate price": *Columbian* (New York), 15 June 1819.

p. 43   "This whimsical new hobby": *Columbian* (New York), 1 June 1819.

p. 43   Mr. Parker on stage: *Star in the West* (New York), 5 June 1819.

p. 43   rink near Bowling Green: Advertisement in the *New York Evening Post,* 18 June 1819.

p. 43   banned the vehicle from public ways: *Genius of Liberty* (Leesburg, Virginia), 7 September 1819.

p. 43   Davis and Rogers reportedly built: Recounted in the *Troy Daily Times,* 9 January 1869.

p. 43   coachmaker Westervelt and clown demonstration: *Western Spy* (Cincinnati), 14 August 1819.

p. 43   exhibited in Georgetown and Norwalk: *Georgetown Gazette,* 1 June 1819; *Norwalk Gazette,* 30 June 1819.

p. 44   "met with so little encouragement": *Northern Whig* (Hudson, New York), 1 June 1819.

p. 44   "A Velocipede made an appearance": *Columbian Museum* (Savannah), 22 June 1819.

p. 44–45   spirited trial in New Haven: *Connecticut Herald* (New Haven), 19 July 1819.

p. 45   velocipedes "possess some advantages": Ibid.

p. 45 "to put common law into practice": *Columbian Register* (New Haven), 10 July 1819.

p. 45 "lingered in and out of occasional use": Charles Pratt, "Pierre Lallement and His Bicycle," *Wheelman Illustrated,* October 1883.

p. 45 "greatly underrated": *Kaleidoscope* (Liverpool), 20 January 1829.

pp. 45–46 "obsolete triffle": *Mechanics' Magazine,* 28 November 1829.

p. 46 Davies implored inventors: Thomas Davies, "On the Velocipede," lecture given at Trinity College, Dublin, in May 1837, reprinted in *Boneshaker,* Autumn 1985.

p. 46 ingenious proposal from Gompertz: *Polytechnisches Journal* (Augsburg), June 1821.

pp. 46–47 velocipede with an improved seat spring, "had as fair a trial": *Mechanics' Magazine,* 21 April and 29 September 1832.

p. 47 "mechanism so simple": *New York Clipper,* 26 September 1868.

pp. 47–48 Drais denounced treadle-driven three-wheelers: *Journal für Literatur, Kunst, Luxus und Mode* (Weimar, Austria), June 1820.

p. 49 "The works of the caricaturists": *Cincinnati Inquisitor Advertiser,* 24 August 1819.

p. 49 "yield to the advantages" of velocipedes: *Repertory of Arts, Manufactures, and Agriculture* (London), vol. 39, 1821.

pp. 49–50 Lord Mortimer: *Albany Argus,* 18 February 1869.

p. 50 creation of special velocipede lanes: *Repertory of Arts, Manufactures, and Agriculture* (London), vol. 39, 1821.

p. 52 "You have given sketches": *Mechanics' Magazine,* 2 December 1843.

CHAPTER THREE   *Wheels and Woes*

p. 53   French-built tricycle: *Kentish Chronicle* (Canterbury), 4 May 1819.

pp. 53–54   tricycle in New York's Battery Park: *Cincinnati Inquisitor Advertiser,* 10 August 1819.

p. 54   treadle-driven four-wheeler in Dumfries: *Dumfries Weekly Journal,* 7 September 1819.

p. 54 Velocimano tricycle by Brianza: *Gazzetta di Milano* (Milan), 25 January 1819.

p. 54 "Wheel carriages, to be impelled": *Kaleidoscope* (Liverpool), 8 June 1819.

p. 54 three tricycles by J. Birch: *Monthly Magazine,* 1 November 1819.

p. 55 "Impossible for an individual to travel": *Mechanics' Magazine,* 21 April 1832.

pp. 55–56 "Not only is it not new": *Antologia* (Florence), vol. 22, May 1826.

p. 56 "or has nature placed a limit": *Mechanics' Magazine,* 26 August 1837.

p. 56 "We occasionally meet with": *Mechanics' Magazine,* 18 May 1839.

p. 56 "sundry schemes for accelerating": *Mechanics' Magazine,* 6 February 1841.

p. 57 American velocipede trade for children: Edwin T. Feedley, *Philadelphia and Its Manufactures: A Hand-book of the Great Manufactories and Representative Mercantile Houses of Philadelphia in 1867* (Philadelphia: E. Young, 1867), p. 529.

p. 58 invention of the late Edmund Cartwright: *Philosophical Magazine,* vol. 53, 1819, p. 425.

p. 58 "astonished the natives of London": *Mechanics' Weekly Journal,* 20 December 1823.

p. 59–60 "A more beautiful piece of workmanship": *Field,* 27 July 1861.

p. 60–61 Sawyer's exhibition and rentals: W. Sawyer, Catalog, ca. 1858. Held by the London Science Museum.

p. 61 Sawyer threatened to leave town: *Dover Telegraph,* 9 August 1856.

p. 62 prince of Wales stopped by: *Illustrated London News,* 17 April 1858.

p. 62 Skeffington claimed to have toured: W. Sawyer, Catalog, ca. 1858.

p. 62   a rider could travel up to 60 miles: W. Sawyer, Catalog, ca. 1863. Held by the British Library, London.

p. 62   human-powered "miniature carriages": *Builder*, 5 April 1856.

p. 63   velocipedes by H. Cadot: Several models were detailed in Cadot's catalog, *H. Cadot, Notice sur les Voitures Mécaniques Suspendues* (Lyon: Lépagnez, ca. 1864). Held by the Municipal Archives of Lyon.

p. 63   "required an engineer": *Brooklyn Daily Eagle*, 25 March 1869.

p. 63   "attained to the rank of a machine": *Great Western Magazine* (Bristol), June 1863.

p. 64   "the rattling and shaking": *English Mechanic*, 26 February 1869.

pp. 64–65   "In these days of invention": *Mechanics' Magazine*, 14 December 1860.

p. 65   formation of a velocipede club: *English Mechanic*, 13 July 1866.

p. 66   Dalzell's son submitted documentation: *Scottish Cyclist*, 20 February 1889.

p. 67   report of a velocipede accident in 1842: *Glasgow Herald*, 11 June 1842.

p. 67   McCall had seen MacMillan: *Bicycling News*, 6 February 1892.

pp. 67–68   "Having made velocipedes thirteen years ago": *Kilmarnock Standard*, 10 April 1869.

pp. 68–69   articles on McCall's design: *English Mechanic*, 14 May and 11 June 1869.

p. 69   "the colporteur that travels": *Hamilton Advertiser*, 29 May 1869.

p. 69   "A merchant in this town": *Hamilton Advertiser*, 10 July 1869.

p. 69   "No little amusement": *Dumfries and Galloway Saturday Standard*, 22 May 1869.

p. 70   early Michaux company correspondence: Michaux letters no. 11, dated 23 January 1868, and no. 40, dated 31 January 1868. All Michaux letters cited are held by the Olivier family.

p. 70   built by a millwright in Strathaven: *English Mechanic*, 6 January and 13 January 1871.

BOXED INSET   *The Draisine's Lingering Influence*

p. 60   Gooch's "Aeripedis": *Magazine of Science*, 16 July 1842.

p. 60   "considerable voyages were performed": *Great Western Magazine*, June 1863.

BOXED INSET   *Mechanical Minds*

p. 64   Gompertz presented two velocipedes: *Scientific American*, 12 August 1848, and *Mechanics' Magazine*, 5 April 1861.

p. 64   advantages of Drais's carriage: *Mechanic's Register*, 11 August 1837.

pp. 64–65   Drais's railroad velocipede: *Mannheimer Morganblatt*, 8 March 1843.

p. 65   "the general speed of the railways": *Great Western Magazine*, June 1863.

CHAPTER FOUR   *The Bicycle Breakthrough*

p. 75   "completely changes the character": *Scientific American*, 30 January 1869.

pp. 75–76   lack of French enthusiasm: *Moniteur Universel du Soir*, 21 April 1867.

p. 76   first Michaux advertisement: *Moniteur Universel du Soir*, 18 May 1867.

pp. 76–78   "It's just Paris at play": *Illustration, Journal Universel*, 12 June 1869.

p. 78   "young men of leisure": *New York Times*, 22 August 1867.

p. 78   in the Bois de Boulogne: *American Artisan*, 11 September 1867.

p. 78   "On your velocipede!": *Le Sport*, 28 July 1867.

p. 78   "A Revolution in Locomotion": *New York Times*, 22 August 1867.

p. 78   Universal Exhibition: Georges de la Bouglise applied to exhibit a "two wheeled velocipede" on 6 October 1865 but was refused. Letter in the National Archives of France, Paris.

p. 78 firms in Lyon and near Grenoble: Cadot (Lyon) and Favre (Voiron).

p. 78 "every one is talking velocipedes": *Vie Parisienne*, 21 September 1867.

p. 78 Paris en masse to Versailles: *Petit Journal* (Paris), 10 December 1867.

p. 81 "Many persons around here": Michaux letter no. 7, dated 22 January 1868.

p. 81 "Make it low": Michaux letters no. 80, dated 18 February 1868, and no. 109, dated 3 March 1868.

p. 81 A customer in Bilbao: Michaux letter no. 53, dated 3 February 1868.

p. 81 "I find your price": Michaux letter no. 257, dated 15 April 1868.

p. 81 "Would you agree": Michaux letter no. 1, dated 2 January 1868.

p. 81 "perfectly and without danger": Michaux letter no. 407, dated 28 April 1868.

p. 81 "Can you tell me": Michaux letter no. 420, dated 2 May 1868.

p. 81 free lessons to purchasers: *Gazette des Etrangers* (Paris), 28 February 1868.

p. 81 women ready to pedal: *Paris-Caprice*, 25 April 1868.

p. 81 not a special gift: *Cincinnati Daily Gazette*, 26 January 1869.

p. 83 only to lambaste Michaux: Michaux letter no. 73, dated 17 February 1868.

p. 83 "As to the colors": Michaux letter no. 45, dated 3 February 1868.

p. 83 "I don't care about the color": Michaux letter no. 230, dated 9 April 1868.

p. 83 "amusement of golden youth": *Vie Parisienne*, 28 January 1868.

p. 83 Michaux workforce swelled: *Evénement Illustré* (Paris), 1 June 1868.

p. 84 Easter parade on Longchamps: *Charivari*, 12 April 1868.

p. 84 velocipedists apprehended a thief: *Gazette des Etrangers*, 10 August 1868.

p. 84 "man, woman and child can play": *Paris-Caprice*, 25 April 1868.

p. 84 Nice to Clermont-Ferrand: *Moniteur du Puy-de-Dôme* (Clermont-Ferrand), 24 May 1868.

p. 84 Michaux's patent claim: Allusion to a patent appears, for example, in *Le Sport*, 4 August 1867.

p. 84 Michaux sons' experience: *Le Sport*, 28 July 1867.

p. 85 no sales before 1867: An Irishman named J. Townsend-Trench recounted in the *Irish Cyclist* of 25 September 1895 that he came across a bicycle while visiting Paris in July 1864. Following it to a blacksmith shop, presumably Michaux's, Towsend-Trench was told by the proprietor that he had "just invented" the machine, and had made six to date, one of which Townsend-Trench said he bought. This account seems plausible, and the Irishman produced a letter with a drawing of a serpentine bicycle, apparently sent to his sister shortly after the incident. Still, this case most likely represents the exceptional sale of a prototype and not the start of systematic commercial sales, which began only in 1867.

p. 85 Michaux starts velocipede production in 1867: The 1862 Land Register in the Archives of Paris first records velocipede production at 29 Avenue Montaigne in 1867.

p. 85 continued his regular business: Michaux billed himself as a locksmith in the 1868 and 1869 city directories.

p. 85 Michaux's 1855 patent: French patent 23576, dated 19 May 1855.

p. 85 Ernest Michaux patents for a miniature steam engine: French patent 61858, dated 11 February 1864; Belgian patent 17536, dated 15 March 1865; British patent 1771, dated 5 July 1865.

p. 85 "the individual who first rode": *New Orleans Tribune*, 19 March 1869.

p. 86 Michaux company charter: Registered on 7 May 1868. Held by the Archives of Paris.

p. 86 Lallement patent of 1866: U.S. patent 59915, dated 20 November 1866.

p. 86–87 Lallement conceived the bicycle in 1862: Lallement testimony in *Pope Manufacturing Company v. McKee & Harrington*, Southern District of New York, 1882.

p. 87 Lallement built and learned to ride: *Wheelman Illustrated*, October 1883.

p. 89 original inventor was an unidentified workman: Testimony from *Oliviers v. Michaux*, Tribunal de Commerce de la Seine, 1869. Held by the Olivier family.

p. 89 "a few who took note": Recounted in "Pierre Lallement and His Bicycle," *Wheelman Illustrated,* October 1883.

p. 89–90 René a fanatic of the bicycle: Testimony from *Oliviers v. Michaux.*

p. 90 debate on malleable cast iron: One discussion on the merits of malleable cast iron in this period can be found in A. Brüll, "Etude sur la Fonte Malléable," *Mémoires et Compte Rendu des Travaux de la Société des Ingenieurs Civils* (Paris), no. 24, October–December 1863.

p. 90 René Olivier met Michaux: Testimony from *Oliviers v. Michaux,* Tribunal de la Seine, 1869.

p. 90 initial experimental batch: Although René Olivier was vague about his initial dealings with Michaux in his court testimony, the Townsend-Trench evidence suggests that Olivier ordered his first six bicycles in the summer of 1864.

p. 90 velocipede sent to Aimé: The entry for 22 October 1864 in the diary of Jules Olivier confirms that his son Aimé was then in Lyon and in possession of a velocipede, presumably the Michaux-built bicycle René had sent from Paris. Diary held by the Olivier family.

p. 90 Gabert collaboration: Testimony from *Oliviers v. Michaux,* Tribunal de la Seine, 1869.

p. 91 Paris to Avignon: Jules Olivier noted in his diary entry for 1 August 1865 that Aimé, René, and Georges de la Bouglise were planning to ride velocipedes from Paris to Tullins (near Grenoble), where the Oliviers' uncle Michel Perret resided. The brothers apparently covered an extra leg from Tullins to Avignon, as Jules noted their arrival in Avignon on 1 September 1865. The brothers also alluded to the Paris-to-Avignon ride in various statements to the press from 1867 on.

p. 91 astonished citizenry gave chase: *Vie Parisienne,* 14 September 1867.

p. 91 Georges dropped out: The entry of 1 September 1865 in the diary of Jules Olivier noted only that his two sons Aimé and René arrived in Avignon on velocipedes.

p. 91 switched to wooden prototypes: In his court testimony, René Olivier stated that he and his brother rode Michaux-built bicycles of malleable cast iron from Paris to Lyon in 1865. In other statements, however, he indicated that they rode Gabert-built diagonal bicycles to Avignon that same year, suggesting that they must have changed bicycles in Lyon, where Gabert was based.

p. 91 visit with uncle, Michel Perret: The entry of 1 September 1865 in the diary of Jules Olivier noted that his sons arrived from Tullins, where they had evidently stayed overnight with their uncle Michel Perret.

p. 91 grueling but triumphant marathon: In an apparent reference to the Paris-to-Avignon ride, the original Michaux booklet of 1868 referred to a "Tour de France" undertaken by three amateurs, in which one made the last leg of 199 kilometers in 23 straight hours; *Notice on the Michaux Velocipede with Pedals and Brake* (Paris: Imprimerie de Lainé et J. Havard, 1868), p. 4. That is the approximate distance between Tullins and Avignon, and the entry of 1 September 1865 in the diary of Jules Olivier appears to confirm that his sons arrived to Avignon from Tullins in one stage. Other papers held by the Olivier family suggest that Aimé traveled some of that distance by train, and that René was the one who rode the entire distance.

p. 91 René made plans to launch an industry: Louis Lockert recalled years later how his classmate, René Olivier, took the lead in the early stages of the Michaux bicycle operation, racing over to the blacksmith's shop as soon as classes were over; Louis Lockert, *Manuel de Vélocipédie: Locomotion, Vélocipèdes, Construction, etc.* (Paris: L. Mulo, 1896), p. 26.

p. 91 family did not approve: Undated letter by Aimé Olivier to his nephew Louis Olivier, ca. 1894. Held by the Olivier family.

p. 91 bank turned down loan: G. O. S. Sanderval, *Mémoires et Notes* (Rennes: Imprimerie Bretonne, 1961), p. 89.

p. 92 "desiring to launch this industry": *Tintamarre,* 16 May 1869.

p. 92 Georges planned machinery: Recounted by Aimé Oliver in *Nature,* 6 August 1892.

p. 92 Georges supervised the operation: René Olivier stated in his court testimony that he put Georges de la Bouglise in charge of overseeing the bicycle operation. This supervisory role appears to be confirmed by several telegrams and a letter in the Michaux correspondence compendium, in which Georges sent Michaux instructions such as when and where to pick up bicycle parts.

pp. 92–93 René's agreement with Michaux: René Olivier's testimony in *Oliviers v. Michaux.*

p. 93 René was the "heart and soul" and Michaux a "pseudonym": From a statement drafted by Aimé Olivier in early 1894, held by the Olivier family. Aimé, who was appealing to his former classmates to support a memorial that would honor René Olivier as the true industry founder, wrote: "One is justly concerned with the erection of a statue to honor the inventor who created the success of the velocipede. The name of Michaux, taken by our schoolmate [René Olivier] naturally draws attention, but that name, like a pseudonym, covers that of Olivier. It is now time to say as much: the success that one attributes [to Michaux] belongs to Olivier."

p. 93 a strong backer finally emerged: In one draft of a letter to his nephew Louis held by the Olivier family, Aimé stated that his father-in-law Jean-Baptiste Pastré was the only one in the family willing to help finance the operation. The entry for 10 December 1869 in the diary of Jules Olivier confirms that Pastré was a major investor in the Compagnie Parisienne.

p. 93 request for wrought iron: Michaux letter no. 122, dated 6 March 1868.

p. 93 contempt for cast iron: Michaux letter no. 299, dated 22 April 1868.

p. 93 production hardly sufficient to meet demand: René Olivier stated in his court testimony from the second half of 1869 that the Compagnie Parisienne was making ten times as many velocipedes as had Michaux in the early going. Peak production was reportedly about two hundred bicycles a week, suggesting an initial output of about twenty serpentine frames a week.

pp. 93–94 "I finally received your velocipede": Michaux letter no. 268, dated 15 April 1868.

p. 94 Cadot received favorable reviews in Lyon: *Progrès,* 7 June 1867; *Salut Public,* 19 July 1867.

p. 94 Jacquier's diagonal models: N. Gallois, *Les Curiosités de l'Exposition Maritime Internationale du Havre* (Paris: E. Dentu, 1868).

p. 96 up to twenty units a day: *Salut Public,* 10 October 1868.

p. 96 Saint-Cloud race results: *Petit Journal,* 2 June 1868.

p. 96 major races in Toulouse: *Gazette du Languedoc* (Toulouse), 26 July 1868.

pp. 96–97 Le Havre races: *Havrais,* 9 August 1868.

pp. 97–99 Castres to Toulouse: *Echo du Tarn* (Castres), 12 July 1868.

p. 99 "To the velocipede, gentlemen": *Echo du Tarn,* 19 July 1868.

p. 99 "It is extraordinary what strides": *Paris Times* (London), 19 September 1868.

p. 99 Favre sold two thousand: A. Favre, *Le Vélocipède: Sa Structure, ses Accessoires Indispensables,* 2nd ed. (Marseille: Barlatier-Feissat et Demonchy, 1868), p. i.

p. 99 post office contemplated tricycles: *Journal des Postes,* November 1868.

p. 99 Hippodrome acts: *Indépendence Dramatique,* 7 October 1868.

p. 100 Bordeaux women's race: *Bordelais,* 8 November 1868.

p. 100 etching of the epic battle: One magazine that reprinted the image was *Harper's Weekly,* 19 December 1868.

p. 100 "year of the velocipede": *Petit Moniteur Universel* (Paris), 16 January 1869.

pp. 100–101 Figurier's assessment of the velocipede: *Année Scientifique,* 1869.

BOXED INSET   *A Letter to Michaux*

    p. 79   "Last year, at the time of the universal exposition": Michaux letter no. 95, dated 22 February
        1868.

BOXED INSET   *Tapping Human Power*

    p. 88   *Hunley*'s career and raising: *National Geographic,* July 2002.

 CHAPTER FIVE   *The American Adventure*

    p. 102   Lallement arrived in U.S.: His name appears in the *City of London* passenger
        list dated 25 July 1865. Held by the National Archives, College Park, Maryland.
    p. 102   Lallement's ride to Birmingham: Recounted in "Pierre Lallement and His
        Bicycle," *Wheelman Illustrated,* October 1883.

    p. 102   contortions provoked laughter": Karl Kron [Lyman Hotchkiss Bagg], *Ten Thousand Miles on
        a Bicycle* (New York: self-published, 1887), p. 141.

    p. 102   "An enterprising individual": *New Haven Daily Palladium,* 5 April 1866.

    p. 103   Lallement retreated to France: The exact date is unknown, but Lallement is listed in the 1868
        New Haven Directory, suggesting that he left after the start of that year.

    p. 103   Hanlon Brothers raced bicycles: *Boston Evening Transcript,* 13 August 1869.

    p. 103   romp through the Boston Commons: *Boston Evening Transcript,* 18 August 1868.

    p. 103   Hanlons' ride through Savannah: *Savannah Morning News,* 23 February 1869.

    p. 103   Hanlons secured American patent: *American Artisan,* 23 September 1868.

    p. 103   Pickering velocipede: *American Artisan,* 21 October 1868.

    p. 103   variety of colors: *Evening Standard* (Bridgeport, Connecticut), 8 February 1869.

    p. 103   "excitement may die out": *New York Coach-Makers Magazine,* February 1869.

    p. 103   "every part made by hand": *Newport Daily News,* 29 January 1869.

    pp. 103–5   price of a new bicycle: *National Chronicle* (Boston), 16 January 1869.

    p. 105   drove down its "exorbitant price": *Reading Gazette and Democrat,* 27 March 1869.

    p. 105   furor erupted in Manhattan: *Frank Leslie's Illustrated Newspaper,* 28 November 1868.

    p. 105   Pearsall brothers' riding school: *Turf, Field, and Farm,* 15 January 1869.

    p. 105   Portland, Maine, specimens: *Portland Daily Advertiser,* 26 January 1869.

    p. 105   Mechanics' Fair in Hartford: *Hartford Daily Times,* 16 January 1869.

    p. 105   hundreds watched indoor velocipede races: *Cincinnati Evening Chronicle,* 12 January 1869;
        Chicago Republican, 14 January 1869; *New Bedford Mercury,* 21 January 1869.

    p. 105   More schools opened: *Syracuse Daily Standard,* 20 January 1869; *Detroit Free Press,*
        28 January 1869; *San Francisco Chronicle,* 29 January 1869.

    p. 105   race in Fall River: *Fall River News,* 25 January 1869.

    pp. 105–6   attorney in Indianapolis: *Indianapolis Sentinel,* 8 January 1869.

    p. 106   Beecher pronounced the sport: *New York Sun,* 29 January 1869.

    p. 106   Dana proposed an elevated bicycle path: *Scientific American,* 30 January 1869.

    p. 106   fifteen velocipedes a day: *Bridgeport Daily Standard,* 8 February 1869.

    p. 106   "is a joke no longer": *Indianapolis Journal,* 15 January 1869.

    pp. 106–8   "It being understood": *Eastern Argus* (Portland, Maine), 2 March 1869.

    p. 108   Witty sole owner of patent: Ibid.

    p. 108   manufacturers settled with Witty: *New York Sun,* 1 February 1869.

    p. 108   reluctantly concluded it was valid: *New York Times,* 15 February 1869.

p. 108 "The monopoly Witty purchased": *Courier des Etats-Unis* (New York), 16 February 1869.

p. 108 Witty collected forty thousand dollars: *Evening Mail* (New York), 13 February 1869.

p. 108 Bicycle makers raised their prices: *New York Sun*, 25 February 1869.

p. 108 Eliot doubled his capacity: *Providence Herald*, 12 February 1869.

p. 108 trade acquired its own monthly: Three issues of *The Velocipedist* were published between February and April 1869.

p. 108 "everything new is called 'velocipede'": *Evansville Journal*, 4 March 1869.

p. 110 "the whole effort of this utilitarian age": *Milwaukee Daily News*, 14 March 1869.

p. 110 "how about sandy roads and steep hills?": *Charleston Chronicle*, 13 February 1869.

p. 110 "poor man's carriage": *Hartford Weekly Times*, 11 January 1869.

p. 110 "era of road travel": *National Chronicle*, 20 March 1869.

p. 110 "the little passenger locomotive": *New Haven Journal and Courier*, 27 February 1869.

p. 110 discouraged use of alcohol: *Hartford Evening Post*, 29 March 1869; *Boston Daily Advertiser*, 21 November 1868.

p. 110 "out into God's light": *Lynn Reporter*, 20 February 1869.

p. 110 Susan B. Anthony's praise: *Newark Evening Courier*, 28 January 1869; *Revolution*, 11 March 1869.

p. 110 "it must be put to practical account": *Harness and Carriage Journal*, December 1868.

p. 110 "the real working, every day velocipede": *Newburyport Daily Herald*, 16 February 1869.

p. 110 "something that can cross the tracks": *Detroit Free Press*, 2 February 1869.

p. 110 "rude contrivances": *Daily State Gazette* (Trenton), 17 April 1869.

pp. 110–11 "The practicality of velocipedes": *Brooklyn Daily Eagle*, 27 February 1869.

p. 111 "beyond the Frenchman's wildest dreams": *Brooklyn Daily Eagle*, 20 January 1869.

p. 111 "the 'feedless horse'": *Providence Journal*, 22 February 1869.

p. 111 "the social system is to be revolutionized": *Boston Evening Transcript*, 2 February 1869.

p. 111–112 applications for velocipede patents: *Daily Journal* (Ogdensburg), 8 March 1869.

p. 112 "this velocipede rush": *National Republican* (Washington), 3 February 1869.

p. 112 Pierre Lallement rink: *Lynn Reporter*, 6 March 1869.

p. 112 novice who tries to "kick his way": *Lawrence Daily American*, 20 February 1869.

pp. 112–13 "Timid Toddlers" and "Fancy Few": *San Francisco Examiner*, 2 February 1869.

p. 113 Chalk "runs into everything": *Brooklyn Daily Programme*, 11 March 1869.

p. 113 Enterprising young men founded rinks: Irving Pearl of New Bedford, for example, established a rink in Richmond and "contemplated" others in Savannah and Nashville; *Evening Standard* (New Bedford), 6 April 1869.

p. 113 "if a man or boy is missed": *New Bedford Mercury*, 22 February 1869.

p. 113 "wheedle money": *Argus and Patriot* (Montpelier, Vermont), 4 March 1869.

p. 113 "Greenhorns come fumbling": *Gardiner (Maine) Home Journal*, 3 March 1869.

p. 113 Eau Claire race: *Eau Claire (Wisconsin) Free Press*, 8 April 1869.

p. 113 thirty to forty dollars a day: *Daily Index* (Petersburg, Virginia), 12 April 1869.

p. 113 "One dollar per hour": *Daily Evening Times* (Newark), 31 March 1869.

pp. 113–14 P. T. Barnum speech: *National Chronicle* (Boston), 10 April 1869.

p. 114 as many as five thousand spectators: That number attended a tournament in Philadelphia, reported in the Philadelphia *Age*, 18 March 1869.

pp. 114–15 lively contest in Lewiston: *Evening Journal* (Lewiston, Maine), 4 May 1869.

pp. 115–17 Master Willie: *Wilmington (Delaware) Commercial Advertiser*, 22 April 1869.

p. 117 five riders on one velocipede: *Albany Argus*, 15 April 1869.

p. 117 Moore stood on one foot: *Boston Post*, 16 March 1869.

p. 117   Carrie Moore's outfit: *Portland Press*, 5 April 1869.

p. 117   production climbed to sixteen thousand: *Galaxy*, April 1869.

p. 117   Hanlons sued Witty: *Brooklyn Daily Eagle*, 12 April 1869.

p. 117   "would destroy the business": *New York Sun*, 25 February 1869.

p. 117   Smith's patent irrelevant: *New York Sun*, 10 March 1869.

p. 117   initial settlement with Witty: *Brooklyn Daily Eagle*, 8 March 1869; decision to pay only the Hanlons: *Scientific American*, 26 June 1869.

p. 117   Witty and Smith joined forces: *New York Coach-Makers Magazine*, July 1869.

p. 117   "wooden-headed" manager: *Sporting Times and Theatrical Review*, 21 August 1869.

p. 117   "with their legs spread apart": *New Albany (Indiana) Daily Ledger*, 10 March 1869.

p. 117   "gratify prurient tastes": *New York Times*, 11 April 1869.

p. 117   Irate citizens clamored: Residents of Amherst, Massachusetts, for example, petitioned the city to close the rink; *Boston Daily Advertiser*, 1 May 1869.

p. 117   most managers shut down their rinks: A rink manager in Washington, for example, sold off his bicycles, originally priced at well over $100, for $18 to $30; *Sporting Times and Theatrical News*, 21 August 1869.

pp. 117–19   velocipedist in Portland: *Portland Press*, 24 February 1869.

p. 119   "clerks struggled with might and main": *Commonwealth* (Frankfort), 30 April 1869.

p. 119   "stuck in the hubs with Spalding's glue": *Indianapolis Sentinel*, 6 May 1869.

p. 119   "half a dozen fruitless efforts": *San Jose Weekly Patriot*, 19 March 1869.

p. 119   "loudly mentioning a place": *St. Paul Dispatch*, 1 May 1869.

p. 119   "Judging from their jaded appearance": *Troy Daily Times*, 1 May 1869.

pp. 119–20   Swift and Boyle ride to Rochester: *Rochester Union*, 30 April and 1 May 1869.

p. 120   better had they walked: *Rochester Express*, 1 May 1869.

p. 120   pedestrian made a stand: *Indianapolis Journal*, 2 April 1869.

p. 120   fines for sidewalk riding: *Lawrence Daily American*, 14 April 1869.

p. 121   Ashmead fought back: *Hartford Courant*, 31 March 1869.

p. 121   fifteen-dollar fine: *Hartford Evening Post*, 17 April 1869.

p. 121   boys arrested in Utica: *Utica Daily Observer*, 19 May 1869.

p. 121   the boy "vented some wrath": *Utica Daily Observer*, 27 May 1869.

p. 121   knocked over a colonel: *Indianapolis Journal*, 1 April 1869.

p. 121   decked a burly Irishman: *Missouri Democrat* (Saint Louis), 25 February 1869.

p. 121   velocipedist scared two horses: *Dayton Daily Ledger*, 9 April 1869.

p. 121   "misfortune to run into a fireplug": *Pittsburgh Gazette*, 15 March 1869.

p. 121   Some medical authorities: *New York Evening Mail*, 8 February 1869.

p. 121   "tender parts of the anatomy": *Elmira (New York) Daily Advertiser*, 27 February 1869.

p. 121   "paternal relation to the bicyclist of the future": *New York World*, 26 April 1869.

p. 121   Dana branded bicycle a failure: *Buffalo Daily Courier*, 4 May 1869.

pp. 121–22   "more laughable than exciting": *Democratic Banner* (Morristown), 10 June 1869.

p. 122   national mile records: Thudium set a mile mark of 3:06 (*Indianapolis Sentinel*, 16 February 1869), and then lowered it by three seconds (*Indianapolis Sentinel*, 16 April 1869). He also purportedly kept up a similar pace over three and even seven miles (*Indianapolis Sentinel*, 28 April 1869), but it is difficult to judge the accuracy of these reports.

p. 122   two miles in eight minutes: *Buffalo Daily Commercial*, 7 May 1869.

p. 122   Brown covered fifty miles twice: *Turf, Field, and Farm*, 23 April and 30 April 1869.

p. 122   one hundred miles in ten hours: *Pittsburgh Evening Chronicle*, 25 May 1869.

p. 122   Messinger rode five hundred miles: *National Chronicle* (Boston), 24 July 1869.

p. 122   outdoor race in Albany: *Albany Argus*, 15 May 1869.

p. 122 mile times in Brooklyn: *Sunday Mercury* (New York), 27 June 1869.

p. 122 race from San Jose to Santa Clara: *San Jose Mercury*, 11 March 1869.

p. 122 race in Newburyport: *Newburyport Daily Herald*, 29 April 1869.

p. 122 Akron to Toledo: *American Artisan*, 7 April 1869.

p. 122 Wheeling to Washington: *Wheeling Intelligencer*, 22 April 1869.

p. 122 Northampton to Boston: *Boston Journal*, 10 May 1869.

p. 122 Indianapolis to Richmond: *Indianapolis Sentinel*, 6 May 1869.

p. 122 "the most senseless mania": *New York World*, 26 April 1869.

p. 124 "superlatively foolish antics": *New York Atlas*, 13 March 1869.

p. 124 commuting in Indianapolis: *Indianapolis Sentinel*, 7 May 1869.

p. 124 bicycle jaunts by moonlight: *Charleston Daily Courier*, 27 May 1869; *Republican Banner* (Memphis), 28 March 1869.

p. 124 "too fascinating a sport": *Sunday Mercury*, 8 August 1869.

p. 124 faith in the bicycle: *Scientific American*, 30 October 1869.

p. 124 "Velocipeding is dead": *Sunday Mercury*, 24 October 1869.

p. 124 transcontinental railroad: *Buffalo Daily Courier*, 10 May 1869.

p. 124 one satisfied Pickering owner: *Boston Evening Transcript*, 29 March 1869.

p. 124 Brownell's rubber tires: *Evening Standard* (New Bedford, Massachusetts), 17 April 1869.

p. 124 Price introduced the wire wheel: *Scientific American*, 12 June 1869.

p. 124 anticipated the high-wheel profile: For example, Soule's velocipede, *Scientific American*, 3 April 1869.

p. 124 Demarest bicycle: *Harper's Weekly*, 13 March 1869.

p. 124 Dexter bicycle: *Brooklyn Daily Union*, 22 February 1869.

p. 124 Witty's geared bicycle: *Brooklyn Daily Eagle*, 19 June 1869; Witty's rear-wheel-drive bicycle: U.S. patent 87999, dated 16 March 1869.

p. 126 "Royalty" Witty: *Evening Telegram* (New York), 26 May 1869.

p. 126 a "great humbug": *Boston Daily Advertiser*, 19 March 1869.

BOXED INSET   *"Bicycles on the Rampage"*

p. 107 "one of the most surprising feats": *Scientific American*, 23 September 1868.

p. 107 "one of the funniest, queerest": *Cincinnati Commercial*, 11 January 1869.

p. 107 "class who love fun": Ibid.

BOXED INSET   *A Victim of the Velocipede*

p. 120 Ehrich and the velocipede: Ehrich's diary in the Louis Rinaldo Ehrich papers, 1865–69, Manuscripts and Archives, Yale University Library.

CHAPTER SIX   *European Development*

p. 127 fifty thousand velocipedes: *Navette* (Tarare), 18 April 1869.

p. 127 "The velocipede is not a fad": *Vélocipède Illustré*, 1 April 1869.

p. 129 "Its fabrication is formidable": *Petite Presse* (Paris), 6 June 1869.

pp. 129–30 "For many years, the founders of the Compagnie Parisienne": *Vélocipède Illustré*, 10 June 1869.

p. 130 "Show me the employee": *Navette* (Tarare), 18 April 1869.

p. 132 riders collided with each other: *Tablettes de Paris*, 28 January 1869.

p. 132   boy's drowning: *Journal de Vienne et de l'Isere,* 27 December 1868.

p. 132   right to risk their own necks: *France du Nord* (Boulogne-sur-Mer), 8 August 1869.

p. 132   hit-and-run accidents: One case is described in *Journal de Maine et Loire* (Angers), 29 January 1869.

p. 132   Dôle ordinance: *Publicateur de Dôle et du Jura,* 14 August 1869.

p. 132   Marseille club: Members list, dated 11 January 1869. Held by the Departmental Archives of Bouches-du-Rhône.

pp. 132–33   Auch to Agen: *Journal de Lot et Garonne* (Agen), 19 February 1869.

p. 133   harassment on the road: In Autun, for example, three velocipedists successively ran into a beam that had apparently been placed in the road to impede their progress; recounted in *Gazette des Bains* (Dieppe), 21 September 1868.

p. 134   ten thousand on the periphery: *Journal du Cher* (Bourges), 24 August 1869.

pp. 134–35   race in Carpentras: *Indicateur de Carpentras,* 4 April 1869.

p. 135   "one of the most pleasant distractions": *Echo de la Mayenne* (Laval), 15 September 1869.

p. 135   race in Thann: *Courrier de Bas-Rhin* (Strasbourg), 29 June 1869.

p. 135   speed of a train: *Salut Public* (Lyon), 11 May 1869.

p. 135   race in Dunkirk, Jacques Pedro: *Impartial de Boulogne-sur-Mer,* 25 September 1869.

p. 135   obstacle races: *Illustration, Journal Universel,* 21 August 1869.

p. 135   women's races drew no contestants: For example, at the announced races in Carcassonne (*Fraternité,* 21 July 1869) and Reims (*Indépendant Remois,* 14 September 1869).

p. 135   no clue how to ride: *Salut Public* (Lyon), 18 May 1869.

pp. 135–36   Moret's style: *Indicateur de Carpentras,* 4 April 1869.

p. 136   women's race in La Réole: *Girondin* (La Réole), 22 August 1869.

p. 136   "Miss America": *Le Sport,* 4 May 1870.

p. 136   wins in Rouen and Blois: *Avenir* (Blois), 3 June 1870.

p. 136   grouch in Fountainebleau: *Nouvelliste de Seine et Marne* (Melun), 24 July 1869.

p. 136   Clermont-Ferrand mayor's refusal: *Auvergne* (Clermont-Ferrand), 19 May 1869.

p. 136   race in Le Neubourg: *Courier de l'Eure* (Evreux), 6 July 1869.

p. 136   Boeuf's freewheel: *Vélocipède Illustré,* 11 November 1869.

pp. 136–37   Ader's tires: French patent 83112, dated 24 November 1868.

p. 137   tires an impractical luxury: *Vélocipède Illustré,* 8 July 1869.

p. 140   Marennes protest: *Journal de Marennes,* 22 August 1869.

p. 140   Oliviers finally won their case: The Seine Tribunal ruled in their favor on 11 October 1869, reported in *Gazette des Tribuneaux,* 6 November 1869.

pp. 140–41   Aimé's letter to Marius: Undated letter, Olivier family archives.

p. 141   he could outrun the machines: *Chronique de Rouen,* 14 November 1869.

p. 141   Paris-to-Rouen race results: *Vélocipède Illustré,* 11 November 1869.

p. 141   Meyer's light bicycles: Advertised at 20 kilograms in *Vélocipède Illustré,* 31 October 1869.

p. 141   wire-wheeled tricycles: *Bell's Life,* 24 September 1870.

pp. 142–43   Roux's geared front hubs: *Vélocipède Illustré,* 4 July 1869.

p. 143   Castera in Le Neubourg: *Courier de l'Eure* (Evreux), 5 July 1870.

p. 143   race around periphery of Paris: *Vélocipède Illustré,* 13 January 1870.

p. 143   Léotard rode forty miles: *Journal de Toulouse,* 30 March 1870.

p. 143   "With the velocipede craze behind us": *Côte-d'Or* (Dijon), 20 May 1870.

p. 144   German sales to Russia: The firm Hoffmann and Lumpp of Stuttgart, for example, advertised in a Saint Petersburg newspaper (*Golos,* 6 June 1869).

p. 144 Italians among the first customers: Several wrote Michaux from Turin in the the spring of 1868 to order bicycles.

p. 144 Favre in Florence: *Nazione* (Florence), 12 September 1868.

p. 144 Florence to Pistoia: *Nazione,* 3 February 1870.

p. 144 sketch of the curious vehicle: *English Mechanic,* 28 June 1867.

p. 144 visit to the Michaux factory: *Field,* 9 November 1867.

p. 144 Charles Bowen: Michaux letter no. 43, dated 21 December 1867.

p. 144 William W. Vine: Michaux letter no. 88, dated 20 February 1868.

pp. 144–45 E. W. Martin: Michaux letter no. 54, dated 6 February 1868.

p. 145 James Collinge: Michaux letter no. 204, dated 31 March 1868.

p. 147 Turner's order: H. W. Bartleet, *Bartleet's Bicycle Book* (London: J. Burrow, 1931).

p. 147 race on Dulwich road: *Sun* (London), 28 January 1869.

p. 147 Mayall arrived in about twelve hours: *Westminster Budget,* 30 July 1897.

p. 147 Mayall felt in "good condition": *Times* (London), 19 February 1869.

p. 147 Liverpool to London: *Liverpool Mercury,* 30 March 1869.

p. 147 Eaton's performance: *Liverpool Mercury,* 5 April 1869.

pp. 147–49 Pascaud's extraordinary riding skills: *Daily News* (London), 7 May 1869.

p. 149 game of tag with Mayall: Ibid.

p. 149 Manchester to Bakewell: *Sheffield and Rotherham Independent,* 17 April 1869.

p. 149 "without violent exertion": *Wolverhampton Chronicle,* 28 April 1869.

p. 149 "agreeable method of taking useful and healthy exercise": *Lancet,* 1 May 1869.

p. 149 "What now seems a folly": Clergyman quoted in *Philadelphia Morning Post,* 26 May 1869.

p. 150 manufacturers in London: *Exchange and Mart,* 2 June 1869; *Court Journal,* 29 May 1869.

p. 150 Phantom introduced: *Exchange and Mart,* 16 June 1869.

p. 150 Peyton's Improved Bicycle: *Ironmonger,* 30 October 1869.

p. 150 Klamroth, London to Edinburgh: *Paisley and Renfrewshire Standard,* 31 July 1869.

p. 151 "There must be something in it": *Era,* 4 July 1869.

pp. 151–53 International Velocipede Exhibition: *Morning Advertiser* (London), 27 September 1869; *Nouvelliste de Rouen,* 13 September 1869.

p. 154 racers connected to carriage trade: Forder worked with Forder and Traves of Wolverhampton (*Sporting Life,* 10 November 1869), while Palmer worked with Palmer brothers of Aston Cross (*Bell's Life,* 2 June 1869).

p. 154 weight penalty: *Sportsman,* 6 October 1869.

pp. 154–55 Palmer vs. Forder: *Sportsman,* 11 August 1869.

p. 155 bicycle had gained much popularity: *Land and Water,* 16 October 1869.

p. 155 "Are these bicycles likely to last": Ibid.

p. 155 "Judging from our own experience": Ibid.

BOXED INSET *Patent Problems*

p. 131 "hesitated at first": Draft of a statement by René Olivier to the Seine Tribunal in connection with his suit against Pierre Michaux in 1869. Held by the Olivier family.

p. 131 Michaux patent inquiry: Michaux letter no. 156, dated 16 March 1868, signed Camille Carrau, attorney in Bordeaux.

p. 131 Witty forbade importation from France: For example, Witty's advertisement in the *Eastern Argus* of Portland, Maine, 21 April 1869, read: "Persons making, using, selling, buying, or importing [bicycles] from Paris or elsewhere . . . render themselves liable to prosecution."

p. 131   "fled without obtaining a patent": *Petit Moniteur Universel,* 28 May 1869.

p. 131   René applied for an American patent: John E. Earle paid a fifteen-dollar application fee on behalf of René Olivier to the U.S. Patent Office on 15 October 1869, just a few days after René received a favorable ruling in his suit against Michaux. René received U.S. patent 97683 covering fork springs on 7 December 1869.

p. 131   Witty turned down an offer: *Eastern Argus,* 9 February 1869.

BOXED INSET   *Women and the Velocipede*

p. 138   Parisian women would sooner shorten their skirts: *Vie Parisienne,* 28 January 1868.

pp. 138–39   Pickering proposed a woman's model: J. T. Goddard, *The Velocipede: Its History, Varieties, and Practice* (Cambridge: Riverside, 1869), pp. 85–86.

p. 139   Calvin Witty's rink: *Brooklyn Daily Eagle,* 16 March 1869.

p. 139   "mere piece of bravado": *Demarest Monthly Magazine,* March 1869.

p. 139   "novel spectacle": *New Haven Daily Palladium,* 12 April 1869.

p. 139   "not altogether such ethereal creatures": *Englishwoman's Domestic Magazine,* 1 June 1869.

BOXED INSET   *The Bicycle in Scotland*

p. 152   Scotsmen obtained the Michaux bicycle: Michaux letter no. 40, dated 31 January 1868, contains an order for a velocipede from E. Houdart of Leith. Several other Scotsmen wrote Michaux for information in the spring of 1868, suggesting that a few Michaux bicycles had probably arrived in Scotland by that summer.

p. 152   the velocipede in Glasgow: *North British Daily Mail* (Glasgow), 12 April 1869.

p. 152   ride from Bonhill to Oban: *Dumbarton Herald,* 18 August 1869.

p. 152   race with steamer: *Public Guide* (Greenock), 13 May 1869.

p. 152   race in Jedburgh: *Border Advertiser* (Galashiels), 13 August 1869.

p. 152   Bathgate prevailed over Klamroth: *Leith Burghs Pilot,* 21 August 1869.

p. 152   Stiles beat Bathgate: *Perthshire Journal,* 2 September 1869.

CHAPTER SEVEN   *The High Mount Prevails*

pp. 159–60   Palmer vs. Prince: *Sportsman,* 5 April 1870.

p. 160   J. T. Johnson: *Bell's Life,* 31 December 1870.

p. 160   Moore at Midland Counties: *Sportsman,* 10 August 1870.

p. 160   "What a revolution": Undated letter by James Moore, held by John S. Moore.

p. 161   Shelton's "gigantic" wheel: *Sportsman,* 1 November 1870.

p. 161   Ariel introduced: *Mechanics' Magazine,* 5 October 1872.

p. 163   Newcastle to Birmingham: *Penny Illustrated Paper,* 12 March 1870.

p. 163   London to Bath: *Field,* 24 September 1870.

p. 163   Aberdeen to London: *Land and Water,* 10 September 1870.

p. 163   "The riders of today": *Field,* 7 June 1873.

p. 164   Keen rode ten miles: *Sporting Life,* 28 December 1872.

p. 164   Moore rode fifty miles: *Bell's Life,* 18 January 1873.

pp. 164–65   "speed-geared" Ariel: *Sporting Life,* 29 February 1872.

p. 165   Moore's fifty-two-inch bicycle: *Sporting Life,* 9 July 1873.

p. 166   Amateur Bicycle Club century ride: *Field,* 2 September 1871.

p. 166 Middlesex club retraced the run to Brighton: *Bell's Life*, 28 September 1872.

p. 166 London to John O'Groats: *Graphic*, 19 July 1873.

p. 166 "mainstay of bicycling": *Field*, 29 June 1871.

p. 167 "jolly as a sand boy": *Bazaar, The Exchange and Mart*, 25 October 1871.

p. 167 longtime rider outlined his objections: *Field*, 1 November 1873.

p. 167 "averse to mounting": *English Mechanic*, 21 November 1873.

p. 167 "Having personally learned": *Field*, 17 October 1874.

p. 169 "universal, easy, and dependable": *The Wheel and the Way* (London: Phantom Wheel, 1871), p. 3.

p. 169 demise of the Phantom: *Field*, 5 October 1872.

p. 169 "I have a geared bicycle": *Field*, 24 January 1874.

p. 169 thirty thousand miles on a Tension bicycle: *Field*, 10 January 1874.

p. 169 "During the holiday months": *New York Times*, 7 November 1874.

p. 169 "happiest hours of my life": *Field*, 12 April 1873.

p. 169 Edinburgh Tricycle: *Field*, 28 November 1874.

p. 170 "as common as umbrellas": Undated letter by James Moore, held by John S. Moore.

p. 170 army of crude bicycles: *Field*, 16 March 1872.

p. 171 had to use the best technology: Ibid.

p. 171 "The difference between the best": *Bazaar, The Exchange and Mart*, 13 December 1871.

p. 171 "amusement, and nothing more": *Field*, 16 March 1872.

p. 171 "upper, middle, and higher classes": *Field*, 6 December 1873.

p. 171 Coventry Machinists' interlaced wheel: *Bicycling World*, 6 November 1896.

p. 172 "The bicycle in England": *Vélocipède*, 1 August 1874.

p. 172 Keen's record fifty miles: *Bell's Life*, 5 December 1874.

pp. 172–73 Whiting beat Keith-Falconer: *Bell's Life*, 30 January 1875.

p. 173 Whiting defended his title: *Bell's Life*, 27 March 1875.

p. 173 Cambridge and Oxford clubs: *Field*, 20 June 1874.

p. 173 Keith-Falconer prevailed: *Bell's Life*, 15 May 1875.

p. 173 Bath to London: *Land and Water*, 25 July 1874.

p. 173 Stanton retraced the route: *Pictorial World*, 29 August 1874.

p. 173 "double century": A. Howard, *Bicycle for 1877* (London: Bicycle Journal Office, 1877), p. 10.

pp. 173–74 "Croppers are not of such importance": *Bicycling News*, 2 June 1876.

p. 174 astonishment in India: *Field*, 11 April 1874.

p. 174 Moore escorted tourists: *Vélocipède*, 4 July 1874; *London Reader*, 1 July 1874.

p. 175 races in Mons, Belgium: *Gazette du Mons*, 21–22 June 1870; *Vélocipède Illustré*, 13 August 1871.

pp. 175–76 clubs in the Netherlands: George J. M. Hogenkamp, *Een Halve Eeuw Wilersport [1867–1917]* (Amsterdam: 1916), pp. 42–48.

p. 176 Geneva's club: *Bicycling World*, 21 February 1880.

p. 176 Florentines performed: *Opinione Nazionale* (Florence), 1 July 1872.

p. 176 Florence vs. Pistoia: *Opinione Nazionale*, 2 September 1872.

p. 176 Milan club entertained: *Spirito Folletto* (Milan), 22 May 1873.

p. 176 bicycles with the latest improvements: *Vélocipède*, 27 June 1874.

p. 177 Moore and Keen in Lyon: *Vélocipède*, 7 March 1874.

p. 177 Paris to Vienna: *Field*, 30 October 1875.

p. 177 Truffault introduced hollow forks: *Révue Vélocipédique*, 15 December 1882.

p. 177 press couriers: *Vélocipède*, 15 January 1874.

p. 177 bank couriers: *Petit Journal*, 24 June 1874.

p. 177 new restrictions in Paris: City ordinance, dated 9 November 1874.

p. 177 race at the Empire Rink: Cited in *National Police Gazette*, 12 June 1880.

pp. 177–78 "dearth of horses," "inherent defect": *New York Times*, 1 November 1872.

p. 178 "Professor Brown" on stage: Referenced in *Bassett's Scrap Book*, April 1913.

p. 178 "velocipede is no longer a toy": *Boston Herald*, 7 November 1875.

p. 179 Hillsboro to London and back: *Madison County Democrat* (London, Ohio), 27 October 1875.

p. 179 Long Distance Championship: *Turf, Field, and Farm*, 27 December 1875.

p. 179 "exhibiting powers of endurance": *New York Sportsman*, 22 April 1876.

p. 181 Stanton's advertisements: *New York Sportsman*, 3 June 1876.

p. 181 "Through Mr. Stanton's endeavors": Ibid.

p. 181 scattered sales to courageous customers: *Bassett's Scrap Book*, April 1913.

BOXED INSET   *Extreme Indoor Racing*

p. 180 Stanton's ride questioned: *Sporting Life*, 7 October 1874.

p. 180 report on Stanton's unsuccessful ride at Lille Bridge: *Land and Water*, 10 October 1874.

p. 180 cycling feat many regarded as the greatest: *Land and Water*, 24 October 1874.

p. 180 Stanton covered 650 miles: *Land and Water*, 4 January 1879.

CHAPTER EIGHT   *The Pinnacle of the High Wheeler*

p. 182 "every quarter of the world": *Bicycling World*, 27 December 1879.

p. 184 ball bearings introduced around 1878: The first ball-bearing patents were issued in Britain to J. H. Hughes (19 September 1877) and Daniel Rudge (8 February 1878); *Bicycle News*, June 1915.

p. 184 Keen's hour record: *Bell's Life*, 9 December 1876.

p. 184 mile and fifty-mile records: *Brentano's Monthly*, May 1880.

p. 185 Stanton's thousand miles: *Land and Water*, 4 January 1879.

p. 185 Waller's record: *Brentano's Monthly*, May 1880.

p. 186 Keith-Falconer's protest: *Bicycling News*, 7 July 1876.

p. 186 Keith-Falconer bested Keen: *Bearings*, 27 May 1897.

p. 186 increase in London clubs: *One and All*, 17 April 1880.

pp. 186–87 provincial clubs ballooned: *Boy's Own Paper*, 1 May 1880.

p. 187 club admission policies: *Boy's Own Paper*, 1 May and 15 May 1880.

p. 187 Bicycle Touring Club: *Daily News*, 24 April 1886.

p. 187 club benefits and services: *Century Magazine*, September 1884.

p. 187 weekend "club runs": *Boy's Own Paper*, 15 May 1880.

pp. 187–88 bicycle production increases: *Times*, 28 May 1877 and 24 July 1878; *Bicycling World*, 15 May 1880.

p. 188 "freaks of ornamentation": *Household Words*, 1881, p. 318.

p. 188 Coventry Machinists' production: *Times*, 28 May 1877.

p. 188 Laumaillé requested a touring bicycle: Michaux letter no. 163, dated 20 March 1868.

p. 188 Laumaillé toured Brittany in 1868: *Cycle* (Paris), 23 January 1892.

p. 188 Laumaillé's ride in Europe: *Illustration*, 18 May 1878.

p. 189 "fearfully and wonderfully made": *Saturday Evening Express* (Boston), 17 November 1877.

pp. 189–90 Pope saw Chandler riding: Recounted in *American Athlete*, 5 October 1887.

p. 190 Pope imported bicycles from England: *Bicycling World*, 15 May 1880.

p. 190 Pope bicycled in Hartford: *National Magazine*, February 1893.

pp. 190–92 Pope emerged with a controlling interest: *Wheel*, 21 May 1897.

p. 192　Hodgson initiated small production: *Bicycling World,* 29 May 1880.

p. 192　"sure to lose my money": Testimony from *Pope Manufacturing Company v. Harry B. Owsley,* Northern District of Illinois, 1884. Held by the National Archives, Great Lakes Region, Chicago.

pp. 193–94　"A gay scene": Quoted in *American Bicycling Journal,* 27 April 1878.

p. 194　Haverhill to Boston: *Haverhill Daily Bulletin,* 26 March 1878.

p. 194　Fitchburg to Boston: *Fitchburg Sentinel,* 19 April 1878.

p. 194　races in the Boston area: The Harvard Athletic Association hosted a three-mile race in Boston on 24 May (*New York Clipper,* 1 June 1878), and a one-mile handicap on 2 November (*New York Clipper,* 9 November 1878). Other races were held in Lynn and Brockton on 4 July (*Lynn Transcript,* 6 July 1878; *Brockton Weekly Gazette,* 8 July 1878) and Framingham on 18 September (*Framingham Gazette,* 20 September 1878).

p. 194　Pope's bicycles still not available: *Wheel,* 21 May 1897.

p. 194　"prostrated rider": *Boston Daily Advertiser,* 20 June 1878.

pp. 194–95　"With park guards unfriendly": *New York Sun,* 19 October 1878.

p. 195　a woeful four minutes: *New York Daily Tribune,* 29 November 1878.

p. 195　three hundred brave Americans: *Bicycling World,* 27 December 1879.

pp. 195–96　Boston sponsored a race: *American Bicycling Journal,* 9 August 1879.

p. 196　bicycles at Harvard College: *Boston Globe,* 9 November 1879.

p. 196　growth of Pope's business: *Bicycling World,* 15 May 1880.

p. 197　Pratt's illustrated account: *Scribner's Monthly,* February 1880.

pp. 197–98　six-day racing in Boston: *Boston Globe,* 6 November 1879.

p. 198　bicycling a "rational substitute": *Boston Globe,* 10 November 1879.

p. 198　twenty-five hundred Americans: *Bicycling World,* 27 December 1879.

pp. 198–99　no entry for the word "bicycle": *Bicycling World,* 7 February 1880.

BOXED INSET　*The Importance of Bearings*

p. 185　Suriray's ball bearings: Advertised in *Vélocipède Illustré,* 21 November 1869, with reference to Moore's triumph in the Paris-to-Rouen race two weeks earlier.

p. 185　first ball bearings: *Bicycle News,* June 1915.

BOXED INSET　*Amateur vs. Professional*

p. 196　amateur athlete and working-class competitions: James McGurn, *On Your Bicycle: An Illustrated History of Cycling* (London: Murray, 1987), pp. 61–63.

p. 197　intermediate category of "promateurs": L. H. Porter, *Wheels and Wheeling* (Boston: Wheelman Company, 1892), p. 8.

CHAPTER NINE　*Growing Safety Concerns*

p. 202　results on the racing track improved: *Longman's Magazine,* March 1884.

p. 202　Keith-Falconer's run: *New Englander and Yale Review,* June 1889.

p. 202　Sutton's twenty-four-hour record: *Longman's Magazine,* March 1884.

p. 202　Bidwell's demonstrations: *American Bicyclist and Motorcyclist,* December 1944, quoted by Carl Burgwardt in *Cycle History* 7, San Francisco: Van der Plas Publications, 1997, pp. 87–93; the corresponding dates are courtesy of Leon Dixon and the NBHAA.

p. 202　a thousand units a month: *Bicycling World,* 1 May 1880.

p. 202 twelve thousand bicycles in U.S.: *Bicycling World,* 17 March 1882.

p. 205 League parade in Boston: *Harper's Young People,* 14 June 1881.

p. 205 Springfield Tournament of 1883: *Harper's Weekly,* 29 September 1883.

p. 205 Balmer's race: *Bicycling World,* 27 December 1879.

p. 205 von Blumen rode a thousand miles: *Bicycling World,* 16 December 1881.

p. 205 Armaindo vs. Prince: *Springfield Wheelman's Gazette,* February 1885.

pp. 206–8 advantages of tricycles: *Popular Science News,* October 1885.

p. 208 bicycles offered distinct advantages: *Popular Science News,* October 1885.

p. 209 Haynes and Jeffries produced Coventry Rotary: Serena Beeley, *A History of Bicycles* (Secaucus: Wellfleet, 1992), p. 42.

pp. 210–12 "There is quite a rage": Quoted in *Cycling,* November 1878.

p. 212 individuals who pedaled for practical purposes: *Longman's Magazine,* March 1884.

p. 212 "When the tricycle was first seen": *Century Magazine,* September 1884.

p. 212 umbrella organization for tricyclists: *Pastime,* 22 June 1883.

p. 214 tricycle meets: *Pastime,* 8 June 1883.

p. 214 Bird rode 222 miles: *Longman's Magazine,* March 1884.

p. 214 tricycle "will supersede the bicycle": *Wheel,* 26 October 1881.

p. 214 Victor tricycles: *Bicycling World,* 28 January 1896.

p. 215 Pope unveiled a tricycle: *Wheelman Illustrated,* October 1882.

p. 216 Lawson's Safety Bicycle: *Cycling,* November 1878.

p. 216 Lawson enlisted Singer and Company: *Bazaar, The Exchange and Mart,* 24 February 1877.

p. 217 Lawson's Bicyclette: British patent 3934, dated 30 September 1879.

p. 217 Bate's chain-drive bicycles: *Iron Age,* 1 April 1897.

p. 219 Adams set the record with a Facile: *Bicycling News,* 5 October 1883.

p. 219 Facile's design praised: *Bicycling World,* 11 May 1883.

pp. 219–20 American Star: *Bicycling World,* 20 April 1883.

p. 220 performances on a Star: William C. Bolger, *Smithville: The Result of Enterprise* (Mount Holly, N.J.: Burlington County Cultural and Heritage Commission, 1980), p. 159.

p. 221 cyclists could reach every hamlet: *Household Words,* 1881, p. 317.

p. 221 CTC benefits and services: *Century Magazine,* September 1884.

p. 221 CTC membership and NCU activities: *Longman's Magazine,* March 1884.

p. 221 armies were contemplating two-wheelers: *Pall Mall Budget,* 21 October 1886.

BOXED INSET   *High-Wheel Accessories*

p. 203 hub lamp preferred: *American Bicyclist and Motorcyclist,* December 1979.

p. 203 take along a Kodak: *American Cyclist,* September 1891.

p. 203 "handy carrier": *Bicycling World,* 8 March 1889.

p. 203 "Safety Handle Bar": *American Bicyclist and Motorcyclist,* December 1979.

BOXED INSET   *The Lallement Patent Again*

p. 208 David Brandon letter: In the scrapbook of Charles E. Pratt, Smithsonian Institution.

p. 209 McKee traveled to Paris: *American Wheelman,* 15 April 1897.

p. 209 "healthy reward to whomever can prove": *Sport Vélocipédique,* 17 September 1881.

p. 209 "I see the one that I made": Lallement testimony, *Pope Manufacturing Company v. McKee and Harrington,* Southern District of New York, 1882.

CHAPTER TEN *The Rise of the Rover*

p. 225 tricycles began to outnumber bicycles: Nick Clayton, *Early Bicycles* (Aylesbury: Shire, 1986), p. 21.

p. 226 "This country needs safety bicycles": *Bicycling World*, 6 November 1885.

p. 226 "get their craniums cracked": *Springfield Wheelmen's Gazette*, July 1884.

pp. 227–28 lady tricyclists interviewed: *L.A.W. Bulletin*, 16 October 1885.

p. 229 Kangaroo praised: *Springfield Wheelmen's Gazette*, July 1884.

p. 229 Ordinary still the leading machine: *Bicycling World*, 20 February 1885.

p. 229 Overman ball-bearing patent: *Cycling Age,* 30 December 1897.

p. 229 endless litigation: *Bicycling World*, 25 June 1886.

pp. 230–32 "Taming the Bicycle": Mark Twain [Samuel L. Clemens], *What Is Man? and Other Essays* (New York: Harper & Brothers, 1917).

p. 232 "bicycle carnival" in Boston: *Outing*, February 1886.

p. 235 Starley explained the Rover: *Journal of the Society of Arts*, 20 May 1898.

p. 236 "practically no resistance": *L.A.W. Bulletin*, 15 January 1886.

p. 240 enthusiastic review of the Rover: *Revue Vélocipédique*, 11 June 1885.

p. 240 Rover's flawed steering: L. H. Porter, *Wheels and Wheeling* (Boston: Wheelman, 1892), p. 79.

p. 240 "The new Rover": *Cycle*, 30 July 1886.

p. 241 "nothing to learn": *Bicycling World*, 27 August 1886.

p. 241 Pope saw no need for the safety: *American Bicyclist and Motorcyclist*, March 1945 (reference courtesy of Leon Dixon and the NBHAA, quoted by Carl Burgwardt in *Cycle History* 7, San Francisco: Van der Plas Publications, 1997).

p. 241 growth of British cycling industry: *Daily News*, 24 April 1886.

p. 241 Pennell reminisced about Humber: *Contemporary Review*, January 1900.

p. 243 Veloce Columbia: Advertised in *Bicycling World*, 13 January 1888.

p. 244 "A sudden desire awoke": *Wheel*, 26 October 1888.

p. 244 first women's bicycle club: *Iron Age*, 13 May 1897.

p. 244 Washington women on bicycles: Cited in *American Athlete*, 24 October 1888.

p. 244 150 defectors to bicycles: *Wheel*, 26 October 1888.

p. 244 "the number of lady riders": *Bicycling World*, 29 March 1889.

p. 244 "cycling for ladies": *American Athlete*, 26 April 1889.

p. 244 "ladies' bicycle clubs": *Wheel*, 26 October 1888.

p. 244 three women completed a century: *Harper's Weekly*, 30 August 1890.

p. 245 "an old woman on a broomstick": *Bicycling World*, 26 June 1891.

p. 245 "It is refreshing": *Brooklyn Life*, 12 July 1890.

p. 245 "remarks calculated to disturb": *Outing*, October 1891.

p. 245 "filled with bitter discussions": *Bicycling World*, 16 December 1887.

pp. 245–46 "hold indisputable sway": *Bicycling World*, 4 November 1887.

p. 246 "The element of safety": *Bicycling World*, 16 December 1887.

p. 246 Du Cros partnership with Dunlop: *Westminster Budget*, 1 May 1896.

p. 246 tires dubbed "steamrollers": *Speaker*, 7 March 1891.

p. 246 improvements to puncture-prone tires: *Wheel*, 6 February 1891.

p. 246 Edge smashed century records: *Speaker*, 7 March 1891.

pp. 246–47 "undoubtedly the tyre of the future": *Wheel*, 6 February 1891.

p. 250 growth of the American trade: *American Athlete*, 20 March 1891.

p. 250 "It is the cleanest": *Wheel*, 4 September 1891.

p. 250   bicycling a social benefactor: *Vélo*, 1 January 1894.

p. 250   Allen and Sachtelben: *Illustrated Sporting and Dramatic News*, 27 September 1890.

p. 250   Osmond switched to safety: *Illustrated Sporting and Dramatic News*, 1 October 1890.

p. 250   "poor man's horse": *Wheel*, 4 September 1891.

BOXED INSET   *Caught Off Guard*

p. 238   Starley articles and interviews: For example, *Journal of the Society of Arts*, 20 May 1898, and *Travel*, 1896, pp. 305–10.

p. 239   Starley initially questioned pneumatic tires: *New Review*, March 1895.

BOXED INSET   *The Memorial Controversy*

p. 248   Michaux conceived bicycle in 1855: The claim was outlined in Michaux's obituary published in *Le Sport Vélocipédique*, 20 January 1883.

p. 248   René Olivier's death in an accident: *Petit Marseillais*, 9 July 1875.

p. 248   Henry Michaux's initial account: *Vélocipède Illustré*, 6 October 1892.

p. 248   committee's plan for Michaux memorial: *Echo de l'Est* (Bar-le-Duc), 22 February 1893.

p. 248   elder Michaux's role disputed: *Revue du Sport Vélocipédique*, 4 March 1893; *Éclair*, 7 March 1893.

pp. 248–49   Henry Michaux denies brother's role: *Éclair*, 10 March 1893.

p. 249   "It's a pity there wasn't": *Bicyclette*, 11 March 1893.

p. 249   Henry Michaux's revised account: *Vélo*, 28 March 1893.

CHAPTER ELEVEN   *The Bicycle Boom*

p. 251   safety gains popularity: *Speaker*, 7 March 1891.

p. 251   a staggering 150,000 bicycles sold: *Wheel*, 4 September 1891.

p. 252   Michelin race from Paris: *Monde Cycliste* (Lyon), 14 June 1892.

p. 252   Safety riders took over races: *Bicycle News*, April 1916.

p. 252   Zimmerman's income: *Bicycling Word*, 20 April 1894.

p. 254   bicycles break trotting records: *National Magazine*, February 1893.

p. 254   Holbein's record: *Illustrated London News*, 28 November 1891.

p. 254   Shorland's record: *Pall Mall Budget*, 2 August 1894.

p. 254   Schock's records: *Illustrated American*, 13 January 1894.

p. 254   Bordeaux to Paris: *Revue du Sport Vélocipédique*, 29 May 1891.

p. 254   Terront won Paris–Brest–Paris: *Nature*, 26 September 1891.

p. 255   encounter with prime minister of China: *Century*, October 1894.

p. 255   Lenz starts trip: *Outing*, August 1892.

pp. 255–58   Elwell organized tours: *Bicycling World*, 4 March 1892.

p. 258   accounts of Elwell's European tours: *Pall Mall Budget*, 20 June 1889.

p. 258   Elwell added a Ladies Tour: F. A. Elwell, *Cycling in Europe* (Boston: League of American Wheelmen, ca. 1899), p. 39.

p. 258   St. Petersburg to London: *Graphic*, 25 October 1890.

p. 258   European armies consider bicycle use: *American Cyclist*, September 1892.

p. 258   Pope's military bicycles: Ibid.

p. 259   bicycle and clean cities: *Arena*, vol. 6 (1892).

p. 259   Pope's new factories: *National Magazine*, February 1893.

pp. 259–61 Pope's headquarters in Boston: *American Cyclist,* April 1892.

p. 261 bicycle relay race: *Once a Week,* 31 May 1892.

p. 264 dozen top-notch racers: *Argosy,* July 1896.

p. 264 municipal workers adopted bicycles: *Illustrated American,* 6 July 1895.

p. 264 New York bicycle police squad: *Nickell Magazine,* July 1896.

p. 264 Roosevelt's praise for bicycle policeman: Theodore Roosevelt, *An Autobiography* (New York: Charles Scribner's Sons, 1925), pp. 182–83.

p. 264 "love of out-of-door life": *Brooklyn Life,* 16 November 1895.

pp. 264–66 Brooklyn bicycle path: *Illustrated American,* 6 July 1895.

p. 266 "Cycling is a furore": *Recreation,* September 1895.

p. 267 LeLong, Chicago to San Francisco: *Outing,* February 1898.

p. 267 "Most cycling women": *Bicycling World,* 10 April 1896.

p. 267 "Dress reform talked of": *Forum,* January 1896.

pp. 268–69 "apology for a bathing suit": *National Police Gazette,* 28 October 1893.

p. 269 "continuance of chastity": *American Athlete,* 27 October 1893.

p. 271 bloomer banned in British Columbia: *Wheel,* 29 March 1895.

p. 271 "legs like anyone else": *Brooklyn Life,* 28 April 1894.

p. 272 the fad hit Newport: *Frank Leslie's Illustrated Weekly,* 16 May 1895.

pp. 272–73 bicycle dances and teas: *Outlook,* 31 August 1895.

p. 273 Tiffany bicycle: *Referee,* 2 January 1896.

p. 273 Diamond Jim Brady: *Toy World,* March 1935.

p. 273 Tsar Nicholas an avid cyclist: *Cycling World Illustrated,* 30 September 1896.

p. 274 saved "every spare penny": *Youth's Companion,* 25 June 1896.

p. 274 bicycles for working girls: *Wheelwoman,* 23 May 1896.

p. 274 "cycling scouts": *Scout,* 1895, p. 48.

p. 275 "tramps" on bicycles: *Brooklyn Life,* 14 September 1895.

p. 275 "will die out altogether": *Brooklyn Life,* 29 June 1895.

p. 275 "cult of the wheel": *Scribner's Monthly,* June 1920.

pp. 275–78 "Heretofore when Lord Willoughby": *Lippincott's Magazine,* May 1892.

p. 278 safety bicycles for children: *Youth's Companion,* 11 June 1891.

p. 280 Pope's progressive labor policies: *National Magazine,* February 1893.

p. 280 Pope's poster contest: *Bicycling World,* 28 February 1896.

p. 280 convict labor to build roads: *Good Roads Magazine,* September 1901.

p. 280 Pope and Good Roads: *National Magazine,* February 1893.

pp. 280–82 Lozier's production: *Sportsmen's Review,* July 1895.

p. 282 Chicago bicycle makers: *Iron Age,* 12 April 1894.

p. 282 experiencing tremendous growth: *American Cyclist,* 1 November 1895.

p. 282 "climax in the cycle trade": *American Cyclist,* 6 December 1895.

BOXED INSET   *The Memorial That Wasn't*

p. 256 "To comrade Olivier": *Bulletin des Anciens Élèves d'École Centrale des Arts et Manufactures,* May–June 1894.

p. 256 Aimé possessed the company books: *Revue des Sports—Le Journal des Vélocipédistes,* 1893, pp. 121–22.

p. 256–57 letter to Louis: Undated letter held by the Olivier family.

p. 257 Lallement died in Boston: Lallement was forty-seven when he died on 29 August 1891; *Boston Globe,* 31 August 1891.

p. 320   Dallas messenger: *Western Union News*, December 1915.

pp. 320–21   heroic delivery in Philadelphia: *Western Union News*, September 1915.

p. 322   Wilson's cycle tour of Bermuda: *Bassett's Scrap Book*, December 1912.

p. 322   Wilson gave a new bicycle: *New York Times*, 14 October 1913.

p. 322   bicycle underused in America: *Bicycling World*, 16 June 1906.

p. 323   bicycle use in France: *Scientific American*, 9 August 1913.

p. 323   "bicycle famine" in London: *Daily News*, 17 June 1917.

p. 323   makeshift tires in Germany: *Scientific American*, 20 January 1917.

p. 323   Liberty bicycles: *Bicycle News*, January 1917.

pp. 323–24   "The cyclist soldier": *Bicycle News*, March 1917.

pp. 324–25   "Ride a Bicycle" campaign: *Printer's Ink*, 19 February 1920.

p. 325   "Everyone's ambition in the States": *Cycling*, 8 January 1920.

p. 325   CTA's promotional movie: *Bicycle News*, September 1926.

pp. 325–27   bicycles used heavily in Europe: *New York Times*, 17 August 1924.

p. 327   Soviet bicycle production program: *Fortune*, July 1946.

p. 327   Great Depression and cheap transportation: *New York Times*, 5 September 1930.

p. 327   "jumping curbs, hurdling ditches": *Consumers Union Reports*, November 1940.

p. 327   Schwinn Aerocycle: *Toy World*, June 1934.

p. 327   Schwinn "cyclelock": *Toy World*, December 1935.

p. 327   adult "change of attitude": *Toy World*, May 1934.

p. 328   Amsterdam commuters: *Christian Science Monitor*, 6 April 1938.

p. 328   "All Hollanders are accomplished": *Travel*, June 1934.

p. 328   "coming into this world on tiny bicycles": Ibid.

p. 328   Copenhagen study: *Transit Journal*, March 1935.

p. 328   European reliance on the bicycle: *Fortune*, September 1933.

p. 328   Raleigh modernized its plant: *Factory*, June 1922.

p. 328   German industry produced: *Foreign Commerce Weekly*, 12 April 1947.

p. 328   Saint-Etienne cycle output: *New York Times*, 2 February 1930.

p. 328   Italy encouraged bicycle use: *New York Times*, 1 November 1931.

p. 330   Chinese peasants adopted bicycles: *New York Times*, 2 July 1935.

pp. 330–32   bicycles could replace Chevrolets: *Time*, 12 January 1942.

p. 332   Victory bicycles: *Science News Letter*, 31 January 1942.

p. 332   Chicago sales and racks: *Consumers Research Bulletin*, April 1942.

p. 332   bicycle registrations: *Scribner's Commentator*, January 1941.

pp. 332–34   Los Angeles recovery rate: *Reader's Digest*, June 1942.

p. 334   Sweden the leading nation: *Foreign Commerce Weekly*, 5 August 1944.

p. 336   Morris workmen cycled: *Fortune*, July 1946.

p. 336   British industry exporting: *Economist*, 22 October 1949.

p. 338   bicycle storage in Japan: *ITE Journal*, September 1981.

p. 340   employers offer incentives to cycle: Pryor Dodge, *The Bicycle* (Paris: Flammarion, 1996), p. 191.

p. 340   Americans make little use: *Traffic Quarterly*, Fall 1997.

BOXED INSET   *Portable Bicycles*

p. 314   Clark's city bicycle: *Scientific American*, December 1919.

p. 315   Moulton foldable suspended frame bicycle: Dodge, *The Bicycle*, p. 182.

p. 315   Strida folding bicycle: *Los Angeles Times*, 5 March 2000.

p. 318   bicycle in Vietnam War: Jim Fitzpatrick, *The Bicycle in Wartime: An Illustrated History* (Washington, D.C.: Brassey's, 1998), pp. 162–88.

p. 318   Seattle police bike squad: *Law and Order Magazine,* April 2002.

p. 318   emergency medical technicians: *American City and County,* March 1999.

CHAPTER FOURTEEN   *Recreational Cycling*

p. 343   "The automobile has divided society": *Bassett's Scrap Book,* June 1912.

p. 343   European touring clubs: *Bassett's Scrap Book,* August 1913.

pp. 343–44   "more or less of a mechanic": *Contemporary Review,* January 1900.

p. 344   bicycle exerts "a good influence": *Fry's Magazine,* January 1907.

p. 344   British royal family on bicycles: *Bicycling World,* 5 November 1910.

p. 344   Golden Sunbeam: Serena Beeley, *A History of Bicycles* (Secaucus: Wellfleet, 1992), p. 88.

p. 346   "streams of riders wending": Quoted in *Bicycling World,* 14 October 1905.

p. 346   Clarion Cycling Club houses: James McGurn, *On Your Bicycle: An Illustrated History of Cycling* (London: Murray, 1987), p. 146.

pp. 346–47   Touring Club of France and the mountain bicycle: *Bicycling World,* 6 November 1902.

p. 347   gold medal went to Terrot: *Bicycling World,* 2 October 1902.

p. 347   Weston spoke disparagingly: *Bicycling World,* 24 April 1902.

p. 347   "Will somebody kindly start a bicycle boom": Quoted in *Bicycling World,* 17 June 1905.

pp. 347–48   a "healthy revival": *Bicycling World,* 2 January 1904.

p. 348   need to win back women: *Bicycling World,* 11 November 1905.

p. 348   "The touring side of cycling": *Bicycling World,* 25 September 1902.

p. 348   misconceptions about the nature of touring: *Bicycling World,* 26 October 1907.

p. 348   "After the first flush": *Bicycling World,* 6 November 1902.

p. 348   "The next big improvement": *Bicycling World,* 10 July 1902.

p. 349   two gears plenty: *Bicycling World,* 31 October 1903.

p. 349   Purely Pleasure Pedalers: *Bicycling World,* 30 March 1907.

p. 349   "pleasures of cycle camping": *Bicycling World,* 4 July 1908.

p. 349   "As a wheelman still active": Quoted in *Bassett's Scrap Book,* June 1913.

p. 349   trips of moderate distance: *Bicycle News,* September 1916.

p. 349   touring a "lost art": *Bassett's Scrap Book,* June 1913.

p. 349   Bassett blamed industry: *Bassett's Scrap Book,* April 1911.

p. 349   inventors focus on motorcycle: *Bassett's Scrap Book,* September 1911.

pp. 349–51   "You experience a rebirth": *Outing,* September 1912.

p. 351   "There is very little pleasure riding": *Cycling,* 8 January 1920.

p. 353   Panel's derailleurs: Raymond Henry, "Joanny Panel," *Boneshaker,* Spring 1993.

pp. 354–55   Caminade alloy frames: *Génie Civil,* 3 October 1936.

p. 355   women's colleges: *Bicycling World,* 24 September 1910.

p. 355   new, affordable accessories: *Steel,* 31 August 1936.

p. 355   factors behind the cycling craze: *Sales Management,* 1 September 1937.

p. 355   rental stands thrived: *Barron's,* 15 March 1937.

p. 355   Boston cycle trains: *Forbes,* 1 December 1935.

p. 355   "Bike to Nature" train: *Railway Age,* 2 May 1936.

p. 356 concern for children's safety: *Sales Management,* 1 September 1937.

p. 356 CTA advertising blitz: *Printer's Ink,* 13 August 1936.

p. 356 CTA initiated programs: *Forbes,* 1 December 1935.

p. 358 women buying a third of bicycles: *Barron's,* 15 March 1937.

p. 358 shorts popular: *Toy World,* November 1934.

p. 358 nude cycling: *Fortune,* September 1933.

p. 358 founding of American hostels: *Knapsack,* Fall 1937.

pp. 358–59 hostels in New England: *Cyclist,* July 1936.

p. 359 hostels across the country: *Cycling Herald,* March 1940.

p. 359 Roosevelt on need for hosteling: *Knapsack,* Fall 1941.

pp. 359–60 Birchmore's world trip: Oliver Hempstone Smith and Donald H. Berkebile, *Wheels and Wheeling* (Washington: Smithsonian Institution Press, 1974), p. 95.

p. 360 Chicago bicycle paths: *Toy World,* August 1935.

p. 360 Central Park cycle path: *Cyclist,* May 1936.

p. 360 Moses paved bicycle paths: *Reader's Digest,* June 1942.

p. 361 "floating through air": *Toy World,* August 1935.

p. 361 "immediate creating of a lightweight": *Toy World,* November 1934.

p. 361 scrambled to unveil lightweight models: *Toy World,* March 1935.

p. 361 Americans coveted British bicycles: *Time,* 5 July 1954.

pp. 361–62 European cycle imports: *American Bicyclist and Motorcyclist,* December 1979.

pp. 363–65 American crazes for ten-speeds and high-risers: Frank J. Berto, "The Great American Bicycle Boom," in *Cycle History* 10, pp. 133–41.

p. 363 banner years from 1972 to 1974: *Machine Design,* August 1974.

p. 368 boom of the 1970s: Richard Ballantine, *Richard's 21st Century Bicycle Book,* pp. vii–viii.

p. 371 Churchill recommended jungle bicycles: *Bicycling World,* 24 October 1908.

p. 371 revamped French touring bicycles: *VTT Magazine,* March 1998.

p. 371 history of the mountain bike: Pryor Dodge, *The Bicycle* (Paris: Flammarion, 1996), pp. 201–5; Paul Rosen, "Social Construction of Mountain Bikes," *Social Studies of Science,* 1993, pp. 486–87.

BOXED INSET *The Founding of International Youth Hostels*

p. 352 founding of German youth hostels: *Knapsack,* Autumn 1937.

p. 353 Schirrmann's letter to Monroe Smith, *Knapsack,* Fall 1945.

BOXED INSET *A Touring Revival*

p. 366 Hemistour and published account: *National Geographic,* May 1973.

p. 366 the Siples carried on: *Adventure Cyclist,* July 1996.

p. 367 Bikecentennial history: *BikeReport,* June 1986.

p. 367 Both couples remain active: E-mail messages from Greg Siple and Dan Burden.

BOXED INSET *Offbeat Recreation*

p. 372 polo played on Star bicycles: *Vanity Fair,* August 1897.

p. 373 "every rider was a trick rider": *Nickell Magazine,* June 1896.

p. 373 "A more thrilling exhibition": *Cosmopolitan,* June 1902.

p. 373 Lee Richardson's closing act: *Nickell Magazine,* June 1896.

p. 376 "Racing has been the most potent force": *Bicycle News,* April 1917.

pp. 377–78 velodromes in the United States: Peter Nye, *Hearts of Lions* (New York: Norton, 1988), pp. 65–90.

pp. 378–80 Taylor's wins and European tour: Ibid., pp. 61, 62–64.

p. 380 racing continued to "hold the attention": *Bicycling World,* 2 September 1905.

p. 380 new six-day format: *Outing,* February 1921.

p. 380 carnival-like atmosphere of six-day races: Ibid.

p. 381 Walthour and motorpacing: Nye, *Hearts of Lions,* p. 72.

p. 381 Kramer's triumphs: *Literary Digest,* 9 September 1922.

p. 381 "Kramer's earnings": *Bicycle News,* April 1915.

p. 381 Kramer's farewell: *Literary Digest,* 9 September 1922.

p. 382 Alf Goullet: Nye, *Hearts of Lions,* p. 77.

p. 382 food consumption of racers: *Illustrated World,* April 1917.

p. 382 golden era of track racing: Nye, *Hearts of Lions,* pp. 102–24.

p. 382 Los Angeles velodrome: *Popular Mechanics,* June 1921.

p. 382 cultural mix at races: *Outing,* February 1921.

p. 382 UCI formed: David Perry, *Bike Cult* (New York: Four Walls Eight Windows, 1995), p. 354.

p. 383 Paris–Roubaix: Editors of Bicycling Magazine, *The Noblest Invention* (Emmaus, Pa.: Rodale, 2004), pp. 134–35.

p. 383 Tour de France conceived: *American Bicyclist and Motorcyclist,* December 1979.

p. 383 inaugural race of 1903: James Starrt, *Tour de France/Tour de Force* (San Francisco: Chronicle, 2000), p. 17.

p. 383 scandals of 1904 Tour: Les Woodland, *The Unknown Tour de France: The Many Faces of the World's Biggest Bicycle Race* (San Francisco: Van der Plas Publications, 2000), p. 12.

p. 384 Tour revamped in 1905: James McGurn, *On Your Bicycle: An Illustrated History of Cycling* (London: Murray, 1987), pp. 158–59.

p. 385 Christophe at forge: Graham Watson, *Tour de France and Its Heroes* (London: Stanley Paul, 1990), pp. 11–12.

p. 387 victories promote brand names: *Literary Digest,* 2 August 1924.

p. 387 racing bicycle largely unchanged: Raymond Henry, "Touring Bicycle Technical Trials in France, 1901–1950," in *Cycle History* 5 (San Francisco: Van der Plas, 1995), 79–86.

pp. 387–90 Super Champion derailleurs and Osgear: Gordon Selby, "History of the Super Champion Osgears," *Boneshaker,* Spring 2000.

p. 390 "Miracle de Bonsecours": Woodland, *Unknown Tour de France,* pp. 92–93.

p. 390 Bartali winner of 1948 Tour: *Gazzetta dello Sport,* 6 May 2000.

p. 391 Coppi rivalry with Bartali: Starrt, *Tour de France,* p. 49.

p. 391 traditions of spectators: *Time,* 16 July 1951.

p. 391 Bobet wins third Tour: *Newsweek,* 8 August 1955.

p. 394 American interest in racing rekindled: Nye, *Hearts of Lions,* chapters 12–13. Joseph Magnani, a native of Belleville, Illinois, was the first American professional to compete in Europe, racing for several French and Italian teams from 1935 through 1948.

p. 397 Simpson's death: Starrt, *Tour de France,* p. 79.

p. 397 cyclo-cross in Italy: *Bicycling World,* 18 April 1908.

pp. 397–98 cyclo-cross history: Gábor L. Konrád, " 'The Tiger': America's Cyclo-Cross Champion Leroy Johnson," in *Cycle History* 11, pp. 137–38.

pp. 399–401 Moser's hour record: Matthew E. Mantell, "What is the UCI?" *Bicycling,* June 1989.

BOXED INSET   *The Hour of the Recumbent*

p. 388   Berthet and Egg rivalry: Chester R. Kyle, "Bicycle Aerodynamics and the Union Cycliste Internationale," in *Cycle History* 11 (San Francisco: Van der Plas Publications, 2001), pp. 118–31.

p. 388   Berthet's initial experiments: *Scientific American*, 17 January 1914.

p. 388   Mochet's Vélocar: Kyle, "Bicycle Aerodynamics," pp. 118–31.

p. 388   Mochet's faired Vélocar: Jacques Seray, *Deux Roues: La Véritable Histoire du Vélo* (Rodez: Editions du Rouergue, 1988), p. 194.

p. 389   Boardman's 1996 record: Otto Beaujon, "Was Bicycle Development Stunted by Organized Racing?" in *Cycle History* 10 (San Francisco: Van der Plas Publications, 2000), pp. 67–76.

BOXED INSET   *Women's Racing*

p. 395   establishment of women's championship races: Perry, *Bike Cult*, pp. 514–50.

BOXED INSET   *The BMX Bicycle*

p. 400   origins of BMX biking: *Popular Mechanics*, March 1974.

p. 400   stripped down old Sting-Rays: Pryor Dodge, *The Bicycle* (Paris: Flammarion, 1996), p. 201.

Conclusion

p. 404   bicycle still a luxury in Africa: *Economist*, 20 January 1990.

p. 406   gasoline used for short trips: Frank Rowland Whitt and David Gordon Wilson, *Bicycling Science*, 2nd ed. (Cambridge: MIT Press, 1982), p. 330. Wilson believes that the percentage of gasoline consumed for short trips has not declined over the twenty-two years since.

p. 407   Bowden Spacelander: Pryor Dodge, *The Bicycle* (Paris: Flammarion, 1996), p. 178.

p. 407   Original Plastic Bike: *Popular Science*, May 1973.

p. 407   Itera plastic bicycle: *Plastics World*, June 1982.

p. 407   Boardman's bicycle at 1992 Olympics: *Economist*, 1 August 1992.

p. 408   lightweight shells: Wilson, *Bicycling Science*, pp. 335–57.

p. 409   Whittingham's record in 2002: *Explore*, March–April 2002.

p. 410   half the adult cycling population: *Technology Review*, October 1983.

p. 411   "many advocates of the power bicycle": *McClure's Magazine*, July 1896.

p. 411–12   varieties of ebikes: *Machine Design*, 15 June 2000.

p. 413   "bicycling is not a fad": *Brooklyn Life*, 23 March 1895.

Acknowledgments

Something like fifteen years went into the research and preparation of this book, which means I have many people to thank for their help, support, or just plain understanding. I would like to start by gratefully acknowledging Kathy McBride, who has been extremely supportive over the years and, in the preparation of this book, offered me insightful criticism as well as her considerable graphic skills. I am thankful to my parents, who instilled in me an appreciation for the past, and to my mother, Patricia Herlihy, in particular, who read the manuscript and offered valuable advice. I appreciate the support I received from my entire family, especially my brother Felix and his wife Lisa Steglich, who helped me gain access to rich sources of historical information in London and New York.

I would also like to thank my editor at Yale, Lara Heimert, for enthusiastically embracing this project from the start and steering it toward a successful completion despite the magnitude of the job. Her insights and guidance have been invaluable. I am also grateful to Phillip King for his brilliant editing and tireless work, to Sonia Shannon for the beautiful layout, and to Keith Condon for his administrative help. I would like to offer a special thanks to my reviewers who were a tremendous help and inspiration: Peter Nye, David Gordon Wilson, and Carolyn Cooper.

The opportunity to curate the traveling exhibition "The Bicycle Takes Off" in 2001–2002 enabled me to prepare much of the material for this book. My sincere thanks to Zachary N. Studenroth, who conceived and organized the exhibition, and to the entire staff of the Lockwood-Mathews Mansion Museum, as well as to the Connecticut Humanities Council for providing major funding. I am grateful to all the lenders and all those who lent their talents, especially Betsy Bailey, Paula Donovan, Steve Marcouillier, and Joe Rivers.

I am also indebted to the international community of cycle historians and collectors, especially to Nick Clayton, who provided a great deal of technical information. Many members of the Veterans' Cycle Club in Britain and the Wheelmen in the United States have been very helpful and supportive to me over the years. Among these are Les Bowerman, Andrew Millward, Hilary Stone, Glynn Stockdale, Andrew Ritchie, Roger Street, Walter Ulreich, and, closer to home, Katheryn Carse, Beth Gorrie, Jim Langley, Tom Maher and Mary Cassidy, Bob and Ruth Sawyer, Lou Schultz, and Jim Spillane and his family. Frank Berto, Sheldon Brown, Michael Kone, Grant Peterson, and Ron Shepherd also helped me better appreciate twentieth-century developments. I would also like to thank Forbes Bagatelle-Black for information related to ebikes, Carole Leone for insights into the human-powered vehicle movement, and Greg Siple for helpful information about cycle touring and for providing wonderful photographs.

I benefited from a number of in-depth studies on nineteenth-century bicycle history. Among these were Roger Street's *The Pedestrian Hobby-Horse* (Christchurch, U.K.: Artesius Publications, 1998), Mark Frost's studies on Willard Sawyer, Keizo Kobayashi's *Histoire du Vélocipède de Drais à Michaux* (Tokyo: Bicycle Culture Center, 1993), and Bruce Epperson's studies on Albert Pope. Other helpful specialized works were Tony Hadland's *The Sturmey-Archer Story*, and Peter Nye's *Hearts of Lions* covering the history of bicycle racing. The proceedings of the annual international cycle history conferences, published by Rob Van der Plas, also gave me a trove of valuable historical information by such academic authorities as Alistair Dodds, Hans-Ehrard Lessing, Glen Norcliffe, Nicholas Oddy, Ross D. Petty, and Paul Rosen.

Numerous libraries and archives were goldmines of information, especially the British Library, the Bibliothèque Nationale de France, the Biblioteca Nazionale in Florence, the Library of Congress, the Boston Public Library, the Harvard Library, and the American Antiquarian Society. I am particularly grateful to the many staff members who helped me with my research. I would also like to thank all those who allowed me access to their personal archives. They include Bruno Olivier de Sanderval (grandson of Aimé Olivier), Dominique Olivier (descendent of Marius Olivier), Caroline Rocherolle (related to Georges de la Bouglise), John S. Moore (grandson of James Moore), and Albert A. Pope (the Colonel's great-grandson). I am also grateful to Pryor Dodge and Lorne Shields for giving me access to their rich collections of bicycle-related graphics and literature.

Finally, I would like to thank my many friends in France who have given me insights and encouragement over the years, including Nadine Besse, Jean-Denys Devauges, Bernard Gougaud, Raymond Henry, Alex Poyer, Rodolphe Rebour, Claude Reynaud, and Gérard Salmon. I am especially indebted to Jacques Seray, who first enlightened me to the depth of bicycle history, and to Pierre Durand and the entire Club Cyclotouriste Mussipontain for providing me with valuable information about the life of Pierre Lallement. I am also grateful for the hospitality and support extended during my visits to France by Jacques Ostier and Brigitte Olivier, Thierry and Arnaud de La Bouillerie, Stacey Benoit, and Constantin and Natasha Federovsky. I also thank Andrew Greene, Peter Townsend, and Phil Saunders in England, as well as Renzo and Anna Maggiori and Fabio, Ilaria, and Mario Noferini in Florence. Without the generous help of all these individuals and institutions this work would not have been possible.

Illustration Credits

University Archives, department of Rare Books and Special Collections, Princeton University Library, p. 2; Trustees of the Boston Public Library, pp. 4 (Rare Books), 9 (reprinted by permission of the Norman Rockwell Family Agency), 19, 46, 48, 57, 70, 100, 106, 112, 134, 162, 189, 199, 203, 220, 233, 238, 245, 255, 262, 266, 268, 272, 274, 279, 296, 298, 315, 326, 334, 346, 356, 362; The Granger Collection, New York, pp. 5, 115, 166, 193, 269, 273, 299, 350, 404, 413; The Library of Congress, pp. 6, 7, 8, 18, 55, 98, 105, 116, 118, 138, 170, 201, 206, 207, 219, 265, 270, 281, 284, 285, 286, 295, 312, 322, 329, 332, 345, 357, 358, 360, 381; Trek USA and Canada, pp. 10, 396; The British Library, pp. 16, 62, 63, 151, 164; By Permission of the Houghton Library, Harvard University, pp. 17, 176; Harvard University Library, pp. 20, 61, 83, 87, 90, 99, 125, 153, 183, 194, 230, 237, 321, 379, 384, 398; The Lewis Walpole Library, Yale University, pp. 21 (unknown artist, "Match against Time or Wood beats Blood and Bone," etching with hand-coloring, 20.3 x 31.6 cm., image, published April 17, 1819, by T. Tegg, 819.4.17), 25 (unknown artist, "The Dandy Charger," etching with hand-coloring, 22.2 x 29.5 cm., sheet, published February 23, 1819, by John Hudson, 819.2.23), 29 (attributed William Heath, 1795–1840, "The Pedestrian Hobbies or the Difference of Going Up and Down Hill," etching with hand-coloring, 19.9 x 31.4 cm., image, published April 8, 1819, by T. Tegg, 819.4.8.1), 34 (Robert Cruikshank, 1789–1856, "Pedestrians traveling on the New Invented Hobby Horse," 1819, etching, 22.4 x 32.6 cm., image, published by J. Sidebethem, 819.0.32), 37 (unknown artist, "Modern Olympics," etching, 23.7 x 37.7 cm., sheet, published February 23, 1819, by John Hudson, 819.2.23.1), 38 (Robert Cruikshank, "The Ladies Accelerator," 1819, etching, 22.8 x 34 cm., image, published by SW Fores, 819.0.35), 49 (Robert Cruikshank, "Collegians at their Exercise! or Brazen Nose Hobbies!" 1819, etching with hand-coloring 21.6 x 32.2 cm., image, published by J. Sidebethem, 819.0.46), 51 (attributed to William Heath, "Every One his Hobby, plate 1st," etching with hand-coloring, 20.7 x 31.7 cm., image, published April 24, 1819, by T. Tegg, 819.4.24.1); Bibliothèque Nationale de France, pp. 28, 95, 128, 137, 146, 310; National Archives, pp. 32 (Northeast Branch, New York, from Equity Case File D-1652, Southern District of New York), 104; Science Museum/Science and Society Picture Library, pp. 33, 68, 215, 236, 247, 304; Pennsylvania Academy of the Fine Arts, p. 41 (gift of Mrs. Sarah Harrison, The Joseph Harrison, Jr., Collection); The Beinecke Rare Book and Manuscript Library,

Yale University Library, pp. 44, 80; The Lorne Shields Collection, pp. 58, 213, 217, 287, 377, 378; Canada National Museum of Science and Technology, pp. 59, 211; © Réunion des Musées Nationaux/Art Resource, New York, pp. 77, 82, 92, 97, 130, 133; Olivier Family, p. 86; Naval History Center, p. 89; DeVincent Collection of Illustrated Sheet Music, Archives Center, National Museum of American History, Smithsonian Institution, pp. 109, 123; American Antiquarian Society, pp. 111, 119; General Research Division, The New York Public Library, Astor, Lenox, and Tilden Foundations, pp. 165, 172, 174, 260; John S. Moore, pp. 142, 161; Brown University Library, p. 145; Claude Reynaud, p. 148; Alexander Turnbull Library, Wellington, New Zealand, p. 168 (photographer Frank J. Denton, Reference Number: G-8609-1/4, Collection Reference no.: PAColl-3042); National Széchényi Library, p. 175; ARCPP, Paris, p. 178; The University of Indiana, p. 186; The Pryor Dodge Collection, pp. 191, 218, 228, 253, 275, 291, frontispiece; Manuscripts and Archives, Yale University Library, p. 195; Quincy Historical Society, p. 198; The University of North Carolina at Chapel Hill Libraries, p. 204; National Medical Library, p. 226; Smithsonian Institution, p. 227; Hess Collection, University of Minnesota Libraries, p. 231; Warshaw Collection of Business Americana—Bicycle, Archives Center, National Museum of American History, Smithsonian Institution, p. 242; Connecticut Valley Historical Museum, 220 State Street, Springfield, Massachusetts, p. 243 (gift of George Hendee, 85.113); Jacques Simon, p. 249; Connecticut Historical Society, Hartford, Connecticut, p. 259; Hilary Stone, p. 289; Northwest Museum of History Collection, K. Ross Toole Archives, The University of Montana, Missoula, p. 293; Glenn Curtiss Museum, Hammondsport, New York, p. 303; Jim Gill, p. 313; Samantha Moranville, pp. 319, 335, 364, 399, 400; Stamford Historical Society, p. 320; Yale University Library, p. 324; Harvard-Yenching Library of the Harvard College Library (photo by Hedda Morrison), p. 330; Poster Collection, DK 40, Hoover Institution Archives, p. 331; Minnesota Historical Society, pp. 333, 359; British Film Institute, p. 337; Stadt Münster/Stadtplanungsamt, pp. 338, 341; Keystone Press Agency, pp. 339 (photo by Wanggengfeng/Imagine China/ZUMA Press/KEYSTONE Canada), 372 (photo by KEYSTONE Press, © Copyright 1965 by KEYSTONE Press), 392 (photo by KEYSTONE Canada); Adventure Cycling, pp. 365 (photo by Dan Burden), 367 (Hemistour photo by Greg Siple), 369 (photo by Dan Burden), 411 (photo by Greg Siple); Rails-to-Trails Conservancy, p. 370; Cannondale Corporation, p. 374; Tony Hadland, p. 389 (from the archives of Arnfried Schmitz, reprinted from *Human Power: The Forgotten Energy*); Kathleen R. McBride, p. 393; University of Massachusetts, Amherst, Special Collections, p. 405; Bicycle Museum of America, p. 408; Arne Hodalic, p. 409; WaveCrest Laboratories, p. 412.

Index